Online Journalism in Africa

"A timely contribution that fills a critical gap in the ethnography of African online media and press practices in evolving political cultures".

—Folu Ogundimu, Michigan State University

Very little is known about how African journalists are forging "new" ways to practise their profession on the web. Against this backdrop, this volume provides contextually rooted discussions of trends, practices and emerging cultures of web-based journalism(s) across the continent, offering a comprehensive research tool that can both stand the test of time as well as offer researchers (particularly those in the economically developed Global North) models for cross-cultural comparative research. The essays here deploy either a wide range of evidence or adopt a case-study approach to engage with contemporary developments in African online journalism. This book thus makes up for the gap in cross-cultural studies that seek to understand online journalism in all its complexities.

Hayes Mawindi Mabweazara is currently a Senior Lecturer in Journalism Studies at Falmouth University, UK. His research on the new media and journalism practice in Africa has been published in a number of leading journals and edited books. Mabweazara serves on the editorial board of *Digital Journalism* and is the Book Reviews Editor of *Ecquid Novi: African Journalism Studies*.

Okoth Fred Mudhai is a Senior Lecturer in Journalism in the Media Department, Coventry University, on a 17-month Post-doctoral Research Associate secondment (2012–14) to the University of Cambridge. He has written extensively and won awards on ICTs. His recent publications include two journal articles in *Journalism: Theory, Practice and Criticism,* a number of book chapters and co-editorship of *African Media and the Digital Public Sphere.*

Jason Whittaker is Head of the Department of Writing at Falmouth University. He has written extensively on William Blake and digital technologies, his most recent works including *William Blake and the Digital Humanities* and *Producing for Web 2.0.* He has worked as an editor and journalist for nearly twenty years.

Routledge Advances in Internationalizing Media Studies

Edited by Daya Thussu, University of Westminster

Online Journalism in Africa

Trends, Practices and Emerging Cultures

**Edited by Hayes Mawindi Mabweazara,
Okoth Fred Mudhai and Jason Whittaker**

Routledge
Taylor & Francis Group

NEW YORK AND LONDON

First published 2014
by Routledge
711 Third Avenue, New York, NY 10017

and by Routledge
2 Park Square, Milton Park, Abingdon, Oxfordshire OX14 4RN

First issued in paperback 2016

*Routledge is an imprint of the Taylor & Francis Group,
an Informa business*

Library of Congress Cataloging-in-Publication Data

Online journalism in Africa : trends, practices and emerging cultures /
   edited by Hayes Mawindi Mabweazara, Okoth Fred Mudhai and
   Jason Whittaker.
      pages cm. — (Routledge advances in internationalizing media
studies ; 12)
   Includes bibliographical references and index.
   1. Online journalism—Africa.   2. Journalism—Technological
innovations—Africa.   3. Citizen journalism—Africa.   4. Social
media—Africa.   I. Mabweazara, Hayes Mawindi, 1977– editor
of compilation.   II. Mudhai, Okoth Fred editor of compilation.
III. Whittaker, Jason, 1969– editor of compilation.
   PN4784.O62O55 2013
   076—dc23
   2013024064

ISBN 13: 978-1-138-68919-0 (pbk)
ISBN 13: 978-0-415-50374-7 (hbk)

Typeset in Sabon
by Apex CoVantage, LLC

Contents

Tables and Figures

Foreword

During the early days of the World Wide Web's development, commentators frequently found themselves immersed in lively debate over the possible implications for journalism. Opposing views and opinions recurrently revolved around imagined scenarios indicative of sharply divergent projections of the future. For some of the more pessimistic critics, the emergence of online journalism posed a grave threat, its gradual consolidation portending to destabilise and almost certainly undermine the financial viability—and professional integrity—of mainstream news organisations. For some advocates, in marked contrast, online journalism promised to usher in a new age of news reporting, one that would help to rewire the planet into a virtual community of global citizens. The celebrated theorist Marshall McLuhan's writings about electronic media, published decades earlier, proved influential for optimistic appraisals, particularly with respect to the way his concept of the 'global village' invited confidence in online journalism's capacity to transcend national boundaries. McLuhan (1962) had boldly prophesised that 'electro-magnetic discoveries' would one day bring together 'the entire human family into a single global tribe' (1962, 8).

That day remains on a distant horizon, but as the contributors to Hayes Mawindi Mabweazara, Okoth Fred Mudhai and Jason Whittaker's *Online Journalism in Africa: Trends, Practices and Emerging Cultures* succeed in documenting, these uneven, contested processes continue to gather momentum across expanding news and information networks. The imperatives shaping online journalism—its affordances as well as its constraints—are being negotiated in converging circumstances of economic, political and cultural factors that often elude adequate scrutiny, namely because they typically seem too obvious or commonsensical to justify sustained critique. From one chapter to the next, however, we see the import of attending to the specificities of diverse African contexts and thereby of necessarily questioning any easy notion that how online journalists go about their work is overtly determined by such factors. At the same time, what counts as impartial news coverage is revealed to be conditioned by highly ritualised—that is to say, legitimised—protocols, such as in the subtle, seemingly ad hoc judgements made regarding how best to cover contentious news stories (whereas alternative perspectives may be ignored due to self-censorship or marginalised, even trivialised in the name of patriotism). Taken together, the chapters make a compelling case for delving into the lived materialities of reportorial forms, practices and epistemologies, showing us wherein lie the challenges—as well as the remarkable potentials—for online journalism as it evolves across multiple digital platforms.

Much of this book's discussion is informed by cautious optimism. We learn how innovative approaches to connectivity are reinvigorating African journalism, some of which resonate with McLuhan's speculative assertions about the recasting of time, space and place in unexpected ways. More often than not, however, they have been crafted with inspired creativity from hard-won experience of exigent pressures, not least the frustrations of improvisations wrested from impoverished resources. In seeking to move debates regarding how to further extend online reporting's capability to engage distant others beyond the soaring rhetoric of the 'global village', *Online Journalism in Africa* maps these shifting conditions of possibility with great insight. The contributors underscore the reasons such a commitment is so significant for the advancement of scholarship as well as why journalism as a public service needs to be at the heart of democratic cultures. In so doing, then, this book helps to point the way forward with respect to how we may begin to make good McLuhan's (1964) conviction that the "aspiration of our time for wholeness, empathy and depth of awareness is a natural adjunct of electric technology" (1964, 21).

Stuart Allan,
Professor of Journalism
at Bournemouth University, UK

REFERENCES

McLuhan, Marshall. 1962. *The Gutenberg Galaxy: The Making of Typographic Man.* Toronto: University of Toronto Press.
———. 1964. *Understanding Media: The Extensions of Man.* New York: McGraw-Hill.

Introduction

Online Journalism in Africa: Trends, Practices and Emerging Cultures

Hayes Mawindi Mabweazara, Okoth Fred Mudhai and Jason Whittaker

Although in the economically developed countries of the North, developments in online journalism have seen a sharp rise in research that interrogates its practice from a variety of theoretical traditions (see Deuze and Dimoudi 2002; Deuze 2003; Singer 2003; Allan 2005; Lowrey 2006; Paterson and Domingo 2008; Fenton 2010), the field largely remains untouched in Africa. Understandably so perhaps: not only is the medium young, but the continent also continues to suffer a number of setbacks related to the 'digital divide'. The research gap thus mirrors the complexities and contradictions with respect to the diffusion and permeation of new digital technologies into African journalism practice (Atton and Mabweazara 2011). A few studies suffer from a kind of anachronistic approach, explaining the 'new' practices and cultures by using the old rather than addressing how journalists are adjusting to the new platforms of practice (Deuze 1998; Atton and Mabweazara 2011). Researchers have, for instance, focused on how traditional media have been repurposing their offline content for the web or how the web functions as a news-gathering and research tool (Berger 2005), as opposed to how it has emerged as an autonomous platform for the practice of journalism.

Similarly, some scholars have preferred to examine the potential impact of new digital media on political participation and democratic struggles in Africa (L. Moyo 2009; D. Moyo 2009). Although the contributions of these studies are by no means insignificant, "especially in a continent where democracy is perennially under threat" (Atton and Mabweazara 2011, 667), what is lacking is a close look at how African journalism has forged new ways of practice in the new media age, particularly how the Internet and its associated interactive digital technologies have offered a new 'stand-alone' platform for the practice of journalism. There are no studies as yet that have focused on the daily practices and characteristics of online journalism in Africa, even as it has become apparent that the Internet and associated digital technologies are no longer just basic tools for the practice of traditional journalism. Rather, they have become an integral part of the profession, and indeed, forms of online or digital journalism are thriving on the continent.

Very little is therefore known about how African journalists are forging 'new' ways to practise their profession on interactive digital platforms, including the web. It is not clear how African journalists have dealt with emerging technological transformations and, more importantly, "how they have adapted their professional notions in terms of which traditions have survived" and which have been redefined (Atton and Mabweazara 2011, 668). As Cottle (2000, 432) puts it, "we need to examine the fast changing ecology of news, its changing industrialised and technological basis and its response to the changing structurations of society".

As Atton and Mabweazara observe, "Few studies have as yet sought to empirically discriminate between what could or should be universal professional values and what might be context-dependent practices of online journalism" (2011, 668). This has meant that professional norms and practices emerging from Western scholarship are applied "out of context, sometimes awkwardly" in Africa (Ibelema 2008, 36). Analytical tools, theories and empirical studies developed in the West might appear to be applicable to the African context—indeed some of the work may be seminal and groundbreaking—but a closer look shows significant differences "requiring nuanced theorising and research" (Atton and Mabweazara 2011, 668) given that much of the research, definitions and applications are often not entirely compatible with the specificities of conditions and experiences in African countries (Berger 2000; Hyde-Clarke 2010).

Thus, adapting the studies to the African context sometimes creates problems as they cover only a small portion of developments in Africa and the wider developing world (Atton and Mabweazara 2011). As Nyamnjoh argues, African journalism research must be located "in African realities and not in Western fantasies" (1999, 15). This intervention is particularly necessary in light of the fact that African journalism is all too often measured against Western professional values and standards; local contextual factors that shape and underlie evolving practices in Africa are often overlooked (Nyamnjoh 2005; Ibelema 2008; Atton and Mabweazara 2011). Although these factors are far too many to outline here, they include sociopolitical, economic and institutional contexts that are markedly different. The majority of African journalists work in significantly under-resourced contexts (including digital technologies), yet despite these challenges and the very problem of defining exactly what delineates online journalism or journalists on the African continent, there is no denying that web-based journalistic practices are revolutionising the way news is reported, disseminated and consumed on the continent. As elsewhere, the African news environment is being shaped and redefined in various ways by emerging technological transformations: "Content, distribution channels, geographical constraints, production values, business models, regulatory approaches and cultural habits are all changing as new media technologies are adopted and adapted" (Meikle and Redden 2012, 1) by emerging and established news organisations.

Against this backdrop, this volume provides a forum for theoretically driven scholarship that either deploys a wide range of evidence or adopts a case-study approach to engage contemporary developments in African online journalism practices. It provides contextually rooted discussions of trends, practices and emerging cultures of web-based journalism(s) across the continent and hence offers a comprehensive research tool that can both stand the test of time as well as offer researchers (particularly those in the economically developed Global North) models for cross-cultural comparative research. As Mitchelstein and Boczkowski (2009) rightly assert, studies of online journalism could benefit from a broader contextualisation that takes into consideration historical dimensions. The book is thus an attempt to make up for the gap in cross-cultural studies that seek to understand online journalism in all its 'contextual complexities' (Fenton 2010).

DEFINING ONLINE JOURNALISM

The findings collected in this volume demonstrate that universal truths about online journalism in Africa are hard to come by. This result connects closely to the very challenges of the notion of 'new technologies' on the African context and the slow rate at which the technologies have percolated into different social contexts as a result of the challenges associated with the notion of the digital divide. The wide-ranging nature of the practices and issues explored in the chapters in this volume capture this complexity.

However, before delving into discussions about online journalism in Africa, it is important to provide a brief overview of what constitutes online journalism in the context of this volume. This is important in order to clarify what makes journalism on the Internet (and associated digital platforms) different from traditional journalism. In our attempt to provide an overview of what constitutes 'online journalism', we remain alert to the fact that there is no absolute agreement about what this concept or practice is. As Steensen (2011, 221) observes, "research on online journalism is flooded by a range of theoretical concepts that are either interchangeable or are interpreted differently by different researchers". Similarly, Kawamoto (2003) notes that some might consider the mere repurposing of content from one traditional medium to a digital medium as having sufficiently met the criteria for online journalism, and yet for others, it is strictly about new communication practices on interactive digital platforms.

Are there differences in the newsgathering practice between online and traditional journalism? Or is the way the story is formatted and disseminated the key differentiating factor between traditional journalism and online journalism? In an attempt to solve the dilemma of definition, Deuze (2003, 206) succinctly defines online journalism as the type of journalism that is produced more or less exclusively for the World Wide Web (as the graphic interface of the internet). Online journalism can be functionally differentiated from other kinds of journalism by using its technological component as a determining factor in terms of a (operational) definition. The online journalist has to make decisions as to which media format or formats best convey a certain story (multimediality), consider options for the public to respond, interact or even customize certain stories (interactivity), and think about ways to connect the story to other stories, archives, resources and so forth through hyperlinks (hypertextuality). This is the 'ideal–typical' form of online journalism, as professed by an increasing number of professionals and academics worldwide.

In this definition, three features at the heart of online journalism are evident. The first is *multimediality*, that is, the ability of the website to carry multimedia functions such as podcasts, social media, YouTube etc. and to offer enough space for text which can form either the main story or analysis of the story, thereby giving readers a choice on how to consume the message. The second feature is *interactivity*, where readers have the opportunity to be active participants in the news story by expressing their views—and in some instances by providing additional context or related input to stories. Related to this is the third feature, *hypertextuality*, which enables various news texts to 'speak to each other'—thereby providing a fuller picture to the user (see Muhammad Jameel Yusha'u's chapter in this volume for a contextualised exploration of these three elements of online journalism).

We embrace this definition in this volume, taking into account possibilities for convergence that allow the more conventional news media to reinvent themselves for online audiences who are increasingly 'on the move' with hand-held mobile devices, especially the mobile phone, which has apparently become the technology of choice on the African continent (Mabweazara 2011; Paterson 2013). However, although we draw on the three technical elements offered by Deuze, the research in this book is far from being 'technicist', that is, reducing the complexities of online journalism in Africa to the three technical elements in ways that exclusively privilege technology over wider social dynamics that underlie the distinctive uses of technologies in specific contexts (Mabweazara 2010). Rather, as the chapters in this volume collectively demonstrate, the book draws on a constructivist approach that acknowledges and embraces the 'social shaping' nature of technology. This approach enables us to see *multimediality*, *interactivity* and *hypertextuality* as not necessarily replacing existing social, cultural and political networks but rather as continuous with and embedded in them (2010). Following this approach, this book demonstrates that the starting point should not be a particular *technological field* but a particular *social context* in which 'new' technologies are used (Heap et al. 1995). We, therefore, need to "examine the multidimensional factors—in everyday work practices and wider social contexts—which structure and constrain the deployment of 'new' technologies by journalists" (Mabweazara 2010, 11). So, online journalism in Africa should be seen as intimately tied to, constrained or enhanced by a broader range of socioeconomic, political and cultural factors.

PROBLEMATISING THE 'NEWNESS' OF 'NEW TECHNOLOGIES' IN AFRICA

The challenges of defining online journalism in the African context also relate to the problematic of the notion of 'newness' in new technologies that mediate online journalism (Mabweazara 2010; see also George Ogola's chapter in this volume). "Although the term *new technology* has been widely used as a collective singular noun, as if it refers to a coherent entity, it is in fact, an enormously general and vague term" (Mabweazara 2010, 13) which needs to be understood and used in its *plural* sense (Lister et al. 2003).

Many writings have made very little attempt to define or problematise the term, consequently leading to generalisations and assumptions in its use (Mabweazara 2010). The term has often been used as if it were self-explanatory and had some universal applicability in diverse geopolitical contexts (Lister et al. 2003). In short, no significant attention has been paid to the 'quality' and form of 'new' technologies in the developing world *vis-à-vis* those in the developed countries.

New technology theorists and other commentators generally tend to be polarised over the degree of new technology's newness, with some arguing that "to place emphasis on the 'new' can be misleading" (Meikle and Young 2012, 2). In the African context, this question is even more convoluted. There is a temptation to simply list the latest developments in media technologies and call these new. This approach is inadequate as it prevents an understanding of what may be different degrees of 'newness' among and across various media (Flew 2002, 9) and contexts. As Meikle and Young observe, a blanket emphasis on technological novelty or the 'new' "obscure[s] the crucial processes of transition, of both adoption and adaption, through which a medium comes to seem part of the furniture" (2012, 2).

The tendency among scholars in the developing world and beyond is to discuss new technologies as if there were some semblance of homogeneity in terms of the nature and form in which they manifest themselves across regions. Lister et al. (2003, 11), however, contend that "calling a range of developments 'new', which may or may not be new or even similar, is part of a powerful ideological movement and a narrative about progress in Western societies" which suggests a polarity in technological advancements between the developed North and the developing South.

These generalisations about new technologies, mainly directed towards the potential they wield, as Sasole (2003, 378) observes, negate the "actual material distribution in the current world order", which suggests an entirely different picture, especially the disparities between the economically developed North and the developing South as encapsulated in the notion of the 'digital divide'.

It is thus important to highlight that the *newness* of new technologies is 'historically relative' and contingent upon a particular context (Lister et al. 2003). In fact, the distinct developments of the mobile phone between the developed and the developing countries offer a good example of this observation. In the economically developed countries, "third generation (3G) mobile phones include broadband Internet connection, multimedia messaging, text messaging, mobile pictures and more importantly location awareness" (de Souza e Silva 2006, 109). In contrast, in a significant number of African countries, mobile phones continue to be used primarily as portable telephone for voice communication; hence, "for cellphone manufacturers like Nokia, Africa offers a market for less sophisticated models of phones" (Mudhai 2003). Indeed, the 'local context' appropriations of these less sophisticated mobile phones in Africa demonstrate the technology's unique position on the continent. The technology's rapid development and penetration rate has situated it as a facilitator of "new modes of participatory journalism in Africa" (Paterson 2013, 2).

Under these circumstances, "affirming that mobile devices are *new* interfaces through which communities are formed seems odd" (de Souza e Silva 2006, 109, emphasis added). This scenario finds support in Paterson's further observation that "some of the technologies having the most pronounced effect on society around Africa now are deemed passé by a Northern news media always clamouring for the latest techno-trends" (2013, 1–2). Thus, "[t]he notion of newness—in reference to 'new' media is a relative concept [that] demands critique, particularly in light of the complex and diverse histories of technological change—change which affects both hardware and software, institutions and practices" (Jankowski et al. 1999, 6).

This understanding sensitises us to the analytical distinction between the 'old' and 'new' technologies but, more importantly, diffuses common generalisations and assumptions by placing new technologies in Africa within context (Mabweazara 2010). As Nyamnjoh (2005, 4) notes, "Africa's creativity simply cannot allow for simple dichotomies or distinctions between old and new technologies, since its people are daily modernising the indigenous and indigenising the modern with novel outcomes. No technology seems too used to be used, just as nothing is too new to be blended with the old for even newer results". For this reason, as Silverstone (1999, 11) notes, "new media technologies [. . .] have to be tested not just against the old, but in the context of both the past and present, against the social and the human". The chapters in this volume examine various contexts within Africa in which the newness of online journalism is captured.

CHAPTER OUTLINES

Although research in this volume suggests that online news is supplemental and not a substitute for conventional ('traditional') forms of news, it is equally clear that online news is assuming a central position in Africa's news diet. Most news organisations have been clearly adjusting to the demands of the new digital era by allocating resources to make content available to their audiences in digital form. Whereas most of the studies echo views of Western journalism scholarship in which scholars have long "accepted the discourse of the [new media] as the major player in redefining and rethinking 'traditional' journalism" (Deuze and Dimoudi 2002, 86), the studies also point to localised appropriations of new digital technologies as defined by the broader social structure in which they are used.

The book is organised into four interrelated parts, all empirically exploring in diverse but related ways the manifestations, implications and professional transformations of African journalism as mediated and facilitated by new digital technologies. The *first section* addresses the structural continuities, shifts and redefinitions of traditional journalism practice in the context of the adoption of online digital practices. Marenet Jordaan considers the South African context for weekly newspapers, paying particular attention to how Facebook and Twitter have an effect on newsroom routines and cultures. Whereas new technologies have brought considerable anxieties for more traditional practices around the world, Jordaan argues that social media have also been accepted in South Africa as valid journalistic tools in recent years. In addition, Jordaan draws on social constructionism paradigms to examine the contrast between journalists' perceived professional uses of such tools, which they believe has not affected their newsgathering culture in any significant way, and the actual practice which, Jordaan argues, is not as immune to social media as the professionals would like to believe. The contribution by Johanna Mavhungu and Hayes Mawindi Mabweazara delves into the challenges, opportunities and successes of the South African mainstream press in an online environment, especially how the new modes and practices have forced traditional media houses to revisit their business plans as journalists reconsider their professional identities. Although access to online platforms cannot be taken for granted in the African context, different models for engagement are emerging, and the authors draw upon interviews with editorial staff to consider how three newspapers in South Africa are reacting to changes taking place in African journalism today.

In contrast to the print-first or text-based approaches to journalism considered by most of the contributors to this volume, Last Moyo instead concentrates on converging technologies and practices in radio journalism in Southern Africa. The past decade, argues Moyo, has seen radical changes taking place in which audiences and producers engage with radio in the region, with digital media making the format potentially more accessible through multiple delivery platforms. At least theoretically, the interaction of audiences with shows via social media sites such as Twitter and Facebook as well as via mobile technologies has made those audiences more visible, but Moyo is rightly critical of commentators' tendency to romanticise such engagements as 'citizen journalism'. Nonetheless, through a close study of mobile and online interactions in Malawi, Moyo is able to explore the role of these technologies in transforming the social and organisational contexts in which radio journalism operates.

Hayes Mawindi Mabweazara's chapter provides a Zimbabwean perspective on the appropriation of social media within the context of mainstream journalism. Focusing on seven newspapers drawn from the dominant state-controlled press and the small but powerful private press, Mabweazara examines how the adoption and use of Facebook is redefining traditional newsmaking practices, including how journalists engage and interact with their sources and readers. The chapter generally affirms findings from previous studies, especially that social media (Facebook in this case) offer journalists a wide range of resources and technological possibilities for connecting reporters to news sources and readers. Mabweazara also dedicates substantial space to the discussion of professional and ethical dilemmas emerging with the appropriation of Facebook in Zimbabwean newsrooms. These dilemmas range from the well-known challenges of moderating User Generated Content (UGC) on the news organizations' Facebook profiles to the controversies surrounding the blurring of the distinction between private and professional life as well as the invasion of ordinary users' personal privacy by journalists. Similarly, overdependence on social media in the context of disproportionate access to digital technologies is seen as engendering an 'elite news culture' that negates news occurrences outside social media platforms.

The *second part* of the book focuses on the ethical and regulatory challenges spawned by online digital practices. Compared to the considerable optimism evident throughout most chapters in this book regarding online engagement with various forms of journalistic practice, Terje S. Skjerdal's contribution on Ethiopian online journalism draws attention to what happens when opportunities are not taken advantage of. In Ethiopia, there has been little improvement or development since the mid-2000s, with fewer new blogs today than in 2005. Online news sites typically are replicas of print publications, and in contrast to the usual approaches to new media governance typically considered, whether formal regulation or self-regulation, Skjerdal examines how a series of informal forms of control, such as IP filtering and the intimidation of individual journalists and bloggers, have become effective in manipulating the media into formats more amenable to governmental demands.

Ylva Rodny-Gumede and Nathalie Hyde-Clarke deal with social media in the context of political journalism by examining how various controversies and investigations may be motivated by the engagement of the public on different social networking sites. Although such sources may be invaluable for journalists seeking public engagement, especially in terms of understanding the motivations of citizens in response to particular scandals and stories, at the same time, such participatory journalism is creating its own difficulties with regard to questions of objectivity and credibility.

The chapters in *section three* variously explore the shifting relationships between politics and journalism as mediated by online digital practices. With an emphasis on coverage of constitutional referenda in Kenya from 2005 to 2010, Okoth Fred Mudhai examines how two leading newspapers in the country have sought to keep up with emerging alternative spaces for networked, public expression. Although the continent has seen real progress with regard to civil liberties and freedom, Mudhai notes how some recent activities against newspapers in Kenya have been seen as a return to an era of extreme media repression—but networked-convergent models of journalism and democracy as typified by Wikileaks have also emerged to provide an alternative that is not as easy to shut down. Nonetheless, as Mudhai also observes, various obstacles remain in the way of an effective form of networked journalism, not least of which is the opposition by many trained in 'traditional' forms of media (whether print or broadcast) to working with colleagues in an environment that still tends to privilege a medium-based approach to the news.

Ahmed El Gody, in "Online Journalism, Citizen Participation and Engagement in Egypt", offers an account of how online reporting in Egypt provides one of the longest examples of not only this kind of journalism in Africa but also of various forums for public engagement that could provide citizens with the means to engage in communication and debate that eventually fed into that country's 'revolution' of January 2011. Although the Egyptian government maintained tight controls over Internet access from the mid 1990s onwards, its decision to commercialise and extend such access nonetheless provided a catalyst for changes in the political scene, with social networking sites being increasingly popular among the near forty percent of Egyptians who had Internet access by 2012. Indeed, suggests El Gody, it is this access to external sources outside of Egypt that may have had a more important role to play initially, with online journalists within the country at first being seen as second-class citizens within their own organisations. By working with groups such as the BBC and *The Guardian*, however, online journalists were increasingly able to engage more democratically with audiences and were thus in a much improved position to convey information about the Egyptian revolution from 2011 onwards.

Similar concerns arise in Sahar Khamis and Katherine Vaughn's chapter on public mobilisation and online citizen journalism in the Tunisian and Egyptian revolutions. The authors consider how a range of new tools, particularly those surrounding social media platforms such as Twitter, Facebook and YouTube, have been transformed in recent years from providing a safety-valve for the complaints of citizens to becoming the means for mobilising and organising protest. By providing forums for free speech and opportunities for networking, the authors argue, such online tools have enabled citizen journalists and political activists to engage in virtual spaces of assembly and to plan and execute the peaceful protests which had an incredibly important role to play in the Arab Spring revolutions in North Africa. What is more, by allowing the documentation of government brutality as well as the outcomes of these various protests, such activists were finally able to move beyond the officially-sanctioned state media which had kept a tight reign on such protests for a long time, and the activists thus communicated more effectively with the wider world. Nagwa Abdel Salam Fahmy also deals with the role of new forms of journalism in Egypt, in this case concentrating on the phenomenon of blogging as a means of dealing with restricted news flows within the country. Blogs, argues Fahmy, are frequently used to disseminate stories that were excluded or 'cut' ('spiked') for various reasons in the traditional media, so that the Egyptian blogosphere has increasingly emerged as able to play an important role in reporting stories not covered elsewhere, so much so that these blogs are increasingly seen as a viable news alternative.

The *last section* of the book looks at the dynamics of the changing interactions and connections between audiences and journalism. In "Online News Media Consumption Cultures among Zimbabwean Citizens: 'Home and Away'", Tendai Chari examines the online habits of local and diaspora Zimbabwean citizens by comparing the online habits of readers in Harare to other western capitals. For Chari, online newspapers create opportunities for spatially disconnected individuals to share memories and identifications; thus, the online newspapers sustain social, cultural and political connections to common spaces and localities. In contrast to pessimistic assumptions about the possibilities for the dissemination of online and digital media across sub-Saharan Africa, Chari indicates ways in which digital newspapers in particular are becoming an integral part of consumption for some Zimbabweans. This chapter therefore argues that the online newspaper has the potential to be a locus for the enactment of new ways of citizenship within the context of digitisation and globalisation, and these results indicate further directions for future research.

"The Internet, Diasporic Media and Online Journalism in West Africa" by Muhammad Jameel Yusha'u draws attention to the complexity of media within a region that comprises countries as diverse as Nigeria, Cape Verde and Sierra Leone. Tracing the emergence of journalism within the region, Yusha'u examines how recent moves towards the deregulation of media environments and the establishment of private media organisations have helped to facilitate the growth of online journalism in West Africa, and he considers the challenges and opportunities offered by such practices in recent years. In particular, Yusha'u considers how the rise of diasporic media online has in part emerged through new citizen journalisms, whereby Africans abroad can not only provide news to local citizens in the region but also serve as watchdogs on corruption, human rights violations and other abuses by various West African governments.

As in the case of Last Moyo's contribution, radio is also the focus of George Ogola's chapter on the media landscape in Kenya, which explores how much social media and online technologies influence institutional journalistic practices and in particular whether the 'community' in community radio is changing. Ogola's conclusion is that although the potential of online platforms has been recognised by a number of radio broadcasters and editors, for the moment, these platforms have not been strongly integrated into daily operations. Indeed, the ubiquity and relatively low cost of mobile technologies have proven to be more important for the stations that Ogola considers.

Marie-Soleil Frere's chapter points to the centrality of online forums in highly sensitive African sociopolitical contexts. Focusing on interactive online discussion forums in Burkina Faso, Frere observes that the participatory forums have stimulated audience interest and have provided an alternative communicative space that counters ingrained editorial and political constraints that have traditionally weighed down on professional journalism. She demonstrates how the vibrancy of discourses generated on the forums has not gone without notice from the authorities. In addition to receiving regular reprimands from the regulatory authority in charge of monitoring media content, the online debates also have a marked influence on political decision-making processes. The chapter aptly highlights the 'local context' appropriations of new digital technologies in Burkina Faso, especially how the country's political sphere shapes and constrains forms of online interactions, including the very nature of traditional journalism itself.

CONCLUSION: THE SIGNIFICANCE OF THIS VOLUME

The value of collecting findings from many nations in this volume, as Paterson (2008, 9) notes, "is not that universal truths about online journalism will emerge, but that a wide range of ideas about what online journalism may and may not be are on offer, and it remains for future scholars to test the durability of these observations in the realms of online production they know best, and those which they have access to". We believe there is a particular value in this multinational collection of research. Whereas findings in one country do not necessarily apply to another, there are inevitable overlaps, and findings in one country can and probably should be tested in other countries beyond the African continent itself.

We hope that this book will inspire all of us in the community of scholars studying and teaching online journalism to acknowledge emerging journalistic practices beyond the Western context, particularly the UK and the US. Collectively, the chapters in this volume provide a rich basis of comparison with developments unfolding in the economically developed world of the North where online journalism has assumed a more defined status than in Africa.

REFERENCES

Allan, Stuart. 2005. "News on the Web: The Emerging Forms and Practices of Online Journalism". In *Journalism: Critical Issues*, edited by Allan, Stuart, 67–81. Maidenhead: Open University Press.

Atton, Chris and Mabweazara, Hayes M. 2011. "New Media and Journalism Practice in Africa: An Agenda for Research". *Journalism: Theory, Practice & Criticism* 12(6): 667–673.

Berger, Guy. 2000. "Grave new world? Democratic journalism enters the global twenty-first century". *Journalism Studies* 1(1): 81–99.

———. 2005. "Powering African Newsrooms: Theorising how Southern African Journalists make use of ICTs for Newsgathering". In *Doing Digital Journalism: How Southern African Newsgatherers are using ICTs*, edited by Berger, Guy, 1–14. Grahamstown: High Way Africa.

Cottle, Simon. 2000. "Towards a 'Second Wave' of News Ethnography". *Communications* 25(1): 19–41.

de Souza e Silva, Adrian. 2006. "Reconceptualising the Mobile Phone—From Telephone to Collective Interfaces". *Australian Journal of Emerging Technologies and Society* 4(2): 108–127.

Deuze, Mark. 1998. "The WebCommunicators: Issues in Research into Online Journalism and Journalists". *First Monday* 12(3). Accessed June 10, 2007. *http://www.firstmonday.dk/issues/issue3_12/deuze/index.html*.

———. 2003. "The Web and its Journalisms: Considering the Consequences of Different types of Newsmedia Online". *New Media & Society* 5(2): 203–230.

Deuze, Mark and Dimoudi, Christian. 2002. "Online journalists in the Netherlands: Towards a Profile of a New Profession". *Journalism, Theory, Practice & Criticism* 3(1): 85–100.

Fenton, Natalie. 2010. "Drowning of Waving? New Media, Journalism and Democracy". In *New Media, Old News: Journalism & Democracy in the Digital Age*, edited by Fenton, Natalie, 3–16. London: Sage.

Flew, Terry. 2002. *New Media: An Introduction*. Oxford: Oxford University Press.

Heap, Nick, Thomas, Ray, Einon, Geoff, Mason, Robin and Mackay, Hug, ed. 1995. *Information Technology and Society*. London: Sage.

Hyde-Clarke, Nathalie, ed. 2010. *The Citizen in Communication: Re-visiting Traditional, New and Community Media Practices in South Africa*. Capetown: Juta & Co.

Ibelema, Minabere. 2008. *The African Press, Civic Cynicism, and Democracy*. New York: Palgrave Macmillan.

Jankowski, Nicholas, Jones, Steve, Samarajiva, Rohan and Silverstone, Roger. 1999. "Editorial". *New Media & Society* 1(1): 5–9.

Kawamoto, Kevin. 2003. *Digital Journalism: Emerging Media and the Changing Horizons of Journalism*. Lanham: Rowman & Littlefield.

Lister, Martin, Dovey, Jon, Giddings, Seth, Grant, Ian and Kelly, Kieran. 2003. *New Media: A Critical Introduction*. London: Routledge.

Lowrey, Wilson. 2006. "Mapping the Journalism-Blogging Relationship". *Journalism: Theory, Practice & Criticism* 7(4): 477–500.

Mabweazara, Hayes M. 2010. "'New' Technologies and Journalism Practice in Africa: Towards a Critical Sociological Approach". In *The Citizen in Communication: Re-visiting Traditional, New and Community Media Practices in South Africa*, edited by Hyde-Clarke, Nathalie, 11–30. Capetown: Juta & Co.

———. 2011. "Between the Newsroom and the Pub: The Mobile Phone in the Dynamics of Everyday Mainstream Journalism Practice in Zimbabwe". *Journalism, Theory, Practice & Criticism* 12(6): 692–707.

Meikle, Graham and Redden, Guy. 2011. "Introduction: Transformation and Continuity". In *News Online: Transformations and Continuities*, edited by Meikle, Graham and Redden, Guy, 1–15. New York: Palgrave Macmillan.

Meikle, Graham and Young, Sherman. 2012. *Media Convergence: Networked Digital Media in Everyday Life*. New York: Palgrave Macmillan.

Mitchelstein, Eugenia and Boczkowski, Pablo J. 2009. "Between tradition and change: A review of recent research on online news production". *Journalism: Theory, Practice & Criticism* 10(5): 562–586.

Moyo, Dumisani. 2009. "Citizen Journalism and the Parallel Market of Information in Zimbabwe's 2008 Elections". *Journalism Studies* 10(4): 551–567.

Moyo, Last. 2009. "Repression, Propaganda, and Digital Resistance: New Media and Democracy in Zimbabwe". In *African Media and the Digital Public Sphere*, edited by Okoth F. Mudhai, Wisdom, J. Tettey, and Fackson, Banda, 57–71. New York: Palgrave Macmillan.

Mudhai, Fred. O. 2003. "Exploring the Potential for Strategic Civil Society Uses of Mobile Phones: Social Science Research Council Sponsored Paper". Accessed April 24, 2007. *http://www.programs.ssrc.org/itic/publications/knowledge report/memos/okoth.pdf*.

Nyamnjoh Francis B. 1999. "African Cultural Studies, Cultural Studies in Africa: How to Make a Useful Difference". *Critical Arts: A Journal of Cultural Studies in Africa* 13(1): 15–39.

———. 2005. *Africa's Media: Democracy and the Politics of Belonging*. London: Zed Books.

Paterson, Chris. 2008. "Introduction: Why Ethnography?" In *Making Online News: The Ethnography of New Media Production*, edited by Paterson, Chris and Domingo, David, 1–11. New York: Peter Lang.

———. 2013. "Journalism and Social Media in the African Context". *Ecquid Novi: African Journalism Studies* 34(1): 1–6.

Paterson, Chris and Domingo, David, eds. 2008. *Making Online News: An Ethnography of New Media Production*. New York: Peter Lang.

Sasole, Sujatha. 2003. "Envisioning a New World Order Through Journalism: Lessons from recent History". *Journalism: Theory, Practice & Criticism* 4(3): 377–392.

Silverstone, Roger. 1999. "What's New about New Media?" *New Media & Society* 1(1): 10–12.

Singer, Jane B. 2003. "Who are These Guys? The Online Challenge to the Notion of Journalistic Professionalism". *Journalism: Theory, Practice & Criticism* 4(2): 139–163.

Steensen, Steen. 2011. "Online Journalism and the Promises of New Technology: A Critical Review and Look Ahead". *Journalism Studies* 12(3): 311–327.

Part I

Online vs. Traditional Journalism Practice

1   Back to the Future

Reinvigorating the 'Newsroom Genre' to Study Social Media Use in Developing Contexts

Marenet Jordaan

It's like asking whether being able to use a dictaphone instead of a shorthand notebook will help journalism or not. I think social media is such a basic part of what journalism should do now. Whether it helps you or not, is irrelevant. It's part of what you do. If I had to answer the question . . . social media is going to be the saving of journalism.

(Chris Roper, editor of the *Mail & Guardian Online* 2011)

INTRODUCTION

Social media are not the new kids on the block anymore. Most of these technologies and platforms, such as Facebook and Twitter, have established themselves as high-profile players in the media and communications landscape over the past decade. Due to high broadband Internet costs and various levels of inequality, the penetration rate of these platforms in developing countries, such as South Africa, has not yet reached the proportions of that in the developed Global North. However, the rate at which citizens access these social media platforms and technologies in South Africa—when compared to the rest of Africa—is steadily rising. Social media enable people to become so-called 'prosumers' of news: they are not just passive consumers but also have a chance to produce, distribute and interact with their own versions of the truth in global public forums.

These digital social interactions have some profound implications for mainstream media organisations and professional journalism. In recent years, research has been done on whether journalists use social media and whether they find these technologies credible. There has been little focus, however, on what the impact of these technologies might be on the routines and cultures within professional newsrooms. This lack of research is especially evident within developing contexts and/or the Global South.

Web-based surveys and content analyses are worthwhile for investigating the rise of social media. However, it remains crucial to speak to journalists— within newsrooms as their natural environments—about their experiences and impressions regarding the permeation of new technological variables such as Facebook and Twitter into these newsrooms.

Following Cottle's (2000) advice, this study proposes that journalism researchers take a renewed look at newsroom studies or newsroom ethnography as methods to investigate the impact of social media as a new variable on professional newsrooms. As discussed below, seminal newsroom studies, such as those by Gaye Tuchman (1978) and Herbert J. Gans ([1979] (2004), might be of value as starting points here. But as Wasserman (2010, 10) argues in his study of tabloid journalism, theoretical debates on journalism and media studies too often ignore conditions in the 'Global South', or what will in this chapter be referred to as 'developing countries'. According to Wasserman (2010, 10), the result is that "[. . .] theoretical frameworks and future predictions are often arrived at by extrapolating the experiences of a limited range of countries and regions to assume universal relevance". It remains critical, therefore, for local researchers in the developing world to investigate the experiences unique to the professional journalists at work in their countries. This is arguably the best way to arrive at a point where theoretical frameworks include a wider variety of views and experiences.

The discussion that follows illustrates one example of how newsroom ethnography within a social constructionist paradigm was employed to investigate whether the professional use of social media, with specific reference to Facebook and Twitter, influences the processes and cultures of news selection and presentation in newspaper newsrooms. The results are based on empirical research done in June and July 2011 at *Rapport,* an Afrikaans-language Sunday newspaper owned by Media24 (subsidiary of international media conglomerate Naspers), and the *Mail & Guardian,* an independent English weekly newspaper owned by *Mail & Guardian* Media Limited.

The study used a combination of qualitative and quantitative research methodologies to triangulate results. The focus was on the newsroom study, with a two-week-long period of newsroom ethnography and semi-structured interviews. The interviews were conducted with a purposefully selected sample of journalists and editors. In order to draw this sample, the researcher conducted preliminary surveys of the Twitter and Facebook usage of the journalists at *Rapport* and the *Mail & Guardian* in Gauteng. This process enabled the researcher to identify journalists who are either very active on social media or who are not active at all and might not even have Twitter or Facebook accounts. Leedy and Ormrod (2005, 206) summarise this as choosing people who are either "typical" of a group or those who represent "diverse perspectives on an issue". A preliminary survey of journalists from both *Rapport* and the *Mail & Guardian* showed that the majority of the journalists have a presence on Facebook and/or Twitter—albeit not necessarily an active one. It can therefore be inferred that this group typically has some kind of social media presence.

To initiate the research and assist with establishing a framework for further investigation during the semi-structured interviews, self-administered questionnaires were distributed to all the journalists and editors in these two newsrooms during June 2011. At the time the research was conducted, limited academic research on professional social media use by journalists existed. Industry studies on the topic as well as guidelines on the design of questionnaires by established media researchers therefore served as starting points for the structuring of this questionnaire. The final questionnaire consisted of four sections on social media use and its relationship to newsroom routines. Questions were mostly based on 'yes' or 'no' answers or a variety of Likert scales (to assess the degree to which a respondent agrees/disagrees with a statement). With 21 questionnaires returned, the response rate was around 67 percent.[1]

Ethnographic principles were applied when visiting each newsroom for one production week at the end of June and the beginning of July 2011. During this period, the researcher took field notes of her own personal impressions and observations, made descriptive notes of journalists' actions and events in the newsrooms and engaged in informal conversations with various journalists and editors.

Fetterman (1998, 1) compares the work of an ethnographer to that of an investigative reporter, with one key difference: journalists look for the unusual, whereas the ethnographer writes about the "routine, daily lives of people". In the weeks spent at each of the newspapers, I attempted to establish what the cultures and the general news routines of the journalists in the newsrooms were as well as what roles social media played in this regard.

Due to time constraints, observation was possible for only a period of one production week at each newspaper. Although this was ample time to gather information about regular routines, such as editorial conferences, this might not have been sufficient time for the journalists to get comfortable enough to see the researcher as part of their natural environment. Relationships were easier to establish at *Rapport* than at the *Mail & Guardian* because I worked there (at *Rapport*) as a journalist between 2005 and 2009 and knew a fair number of the journalists and editors. It must be noted, however, that I worked in a satellite office (in Pretoria, not the head office in Johannesburg) and was therefore not part of the day-to-day editorial conferences. However, I was still known to some as a journalist, not an academic. This perception might have contributed to my particular awareness that I should not be, for lack of a better word, "friendly" with the journalists when it came to data capturing and analysis.

This prior relationship with the *Rapport* news office also initially made it easier for me to schedule semi-structured interviews with journalists and editors in this newsroom. I did these 15 interviews in the two different newsrooms during the same period that I made the ethnographic observations in each newsroom.

Although the study is limited in scope, it important to emphasise that the aim of this chapter is to highlight the importance of the newsroom genre as a research paradigm for the exploration and description of how new technologies are accepted within traditional professional newsrooms. The term 'newsroom genre' as used here refers to the exploration and investigation of phenomena within a newsroom using methods that are based on ethnographic principles. As explained by Schultz (2007, 191), newsroom studies involve the study of "journalistic practices in news organisations and on newsbeats". According to Schultz (2007, 191), such studies have provided media and communication researchers with "important insights on the inner workings of media research". Newsroom studies therefore include direct contact with journalists within their natural environments. This contact consists not only of formal interviews but also of participant observation and informal conversations.

In presenting the results of my study, I also hope to contribute knowledge to the debate on whether social media is seen as an opportunity or a threat by newspaper journalists in South Africa. The latter issue, however, is not the main focus of this chapter.

THE SOUTH AFRICAN NEWSPAPER LANDSCAPE

> *The newspaper industry enters 2012 neither dying nor assured of a stable future.*

These opening words in the essay on newspapers (Edmonds et al. 2012) in the *State of the News Media 2012* report ring true not only for American journalism. If we look at the World Association of Newspapers and Newspublishers' World Press Trends for 2012, it might still look as if global newspaper circulation is rising, but these increases are fuelled mainly by growth in China and India (In Publishing 2012).

The South African newspaper industry has not been immune to the forces that have been putting its global counterparts under immense pressure. A tough economic climate, lack of advertising revenue, declining readership and a steady rise in the Internet penetration rate make it increasingly difficult for newspapers to remain competitive.

The South African Audit Bureau of Circulations reports on its website on 14 August 2012 that circulation of local daily newspapers declined by 5.5 percent (equivalent to 414,000 copies) from 2008 to the second quarter of 2012. The circulation of weekend newspapers also declined by 2.6 percent annually since 2008. In contrast, weekly newspapers recovered to their 2008 levels after a dip in 2010.

Rapport, the widest reaching Afrikaans (weekend) newspaper, and the *Mail & Guardian,* an independent investigative weekly, differ in terms of target market and ownership. However, they have similar deadlines and production routines, which is what this study focused on. Therefore, these newspapers served as good case studies for an exploratory study into how newspaper newsrooms might react to the introduction of a new variable: social media.

AFRICA AND SOCIAL MEDIA USE

As mentioned in the introduction, there might be millions of Facebook and Twitter users in some African countries (such as Egypt, Nigeria, Kenya and South Africa), yet the penetration of these media is generally very low.[2] This low penetration rate can for the most part certainly be ascribed to the low Internet-penetration rates on the continent. The International Telecommunications Union (ITU) reports on its website (in its statistical highlights for 2012) that fixed-broadband penetration in Africa was only 0.2 percent at the end of 2011, compared to 12 percent in China and 35 percent in the Global North (such as France and the Netherlands). Mobile broadband penetration rates in Africa are slightly higher at five subscriptions per 100 inhabitants, compared to 10 percent in other regions. According to the ITU, "major differences in Internet bandwidth per Internet user persist between regions: on average, a user in Europe enjoys 25 times as much international Internet capacity as a user in Africa."

South Africa is at the forefront of social media use on the continent. A leading technology research company, World Wide Worx, reported on its website on 4 September 2012 that both Facebook and Twitter had grown in South Africa in the previous year at a rate of 100,000 new users every month. This *South African Social Media Landscape Study* by World Wide Worx also found that both Facebook and Twitter have "crossed the urban/ rural divide"; in other words, rural adults using these social media are catching up to the urban adults. Another industry study by Strategy Worx Consulting reported on its website on 22 August 2012 that around 75 percent of Internet users in the country had Facebook accounts, and 18 percent were using Twitter.

The role of cell phones in social media use on the continent should not be ignored and arguably needs further study. The ITU reports that by the end of 2011, there were 105 countries worldwide with more mobile-cellular subscriptions than inhabitants. These include African countries such as Botswana, Gabon, Namibia, the Seychelles and South Africa. Strategy Worx Consulting wrote on their website on 22 August 2012 that of the around 5.3 million South Africans with Facebook accounts at the time of reporting, around 4.5 million accessed these accounts on their cell phones. In this industry study on social media and mobile use in South Africa, Strategy Worx found that adoption of social media in South Africa is driven by an increase in the use of smartphones.

It is noteworthy that whereas Facebook and Twitter dominate worldwide (and are the focus of this study), Africa is also seeing growth in local and regional social networks, which are often better geared for mobile use. The technology website Memeburn reported in September 2012 on two such networks: MixIt and 2go. According to Memeburn, 2go has seen impressive growth across Africa since its 2008 launch: nine million monthly users in Nigeria, 1.5 million in South Africa and 300,000 in Kenya.

It would follow that the use of social networks for mobile use—and its influence on professional journalism—should also become the focus of local media and journalism research.

NEWSROOM ETHNOGRAPHY—RENEWED

Newsroom studies remain valid for investigating and describing the influence of external factors, such as the introduction of new technologies, on the newsroom. Hermans et al. (2009, 139) have found that the Internet, for instance, has brought changes to news flows, daily journalistic routines and professional accountability. Cottle and Ashton (1999, 22) used a newsroom study to make a case against technological determinism when they studied the influence of new technologies on news production at the British Broadcasting Corporation. Another recent example is the work of Sue Robinson (2011), who did a year-long ethnographic study at a Wisconsin-based newspaper in the United States as it shifted its focus from a daily print product to online. I agree with this author that news ethnography specifically has shown to "reveal the deep context of . . . transformations in ways that would show the values, routines and attitudes behind new manifestations of journalistic work" (Robinson 2011, 153).

Despite the validation and relevance of the aforementioned study and other related research, modern newsroom studies are not as comprehensive and do not appear at such regular intervals as when Tuchman (1978) did her ten-year long research. This is why Schultz (2007, 191) argues for a "re-invigoration" of the newsroom genre. According to Schultz (2007, 191),

> [. . .] news ethnography is a key method for studying the processes and norms guiding the producers and the production, but as most of the studies are Anglo-American and were conducted around the 1970s, we need more research on the everyday processes of news work in different cultural settings in order to understand the diverse, globalised journalistic cultures of the 21st century. [. . .] Naturally, a re-invigoration of the newsroom genre means complementing the previous findings as well as trying to improve the analytical frameworks used in the past.

Wright (1995, 100) says early newsroom studies adopted the functionalist approach to analyse mass media organisations and to examine patterns within those organisations. According to Boyd-Barrett (1995, 73), the system-focus of functionalism "tends towards a rather mechanical way of asking and addressing questions". Boyd-Barret (1995, 73) argues that it lends itself better to the theoretical than to the practical or empirical levels of inquiry and that it is not "well suited to the subtleties and ambivalences of social, cultural and economic processes". Cottle (2000, 21) also criticises early researchers such as Tuchman (1978) and Gans ([1979] 2004) for their view of news as an "organizational and bureaucratic accomplishment of routine", which he terms "organizational functionalism".

Although some of the fundamental principles of early researchers such as Tuchman and Gans can be appreciated and adopted in context, their approaches tend to be limited and too narrow for a study that incorporates the flexibility of new media technologies. In making this statement, I remain cognisant of the fact that studying the impact of technologies on newsmaking was not part of these researchers' objectives—hence the validity of renewing these studies. Therefore, the present study adopted an alternative approach to newsroom study.

Berkowitz (1989) compares the methodological differences of what he refers to as the "naturalist paradigm" with the positivist (or dominant) paradigm when doing newsroom research. According to Berkowitz (1989, 1), naturalism begins in a "less-structured manner", with background about the problem to be studied. The method moves to data collection within the context of the situation "as the study evolves" (1989, 1). Berkowitz (1989, 4) emphasises that it is "unavoidable in an interactive situation" that the researcher working within a naturalist paradigm will interact with the people he or she studies. The research can therefore never be completely objective (Berkowitz 1989, 4). Guba and Lincoln (1982, 238) also describe the aim of gathering knowledge during naturalistic inquiry as developing a series of "working hypotheses" that describe each individual case. According to them, one can never generalise because phenomena are always studied within a certain context and time frame. Guba and Lincoln (1982, 234) say that "[. . .] finding a paradigm that can tolerate real world conditions surely makes more sense than manipulating those conditions to meet the arbitrary design requirements of a paradigm".

Following this argument, I adopted a social constructionist approach for my newsroom study to work within the critical, or naturalist, paradigm. In adopting this approach, the study views reality as a social construct and sees the media as an entity which helps to create and construct various realities.

To work with social constructionism as a theoretical framework, it was necessary, according to Burr (2003, 3), to be "ever suspicious of our assumptions about how the world appears to be". Burr (2003, 4) says that instead of deriving our knowledge of the world from the natural world as it is, we should understand that knowledge is constructed when people interact with each other. Gergen (2009, 58) argues that constructionists give voice to the cultural traditions of which they are a part when they select phenomena to study. It is therefore important to note that the researcher working in this paradigm is part of a society in which social media usage is currently a cultural by-product of a specific period in time.

According to Burr (2003, 149), social constructionist research usually shows a preference for qualitative methods of inquiry partly because they are viewed as "less likely to decontextualize the experience and accounts of respondents". Burr (2003, 152) emphasises that researchers who work within a social constructionist framework will view objectivity as impossible because everyone approaches the world from some perspective, and the assumptions embedded in this perspective will inform the questions he or she asks about the world. One should therefore take note that researchers who adopt the social constructionist paradigm should acknowledge their own responses to and involvement in the research process—even more so when doing ethnographic research.

Similar studies have used the social constructionist approach for newsroom studies. Paulussen and Ugille (2008, 37), for instance, contend that social constructionist approaches "provide an appropriate theoretical framework to reveal [. . .] contextual factors that help us understand more profoundly how mainstream news media are dealing with user generated content and citizen journalism". In this sense, social constructionism is especially useful as a research paradigm when working with social media because these technologies also enable consumers to challenge and to influence the realities shaped by the media.

Mabweazara (2011) also employs the social constructivist approach to technology in his study of the influence of mobile phones on the everyday routines of mainstream journalists in Zimbabwe. He acknowledges that "journalism (and research into journalism) is not performed in a vacuum, independent of the shaping impact of contextual influences" (2011, 694).

The use of Bourdieu's field theory, and specifically the *habitus* concept, might serve to try to bridge the gap left by earlier newsroom studies that focused mostly on structure and routine. A complete analysis of Bourdieu's field theory falls beyond the scope of this chapter, but it is important to take note of the field concept described by Bourdieu (2005, 30) as "the site of actions and reactions performed by social agents endowed with permanent dispositions, partly acquired in their experiences of these social fields". Schultz (2007, 190) argues that the field perspective contributes a "promising analytical framework to re-invigorate the genre of news ethnography". In Bourdieu's (2005, 33) terms, it is not enough to have knowledge of the world that surrounds the journalistic field because "[. . .] part of what is produced in the world of journalism cannot be understood unless one conceptualizes this microcosm as such and endeavours to understand the effects that the people engaged in this microcosm exert on one another". Benson and Neveu (2005, 3) argue that the concept of *habitus* expresses a "reasonable hypothesis". They argue that "individuals' predispositions, assumptions, judgments, and behaviours are the result of a long-term process of socialization, most importantly in the family, and secondarily, via primary, secondary, and professional education" (Benson and Neveu 2005, 3).

Bourdieu (1990, 61) argues that the *habitus* will defend itself against change by rejecting information—"if exposed to it accidentally or by force"—capable of calling into question the information that is already part of its history and make-up. Following Bourdieu's reasoning, one might therefore assume that changes within the newsroom will be met with resistance from the journalists within. This view is supported by, for instance, Ryfe's 18-month long ethnographic study of an American daily newspaper where a new editor was brought in to introduce new news-gathering and reporting practices (Ryfe 2011). He found that the culture of professionalism in the newsrooms is "remarkably resilient and resistant to change" and that the resistance to change is "institutional and cultural" (Ryfe 2011, 166). According to Ryfe (2011, 166) "deviations from their basic routines and practices may threaten journalists' ability to find and transform information into news, and may also trouble deep-seated conceptions of identity and value within the profession".

Social media may also be viewed as an agent of change within newspaper newsrooms. One could thus argue that an investigation of newsroom culture, or *habitus,* will contribute essential knowledge to ethnographies that explore the impact of social media on newsrooms.

Despite the usefulness of the newsroom genre, this methodology is not without its drawbacks for exploring social media influences. Mabweazara (2010, 665) discusses the challenges of using ethnography to research the use of new technologies by journalists, for instance, "how to observe a journalist browsing the internet, writing a text message on his/her mobile phone or engaging in a mobile phone conversation, without being deemed too intrusive and relating these practices to the object of one's study". Although these were key challenges in the present study, the newsroom layouts at the *Rapport* and the *Mail & Guardian* made observing journalists at work behind their desks equally difficult.[3]

A researcher would need to spend a considerable amount of time in a newsroom to almost become invisible and/or gain the trust of the journalists. He or she would arguably then get a far more comprehensive picture of the daily routines and culture in the newsroom. Such research, however, is expensive and often deemed intrusive by time-pressured working journalists. I am of the opinion that more needs to be done to convince practicing journalists that the findings of such research will be of value to them as well. This might go a long way toward facilitating better access for researchers—and perhaps even public funding. Although the latter suggestion might be an ethical minefield, I would argue that in a developing context, it is often a necessity to enable proper research.

Despite my aforementioned reservations regarding the newsroom genre, I am confident that the triangulation of research methods used in this study enabled the validation of the results summarised below.

SUMMARY OF RESULTS: TRACKING
TRENDS AND MAKING FRIENDS

As discussed above, a successful newsroom study focuses on observing and interviewing journalists within their natural environments. This study was no different. Without the time spent in the newsroom, drawing conclusions and answering the research questions posed by this study would arguably have been nearly impossible. Close-ended questionnaires alone would not have provided the findings necessary for in-depth analysis of themes and issues related to professional social media use. I contend that journalists often become self-reflective about their own practices only when directly confronted with questions about such practices and routines.

More specifically, the use of ethnographic principles enabled the researcher to identify where the journalists' perceptions of their own actions and behaviours differed from reality (as observed by the researcher). The use of these principles also provided the opportunity to observe the journalists within a group setting (such as editorial conferences) and thus to draw conclusions about the influence of newsroom culture on the professional use of social media in these two newsrooms.

The majority of the journalists at *Rapport* and the *Mail & Guardian* who took part in this study indicated that they did not feel they had adapted their schedules, news typologies, beat structure or relationships with sources according to their professional use of Facebook and Twitter. One senior journalist at the *Mail & Guardian* summarised the general sentiment as follows:

> It is giving social media too much importance to say that it has changed the news agenda. It has probably had an influence, but a very minimal influence [. . .] It's a communication tool. It's all it is. Like a telephone or an Internet account or an RSS[4] feeder.

Most of the journalists also rated Twitter and Facebook the lowest as sources during the newsgathering process—when compared to documents, first person encounters, electronic research, public events and publicity agents. The news editor at the *Mail & Guardian* said he does not know of any stories their newsroom picked up on Twitter that they would not have picked up as quickly on the telephone or the newswires. "I don't think it offers any major advantages in terms of access to news developments," he said.

Working within a social constructionist paradigm, however, I had to critically examine and question some of these responses—especially after the week of ethnographic research at each publication. The journalists, for instance, believed that they were gathering most of their information for news articles from personal contact with sources. A *Mail & Guardian* journalist said that social media create the space for a one-on-one conversation with someone you have never met. "It's not substitution for a one-on-one," she said. A junior journalist at *Rapport* agreed when she said that she might "find someone on Facebook, but will still make an appointment to see that person. It [Facebook] just makes that initial contact easier."

Some journalists were also very sceptical about using Facebook or Twitter as a means of engaging with sources. One assistant editor of *Rapport,* for instance, explained that social media take "[. . .] telephone journalism one step further. How you have to write your story, is by going out and looking someone in the eyes [. . .]. I have seen too many mistakes from [using] things that have been on Facebook".

Not only more seasoned journalists questioned social media as a tool to engage with sources. One intern at the *Mail & Guardian* said he was "uneasy" about using social media as a journalist because people often just put "random" thoughts on it, and those can be used out of context. Some younger journalists were especially concerned with these media's ability to reach a wider audience, especially in developing countries such as South Africa. One *Mail & Guardian* journalist said he sometimes feels that

> [. . .] South African journalists take it a little bit too seriously and are losing touch with reality on the ground, and the people on the ground who aren't on Twitter. Twitter can explode with a story [. . .] but you actually feel this is a very small segment of a population. Not everybody feels this way, so while it feels like a huge event to you, it is a small ripple in a huge pond.

Journalists did not factor in social media when talking about what determined the way they planned their days and weeks. Although clearly encouraged to do so by their editors, journalists did not often present ideas or follow-up ideas that originated from social media. In the questionnaires, most journalists said they find story ideas on Facebook or Twitter every few months—and the rest reported doing so even less often.

However, the majority of journalists (almost 50 percent) said that they often (daily/weekly) use Facebook—and to a lesser extent Twitter—as a means to find sources. This is despite the fact that they were adamant about spending their days outside the office having coffee with their sources. It was also observed that the majority of the journalists (especially at *Rapport*) spent most of the week actually in the office and sometimes finished articles without meeting a source in person at all. Although social media cannot be seen as the only factor contributing to office-bound journalism, observations such as this led the researcher to question the journalists' perceptions regarding their own actions more critically.

It was also observed that some of the time the journalists spent at the office was spent on social media. This observation was confirmed through informal conversations with journalists at both publications. Most journalists, especially at *Rapport*, admitted that they open Facebook and Twitter the moment they get to the office and often keep it open throughout the day. Even journalists who believed that social media did not apply to story ideation and sourcing admitted that they spent some of their time at the office using social media. As remarked by the assistant-editor of *Rapport*, this might be a further indication that the traditional image of a journalist hitting the pavement to track down sources and stories is slowly fading.

Much of what the journalists used Facebook and Twitter for can be summarised as 'trend tracking'. Browsing social media in this manner might appear like a waste of time. In an informal conversation on the use of social media, a senior reporter at *Rapport* explained thus: "I don't always know where the line is between when I am working and when I am just looking at trash".

But the present study demonstrated that trend tracking appeared to aid some of the journalists when it came to staying informed (in general and about specific topics they were reporting on). The editor-in-chief of the *Mail & Guardian* told me that he used social media to stay in touch with what is going on outside his newsroom to get a sense "of where people are addressing the right things and where they are addressing the wrong things". One journalist at *Rapport* also said that part of the allure of social media—specifically as a professional reporting tool—is that you "play around". He said, "Ninety-five percent of the stuff is fluff and five percent are stories. But that's the way research has always been".

Social media also afforded journalists the opportunity to engage with their audiences in a more personal manner. A senior journalist at the *Mail & Guardian* explained that social media "open up the debate. It makes things more democratic. I think in the past it was a little [like] one way traffic. With the coming of social media there is a lot more interaction".

Journalists also actively used social media to promote themselves and their work. Although the topic of self-promotion and branding was not investigated in depth in this study, it was apparent from the interviews that journalists considered this to be an important aspect of using social media as a professional tool. Even the news editor of the *Mail & Guardian,* who openly did not support social media as a professional newsgathering tool at the time, said the one thing he thinks it can be valuable and professionally useful for, for the newspaper, is to promote stories.

In the context of the typification of news (as described by Tuchman 1978), the findings of this study indicate the necessity for the bulk of the news constructed by newspapers today[5] to be reclassified as 'developing news' rather than 'hard news' because of the advent of social media. Tuchman (1978, 50) found that journalists use different story types to describe the practical tasks involved in producing those stories and the synchronisation of their work with likely news occurrences. She (1978, 51) distinguishes between hard news, soft news, spot news, continuing news and developing news. The journalists in this study do not see themselves as writing 'soft news'. Yet they refer to what they do as analysis and interpretation of emerging events-as-news (developing news) rather than of breaking news (hard news). A senior journalist at *Rapport* for instance noted that

> [...] nobody is going to get breaking news from the newspapers anymore
> [...] They [newspapers] will have to switch to analysis and in-depth and
> more lifestyle stuff. This does not mean fluffy, pink-around-the-edges

stuff. It basically means stuff that is approached more narratively [sic] and with a bit more analysis.

All my research methods substantiated the argument that newsroom culture, or collective *habitus,* played a significant role in journalists' acceptance of social media as a professional tool. Journalists at *Rapport* and the *Mail & Guardian* experienced their newsrooms as open and encouraging towards the use of social media. Specific emphasis was placed on the influence of the two newspapers' editors and the way they personally adopted and employed social media. A junior reporter at *Rapport* said about *Rapport*'s editor: "[. . .] when you see her, she is on that phone looking at Twitter feeds". Some journalists at this paper emphasised that it was the editor herself who introduced them to Twitter and showed them how to use it. An online junior subeditor at the *Mail & Guardian* said they should start a fan page on Facebook for *Mail & Guardian*'s editor-in-chief because of his social media following. At the time of writing, he had around 21,000 followers on Twitter—making him one of the most influential journalists in the country. This editor said many of the *Mail & Guardian* journalists are on Facebook having serious discussions with office-bearers and colleagues, without thinking they are using social media as a professional tool. "They just think they are on Facebook," he said.

The lack of support for social media usage from some senior staff members did not seem to deter the journalists from using these media. Despite the lack of formal social media policies at the time of research, the newsroom cultures indicated an environment where the professional use of social media would flourish without fail. It is important to add here that the ethnographic research showed that social media rarely featured in editorial news conferences. Whereas the journalists said that ideas originating from social media were encouraged, the study did not indicate any significant news-related conversations that involved social media at both newsrooms. It was, however, observed that the newsroom cultures at *Rapport* and the *Mail & Guardian* openly encourage the use of social media such as Facebook and Twitter. None of the journalists were restricted regarding the time they spent on social media. Most of the journalists felt comfortable using these media, and especially at the *Mail & Guardian,* they knew what their institutions expected of them when interacting via these media. At the time of study, the journalists at the *Mail & Guardian* had already taken part in a workshop run by the online staff on social media as a reporting tool as well as on the ethics involved. They were all aware of their editor's viewpoint on social media use. According to this editor-in-chief of the *Mail & Guardian*, journalists cannot separate the personal and the professional on social media, and "you need to manage your personal presence online in a way that is consistent with your professional responsibilities and the parameters within which your organisation is able to roam". In February 2012 (around six months after the completion of the fieldwork for this study), the newspaper introduced an ethical code on social media use—one of the first for a print publication in the country. At *Rapport*, efforts to establish a social media policy were more disjointed. Journalists also had differing viewpoints on how to manage their personal and professional profiles on social media.

Overall, the journalists at *Rapport* and the *Mail & Guardian* viewed social media as a supplement to their work rather than as a threat. That being said, they were aware that the immediacy and reach of social media such as Facebook and Twitter challenge the traditional role of journalists. They believed that their role as gatekeepers was still valid, particularly to aggregate and interpret the massive influx of information that their audiences had to deal with. They felt that journalists should help a person to make sense of all the noise by filtering through the information and presenting that which is most important in the order of most importance. A journalist at the *Mail & Guardian* told me that the role of a journalist

> [. . .] has probably changed in that the journalist still has to distil all these things and make sense of them and help people make sense of them [. . .] You probably have to be more media savvy now as a journalist and be able to be on that many platforms, but what you still have to be able to provide is a role of something more considered or slightly more authoritative.

Facebook and Twitter have, therefore, become a natural part of the lives (at a personal as well as professional level) of the majority of the journalists at *Rapport* and the *Mail & Guardian*. The journalists might have viewed these media as separate from their usual activities, routines and cultures within the newsroom, but from a social constructionist point of view, I would argue that being immersed in social media forced the journalists to alter the way they approached news selection and presentation even if they did not reflect internally about it.

FINAL THOUGHTS

I concur with Wasserman (2009, 114), who says that a critical global journalism would have to incorporate the study of new media technologies "on a practical, but also on a reflective intellectual level." Wasserman (2009, 114) says

> Critical approaches to media globalisation will puncture the often exaggerated and technological-determinist views of the potential of new media technologies for journalism, by studying the use of these technologies within the overarching structural economic conditions as well as their actual everyday use. This would mean taking into account the enormous disparities worldwide regarding access to the Internet, for

example, but also the creative ways in which people in the South appropriate and adapt technologies to suit their various socio-cultural and economic settings.

I would argue that in order to reflect intellectually about the influence of these technologies on professional journalism, knowledge and insight on the impact on a practical level would first need to be gained. Although my study was limited in scope, it was clear from the outset that a researcher has to familiarize herself with the context and culture within a newsroom to properly describe journalists' responses. One also has to critically examine the responses of journalists during formal interviews and questionnaires— because they are often more guarded during such interrogations or do not want to spend too much time reflecting about their daily routines. Their actions and routines, however, can be observed and described by doing newsroom ethnography. Attending daily newsroom conferences, observing journalists at work or engaging in informal conversations arguably deliver much richer research data—especially concerning attitudes, assumptions and change.

Therefore, I believe the importance of newsrooms studies for exploring the introduction of new technologies into mainstream or traditional newsrooms cannot be overstated—especially in developing contexts where ethnographic journalistic research are usually not that common. This type of research takes more effort on the part of the researcher and the journalists who have to open their newsrooms to a stranger. This research approach is also expensive and time-intensive, and the findings are not easy to quantify. However, empirical research of this nature will be worthwhile for the journalism academy worldwide, especially once cross-country research relationships can be developed and theoretical frameworks established. Journalism practitioners might also find value in findings from such studies, such as why some journalists are still wary of professional social media use.

One cannot ignore the role social media play in journalism anymore. The editor-in-chief of the *Mail & Guardian* explained that social media

> [. . .] are a kind of natural environment for journalists. We are all gossipy people. We all love data—there are masses of data out there. We are all a bit egotistical [. . .] [Social media usage] says I'm not only a broadcaster, this is not just a one way process, you don't have to just listen to what I have to say, I am responsive, I am an engaged part of the community, I will respond if you are someone who's been talking to me for a while and you have something interesting to say.

The question, therefore, is no longer whether journalists *are* using social media—not even in the African context. How professional journalists within their natural environments react to the introduction of these media is what should be investigated now.

NOTES

1. For consistency and analysis purposes, the researcher estimated how many journalists and editors would have been in the office if *all* the staff were present given that the number of journalists present varies every week.
2. For recent statistics and analysis, visit www.alexa.com, a website that provides free global web metrics.
3. At *Rapport*, journalists have individual offices and often close their doors. At the *Mail & Guardian*, there is an open-plan office; however, I had to work harder for access because I was a newcomer to this news office.
4. RSS refers to "Really Simple Syndication", a web format that is used to aggregate and publish various types of information that are regularly updated, such as blogs and news postings.
5. This is especially true in the case of weekly and weekend newspapers, which now compete not only with other traditional media, such as daily newspapers, to break news, but also with social media.

REFERENCES

Benson, Rodney and Neveu, Erik. 2005. "Introduction: Field Theory as a Work in Progress". In *Bourdieu and the journalistic field,* edited by Benson, Rodney and Neveu, Erik, 1–25. Cambridge: Polity.

Berkowitz, Dan. 1989. "Notes from the Newsroom: Reflecting on a Naturalistic Case Study". Paper Presented at the Annual Convention for the Association for Education in Journalism and Mass Communication Annual Convention, Washington, 10–13 August.

Bourdieu, Pierre. 1990. *The logic of practice.* Cambridge: Polity.

———. 2005. "The Political Field, the Social Science Field, and the Journalistic Field". In *Bourdieu and the Journalistic Field*, edited by Benson, Rodney and Neveu, Erik, 29–47. Cambridge: Polity.

Boyd-Barrett, Oliver. 1995. "Early Theories in Media Research". In *Approaches to Media: a Reader*, edited by Boyd-Barrett, Oliver and Newbold, Chris, 68–76. London: Arnold.

Burr, Vivien. 2003. *Social Constructionism.* New York: Routledge.

Cottle, Simon. 2000. "New(s) Times: Towards a 'Second Wave' of News Ethnography." *Communications* 25(1): 19–41.

Cottle, Simon and Ashton, Mark. 1999. "From BBC Newsroom to BBC Newscentre: On Changing Technology and Journalist Practices". *Convergence, 5*(3): 22–43.

Edmonds, Rick, Guskin, Emily, Rosenstiel, Tom and Mitchell, Amy. 2012. "Newspapers: Building Digital Revenues Proves Painfully Slow". *State of the News Media 2012*. Accessed September 10, 2012. http://stateofthemedia.org/2012/newspapers-building-digital-revenues-proves-painfully-slow/.

Fetterman, David M. 1998. *Ethnography: Step by Step*. London: Sage.

Gans, Herbert J. [1979]2004. *Deciding What's News: A Study of CBS Evening News, NBC Nightly News, Newsweek, and Time.* Evanston: Northwestern University Press.

Gergen, Kenneth J. 2009. *An Invitation to Social Construction.* London: Sage.

Guba, Egon G., and Yvonna, Lincoln S. 1982. "Epistemological and Methodological Bases of Naturalistic Inquiry". *Education technology research and development* 30(4): 233–252.

Hermans, Liesbeth, Vergeer, Maurice and d'Haenens, Leen. 2009. "Internet in the Daily Life of Journalists: Explaining the Use of the Internet by Work-Related

Characteristics and Professional-Opinions". *Journal of Computer-Mediated Communication* 15(1): 138–157.

In Publishing. 2012. "World Press Trends 2012". Accessed September 10, 2012. http://www.inpublishing.co.uk/news/articles/world_press_trends_2012.aspx.

Leedy, Paul D. and Ormrod, Jeanne E. 2005. *Practical Research: Planning and Design*. New Jersey: Pearson.

Mabweazara, Hayes M. 2010. "Researching the Use of New Technologies (ICT's) in Zimbabwean Newsrooms: An Ethnographic Approach". *Qualitative Research* 10(6): 659–677.

———. 2011. "Between the Newsroom and the Pub: The Mobile Phone in the Dynamics of Everyday Mainstream Journalism Practice in Zimbabwe". *Journalism, Theory, Practice & Criticism* 12(6): 692–707.

Paulussen, Steve and Ugille, Pieter. 2008. "User Generated Content in the Newsroom: Professional and Organisational Constraints on Participatory Journalism". *Westminster Papers in Communication and Culture* 5(2): 24–41.

Robinson, Sue. 2011. "Journalism as Process: The Organizational Implications of Participatory Online News". *Journalism & Communication Monographs* 13(3): 137–210.

Ryfe, David M. 2011. "Broader and Deeper: A Study of Newsroom Culture in a Time of Change". In *Cultural Meanings of News: A Text-Reader*, edited by Berkowitz Daniel A., 165–177. London: Sage.

Schultz, Ida. 2007. "The Journalistic Gut Feeling: Journalistic Doxa, News Habitus and Orthodox News Values". *Journalism Practice* 1(2): 190–207.

Tuchman, Gaye. 1978. *Making News: A Study in the Construction of Reality*. New York: The Free Press.

Wasserman, Herman. 2009. "Extending the Theoretical Cloth to Make Room for African Experience". *Journalism Studies* 10(2): 281–293.

———. 2010. *Tabloid Journalism in South Africa: True Story!* Bloomington: Indiana University Press.

Wright, Charles. R. 1995. "Functional Analysis and Mass Communication Revisited". In *Approaches to Media: A Reader*, edited by Boyd-Barrett, Oliver and Newbold, Chris, 95–102. London: Arnold.

2 The South African Mainstream Press in the Online Environment

Successes, Opportunities and Challenges

Johanna Mavhungu and Hayes Mawindi Mabweazara

INTRODUCTION

South Africa as a developing and emerging market in the global economy has made steady advances in the use of 'online media'. New media platforms are contesting the traditional forms of news dissemination and the rules of journalism as an authoritative field of unique expertise. The new platforms have made it easy to publish and access content free online and have thus caused one of the biggest disruptions to the production and consumption of news as well as to the financial livelihood of most traditional media houses (Bosch 2010; McNair 2010; Mitchelstein and Boczkowski 2009; Paterson and Domingo 2008).

Although newspaper circulation has generally been declining in most parts of the world, South Africa only witnessed a decline in some traditional and established newspapers from around 2011 (Myburgh 2011). Whereas online ad-spend is rising and more South Africans are accessing the Internet, a number of media houses note that it is still not sufficient in comparison to the cost of investment incurred annually (Nielsen 2011). Thomas and Mavhungu (2012) observe that in 2012, there were 10 million monthly web browsers; however, only 3.3 million users were consuming news online. With a population of 51,770,560 (Stats SA 2012), this means online users are an affluent minority with access to the Internet on their computers and smartphones.

By late 2012, South Africa's broadband penetration rate was hovering around 7 percent, constituting around 2,000,000 Vodacom subscribers, 700,000 Telkom ADSL users and 700,000 MTN broadband users (Thomas and Mavhungu 2012). Although advertising growth is evident, access and the cost of broadband still curtail widespread use, and this presents a threat to the growth of online media in South Africa.

Scholars in media management and economics have debated issues of viability and the sustainability of business models since the rise of the Internet (McLellan and Porter 2007). Kung (2010, 57) contends that "[. . .] at an organizational level, the strategic challenges facing the media industry crystallize down to one pressing requirement: finding the right business model". Kung further submits that although it is relatively easy to explain what a business model is and to give examples of good ones, it is far harder to instruct media managers on how to develop their own. For Kung, "If the best corporate and consulting brains around are challenged by this issue, we must, alas, be modest in our aspirations in this respect; and, if we do have answers, we should probably think about becoming venture capitalists" (2010, 57). Kung's views are true of the experiences of most South African newsrooms, including the case studies explored in the present study. They are all struggling to find the appropriate business models.

Against this backdrop, the present study seeks to critically engage with online journalism practices and business cultures in South Africa. Drawing on in-depth interviews with editors and key editorial staff involved in online news production and strategic planning at three mainstream newspapers in South Africa (*The Times,* the *Mail & Guardian* and the *Daily Dispatch*), the chapter provides a contextualised understanding of how online adoption processes play out in South African newsrooms. It seeks to understand how commercial mainstream newspapers in the country are reacting to the threats and opportunities posed by the online environment. The chapter focuses on the viability and sustainability of adopting an online news website and on the leadership and management strategies adopted by editors in the selected newsrooms.[1] In doing so, it examines the content, revenue models, convergence strategies and market approaches adopted by the newsrooms.

At the time of conducting research for this study between 2009 and 2010, the three newspapers were at advanced stages of implementing and developing convergence business strategies within their newsrooms. Further, despite economic challenges, the circulation and revenue figures of the newspapers have either been stable or showing improvement, and the level of professional and editorial intervention at the papers' online versions has increased steadily over the years. However, the rising use of new media has largely been explained from a technicist point of view, which tends to obfuscate the deeper implications of the socioeconomic context in which the actual appropriations of digital technologies by the traditional media are situated (Mabweazara 2010). Studies often give the impression that such technological developments and their assimilation by the news media are profitable (see Berger 2005). In particular, there is very little research on the impact of new media on how consumers generally perceive news on digital platforms and on the related business implications.

Furthermore, there is a lack of research about online media use, a critical aspect of understanding the impact and how online news media are consumed in South Africa. Although South Africa has one of the most robust online news websites in Africa, there are 15 percent online users, and 3.3 percent of the 15 percent read news online (SAARF 2011). The major proportion of online use is apportioned to social networks such as Twitter and Facebook.

A key question that is facing print media conglomerates the world over forms the basis of this study, namely, 'Are we witnessing the death of the newspaper?' In attempting to address this question, the chapter identifies successful 'new media' business models in South Africa and outlines the trends in the development of online news media in the context of the broader global framework. Although it remains true that hardly any online editorial entities across the developed and developing countries generate enough revenue, the study highlights two local examples with strong indications and potential for success in the long-term.

ONLINE MEDIA TRENDS IN SOUTH AFRICA

As elsewhere in Africa, the appropriation of online platforms by media houses in South Africa gained momentum in the 1990s as the Internet steadily permeated everyday life globally (Mitchelstein and Boczkowski 2009). However, only recently has the technology impacted the boundaries of professional journalism (McNair 2010; Bosch 2010). Rapid developments in online news (and information) and the rising use of social media by journalists and citizens alike are redefining the boundaries of the profession.

However, the proliferation of online news media in the English language press has created a vast amount of competition locally and internationally. The cost of going online is no longer prohibitive. Technology, with the availability of open source software, has made access to online media easier. An example of this is the *Daily Maverick,* one of South Africa's newly established and growing online newspapers developed on WordPress 2.8. Nonetheless, the biggest barrier to online websites in South Africa is the availability of advertising and the ability to generate meaningful revenue to remain viable.

Research by Rhodes University's Sol Plaatje Institute for Media Leadership (SPI) on new media business models for independent commercial print media in South Africa (2009–2010) points to the dilemma of supplementing, complementing and even replacing the traditional versions of newspapers by using online platforms (Bosch 2010). No South African newspaper to date has closed their print in favour of an online (web) version. Rather, most newspapers use their websites to supplement and complement their traditional version. As Bosch (ibid) contends, digital journalism is a supplement and not a complement or replacement for print or broadcast news media in South Africa.

In general, the online landscape is a plethora of English medium news websites. Nearly all print publications, including small independent and community newspapers, have an online website, but very few have a digital edition of their print version. Recent developments have seen the emergence of new news websites and mobisites (websites hosted on a mobile phone) such as the *Daily Maverick*,[2] *Zoopy, Memeburn* and many others. According to Bosch (ibid), despite the popularity of online news, print newspaper circulation is on the increase. However, between 2011 and 2012, print has been on a steady decline, and advertising is down; most newspapers are either holding their position in the market or declining, with a few titles such as *The Times* growing their circulation steadily (ABC 2011).

Online news websites have become synonymous with free access to news and information worldwide, and the trend is evident in South Africa by the low numbers of subscribers for digital editions. Arguments about free and 'paid-for' content have been debated at conferences and in the media, and two main arguments have revolved around whether newspapers should introduce paywalls and 'paid-for' content as well as the challenges posed by the prohibitive access and affordability of broadband in Africa.

Media houses are scrambling to generate revenue from online media platforms, and this is a major challenge for Western media (McNair 2010), and the situation bears some truth for media houses in South Africa. Similarly, between 2007 and 2010, newspapers in North America and Europe lost a large portion of their markets, and some scholars and practitioners believe that the emergence of social media and technology are responsible (Vujnovic 2011). The decline in circulation and advertising put pressure on online profitability, an area where very few sustainable cases have been documented worldwide because digital subscriptions are insufficient to replace revenue from advertising (ibid).

The cases (*The Times,* the *Mail & Guardian* and the *Daily Dispatch*) presented in this study reflect different views about a viable and sustainable revenue generation model, which is based primarily on their existing traditional business models and how they best position their media products online. *The Times* was launched in 2007 by AVUSA (now known as Times Media Group), one of South Africa's media conglomerates, as a sister paper to the biggest Sunday newspaper, the *Sunday Times*. Since its inception, the paper's circulation has risen tremendously, and with the implementation of its online strategy, it leads trends online.

The *Mail & Guardian* and the *Daily Dispatch* were established in print form pre-1994, before South Africa transitioned into a democratic state. Like *The Times*, the *Mail & Guardian* and *Daily Dispatch* have established vibrant online platforms that benefit from the reputable history of their print versions. All the newspapers' online versions provide space for discussion and debate around heated socioeconomic issues (Bosch 2010).

As well as providing a brief background of each of the newspapers, the sections that follow discuss in-depth how the three newspapers are managing their transition to the online environment, including the ensuing business models as well as the challenges they are facing. The discussion also highlights trends in content, revenue models, convergence strategies and market barriers.

Table 2.1   *The Times* facts

Print started	2007
Online website started	2010
Circulation	142,024 (ABC 2011)
Digital edition	No digital edition
Readership	313,000 (SAARF 2011)
Frequency of publication	Daily
Online editorial staff	14
Owners	Times Media Group
Website	www.TimesLive.co.za

THE TIMES, MAIL & GUARDIAN AND DAILY DISPATCH: SUCCESSES, OPPORTUNITIES, CHALLENGES

The Times

The Times, owned by AVUSA Limited, is one of the early adopters and leading innovators in South African online news platforms. The Audited Bureau of Circulation figures for July–September 2011 note a 4,567 rise in the paper's circulation in comparison to the same period in 2010, thus making the paper one of the fastest growing dailies in South Africa. A 2010 financial report observes that *"The Times,* having established itself in the market, enjoyed 132 percent growth in revenue over the prior year, on the back of advertising support from major retailers. The title's losses narrowed to R25 million from R39 million reported [the previous] year" (Avusa 2009).

The Times' strategy is closely defined by its relationship to its sister paper, *The Sunday Times.* This relationship with the well-established *Sunday Times* has helped the paper secure advertising revenue much quicker. As a former editor-in-chief of the paper explained in a personal interview (24 July 2009), "We didn't actually need to make that massive investment. We started getting ad revenue on day one. There were a lot of people who made deals across the two products, and the revenue picked up from there". The institutional power of a big corporation such as the Times Media Group has made it possible for the print version of the paper to flourish in an environment where newspapers globally are losing revenue and readers.

Mail & Guardian

Nicholas Dawes took command of the newsroom as editor-in-chief in June 2009. He inherited a newspaper that is challenging international trends in many ways, including circulation. In the second-quarter of 2009, ABC results for the *Mail & Guardian* showed the biggest growth in the weekly newspaper category. The rise in average sales of 2.17 percent saw the

Table 2.2   *Mail & Guardian* facts

Print started	1985 was called *The Weekly Mail*
Online website started	1994 was initially known as the *Electronic Mail & Guardian*
Circulation	45,692 (ABC 2011)
Digital edition	117 (ABC 2011)
Readership	383,000 (SAARF 2011)
Frequency of publication	Weekly
Online editorial staff	14-16 (excluding freelancers)
Owners	Mail & Guardian Limited
Website	www.mg.co.za

circulation rising to 51,166. This was secured via growth in subscriptions and a concomitant decrease in third-party bulk distribution. However, in the last quarter of 2011, print circulation had dropped to 45,692 (ABC 2011).

The paper continues to experiment and innovate with its business model, which combines the traditional newspaper and 'new media'. The digital version of the *Mail & Guardian* was founded in the mid-nineties as one of Africa's first online news sites. In 2008, it launched a new independent online version (*Mail & Guardian Online*) to keep up to date with international trends and to enable interactivity through multimedia platforms (Wolmarans 2009). Wolmarans further notes that the *Mail & Guardian Online* is innovating with mobile media and other gadgets such as the iPad, although revenue from these platforms is far from substantial at the current stage. The editor concurs, noting that "[online] is the one area of the budget that actually is increasing in the middle of the recession—for capital, or training and also for people. So all other aspects of our budget have been cut in the peak of the recession, and online budgets are up" (personal interview 5 August 2009).

Investment in digital platforms at the *Mail & Guardian Online* is increasing steadily, and innovation seems to be rising, with the development of other new media services such as a separate website for investigative journalism, mobile news services and an iPad, Kindle and iPhone edition of the paper. There are a number of digital offerings for readers using the paper's website for news. In addition, the editors of the paper have been exploring possibilities and ways of introducing 'paid-for' content options, and there is strong belief that their investigative journalism tradition will set them apart from their competitors and eventually translate into meaningful online revenue.

Daily Dispatch

As with *The Times,* the *Daily Dispatch* is owned by Johannesburg-based Times Media Group. It is located in a predominantly rural province of the

Table 2.3   *Daily Dispatch* facts

Print started	1872
Online website started	1997
Circulation	28,041 (ABC 2011)
Digital edition	304 (ABC 2011)
Readership	261,000
Frequency of publication	Daily
Online editorial staff	2
Owners	Times Media Group
Website	www.dispatch.co.za

Eastern Cape. Since 2009, the paper has experienced a steady decline in circulation. According to Bloom and Mavhungu (2009), the paper experienced a 5.2 percent decrease in circulation over the first quarter of 2009, falling from average copy sales of 32,919 to 31,195. In 2011, the circulation plummeted to figures below 30,000 (ABC 2011), taking the newspaper below their average performance. The paper has faced pressure from management to generate revenue from its online version, which is available on subscription for 40 ZAR (5 USD) a month. Although their print version has declined, *Dispatch Online* has generated a significant user base online.

In 2010, the daily was shaken by retrenchments that saw massive downsizing of their online staff. *The Dispatch* Online team of five people was reduced between 2010 and 2012 to two staffers. This impacted the capacity of the team to produce the type of online journalism that had won the paper a number of awards. Nevertheless, the paper has managed to establish a truly converged newsroom—convening diary meetings together as well as sending multimedia journalists on assignments with the print journalist (Moodie 2010).

According to a former *Daily Dispatch* and *Dispatch Online* editor, the paper has held steady in its annual revenue; it was only in June and July 2009 that the real effects of the recession began to be felt in South Africa's Eastern Cape region. The editor believed in 'paid-for' content and was confident of the existence of a market base on the premise that if the paper's circulation is 30,000 and its readership 300,000, it is therefore only reaching 10 percent of its readers who are buying the hard copy. He further argued that if one looks at the research measuring the number of readers willing to pay for the content, it is preferable to have a fraction of those paying than the current situation where everything is free. In his words, "If we go for the paid-for [online] model [. . .] they either walk away and they just don't worry about news anymore, or they come back to the [print] paper, or they pay for online" (personal interview 12 August 2009). He also asserts that the *Daily Dispatch* is a unique product: "it's [. . .] content [. . .] is available nowhere else on the planet", which implies that it's the type of content that people will pay for.

BUSINESS MODELS FOR A CONVERGED MEDIA HOUSE

Emerging online newspaper business models in South Africa, like their counterparts in the US, also depend on advertising revenue as their main source of income (Mitchelstein and Boczkowski 2009; Vujnovic 2011). Google Ads/Adworks are major players in the online advertising sector and a 'middleman' for most online news services. Businesses work and do business with online news websites via Google instead of directly approaching local online organisations. As one senior editor at the *Mail & Guardian* explained, "Clients who [. . .] would traditionally come to you with their inventory, say, well, I get it anyway because Google is on the site [. . .] and you end up getting a fraction of [the revenue] you used to" (personal interview 5 August 2009). He further argued that in the online advertising market, new business models have to work on old advertising because most of the online news services, including the *Dispatch Online*, depend on Google for a large percentage of their advertising revenue.

The *Mail & Guardian* acquired 65 percent of their website from their largest shareholder MWeb in 2008. This shift in their business strategy meant that the paper could begin to strategically shape its online business model.

Although the editors of both the *Mail & Guardian Online* and the *Dispatch Online* firmly believe in introducing a 'paid-for' content model, one of the main challenges facing 'paid-for' online content in South Africa is the non-existence of a suitable, accessible and convenient payment system that can transfer small payment amounts instantly. M-Pesa mobile money (a mobile phone-based money transfer and microfinancing service) has not taken off like in other African countries such as Kenya, for example (Van Noort and Mavhungu 2010). Instead, the *Mail & Guardian* and the *Dispatch Online* have settled for a credit card payment system as well as electronic bank transfers. The implications here are that only those with credit cards or time and access to make an electronic payment can access the digital news content; hence, the market is limited.

The *Dispatch Online* has introduced a monthly subscription to their online digital newspaper version. The Eastern Cape province publication has been a local trailblazer in the online landscape, and one of its former editors believed that possibilities were endless because of the paper's unique selling point, i.e., local content specifically targeted at the rural and urban parts of the Eastern Cape. The former editor's 'localisation' strategy and stated drive to be the world's number one online source of news in the Eastern Cape generated between 125,000 and 130,000 visitors a month to the paper's website as of August 2009. Before the relaunch in early 2008, the site was attracting 30,000 visitors a month. The 400 percent rise in traffic has been brought about not only by an overhaul of the site but by an approach to 'convergence' that is "arguably the most progressive in the South African newsprint environment" (personal interview 12 August 2009).

The *Daily Dispatch* provides a unique South African convergence story. From 2008, the newspaper developed a converged newsroom where the news editors of the print edition and the online version convened the daily news conference together with their teams. This recipe saw an improved newsroom and worked well for their multimedia reporting. The team won awards, including the Digital Journalism Award for 2011 in the CNN Multichoice African Journalist Awards. What made the editor confident about the 'paid for' content model were encouraging findings from audience research commissioned by the paper. One of the critical findings of the audience research was that local readers were prepared to pay for content online, and they specified an acceptable figure of between 38 and 40 ZAR monthly (about 5 USD). This figure was seen as profitable, as the editor explained: "if over the course of a year we monetise just 10 percent of our existing unique user base at 40 ZAR, it amounts to 4.5 million more on revenue [per year] than we are making at the moment" (personal interview 12 August 2009). Indeed, the paper is now charging 40 ZAR for a monthly digital subscription, which was confirmed as profitable by the online editor.

All three online websites explored in the present study use multimedia applications to optimise content delivery; this includes the use of video and podcasts suited for their audiences. The *Mail & Guardian Online* has been online longer than the *Dispatch Online* and *The Times*. Nonetheless, the success of the *Mail & Guardian Online* website is not dependent on complex multimedia functionality but on their relevance to the target market and branding. As one of the paper's senior online editors explained,

> Remember you are thinking about the problem in journalistic terms as well as business terms [. . .]. Video's very expensive, and if you've got a brand like the *Mail & Guardian,* which is all about superb journalism, as soon as you have some half-arsed news generated video that some journalist has cut together out there, that journalism standard drops automatically (personal interview 5 August 2009).

The senior editors of all three newsrooms tailor their innovations to their readers' content expectations as established through their print versions. This includes investigative reporting for the *Mail & Guardian* and 'localised' content for the *Daily Dispatch*. Online innovation is also aimed at retaining brand loyalty, boosting web traffic and remaining competitive in a space flooded by user-generated content and new entrants (Vujnovic 2011). In this sense, the 'new medium' is not neutral; its content determines readers' responses (Chyi and Yang 2009; Mitchelstein and Boczkowski 2009).

The *Mail & Guardian* and the *Daily Dispatch* have implemented paid-for models for their digital editions, which can be subscribed to through a credit card or an electronic bank transfer on a month-to-month subscription rate or a fixed rate of six to twelve months. Subscription to the newspapers' digital editions is also audited by the Audit Bureau of Circulations. Although their subscription base has been low, the newspapers show potential for self-sustainability. As an urban-based English newspaper, *The Times* is different from the other two case studies because its content is not targeted to a niche market.

Senior editors from the three papers collectively suggested that another way to monetise their content is to aggregate information that they have reported in previous years and produce packages such as in-depth sections titled "Health in South Africa (2009–2012)". It remains to be seen whether the packages will attract more readers.

Digital copies, advertising revenue and annual budgets for website financing from big media organisations are part of a revenue-generation model. To diversify these revenue streams and ensure that they meet costs and generate profits, the media houses will have to increase the sales of their digital editions. Further research in the form of an economic analysis is required to assess whether revenue from online news websites translates into profitability. The research would inform issues of financial sustainability as an area for future research and one that requires a comparative analysis of the economic value chain of both the traditional and the online newspaper versions. Mitchelstein and Boczkowski (2009) state that profitability has been premised on complicated decisions based on how much cost is attributed to the online site versus the old-media operations (2009, 565). In addition, some scholars suggest that this initial lack of profitability resulted from an inadequate business model (ibid).

A number of conclusions can be drawn from the above: First, online payment models are difficult to implement, especially without exclusive, sought-after content. Second, it is important to have a newsroom that understands the necessity of cross-platform convergence. Finally, a news website should be designed with a thorough understanding of its target readership, have the ability to pull them in and encourage them to return.

CONVERGENCE AND HUMAN RESOURCE SYSTEMS

One of the key findings of this study is that the concept of converged (print/online integration) newsrooms has become a non-negotiable ideal. All the media houses concurred that their newsrooms have adopted and adapted to a converged environment. For example, journalists at *The Times* are asked during recruitment if they can perform and deliver news content using multimedia platforms (personal interview 24 July 2009).

The successful implementation of convergence strategies rests on the management and leadership styles of the editors. Their approach to leadership favours positive reinforcement. They choose to encourage their staff to report using the various multimedia platforms available in the newsroom. Most staffers at the online newsrooms are young and techno-savvy, hence contributing to the 'juniorisation' of newsrooms—a predominant South

African phenomenon in which young reporters and editors run newsrooms (Bosch 2010).

On the job training is also essential in this environment because there are multiple features to learn and use, and online technology is constantly changing. Nevertheless, most journalists working in online newsrooms are either self-taught or learn from one another on the job (see Berger 2005).

One senior editor at *The Times* advocated for the integration of old and new media structures of the newsroom by creating an open space newsroom that enhances communication between management and reporters. As he explained,

> The managers will sit in the open and in the middle of the newsroom, and that'll be the end of poor communication [. . .]. So the geography of it is vital. It's also this sense of everybody immersed in the process without exception, which I think is quite important. You've got to flatten structures in this environment. (personal interview 24 July 2009)

Communication within the newsroom is essential, and both the *Mail & Guardian* and the *Dispatch Online* editors concurred that it works to keep the productivity flow high. The extract below explains how a converged newsroom functions at the *Daily Dispatch:*

> We have a designated video person that goes out to a breaking news story, [he's] basically self-taught, like all of us. He's very good. But he will then go out with the reporter to the scene [. . .] Once they've got a handle on the situation [. . .] sort of figured out what the hell's going on, I could use the reporter directly as a source for the blog [. . .] That kind of immediacy, it's when the reporter gets there, he's the eyes, and I trust him to give me feedback that I can put on the blog. I would expect him at that stage also to try and talk to official sources, like paramedics or the police spokesman or whatever [. . .] At that stage, once I've got that kind of confirmation, [. . .]. I'll put up a second blog and [send out an alert] on Twitter [. . .]. (personal interview 14 August 2009)

Unlike the *Daily Dispatch* and *The Times*, the *Mail & Guardian* has a weekly news cycle that makes it difficult to practise similar convergence strategies. News content is generated from news agencies such as the South African Press Association (SAPA). They pay for these and have to create value for their paper out of what they receive from the news agencies and not duplicate it.

It is clear that the newsrooms are moving towards training their journalists to become platform-agnostic. Human resource systems are being reworked to reflect this philosophy, and editorial staffers are encouraged to work for the brand rather than the medium. Brand building is aimed primarily at gaining and retaining more readers for the purposes of growing advertising revenue. Some researchers link the growing importance of advertising revenue to concerns about the increased blurring of commercial and editorial content in the online environment (Chyi and Yang 2009, 566).

The online products developed by the media houses lean towards project-based journalism, 'packaged journalism', as some interviewees called it. According to Trench (cited in Bloom and Mavhungu 2009), the packages are mini-sites within the main site that focus on specific stories and use the tools of the web to offer audiences a 360-degree view. An example is the award-winning 'Dying to Live' project, where the *Daily Dispatch*'s investigative team spent nearly four months attempting to understand the spate of fatal attacks on Somalis in Eastern Cape townships. The mini-site includes a diary, an archive of print stories on the subject, photo essays by the publication's photographers, video footage, audio files, maps detailing where the incidents occurred and timelines. News products are no longer developed in isolation for print or online media but are developed to suit both mediums and to give mileage to the stories covered in the print edition. In keeping with their community news orientation, the *Dispatch Online* is planning to 'mine' their community features and build social networks that create communication bridges online. These social networks target young people who are not reading the print version of the paper.

The *Mail & Guardian* is aiming to develop innovative interactive content which their readers can engage with. As Bosch (2010) observes, the paper's blog site 'Thought Leader' has an interesting array of opinion-leading blog posts with critical political commentary that engages the readers and authors of the blog posts. One notes that the *Mail & Guardian* is slightly similar to the *Dispatch Online* because it uses 'packaged journalism' and other interactive forms of reporting online to maintain their in-depth news and analysis brand.

PRODUCTIVITY IN A CONVERGED NEWSROOM

Some editors measure productivity using a qualitative assessment as opposed to quantitative, i.e., the number of stories written or reported. In all the newsrooms studied, journalists are encouraged to make use of online platforms such as blogs. They are assessed according to what they are capable of and how close they are to achieving that as opposed to how many stories they churn out. Editors are also involved in the digital practices and processes, such as posting material on blogs; thus, they lead by example. One of the editors at the *Dispatch Online* noted that the advantage of an online platform is that we can explore and experiment, and if one makes a mistake, you can easily correct it unlike in print.

Communication and an open and transparent working environment were also highlighted as key elements of a well-functioning converged newsroom. It is very difficult for the editors to separate their work on the print version from the online version because they all see what they do as delivering content for different platforms. As one *Mail & Guardian* senior editor explained, the differences between online and print, especially for a weekly paper, are the 'work curves':

> Say you're writing for the print news section. You start off at the bottom of the curve on a Monday or on a Friday actually, and you know you've got a rough idea of what's going to be in your diary. On Monday you're required to harden that up for conference and have a little bit more information. On Tuesday you're supposed to be working steadily but you probably aren't too frenzied yet. On Wednesday you start to get into a panic, you have to make pretty sure that you're locking off your sources. Some people will file by Wednesday night. If you're writing the lead, things will peak at kind of 3 o'clock on a Thursday afternoon. The paper will go to bed at five [pm] and then [the curve] falls off a cliff [. . .] obviously the online environment has long curves like that; [but it also] has day- long curves and it has 15-minute curves and Twitter-shaped five-minute curves. So there are those sorts of differences. The other difference is that some of the structures around how much you express your own opinion, how much you insert yourself into what you doing, are different. There are all sorts of debates around that stuff. But in terms of management of newsrooms, the problem that we face is 'management of newsrooms', not 'problems of digital newsrooms'. (personal interview 5 August 2009).

The editor concludes by highlighting how journalists remain journalists whether they are in print or online. This echoes researchers who argue that absent from online research within studies of the market environment is the examination of the role that labour processes and conditions play in online news enterprises (Mitchelstein and Boczkowski 2009). Future scholarship might examine how newsroom production has changed in Africa and what implications this has on the working conditions and remuneration of journalists.

CONCLUSION

The media houses in this chapter embrace varied methods of generating revenue online. Advertising is the main source of revenue, followed by subscription to digital editions of the print version. Increasing unique users and web page impressions are critical to managers and advertisers (Vujnovic 2011). As with newspapers in the US, new media business models are not innovating on e-commerce, and initiatives to drive up digital subscriptions are not visible (Mitchelstein and Boczkowski 2009).

The case studies highlight difficulties related to competition because of easy access to online publishing. However, costs associated with marketing, recruitment and editorial production separate the small independent operations from established players. A significant requirement is financial and human resource investment, both of which are essential for the success or failure of news organisations venturing into online platforms. Kawamoto (cited in Chyi 2005) asks, "is there value to maintaining digital media when profitability is not achievable?" In response to this question, Chyi (2005) argues that there is value because digital media have become such a compelling instrument of disseminating and consuming news.

Enhanced multimedia functionality and strategic use of social media and project-based journalism are becoming features of all three of the newspapers studied, and with this is a leadership strategy that encourages journalists to report for the brand instead of a specific medium.

NOTES

1. For ethical reasons, we have decided to anonymise all the names of the interviewees involved in the study in order to protect them from possible identification.
2. *The Daily Maverick* is set to shake up the local digital journalism scene with the launch of a new daily news-based iPad app, which it describes as "South Africa's first daily newspaper specifically designed for the iPad" (Pepetta 2011).

REFERENCES

AC Nielsen. 2011. *Total Adspend: All Media Types (Excluding Self-promotion).* Unpublished report. Johannesburg: AC Nielsen.

Audited Bureau of Circulation (ABC). 2011. *Weekly, Daily and Weekend Newspapers Audited Circulation.* Unpublished report. Johannesburg: Audited Bureau of Circulation.

Avusa. 2009. Audited Condensed Group Financial Results for the Year ended 31 March 2009. Accessed August 12, 2009. http://www.avusa.co.za/PDFs/Avusa-Advert-May-09E.pdf.

Berger, Guy. 2005. "Powering African Newsrooms: Theorising how Southern African Journalists make use of ICTs for Newsgathering". In *Doing Digital Journalism: How Southern African Newsgatherers are using ICTs*, edited by Berger, Guy, 1–14. Grahamstown: High Way Africa.

Bloom, Kevin and Mavhungu, Johanna. 2009. *Successful 'New Media' business models: Case studies of independent commercial print media in South Africa.* Grahamstown: Sol Plaatje Media Leadership.

Bosch, Tanja. 2010. "Digital Journalism and Online Public Spheres in South Africa". *Communicatio: South African Journal for Communication Theory and Research* 36(2): 265–275.

Chyi, Iris H. 2005. "Willingness to Pay for Online News: An Empirical Study on the Viability of the Subscription Model". *Journal of Media Economics* 18(2): 131–142.

Chyi, Iris H and Yang, Jacie M. 2009. "Is Online News an Inferior Good? Examining the Economic Nature of Online News among Users. *Journalism & Mass Communication* Quarterly 86(3): 594–612.

De Kock, Rick. 2011. "Africa=Social + Media + Revolution. The Media Online". Accessed January 20, 2012. http://themediaonline.co.za/2011/12/africa-social-media-revolution/.

Deuze, Mark. 2007. *Media Work*. Cambridge: Polity Press.

International Research and Exchanges Board (IREX). 2010. *Media Sustainability Index: Development of Sustainable Independent Media in Africa*. Washington DC: International Research and Exchanges Board.

Kung, Lucy. 2010. "Why Media Managers Are Not Interested in Media Management—And What We Could Do About It". *JMM: The International Journal on Media Management* 12(1): 55–57.

Mabweazara, Hayes. M. 2010. "'New' Technologies and Journalism Practice in Africa: Towards a Critical Sociological Approach". In *The Citizen in Communication: Re-visiting Traditional, New and Community Media Practices in South Africa*, edited by Hyde-Clarke, Nathalie, 11–30. Capetown: Juta & Co.

McLellan, Michele and Porter, Tim. 2007. *News, Improved: How America's Newsrooms Are Learning to Change*. Washington: CQ Press.

McNair, Brian. 2010. "Managing the Online News Revolution: the UK experience". In *News Online: Transformations and Continuities,* edited by Miekle, Graham and Redden, Guy, 38–52. New York: Palgrave MacMillan.

Mitchelstein, Eugenia and Boczkowski, Pablo J. 2009. "Between Tradition and Change: A Review of the Recent Research on Online News Production". *Journalism, Theory, Practice & Criticism* 10(5): 562–582.

Moodie, Gill. 2010. "So Long and Thanks for all the Awards". Accessed January 14, 2011. http://www.bizcommunity.com/Article/196/15/53906.html.

Myburgh, James. 2011. "SA's Daily Newspapers in Decline". The Media Online. Accessed June 21, 2012. http://themediaonline.co.za/2011/11/sas-daily-newspapers-in-decline/.

Paterson, A. Chris. and Domingo, David. 2008. *Making Online News: The Ethnography of New Media Production*. New York: Peter Lang Publishers.

Prensky, Marc. 2001. "Digital Natives, Digital Immigrants". *On the Horizon* 9(5): 1–6.

Singer, B. Jane, Hermida, Alfred, Domingo, David., Heinonen, Ari., Paulussen, Steve., Quandt, Thorsten., Reich, Zvi, Vujnovic, Marina et al. 2011. *Participatory Journalism: Guarding Open Gates at Online Newspapers*. Oxford: Wiley-Blackwell Publishing.

South African Advertising Research Foundation (SAARF). 2012. *SAARF AMPS*. Unpublished report. Johannesburg: South African Advertising Research Foundation.

Statistics South Africa. 2012. *Census 2011 Key Highlights. Released results*. Johannesburg: Statistics South Africa.

Thomas, Howard and Mavhungu, Johanna. 2012. "Investigating a Sustainable Business Model for Community Television in South Africa". Pretoria: Research paper presented to the Department of Communications.

Van Noort, Elvira and Mavhungu, Johanna. 2010. *A Qualitative Study of Sustainable & Sustainable Mobile News Services in South Africa*. Grahamstown: Sol Plaatje Institute for Media Leadership, Rhodes University

Vujnovic, Marina. 2011. "Participatory Journalism in the Marketplace: Economic Motivations Behind Practices". In *Participatory Journalism. Guarding Open Gates at Online Newspapers,* edited by Singer, Jane B. et al., 139–154. New York: Wiley-Blackwell.

Wolmarans, Riaan. 2009. "The Money Game: A South African Perspective". In *Doing Digital Media in Africa: Prospects, Promises and Problems,* edited by Mdlongwa, Francis, 34–40. Johannesburg: Konrad-Adenauer-Stiftung.

World Association of Newspapers and News Publishers (Wan-Ifra). 2010. *Financially Viable Media in Emerging and Developing Markets*. Paris: World Association of Newspapers and News Publishers.

3 Converging Technologies, Converging Spaces, Converging Practices

The Shaping of Digital Cultures and Practices on Radio

Last Moyo

INTRODUCTION

This chapter seeks to conduct a comparative critique of the uses of Internet and mobile phone by Capital radio and Dzimwe community radio in Malawi. Located in Blantyre's mosaic of telecommunication networks that provide the backbone for Internet and mobile phone platforms, Capital radio has a fairly good uptake of digital media technologies that merit academic interest and curiosity. The station is privately owned and is Malawi's flagship for hard-hitting news and current affairs programming. This feat is in part traceable to its owner Laudin Osman, who is a revered veteran radio journalist in the country. Dzimwe community radio, on the other hand, represents the other end of the spectrum. It is basically a rural radio station that caters to rural audiences mainly from the Mongochi district, although its broadcast footprint extends to other places such as Ntcheu, Dedza and Balaka. As a community radio station, it is branding itself on development-oriented programming that focuses on health, agriculture, conservation and sustainable development. However, community funding for the station is weak because of widespread poverty in Mangochi. Inevitably, the station therefore depends largely on donor aid for resources such as computers, mobile phones and capital. Agencies such as the United Nations Education, Scientific and Cultural Organization (UNESCO) and Farm Radio International have also played a major role in the past. For example, in 2010, the station had four computers and five mobile phones donated by Farm International and other NGOs.

The chapter specifically examines the uses of the Internet, social networking sites and mobile text-messaging by the two radio stations. It also critiques the social affordances of these so-called "technologies of freedom" (Morriset 2004) in democratizing participation for radio publics. Three central questions underpin the study: a) To what extent do institutional and organizational contexts shape the uptake and uses of the Internet and mobile phones by radio journalists? b) How do uses of the Internet and mobile phones in turn influence institutional cultures and organizational practices? c) To what extent, if at all, does radio convergence reconfigure traditional radio to create new spaces that augment audience participation?

Through the examination of the institutional and organizational contexts of digital media uptake and use on radio, the chapter directly engages with the liberatory myth behind new digital media technologies. The aim of such a critique is to critically analyse the complex questions of technology, agency and structure in the deployment of digital media technologies in organizational and institutional spaces. To do this, the chapter recasts organizational and institutional contexts as a structure within which journalistic agency in using the Internet and mobile phones can be understood. As structures, radio organizations and institutions shape and give character to the new technologies that are used by journalists. However, organizations and institutions must not be seen as static because they are "both the medium and the outcome of . . . [professional, social, commercial, and political] practices which constitute [them]" (Giddens 1981, 29). Giddens's concept of "the duality of structure" (27) can therefore help us to understand radio organizations and institutions as simultaneously material and symbolic even though common sense characterizes them as physical and concrete entities. As spaces, both are arguably symbolic products of discursive practices by the agency that occupies them. To that end, the chapter also engages with the agency of radio journalists, their practices and actions and how, in turn, these impact radio's organizational and institutional spaces as well as broaden democratic participation by audiences.

A JUSTIFICATION: WHY CHANGES IN DIGITAL RADIO CULTURES AND PRACTICES MATTER

The Internet and mobile phones are changing the face of radio across the world, especially in the technologically advanced countries of the North (see Gordon 2012; Crisell 2004; Carlsson 2006; Buckly 2000). Theoretically speaking, radio is changing as a technology or medium, and these changes have also brought about changes in radio practices and cultures, especially in the production and dissemination of news. Technological convergence in radio also seems to carry the promise of democratizing and opening up radio to audiences, publics and citizens. For example, digital technologies like the Internet and mobile phones have arguably multiplied and pluralized radio spaces. Radio is now a virtual space, network space and mobile space while at the same time remaining a physical space when conceptualized as its studio format where citizens can participate in public debate. This pluralisation of spaces by new media technologies is subverting the old notion of radio as a unified and bounded medium—hence, its greater accessibility through newer means that traverse the traditional methods of radio access and consumption. Radio as a space is now much more open, permeable, dispersed and fluid, thus making it more accessible in time and space through informal spaces of content production and consumption. Greater accessibility of radio to audiences therefore means that digitization and technological convergence can potentially make radio in Africa more participative within and across social divides. The multiple platforms of websites, social media, podcasts, online and mobile streaming should, in principle, make radio vertically and horizontally accessible within and across social classes.

Whereas convergence of media and communication technologies has been largely a characteristic of late modern societies of Western and some Eastern countries, Africa has a slightly different experience. Radio remains, at the very best, traditional for most people who still receive it through the simple mode of traditional broadcasts. However, the ever-increasing convergence between telecommunications, broadcasting and computing in the continent means that there are some interesting changes in the form, content, practices and cultures in radio. In addition to Ethernet broadband, wireless mobile Internet is accelerating Africa's digital revolution in a way that enhances the availability, affordability and accessibility of the digital media beyond the elite classes and elite institutions. A significant minority of radio stations and their publics have mainstreamed these technologies into their cultures and practices. For example, in a recent study conducted in Southern Africa on radio convergence by Moyo (2011) covering four countries, it was more than evident that the use of the digital media by radio and its publics was reasonably high in the region. The uptake and use of the Internet and mobile platforms in South Africa, Zambia, Zimbabwe and Malawi by private, community, public and state radio stations was, at least in principle, making the radio institution more accessible through the multiple digital platforms of webcasting, social media, podcasting and mobile streaming.

THEORETICAL MUSINGS: TOWARDS A CRITICAL THEORY OF DIGITAL RADIO CULTURES

This section discusses a theoretical formulation that can be used to conceptualize structure, agency and technology in journalistic practices at Capital Radio and Dzimwe Community Radio. To this end, the article takes an interdisciplinary stride that fuses technological constructionism (Flew 2005; Paschal 2001; Feenberg 1999) with organizational and institutional theory (see Hall 1999; Hassard 1990; Carpentier 2011). The purpose of such a theory is to unlock the complex structures and processes within which radio convergence takes place and how it is negotiated by journalists to produce new radio cultures and practices that, in turn, impact those spaces.

The critical theory of radio cultures locates itself between the traditional theoretical positions of technological instrumentalism and technological substantivism (see Feenberg 1999). For example, the former generally romanticizes the impact of digital technologies on institutions and society. Its theoretical postulations are at best deterministic and utopian. Digital media technologies like the Internet and mobile phones, for example, are always regarded as neutral, serving no function other than that for which they were made. In this formulation, digital technologies are regarded as completely value free, and their application in state radio, public radio, private commercial radio and community radio stations must always produce similar outcomes. This claim is based on nothing but digital media's perceived intrinsic affordances of digitization, interactivity, multimodality and convergence (see Lister et al. 2003). Technology in this school of thought is therefore "seen as neutral because it stands under the very same norm of efficiency in every context" (Feenberg 1999, 6). The latter view of substantivism holds a dystopian view of technologies and sees the Internet and mobile phones as being appropriated by a journalism profession that is always structurally and ideologically in service of political and economic power. Like instrumentalism, substantivism also takes an extreme but rather essentialist position to digital technologies. It argues that the sole purpose of technology is subordination and domination. All technology is simply ideology in a material form. All media technologies, for example, "have been shaped by the nature of capitalism, and all of them have been used for forms of communication that are deeply marked by the kind of society in which they developed" (Sparks 2003, 34).

The problem with the two theories is that they undermine the complex questions of media technologies, agency and structure, thus making the impact of new media technologies always predictable. The critical theory of digital cultures seeks to engage much more with these questions and argues for a 'social shaping' thesis (see Paschal 2001) in individual and institutional uses of digital media technologies. Technologies are always socially and historically contingent in their design and usage, and questions of power and domination are central. Organizations and institutions as structures that undergird technological practices by journalists are sites of an ideological power struggle between actors. Although the critical theory of digital cultures is informed by Marxism, it nonetheless shuns vulgar Marxist conceptions of structure that it sees as rigid and fixated. Instead, Giddens's notion of "structuration" is seen as enhancing the theory's analytical currency because it "implies a process and not a steady [or fixated] status" (Sewell 1992, 9). Structuration acknowledges agency, the fact that "structures have no existence apart from the practices that make them" (9). Based on the materialist and hermeneutic notions of structure, the critical theory of digital cultures acknowledges a 'duality of structure' and conceives institutions and organizations as at once physical and symbolic as well as rigid and flexible.

The central argument in the critical theory of digital cultures "is that [media organizations] and institutions shape actions [. . .] by media professionals" (Lecours 2005, 15). Institutionalism itself is "based on the assumption that a historically constructed set of institutional [and organizational] constraints structure the behaviour and choices of [media] actors" (Beland 2005, 25). Digital media technologies are not used in a vacuum but within contexts of these structures (i.e., institutional contexts, organizational contexts and social contexts) and processes and ideologies (news production routines, professional values). Theoretically speaking, therefore, structures, processes, resources and professional ideologies are seen as central in the tailoring of digital cultures, practices and spaces in radio. They add to the character of technologies and give meaning to practices by radio journalists. Institutions and organizations as structure represent norms, social orders and the value systems for actors and the technologies they use.

Although organizations and institutions share characteristics at some point, organizations are perceived as representing physical structures or spaces where technologies are deployed for specific ends. Organizations are essentially "empirical facets of the underlying [institutional] modes and rules" (Morgan 1990, 25). As production spaces, organizations are not neutral places but highly ideological because they are also symbolic constructions. They are "realms of activity that are characterized by particular forms of myth-making or models of action that give form to contextually based systems of meaning" (19). Organizations as structures are 'enacted domains', and organizational practices "represent a continuous process of enactment" (22) that is informed by institutional myths and power relations. The shape that organizations take and priorities about which technologies are used and how are always arbitrary questions because of structuration. For example, power relations within radio organizations and between organizations and institutions underpin the transformative agency of digital media technologies.

INSTITUTIONAL MODELLING OF DIGITAL CULTURES

This section explores the radio broadcasting institution in Malawi in which Capital Radio and Dzimwe Community Radio are actors. Based on the preceding theoretical discussion, the central argument it advances is that the broadcast institution in Malawi forms the structural conditions that simultaneously create opportunities, bottlenecks and blockages for the appropriation and creative use of the Internet and mobile phones by radio journalists and their publics. The development of digital cultures and practices in radio are therefore seen as taking place within a power dynamic epitomized by the broader institutional regime of radio broadcasting, where the creative agency of journalists in using digital technologies is negotiated. Technologies do not just happen to be there in media as sites of production; instead, their presence or absence apart from the material question of affordability reflects the decisions of powerful actors that shape technological possibilities in media institutions. Through the twin processes of policy and regulation, the broadcasting institution is seen as representing a top-down force which arguably shapes what is technologically, legally, professionally and ethically possible for radio news practices and cultures in the newsrooms of the two radio stations.

In modern day Malawi, the radio broadcasting institution is a product of the Communications Act (1998) and the Malawi ICT Policy (2003). In the age of convergence, these two policies have been central in the modernization of broadcasting and telecommunications, especially through strategic interventions that promote technological diffusion that is driven by the new wave of digital technologies. Both policies are informed by the need to take Malawi into the information society where broadcasting, telecommunications and computing converge and create a multiplicity of interactive platforms for media and citizens. Similarly, the role of the state and the market is seen as fundamentally important in shaping the radio broadcasting institution by both policies, especially in terms of the provision of infrastructure, telecommunications and mobile networks and end-user technologies, which in the digital age have become inseparable from radio. For example, through the regulation of the merging platforms of broadcasting, telecommunications and computing industries in the country, the state influences not only what digital media technologies are available for use by the journalists and the public but also the amount and diversity of players in radio broadcasting as an institution. Hence, the Communications Act foregrounds the principle of creating an open and competitive broadcast and telecommunications market that is based on the full respect of users' choices, fair pricing and the quality of services.

The Malawi Communications Regulatory Authority (MACRA), an independent regulatory body in the convergence environment, was also constituted through the Communications Act. To date, there are over 20 radio stations that compete in news and current affairs provision and use some of the new cutting edge technologies, which are a product of the new institutional conditions. Apart from Capital Radio, other major players in the radio broadcasting institution, such as Zodiak, Star FM, Radio Islam, and Maria FM, also use websites, social media and mobile phones in many different ways to promote interactive journalism. However, as part of the institutional conditions, there are variations in the digital media uptake and use between private, public and community radio stations in the country. Greater uptake and use is often more pronounced in private commercial radio and in some community radio stations mainly because of their access to funding from advertising and donors. Dzimwe Community Radio enjoys a degree of access and use of the Internet and mobile phones, but only to a limited extent compared to Capital Radio. As I argue later, advertiser and donor funding cannot be entirely celebrated as both impact negatively the question of professional autonomy and audience participation in the usage of digital media technologies.

MACRA also plays a crucial role in creating an enabling environment, especially through the licensing of mobile networks such as Telekom Networks Limited (TNM) and Airtel. These provide voice calling, text messaging and mobile Internet, which are important interactive platforms for radio and its publics. Consequently, the mainstreaming of the Internet and mobile phones into radio's institutional cultures and practices has also been largely influenced by how accessible digital media are to radio and audiences. Malawi has a population of just over 15 million people, and of these, about 716,400 have access to the Internet and 112,000 use Facebook, whereas slightly over 3 million have access to mobile phones. The availability, accessibility and affordability of these digital technologies to audiences create the institutional conditions that are seminal to radio's newer digital cultures and practices. The presence of the digital newsroom practices and cultures in Malawi must therefore be seen as always subject to market and regulatory forces that create or limit digital opportunity to radio journalists and the public. Policy and regulation have ramifications for the radio and telecommunications market structures and the types and levels of competition between radio broadcasters in the provision of news through newer digital platforms like webcasts, podcasts and social media.

Apart from regulation, the use of the new forms of digital media technologies and their adaptation into mainstream radio news practices and cultures are also largely guided by an economic rationale of the radio broadcasting institution. As argued by Hall (1999) changes in institutional cultures and practices are normally based on strategic financial considerations in terms of benefits that can be accrued. For example, in radio broadcasting, such changes could be influenced by how much revenue can be generated from the new platforms of online and mobile advertising. Although as stated earlier, the major players in the radio industry in Malawi are online, mobile and online advertising were not major strategic considerations in decision-making regarding the uses of these digital platforms for Capital Radio and Dzimwe Community Radio. However, this does not mean that other stations completely ignored the economics of using the Internet and mobile radio.

The deregulation of radio broadcasting in Malawi has also been central in indirectly shaping the institutional conditions of new digital cultures and practices in radio. The country, for instance, liberalized its radio broadcasting institution in the mid-nineties after the collapse of the one-party state that maintained an authoritarian grip on broadcasting and limited any possibilities of a technologically robust radio industry. Such historical transformations came with big changes in power relations between competing political forces, which culminated in new ways of imagining and organizing the broadcast media and its technologies. As a result, the change to multi-party democracy in the mid-nineties influenced the structure and organization of broadcasting in the country, including the types of broadcasting technologies available to radio stations and their audiences. The three-tier broadcasting system and the fairly pervasive new digital media networks, as demonstrated earlier, are products of this democratic wave that not only emphasized the liberalization of radio airwaves but also access to related technologies for radio and its publics, as seen in the two core policies referred to earlier.

Although MACRA has been a product of a democratic dispensation in Malawi, it is imperative to note that its regulation of the radio broadcasting institution and related media technologies has not always been democratic in the sense of defending the public interest. For example, more recently, the body was accused of political bias in favour of the government and ruling party, whereby some radio stations have been denied licences or threatened with the withdrawal of licences.[1] For example, Capital Radio was threatened by MACRA over Straight Talk, a current affairs talk show programme that it argued was too critical of the late President Bingu Wa Mutarika. This programme extensively uses e-mail, social media and mobile texting to create robust public debate in the discussion of public affairs. At the peak of the national protests in 2011 when Capital Radio led public debate, MACRA was ordered to block digital platforms like the Internet, Facebook and Twitter and banned coverage of the political events by radio stations. These protests came in the wake of the Arab Spring, and citizens and institutions in Malawi also extensively used social media and mobile phones to mobilize themselves and engage in strategic political action.

As the custodian of the broadcasting institution, MACRA under the government of Bingu Wa Mutarika clearly represented the interests of the state and the political elite, not those of the citizens. Its interference with the freedom of expression of journalists and the denial of access to radio frequencies as a technology (or licences) to some radio stations shows how the regulator curtails the editorial autonomy and technological agency of the radio institution in very complex and subtle ways. Such actions delimit the arena of political and technological possibilities in the radio industry. Needless to say, from mobile phone networks to Internet Service Providers (ISPs), MACRA has also created a communications technological regime that sometimes undermines the convergence of broadcasting and telecommunications so as to undercut any technological transformations in radio broadcasting that are seen as a threat to political power. As Freedman (2008, 1) argues, through regulation, politicians "seek to inscribe their own values and objectives on the [policy] possibilities facilitated by a complex combination of technological, economic, and social factors".

As a regulatory body, MACRA is therefore at once a political regime and a technological and cultural regime. In the ever-changing balance of power between competing social forces, including the state and citizens in Malawi, MACRA is a gatekeeper of the political, cultural and technological 'order' in the country. This order sees to the manifestation of elite hegemony through the radio institution. Invariably, the regulatory body therefore forms the structural and institutional boundaries of acceptable norms, values, communications technologies, spaces and practices.

ORGANIZATIONAL MODELLING OF DIGITAL CULTURES

Whereas I have demonstrated the minimal access to digital media technologies at Dzimwe Community Radio, Capital Radio was relatively well resourced in terms of computers and mobile phones. Easy access to these networks in the newsroom facilitated consistent use of these technologies by journalists in the production and dissemination of news content. Apart from the website that was one of the central spaces where news is disseminated by the station and consumed by the audiences, Capital Radio also used social networking sites such as Facebook and Twitter and some FrontlineSMS prototype to interact with audiences. All these new platforms facilitated interactive communication between Capital Radio and its audiences, sometimes blurring the lines between news production, dissemination and consumption. The Internet and mobile phones created informal spaces of user-generated content in time and space that sometimes served as pointers to news ideas and informative feedback to news bulletins at the station. However, using the critical theory of radio convergence, I want to move beyond the question of the affordances of these technologies to engage more with the organizational context of the two radio stations. This theory allows us to engage with two distinct issues on digital media technologies in both stations.

On the one hand, this theory provides a constructivist critique of technological convergence in a way that acknowledges journalistic creative agency and the newer spaces created to expand radio's reach. On the other hand, the theory goes beyond the facial impressions of what seems to be happening by helping to analyse radio's organizational and institutional contexts as key places of its use of new digital platforms, especially in relation to the broader question of the capitalistic mode of production. Particularly, how it has inscribed its values across the news production, dissemination and the consumption chain on radio. As Couldry and McCarthy (2004, 4) contend, a "spatially sensitive analysis of media practices [must] reveal forms of inequality and dominance" since "all social processes, are inherently stretched out in particular ways, and not others".

As argued earlier, organizations are generally sites of production where professionals have to negotiate their creative agency on digital technologies with myriad other interests. However, whereas organizations in their material and discursive formations are always tied to the interests of owners and, by extension, to the broader interests of the business elite, there is always some relative autonomy for the professionals. This autonomy is both a source of internal contradictions and journalistic creative agency that gives rise to change in institutional cultures and practices.

In Capital radio, the availability of the Internet and Frontline SMS technologies and the attendant practices must also be seen within a context of an asymmetrical power structure within the organization. The availability of these technologies was largely a product of competing interests between owners, management and professionals. For example, journalists largely perceived digital platforms in terms of the professional affordances associated with them, whereas management emphasized commercial imperatives. To owners and management, some of the considerations, although not of primary concern, were on how the Internet and mobile phones could also accrue financial benefits to the organization by way of delivering audiences to advertisers. For example, to reduce the costs of Internet use by the newsroom, the station's advertising department created a barter trade deal with an Internet Service Provider (ISP), Skyband, where the ISP could advertise online and offline for free while it provided bandwidth to the station. According to management, this ensured that the professional interests of journalists to use the Internet were met with as little cost to the organization as possible since the Internet platforms were not considered mainstream by advertisers and sponsors of programmes. The station director (2010, Interview) associated the use of new digital platforms such as the Internet and Facebook mostly with the youth, who in Malawi were not particularly attractive as a niche market to big sponsors of news and current affairs programming. However, other advertisers and sponsors still funded Capital Radio's entertainment programmes, such as musical shows which targeted the youth as big users of Facebook in such shows. The uses of the new digital media on radio therefore reflect a hierarchical flow of power in decision-making where the invisible hand of the market influences the types of decisions made by managers.

Capital Radio's audiences were also evidently using the station's digital platforms to access radio and perhaps also to participate in its programmes. For example, the radio station's website had a total of 939,000 page views and 50,000 visitors by June 2010 since its inception in 2006. The average number of visitors per day was shown to be 225 people.[2] To a certain extent, these statistics indicate that radio publics may no longer just be dependent on traditional terrestrial broadcasting to access radio content and participate in its programmes. It can be argued that at the organizational level, the Internet has brought about new channels for radio through which audiences can access, consume and perhaps even participate using the panoply of the new digital platforms. However, as Carpentier (2011, 13) advises, there is a difference between "access, interaction, and participation" because access to radio and interaction with journalists through these digital technologies is not synonymous with participation in the radical sense of the word. I shall return to this issue.

Dzimwe Community Radio did not have Internet in the newsroom. The station represents a typical rural community radio station that is plagued by numerous digital divides of a technological, economic and social nature (Moyo 2009). However, the station depended on its mobile phone handsets to receive text messages from its rural audiences. This demonstrated the creative agency of journalists and their audiences. This agency is in spite of the rurality and remoteness of Mangochi and its very skeletal telecoms networks, on the one hand, and the multiplicity of its pervasive digital divides, on the other hand. The station also creatively generated content mostly through the Radio Listening Clubs that also used mobile phone texting to participate in radio programmes. As one manager at the station explained, "audiences use mobile telephony specifically in two different ways—the first way is they call the station to give feedback or comments in live programmes. Secondly, they send us SMS with comments on news and current affairs" (2011, Interview). The station claimed that they received about 15 SMSs from audiences per programme.

Although Capital Radio's uptake of the digital media platforms was comparatively high, it is imperative to note that the station's organizational context was one that is largely underpinned by the commercial interests of profit maximization. The uses of the Internet and mobile phones on the station and their associated affordances must therefore be located within the context of capitalistic production and the efforts to promote consumption by the market forces. To that extent, political economy questions regarding the models of ownership, funding and financing of the station and the way they impact the creative agency of journalists and audience participation require some serious critical reflection. Digital media do not always "challenge the social relations associated with capitalist rationalization"; rather, they "reinforce them and expand the scale on which they operate" (Andrejevic 2007, 197). To that degree, radio convergence in Capital Radio was not merely about the convergence of technologies but also about the mutation and mobility of capital into newer spaces of digital capitalism.

This mobility of capital culminates in the convergence of spaces (the market and the political/cultural public spheres), practices (consumption and civic participation) and identities (citizen and consumer) in radio. In late modern societies, this conflation of spaces, practices and identities is said to be symptomatic of the fluidity and reflexivity that is supposedly typical of the age of mass consumption. In Malawi, however, the experiences of converging spaces, practices and identities do not demonstrate mass consumption because many still remain poor. However, the corporate forces are relentless in their pursuit for niche markets, mostly among middle and high-income classes. These are the classes that have money to afford consistent and meaningful use of the Internet and mobile phones. The middle and high-income classes enjoy the same mobility as capital itself through these technologies. Hence, one of the most frequent advertisements on Capital Radio's website was that of the Baobab Travel Agency, which targeted those seeking to travel to "beach holidays in Zanzibar, safaris in Kenya, or any of our wonderful destinations right here in Malawi".[3] It is therefore imperative to underscore the commercial environment within which the new digital media technologies were deployed to advance the professional interests of journalists while also creating new modalities of expression for advertising and sponsorship.

The dominance of advertising and sponsorship therefore had clear imprints on Capital Radio because of its ownership and funding model, which hinge on profit making for the owners. In that context, it can be argued that digital technologies as technologies of freedom had no more power for journalists and their audiences than the foundational structures of Capital Radio's commercial model could allow. The central line of argument here is that the age-old questions around the ownership and the funding and financing models of media also underpin decisions of not only what audiences can participate in but also when, how and through what technologies. How we organize and fund radio is central in the distribution of power in radio, and power itself is a critical factor in shaping radio through priorities given to its new technological platforms of access and delivery. These technologies can either create radio as a genuine participatory space or a space of selling and consumption.

In Capital Radio, the ratings of the most popular programmes of the station, such as Sunday Round Table and News Talk, tended to attract numerous advertisers and sponsorships, who then competed for air space with the audience. In Sunday Roundtable, for example, the Bank Sponsors of the programme always swamped public debate on politics by citizens with commercial messages that also reduced spaces for where and when audience messages coming through Facebook and text messaging could be read by the programme presenters on the air. Thus, as noted by Golding and Murdock (1998, 19), "different ways of funding and financing media have traceable consequences for the range of representations and discourses accessible in [the public sphere]". Capital Radio is a clear example of how advertisers manipulate the popularity of political programming and recast it as a space for selling and not for radical democratic participation. In that sense, the persistent spectra of powerlessness in mediated communication continue to affect audiences in spite of the promise of the new media.

Although there was no evidence to suggest that advertisers influenced the general programming in terms of the selection and exclusion of issues, they, however, clearly influenced whose voice is heard through new media platforms, when and for how long. This is because the radio programmes had a clear template for advertising spaces, whereas the participation from audiences through SMS, Facebook and emails crowded the remaining spaces. Dzimwe Community Radio also faced similar funding and financing pressures, which impeded the mainstreaming of digital media on community radio in a way that enhanced heightened forms of community participation and involvement normally associated with the community radio model. The use of digital media in the station by journalists was largely influenced by donors like Farm Radio International, who provided computers, mobile phones and funding for some programmes with a specific focus on agriculture, development, health and sanitation. For example, the station's five mobile phones, as stated earlier, were provided by donors and were mostly used in programmes that are sponsored by those donors. Their donor dollar power often overrode community participation in decision-making about the type of discourses the community might need in their radio station. As a result, one could argue that donors have usurped the agenda-setting on kinds of participation by audiences and the types of discourses prioritized. This 'donorisation' of the community radio programming and the digital infrastructure through which audiences and journalist practices find articulation is not fundamentally different from the corporatization that we saw in Capital Radio. Uses of these digital media by journalists and audiences were not merely based on professional interests and the need to participate in programmes by audiences. Hence, Carpentier (2011, 14) argues that "participation is always situated in particular processes and localities, and involves specific actors *interacting within a context of power*". In other words, radio's organizational contexts as seen in Capital Radio and Dzimwe Community Radio are ones that are characterized by competing interests, such as those of advertisers, sponsors, professionals, donors and audiences. The dynamic of these relationships characterizes the agency of the Internet and mobile phones in radio and the colour that audience participation takes in terms of its scope and depth.

Willems (2013) also points to the obstinacy of the corporate logic in regulating participation, even in the age of digital technologies. For example, as a privately owned commercial radio station, Capital Radio is owned by shareholders who, above all else, are interested in profit maximization. Although the station allowed audience participation in its current affairs programmes through text messaging, social media and mobile texting, this was always negotiated within the politics of advertising and sponsorships as the lifeblood of corporate radio. Through the corporatization of radio, the technological convergence of traditional radio and the new digital media enhances forms of audience participation on the radio but, as stated earlier, in a way that dilutes politics with market imperatives. Audiences are free to use the Internet and mobile phones to participate in public debates on the radio, but in the process, they cannot eschew the hidden hand of the market, which recasts them as consumers in their sacred civic moments. Andrejevic's (2004) concept of "digital enclosures" is very fitting here to demonstrate how technological convergence in radio serves to create new spaces for capitalistic expansion through advertising. He argues that "the contemporary deployment of [digital media] exploits participation as a form of labour. Consumers generate marketable commodities by submitting to comprehensive monitoring" (64). For example, one manager at Capital Radio also stated that Facebook was one critical tool for surveillance of audiences as a commodity that they sell to advertisers (2010, Interview). Facebook provides users' personal data on age, education, employment and interests, and all these details are usually readily available to the station. This data subsequently influenced types of programmes that targeted an imagined audience of the youth who constituted the majority of the station's 4000 Facebook users who consistently listened to certain musical programmes, like Top of the Pops and Groove Lounge.

Although the advent of technologies like the Internet and FrontlineSMS has clearly culminated in greater audience activity and involvement in news, it is also important to note that the nature of their participation is not direct, but mediated. It is therefore still subject to the processes of selection and exclusion that take place in news production by the radio journalists in both stations. Despite efforts toward the institutionalization of participatory cultures at Capital Radio and Dzimwe Community Radio, the stations still held diary meetings. These meetings must be understood as performing various functions and serving different objectives in any given situation. They can at once play the roles of facilitating, amplifying, or even filtering, policing and gate-keeping audience participation. Text messages about potential news stories from audiences are either attributed or denied some news value by journalists who exercise professional power over the audiences. Although radio convergence has opened the radio to audiences, "limited access to the site of [radio] production helps to naturalise the way stories are framed and the facts presented" (Andrejevic 2004, 198). Finally, this finding shows the limited power of digital technologies when used by audiences to participate in 'invited spaces' (Cornwal 2002) as opposed to when audiences invent their spaces to speak back or create counter public spheres that contest the voices of mainstream radio. Even with the most powerful technologies, when participation is invitational, it is always invariably conditional and restricted (see Dahlgren 2011).

CONCLUDING NOTE: DIGITAL TURN AND DEMOTIC TURN NOT SYNONYMOUS WITH A PARTICIPATORY TURN ON RADIO

The Capital Radio and Dzimwe Community Radio case studies show that greater access to radio through new digital technologies has not necessarily translated to meaningful participation by audiences, although there is some degree of opening up of the journalism profession to informal processes of content production by the public as journalists change their practices on news gathering and production. Although digital media have certainly opened up more spaces of interaction between audiences and journalists, the latter remain firmly in control in terms of the terms of engagement. Although radio convergence has brought about what others have referred to as a 'demotic turn' (Turner 2009), which essentially refers to the growing visibility of ordinary people in the mainstream media, that visibility is not synonymous with audience and citizen participation that is radical and not subjected to the disciplining order of the age-old organizational and institutional cultures preponderant in capitalist societies. The Capital Radio case study shows that digital media platforms have brought about greater visibility of an active audience, which can hardly be said to be representing a demotic turn on radio due to the pervasive digital divide in Malawi. This divide has a social, economic and geographic character and has created an information and communication class structure where the information-haves enjoy more access to radio and other media through a multiplicity of digital platforms, whereas most people remain in the margins. Again, this small class of what I perceive as only an active audience cannot be reconstructed as a participative radio public because of the pervasive corporatization and donor influence on radio spaces in a way that undermines the transformative agency of participatory action. As argued earlier, advertisers, sponsors and donors of radio programmes undercut audience participation through the new digital media by turning radio into a marketing or development advocacy space instead of a civic space.

NOTES

1. See "Community radio stations told to stop airing news reports", Pambazuka News, http://pambazuka.org/en/category/media. Last checked 9 June 2012.
2. Reports by Google Analytics provided by Capital Radio.
3. Baobab Travel Agency, http://www.baobabtravel.net. Last checked 1 October 2012.

REFERENCES

Allan, Stuart. 2006. *Online News*. Buckingham: Open University Press.
Andrejevic, Mark. 2004. "The Webcam Subculture and the Digital Enclosure". In *Media Space: Place, Scale and Culture in a Media Age,* edited by Couldry, Nick and McCarthy, Anna, 193–208. London: Routledge.
Beland, Daniel. 2005. "Ideas, Interests and Institutions: Historical Institutionalism". In *New Institutionalism Theory and Analysis*, edited by Lecours, Andre, 29–50. Toronto: University of Toronto Press.
Buckly, Steve. 2000. "Radio's New Horizons: Democracy and Popular Communication in the Digital Age". *International Journal of Cultural Studies* 3(2): 180–187.
Carpentier, Nico. 2011. "The Concept of Participation. If they have Access and Interact, do They Really Participate?" *Communication Management Quarterly* 14(2): 164–177.
Carlsson, Ulla. 2006. *Radio, TV & Internet in the Nordic Countries: Meeting the Challenges of New Media Technology*. Stockholm: Nordicom.
Communications Act of Malawi, 2012. Accessed 20 September 2012. http://www.wipo.int/wipolex.
Cornwall, Andrea. 2002. *Making Spaces, Changing Places: Situating Participation in Development, Institute of Development Studies, Working Paper, No. 170.*
Couldry, Nick and McCarthy, Anna. 2004. *Media Space: Place, Scale and Culture in a Media Age*. London: Routledge.
Crisell, Andrew. 2004. *More than a Music Box: Radio Cultures and Communities in a Multi-Media World*. New York: Berghahn Books.
Dahlgren, Peter. 2011. "Parameters of Online Participation: Conceptualizing Civic Contingences". *Communication Management Quarterly* 14(2): 87–109.
Feenberg, Andrew. 1999. *Transforming Technology: A Critical Theory Revisited*. Oxford: Oxford University Press.
Flew, Terry. 2005. *New Media: An Introduction*. Oxford: Oxford University Press.
Freedman, Des. 2008. *The Politics of Media Policy*. Cambridge: Polity Press.
Giddens, Antony. 1981. "A Contemporary Critique of Historical Materialism". In *Power, Property and The State*, edited by Giddens, Antony, 67–86. London: Macmillan.
Golding, Peter and Murdock, Graham. 1998. "Culture, Communications and Political Economy". In *Mass Media and Society*, edited by Curran, James and Gurevitch, Michael, 56–82. London: Arnold.

Gordon, Janey. 2012. "Community Radio, Mobile Phones and the Electromagnetic Spectrum". In *Community Radio in the 21st Century*, edited by Gordon, Janey, 115–129. Oxford: Peter Lang.

Hall, Richaer H. 1999. *Organisations: Structures, Processes, and Outcomes*. New York: Prentice Hall.

Hassard, John. 1990. "An Alternative to Paradigm Incommensurability in Organization Theory". In *The Theory and Philosophy of Organisations: Critical issues and New Perspectives*, edited by Hassard, John and Pym, Denis, 1–13. London: Routledge.

Jenkins, Henry. 2006. *Convergence Culture: Where Old and New Media Collide*. New York: New York University Press.

Kalodzy, Janet. 2006. *Convergence Journalism: Writing and Reporting Across News Media*. New York: Rowman & Littlefield.

Lecours, Andre. 2005. *New Institutionalism Theory and Analysis*. Toronto: University of Toronto Press.

Lister, Martin, Dovey, Jon, Giddings, Seth, Kelly, Kieran and Grant, Iain. (2003). *New Media: A Critical Introduction*. London: Routledge.

Malawi Information and Communication Technologies Policy (ICT), 2012. Accessed 30 September 2012. http://www.share4dev.info.

Morgan, Gareth. 1990. "Paradigm Diversity in Organizational Research". In *The Theory and Philosophy of Organisations: Critical Issues and New Perspectives*, edited by Hassard, John and Pyn, Denis, 13–29. London: Routledge.

Morriset, Lloyd. 2003. "Technologies of Freedom?" In *Democracy and New Media*, edited by Jenkins, Henry and Thorburn, David, 21–32. Cambridge, MA: MIT Press.

Moyo, Last. 2009. "The Digital Divide". In *Digital Culture: Understanding New Media*, edited by Creeber, Glen and Martin, Royston, 122–138. London: Open University.

———. 2011. *New ICTs and Radio Convergence in Southern Africa*. Johannesburg: Unpublished report.

Paschal, Preston. 2001. *Reshaping Communications*. London: Sage.

Sewell, William. H. 1992. "A Theory of Structure: Duality Agency and Transformation". *American Journal of Sociology* 98(1): 1–9.

Sparks, Colin. 2003. "Inside the Media". *International Socialism* (98): 24–51.

Turner, Graeme. 2009. *Ordinary People and the Media: The Demotic Turn*. London: Sage.

Willems, Wendy. 2013. "Participation—In what? Radio, Convergence and the Corporate Logic of Audience input through New Media in Zambia". *Telematics and Informatics* 30(3): 223–231.

4 Zimbabwe's Mainstream Press in the 'Social Media Age'

Emerging Practices, Cultures and Normative Dilemmas

Hayes Mawindi Mabweazara

INTRODUCTION

African newsrooms are (as elsewhere) experiencing the transformative 'impact' of new digital technologies at a number of levels, including the way they generate and disseminate news. Indeed, as Accone aptly puts it, "[t]he impact of the Internet has been as significant on media consumption as it has on production" (2000, 69). Social media platforms in particular have been key in transforming "the [. . .] landscape of newsgathering [as well as] the resulting journalistic products, relationships, routines, and culture" (Robinson 2011, 1123). The interactivity and 'viral connections' engendered by social media have facilitated a rise in User Generated Content (UGC), which has impacted upon the broader ecology of the news media as well as challenged "the traditional definition of journalism" (Esipisu and Kariithi 2007).

Although African newsrooms (along with their journalists) have been adapting to these changes in various ways as broadly indicated in the chapters in this volume, few studies have, however, sought to empirically examine the practices and cultures emerging with the adoption and appropriation of social media by mainstream journalism in Africa. Naturally, this has meant that professional norms and practices that emerge in the context of Western experiences, where digital technologies have long impacted on traditional journalism, "are applied out of context, and sometimes awkwardly in Africa" (Ibelema 2008, 36).

Against this backdrop, this chapter is an attempt to contribute an African, particularly Zimbabwean, perspective of how mainstream print newspapers are responding to the wave of changes spawned by social media. It examines how leading print newsrooms drawn from the dominant state-controlled Zimbabwe Newspapers Group (Zimpapers) and the small but powerful privately owned Alpha Media Holdings (AMH) are adapting and adjusting to the interactive and participatory platforms associated with the 'social media era'. The chapter specifically examines how the adoption and use of Facebook (one of the defining social media platforms)[1] is influencing the way the newsrooms generate and disseminate their news. It explores the patterns and trends in the adoption and appropriation of the platform, examining how journalists use it to connect with sources and readers, including its general implications for practices and professionalism.

Although primarily focused on *Facebook,* the chapter interchangeably uses this term with the generic catchword *social media,* which encompasses the characteristic functions of the technology (loosely summed up as the interactions people create, exchange and share), all built on "the ideological and technological foundations of Web 2.0, which allow the creation and exchange of user-generated content" (Kaplan and Haenlein 2010, 61). Facebook particularly allows users to 'friend' other users, share text updates (branded status updates), photos and private messages, with a large emphasis on interacting online through 'liking' and commenting on the 'status' of friends (Sherwood and Nicholson 2012). The platform is therefore a "complex space, a site of multiple convergences and modes of interaction" that offer a good example of "[the] converged media environment" (Meikle and Young 2012, 59).

To illuminate the practices and cultures emerging with the adoption of Facebook in the newsrooms, the study draws on a constructivist approach to technology, which understands social media "as a socially constructed multifaceted reality, and not a monolithic element that [. . .] imposes its own logic to social actors such as media companies" (Domingo 2008, 19), as technological determinists would suggest. The chapter is thus premised on the view that to understand the 'impact' of social media on journalism practice in Africa, we must place "journalists into a critical and analytical context and begin to question the immediate and wider social context" (Mabweazara 2010, 12) in which they deploy and appropriate the technologies. It demonstrates that interactive digital technologies are, in fact, socially and culturally shaped and that the nature and form of their appropriation is inextricably embedded in the context in which they are deployed. As Paterson (2008, 1) contends, "Any technological development is embedded in an adoption process where social subjects make conscious or unconscious decisions that an observer can trace".

CONTEXT OF THE STUDY: THE ADOPTION OF INTERACTIVE DIGITAL TECHNOLOGIES IN ZIMBABWEAN PRINT NEWSROOMS

Although most newsrooms in Zimbabwe (across the divide of the state and the privately owned press) have been slow to embrace interactive digital technologies due to various reasons related to connectivity challenges and the well-documented notion of the 'digital divide', recent years have seen an intensification in the adoption and use of the technologies to reinforce links with sources and readers—albeit in disproportionate ways (Mabweazara 2011a).[2] Thus, while Zimbabwe has endured a lengthy period of under-investment as a result of a protracted political and economic crisis, it has a relatively reliable telecommunications infrastructure that makes Zimpapers and AMH's newsrooms "part of the global information society dream" (L. Moyo 2009, 58).

Whereas all the newspapers assumed an online presence in the late 1990s, in 2007, AMH's newspapers took the lead in the adoption of UGC by refurbishing and furnishing its newspaper websites with interactive features that enable readers to comment and contribute content to the newspapers (Mabweazara 2011b). The newsrooms also gradually strengthened their use of social media (Facebook and Twitter in particular) to reinforce links and connections with readers and news sources in ways that signify a profound paradigm shift in the practice of journalism in Zimbabwe.

Similarly, after an initial phase of resistance and scepticism, in 2010, Zimpapers joined the 'digital migration trail', beginning with an initial overhaul of its newspapers' websites to incorporate interactive features as well as embracing social media in the generation and dissemination of stories. Although the slow adoption of interactive digital platforms by Zimpapers can squarely be attributed to the prolonged economic challenges faced by the country since the turn of the century, it can also be connected to an innate culture of conservatism linked to general concerns about the public's responses to its partisan editorial content (Mabweazara 2011a; 2011b).[3]

Like journalists elsewhere, Zimpapers newsrooms "wasted a lot of time wringing their hands about the Internet and wishing it would disappear. Unsure what could be done with it [. . .] they closed their eyes and pretended it wasn't there" (Peters 2011, 159). As Zimpapers' Group Online Editor explained, "There were fears at the beginning, so we went through a period of testing before we first introduced the interactive website [. . .]. Gradually, everyone acclimatised to the changes [. . .]". This change in attitude has seen all Zimpapers newspapers striving to 'play catch-up' in a radical shift from established practices and cultures that clearly demonstrate fear of "court[ing] obscurity and potential irrelevance" (Peters 2011, 155) by disregarding the changes and dynamics ushered by contemporary developments in interactive digital technologies.

As part of efforts to actively participate in the digital revolution, in 2011, both Zimpapers and AMH hired Group Online Editors "with a number of evolving responsibilities, including repurposing print content for the web; using social media to engage and deliver content to their audiences; as well as filtering User Generated Content emerging from [all interactive platforms]" (Mabweazara 2013, 137). The Online Editors work closely with senior editors, ensuring that the digital platforms of each newspaper (websites and various social platforms) not only reflect the editorial thrust of the news organisation but also offer engaging interactivity that enrich user experience.

Overall, the structures in place across both Zimpapers and AMH indicate elements of gradual transition and adaptation to the era of interactivity and participatory digital journalism. Although they have yet to standardise their online operational procedures, the news organisations are "far from being mired in 'backwardness' or passively awaiting external salvation in regard to attempts to use [digital technologies]" (Berger 2005, 1). As Accone aptly avers, despite challenges, "African journalists should hardly be viewed as second class Net-izens. They have moulded Internet tools to suit their specific needs, devised ingenious technical solutions to overcome the idiosyncrasies of their situations" (2000, 69). There is, therefore, a spirit of participation in the digital revolution, and as Nyamnjoh rightly advises, "the way forward is in recognising the creative ways in which [the news organisations] merge their traditions with exogenous influences to create realities that are not reducible to either but enriched by both" (2005, 4).

The present study thus closely examines how selected newspapers from Zimpapers and AMH are adjusting to the 'social media age'. In particular, it explores how the newspapers and their journalists are appropriating Facebook in their day-to-day newsmaking routines. The chapter examines how the interactive and participatory cultures associated with the platform are impacting and transforming established cultures and practices within the newsrooms, including how journalists generate and disseminate their stories. It also looks at the normative dilemmas emerging with the use of social media and how journalists are handling the new context in which "strangers contribute directly to something [they] alone once controlled" (Singer et al. 2011, 1).

METHODOLOGICAL APPROACH

The empirical data used in this study were gathered through newsroom observation and in-depth interviews with journalists over a period stretching between May 2008 and December 2012. The data gathering process focused on newspapers selected from the dominant state-controlled Zimpapers: two dailies (*The Herald* and the *Chronicle*) and two weeklies (*The Sunday Mail* and *The Sunday News*) as well as newspapers from the privately owned AMH: two weeklies (*The Zimbabwe Independent* and *The Standard*) and a daily (*NewsDay*).

The research deployed a triangulated approach involving the use of multiple cases (newsrooms) and informants as well as data collection procedures (observation and in-depth interviews). Although observations were mainly conducted within the newsrooms to ascertain how the news organisations and their journalists are deploying and appropriating social media (among other digital technologies), a greater part of this approach also involved forms of 'virtual ethnography' (Hine 2000), that is, observing journalists' activities and interactions with readers on Facebook. This provided the necessary first-hand experience of emerging cultures and practices.

The interviews with the journalists were mostly conducted in situ at their desks in the newsrooms. The setting facilitated direct access to their experiences and interactions with social media. Journalists illustrated their responses to particular questions by instantaneously referring to specific aspects of their use of Facebook. They also made relevant connections between the platform and specific news production contexts, including linking the technology to the generation of specific stories. Likewise, interviewing the journalists in situ made it possible for me to make reference to particular activities and practices that I observed from a distance without capturing nuance.

In total, 110 journalists were involved in the study through interviews, observations or a combination of the methods. Interviewees were purposively selected using convenience sampling rather than random sampling. Given the nature of some of the data generated from the study and the likelihood of it being recognisable to other people, I have deliberately avoided using the journalists' names, preferring instead to use their generic titles in order to protect them from possible identification. Further, in cases where journalists specifically requested anonymity, I have completely anonymised their responses, avoiding any mention of their title or news organisation.

Understanding how social media is transforming the practice of journalism in Zimbabwe requires a brief contextualisation of emerging research on the connections between social media and journalism.

SOCIAL MEDIA AND TRADITIONAL JOURNALISM: A BRIEF THEORETICAL OVERVIEW

Although theorisation on social networking sites (and their appropriation) in journalism is dominated by Western scholarship, there is general consensus that these interactive platforms—with their emphasis on peer production, interactive dialogue, collaboration and social connections—have led to significant changes in the profession across the globe (Lowery 2009; Picard 2009; Bruns and Highfield 2012; Canter 2013; Meikle and Young 2012; Gulyas 2013). Alongside other digital technologies, social media have not only resulted in an increasingly active audience but also transformed the way people receive and share information, including how they interact with journalists. Although there is no doubt (especially in Africa) that active participation in social media platforms such as Facebook is limited to a "self selecting" (Newman 2009) elite social group, "more and more journalists across [socio-economic divides] are discovering the relevance of [the interactive platforms] to their lives and work" (Kelly 2008, 12). Indeed, news organizations alongside their journalists are "increasingly turning to social networking tools in their efforts to compete in a challenging and fast-changing media landscape" (Emmett 2008, 41; see also Peters 2011).

In the context of day-to-day journalistic routines, it is widely believed that the interactivity and connections facilitated by social media enable journalists to access information, ideas and feedback from their sources and readers in ways that differ markedly from the "arms-length" operations of traditional mass communication (Picard 2009, 11). In this sense, social media is seen as "expand[ing] the range of participants available to engage in news [production], dissemination [. . .] and commentary" (Bruns and Highfield 2012, 21). The surge in the practice of user-led sharing and discussion of news stories by ordinary citizens (and journalists) on social media platforms—which could be described as "random acts of journalism" (29)—"allows journalists to gather first-hand material" (Gulyas 2013, 272), especially if they are physically remote from the scenes and issues raised by the readers. Gulyas further observes that social media "can enhance the degree of authenticity [in stories], as it takes journalists closer to [news sources and] where the [stories are] actually happening" (272).

Facebook, in particular, has proved useful "beyond [its] original target college audience" (Kelly 2008, 12), thus demonstrating "how technologies are shaped and acquire their meaning in the heterogeneity of social interactions" (Bijker 1995, 6). The gradual transformation of the technology into a platform that accommodates journalistic routines and practices points to the fact that, "one should never take the meaning of a technical artefact or technological system as residing in the technology itself" (6); rather, we should consider the 'social shaping' nature of the contexts in which the technology is adopted and deployed.

In general, Facebook has augmented and reinvented the means by which news organisations interact with their sources and readers as well as the way readers interact and relate with one another (Kelly 2008). The technology has also made it easier for journalists and ordinary citizens "to find stories and news sources of interest to them, and share that material with other interested parties" (Peters 2011, 155).

These observations connect with general observations about the influences of interactive digital technologies on the practice and culture of journalism. Writing from an American context, Pavlik argues that we are seeing the emergence of a "two-way symmetric model of communication [in which] the flow of communication is [. . .] much more a dialog between both or all parties to communication" (2000, 235–236). For Pavlik, the interactivity of the new media is "bringing about a shift in the relationships between or among news organisations and their publics" (2005, 246). Pavlik's observations chime with Singer et al.'s (2011, 1) view that "The twenty-first-century newspaper is essentially never complete, neither finished nor finite [. . .]. Nor are journalists the only ones determining what gets recorded. A great many other people also contribute content, representing their own interests, ideas, observations and opinions". Bruns and Highfield similarly contend that journalists' adoption of participatory and interactive technologies such as Facebook turns their "stories from finished products into the unfinished" (2012, 30), even if they claim to have the complete story.

Writing about interactive digital technologies from an African perspective, Mudhai (2004) and Kupe (2003) submit that interactivity has enabled African journalists to move closer to engaging with readers. They argue that interactivity is changing news production processes and our understanding of who produces news. Taking this argument further, D Moyo (2009) suggests that the ability to engage with news and with other news consumers is giving African readers greater influence over the material covered in the newspapers while at the same time providing journalists with an opportunity to access ideas and leads from the readers.

It is important, however, to note that practices emerging with social media are not without normative implications for the profession. As Canter (2013, 604) puts it, "[t]he rise in participatory journalism has led to new challenges for journalists as they strive to negotiate the often murky waters of user-generated content". In particular, the underlying logic of "openness and participation" (Lewis 2012, 840) characteristic of social media entails that traditional editorial 'gatekeeping' structures in the newsmaking process are challenged as "authority is dispersed and shared" (Gulyas 2013, 272) among both professionals and ordinary citizens. Writing about the consequences of these challenges in relation to Facebook, Peters argues that the platform "provides no good way for its users to assess whether what they're getting at any given time is relevant, intelligent, or accurate" (2011, 155). He observes that journalists cannot independently

> [. . .] assign a specific value to a source or to a piece of information, and [they] can't consider the value that other users have assigned to a source or a piece of information, other than by the comments or 'likes' that it has received. (157)

These challenges are seen as undermining and altering traditional journalistic values such as accuracy and objectivity. The changing values also represent the reshaping of journalism itself, where the traditional construct of the journalist as the verifier of information is being altered by a more "iterative and collaborative approach to reporting and verifying news" (Hermida 2012, 665).

Beyond the foregoing normative implications, journalists' dependence on social media and UGC in news reporting is also seen as portending "the decline of the maker culture" (Peters 2011, 155). The ready availability of information/content on platforms such as Facebook encourages journalists to become "data consumers rather than creators" (155). Peters warns that "news organizations that become too integrated with social media risk losing the very things that made them vital" (159), that is, sourcing and verifying news in situ outside digital platforms.

The burden of moderating volumes of UGC on news organisations' social media platforms is also seen as a key challenge. Singer et al. (2011, 3) observe that "[w]hen journalism becomes 'participatory', the volume of transmitted information rapidly surges to flood levels, swamping traditional approaches to winnowing and the like". Correspondingly, Canter (2012) points to the "confusion surrounding moderation or non-moderation of comments and the potential legal implications". According to Bruns and

Highfield, the challenges of moderating or 'gatekeeping' readers' comments on social media platforms such as Facebook have seen most of the UGC becoming little more than "random rants which are neither policed nor engaged with by journalistic or editorial staff" (2012, 17).

The rest of the chapter presents the findings of the study. The first part focuses on the adoption and appropriation of Facebook in newsmaking practices and routines. The second part examines how the technology is redefining traditional connections between journalists and readers, whereas the third section discusses the threats and ethical challenges posed by social media to established normative practices of journalism. The chapter concludes with a reflective overview of the study's findings.

THE ADOPTION AND APPROPRIATION OF FACEBOOK IN EVERYDAY NEWSMAKING ROUTINES

Although entertainment reporters were among the early adaptors of Facebook (and other social media platforms) across all the newsrooms studied (see Mabweazara 2011a), this study indicated that journalists across all newsbeats are increasingly taking the platform seriously in their day-to-day business, including newsgathering and reporting. Journalists related the increase in the use of the platform to general changes in attitude towards social media by senior editors across all the newsrooms. As one reporter at *The Standard* explained, "Whereas Facebook was initially seen as a waste of valuable company resources, including time by most editors, attitudes have since changed; those very editors now have an active presence on the platform". Although not codified as formal policy, this change in attitude by senior editors has seen more journalists across age lines discovering the relevance of the interactive platforms in their work and private lives. Editors persistently encourage their staffers to actively use the social media in their day-to-day newsmaking routines. One senior editor at *The Herald* explained thus:

> With the surge in the number of public personalities, including politicians using social media, *it's taboo to have a journalist who is not on Facebook* [. . .] you have to be on some form of social media. It's an expectation [. . .]. Time without number; you have editors assigning reporters to stories based on comments on Facebook. You have desk editors saying *"we carried this story yesterday and this is the feedback, can you please do a follow up"*. (emphasis added)

Expressing a similar view, a senior assistant editor at the *NewsDay* stated,

> We encourage all our journalists in the newsroom to have a Facebook or Twitter account [. . .]. It's more or less policy because even the chairperson of AMH is active on social media. He uses Facebook and tweets

if something of interest happens and expects everyone in the newsroom to pick it up, especially the editor [. . .]. That has obviously put everyone on their toes [. . .].

This shift towards the use of Facebook as an everyday tool has seen the emergence of new practices and routines of newsmaking. Journalists, for example, highlighted that they use the platform to 'crowd source' story ideas, comments and general insights from sources scattered across the globe, consequently supplementing or even supplanting their traditional news sourcing strategies.

Across all the newsrooms, journalists gave vivid accounts of how they use Facebook to generate stories. In particular, they described how they deployed the platform to locate sources, track trends and engage in conversations that sometimes led to stories that would have otherwise remained hidden. This use of Facebook included lurking on prominent personalities' profiles, hoping, as one senior political reporter at the *NewsDay* explained, "to sniff out ideas for the next diary or even comments and quotes for stories already in progress". Journalists across news beats branded Facebook "a fertile hunting ground for story ideas", as one reporter at *The Zimbabwe Independent* put it.

Further explaining the centrality of Facebook as a newsgathering tool, a senior entertainment reporter at the *Chronicle* stated,

> Sometimes you can actually pick stories from Facebook [. . .] like if you get an artist writing on his or her [wall][4]: "I had a boring show", that is a scoop on its own! You quickly initiate communication with them and ask how big the show was, what went wrong and so on. In fact, a couple of weeks ago, a South African musician was publicly 'dumped' by his girlfriend on Facebook and the *Sowetan* tabloid made a big story out of it [. . .]

Journalists also highlighted that they received updates through Facebook on diverse issues of interest to their beats. They noted that the social platform was an invaluable reporting tool that instantaneously connected them to key sources and stories that would otherwise take days or weeks to surface. A news reporter at *The Sunday Mail* aptly explained this development:

> In some of our stories reporters talk to government ministers on Facebook [. . .]. They actually engage directly and publicly debate. Just yesterday, I followed a reporter who was debating with the Minister of Education about the 70 thousand teachers who are said to be relocating to other countries [. . .]. *So the benefit of using social media is that we have come closer to the sources of news* (emphasis added).

This extract echoes Gulyas's observation that social media use "allows journalists to gather first-hand material from the ground" (2013, 272).

From the above, it is clear that (as elsewhere) the adoption and use of Facebook in Zimbabwean print newsrooms is reshaping the way journalists conduct their daily business. The technology connects reporters to a range of sources and fosters trust and norms of reciprocity that are key antecedents to effective reporting (Mabweazara 2011a). Thus, the short messages left by friends on the reporters' Facebook 'walls' or 'timelines' call attention to what is happening on the social scene, hence providing them with a conduit "to tap into the popular mood" (Newman 2009), with the potential to enrich as well as amplify their scope of news coverage (Gulyas 2013).

EMERGING INTERACTIVE AND PARTICIPATORY CULTURES

As with the newspapers' interactive websites, which enable readers to directly engage with news content (Mabweazara 2011b), the study also revealed that the interactive features of Facebook (Kelly 2008; Lowery 2009; Meikle and Young 2012) play a key role in stimulating and strengthening the newspapers' connections with their readers and sources. Whereas for the traditionally conservative state-controlled Zimpapers (with its entrenched "arm's length" (Picard 2009, 11) connections with readers), the interactivity of Facebook has facilitated new connections, for AMH, the platform has revitalised and strengthened established connections with the newspapers' readership and former loyalists. In both news organizations, the interactivity of Facebook is therefore modifying the traditional 'top-down' journalistic culture by establishing a more 'open' and collaborative culture (Hermida 2011) that allows readers to contribute in various ways to their news reporting.

We are therefore seeing the "emergence of a two-way symmetric [journalistic] model" (Pavlik 2000, 235) in which the newspapers' Facebook pages serve the dual purpose of 'funnelling' readers to stories on the newspapers' websites as well as providing them with an open platform to deliberate over news content. Thus, Facebook can be seen as a complex space "of multiple convergences and modes of interactions" (Meikle and Young 2012, 59), collectively redefining the connections between newsrooms and their readers. As the Group Online Editors of Zimpapers explained,

> We figured readers were running away from us. At the same time we realized they were creating their own stories and news on Facebook, so we decided to invade their space [. . .] and directly engage with them [. . .]. It has worked!

To directly engage with readers as well as increase traffic to the newspapers' websites, the news organisations post catchy snippets of topical news stories on Facebook peppered with commentary that overtly cajoles readers to visit the newspapers' websites for full stories. They also directly encourage readers to air their views and comment on the issues covered in the stories. AMH's Group Online Editor explained this practice as follows:

> Our aim is to ignite reader-engagement by provoking responses to our stories. So we introduced what we call 'cliff hangers' where you post the most topical or controversial part of a news article on Facebook with a link to the full story on the newspaper's website. We then pose a question to inspire debate. You, therefore, find posts like "Two Masvingo Chiefs are demanding 2000 head of cattle from Econet Wireless for desecrating their ancestral shrine while erecting a base station on Sviba Hills. *Do you think their demand is justified?*" or "The Battle of Zimbabwe! Highlanders vs. Dynamos football club: *Who will walk away victors?*" (emphases added).

Observations further indicated that readers are embracing the interactivity of the newspapers' Facebook profiles in similar ways to the comments sections of their news websites. They actively comment on stories and take journalists to task for stories perceived as poorly researched, lacking balance or simply taking issue with various centres of power in connection to issues prompted by news stories. The challenge for the news organisations, however, was that readers do not always remain on topic in their engagement with the news content and with one another, and in some cases, their comments tend to be abusive.

However, the interactive and participatory practices engendered by the newspapers' Facebook profiles pointed to a significant transformation of journalism itself. In particular, the practices led to the challenging of the traditional construct of a journalist as wielding a monopoly on 'wisdom' by an alert readership that scrutinises and dissects stories in an "iterative and collaborative approach to reporting and verifying news" (Hermida 2012, 665). This development was aptly illustrated by an assistant editor at *News-Day* in a newsroom interview in which he directed me to a heated Facebook conversation between his editor-in-chief and readers:

> I will show you a good example of what I mean [. . .] an exchange between our very own editor-in-chief and readers on Facebook following his response to the criticism of a story we covered about the government's plans to construct a new capital city near the president's rural home by the notorious *Herald* political columnist, Manheru.[5] Look [directing me to his Facebook profile]:[6]

> **Editor-in-chief:** Manheru intrigues me. He attacks *NewsDay* for reporting on the planned new capital city, a story which was confirmed by Minister Chombo. Why not attack Chombo? The Minister availed a

video on the project to the newspaper. Manheru should not abuse public space.

Respondent 1: If I read correctly Manheru was saying the story is not a secret, maybe I did not read the article comprehensively. He says, "The visit was open to media. . . . " and his argument is that it's an old story . . . not that it's a false story. That's my view.

Respondent 2: How are you Cde [Editor]? I kindly urge you to read Manheru's article again. *This time without emotions, read it as if you are someone [who works at the] Rainbow Towers Hotel [or at] Telecel mobile network [. . .].*[7] *You have been caught offside again [Cde Editor].* (Emphasis added)

Respondent 3: Journalism has gone to the dogs—gutter press!!

Respondent 2: [in direct response to Respondent 3]: Manheru's analysis exposes Zimbabwean journalism. Manheru also questions: "Which is nearer to Mount Hampden Zvimba communal lands or the Prime Minister's Mabelreign home?"

Respondent 3: [cajoling the editor-in-chief to respond to the comments]: [. . .] *all that is left to say is "where is [Cde Editor]"* (emphasis added)

Editor-in-chief: I am not even in Zimbabwe [. . .]. I have been away since Thursday.

This exchange is a classic example of how Facebook is enabling readers to directly engage with journalists in hitherto unprecedented ways. In the extract above, readers offer a critique of a story carried in *NewsDay* against the backdrop of a scathing review of the same story by a popular columnist (Manheru) in the state-controlled *Herald* newspaper. The conversation further demonstrates how social media is somewhat 'reforming' traditional journalism in Zimbabwe by bringing it 'back to reality'—reconnecting it with a disillusioned readership. Explaining this shift in practice, a senior desk editor at the *Chronicle* stated, "As you may know reporters tend to go for professional commentators [. . .] but with the emergence of these online spaces, anyone with his facts right can throw in their opinions. This is a complete *shift from tradition*" (emphasis added).

This transformation was especially significant in the context of the polarization of the press in Zimbabwe, which obstructs journalists from impartially reporting news, including adhering to the professional normative values of journalism such as balance, impartiality and fairness (Mabweazara 2011c). The interactive and participatory cultures engendered by Facebook can, therefore, be seen as shaking up traditional journalism and turning journalists back to the 'orthodoxy' of the profession. It is giving journalism *renewed human perspective* that has been lost over the years in the morass of the deeply polarized political spectrum in which the press in Zimbabwe operates. As noted earlier, this cultural shift is particularly defined in the state-controlled newsrooms, which have long "cultivated a professional distance from their readers" (Singer et al. 2011, 7). The newsrooms now find themselves entangled in a context in which their hegemony is not only challenged but also subjected to close scrutiny by their readers. As the Zimpapers' online editor explained, "Times are changing. It's clear people want their input and opinions to be considered in what we do as journalists [. . .]. We just have to be part of the game". This marks a radical break from the dominant top-down journalistic ethos to a more conversational practice in which readers actively engage in the production and reception of news (Hermida 2012).

In general, these findings reinforce the fact that the functions of technologies (the interactivity and participatory practices associated with Facebook in this case) are not fixed in the technology itself; rather, they are a site of interpretive work (Bijker 1996) that is entrenched in the complexities of the social interactions associated with the use of the technology.

THREATS TO ESTABLISHED CULTURES, PRACTICES AND PROFESSIONAL NORMS

The appropriation of Facebook in the generation and dissemination of news by journalists in the newsrooms studied was, however, not without negative professional implications. As Robison reminds us, "[n]ew demands in long-established [journalistic] cultures inevitably create tensions" (2011, 1126) which threaten traditional normative standards and practices. In this study, some of the normative concerns related to the generic crises facing contemporary journalism globally. These included the controversies surrounding the invasion of personal privacy (for both journalists and ordinary citizens), the inadvertent advancement of an 'elite news culture' (Mabweazara 2011a; 2013) that ignores large parts of human existence outside social media platforms (and other digital spaces) as well as the well-known challenges of verifying and 'gatekeeping' volumes of UGC emerging from the platforms. I discuss these issues in turn below.

In reflecting on the professional challenges emerging with the use of Facebook, a number of journalists underlined the dilemmas they faced in negotiating the platform's tendency to blur the line between the *professional* and the personal *subjective individual*. They spoke about the difficulties they faced in publicly expressing their personal opinions on controversial issues generated by friends and family on the platform. A number of journalists described how this put them in the spotlight and subjected them to scathing criticisms from their employers and the public precisely because of the general expectation that journalists should maintain a public deportment that does not put into question their impartiality. One senior news reporter at *The Zimbabwe Independent* lucidly explained this point:

Although, like anybody else, I'm tickled and provoked by some of the issues raised by my friends on Facebook, *I deliberately avoid commenting on those issues I think would put me on a tight spot. I try not to expose my personal convictions, in case I'm generally perceived as impartial and lacking objectivity in my work.* I can only pose more questions and provoke further comments from friends [. . .]. If personal or interesting issues that I think could lead to a good story arise, I follow up behind the scenes by sending particular individuals private messages [. . .]. Thank God Facebook allows for that! (emphasis added).

The 'self-censorship' highlighted in this extract points to the challenges journalists face in negotiating the tensions between private life and work on Facebook. The platform is seen as intruding into aspects of their private life, "leading to a blurring of the distinction between private and professional life" (Mabweazara 2013, 146). Most journalists expressed their frustration at how this implicitly stifled their personal freedom. As one junior sports reporter explained,

You will understand that as long as you are in formal employment the voice on your Facebook 'wall' will always be linked to your employer [. . .]. Personally, I don't know how many times I've been asked why I write so passionately about Dynamos Football Club on my Facebook profile by my desk editor [. . .]. It's worrying.

These concerns point to the broader crisis facing journalism in the era of digital technologies, which has seen the right to personal privacy and space coming under unprecedented threat (Mabweazara 2013).

Linked to the challenges of navigating personal privacy were ethical questions associated with journalists using material posted on individuals' Facebook profiles in news stories without their consent or knowledge. As noted earlier, journalists tended to lurk on prominent personalities' profiles for story ideas, completely disregarding issues of privacy. When probed about this ethical dilemma, a number of reporters pointed to the fine line between privacy and public life on Facebook. One entertainment reporter at *The Standard* explained thus: "If an artist posts something of interest on their Facebook profile, I would definitely use it because [. . .] It's already 'public knowledge' and, irrefutably, they are the main source of that comment". Similarly, a senior desk editor at *The Sunday Mail* stated, "Facebook is an open forum [. . .]. I'm sure if one wants to keep his or her privacy they would shun the platform because it's all, in a sense, about exposing yourself to people [. . .]. More or less like strip tease [quips]".

These findings contrast sharply with some observations in Western countries; for example, writing from an Australian context, Sherwood and Nicholson (2012) observe that an overwhelming majority of print journalists do not use Facebook in their everyday work routines as they see it as a private platform. The "journalists explained that they would have no hesitation in using something written on Twitter as a source, as it was public, but they would not use something written on a private Facebook page" (13).

The absence of codified policy guidelines on how journalists should use and conduct themselves on social media platforms appeared to exacerbate the ethical challenges across the news organisations studied. Whereas Zimpapers has a detailed set of guidelines for its web-content users,[8] it does not specifically address how its staffers should use social media as a journalistic tool. This policy vacuum also contrasts with the scenario in the West where most news organisations have developed clear policy guidelines for their staffers. For example, as early as September 2009, *The Washington Post* had published social media guidelines, which outlined how its journalists should conduct themselves on the platforms as well as the "potential hazards" associated with using the technologies.[9]

The increase in the use of social media as a source of news and story ideas by journalists in the newsroom studied also appears to have impacted *news access and sourcing patterns*. From observations and interviews, it was clear that Facebook (alongside other digital platforms) promoted the sourcing of stories from an elite minority with the access and means to maintain sustained visibility on social media. This "over-accessing to the media" (Hall et al. 1978, 58) by a few techno-savvy individuals inadvertently leads to the 'annihilation' of those existing on the margins of digital platforms. As the Glasgow University Media Group (1980, 114) asserts, "[a]ccess is structured and hierarchical to the extent that powerful groups and individuals have privileged and routine entry into news itself and to the manner and means of its production". This underlines the fact that technology is "not a neutral agent"; rather, it reinforces "traditional norms as much as to enact change" (Robinson 2011, 1135).

The deployment of Facebook by entertainment reporters provides a good example of the implications of social media on news access and sourcing. As some journalists explained, the tendency to rely on Facebook for story ideas and communication with sources limited the scope of the stories covered to the interests and agendas set by a few 'self-selecting sources' with sustained access and knowledge of how to effectively use social media. An entertainment editor at *The Sunday News* explained thus:

> [. . .] the problem with sourcing stories from social networking sites is that it slants your stories towards the more affluent and educated [. . .]. In fact, the whole process of interviewing people 'digitally' leads to journalists missing a lot of good ideas outside these networks [. . .] *Remember there are many entertainers in this very country who are semi-literate and can't tell the difference between the mouse and the keyboard of a computer, let alone, these social networking sites.* (emphasis added)

This response highlights the limitations of journalists' overreliance on social media, especially its potential to marginalise stories from sources that are not digitally connected. It further reinforces the social impact of the 'digital divide' in Africa, in particular the question of access to technology, which also includes "(digital) skills or competencies and media or technology use and applications" (van Dijk 2006, 224). Consequently, those who actively engage with social media become the "primary definers" (Hall et al. 1978, 61) of news. They set the agenda for issues covered by the reporters, especially in a context where journalists constantly work against the clock in order to meet the required story quotas.

Although it is indeed reductionist to attribute "elite news access" (Mabweazara 2013, 144) to Facebook alone, it seems clear from the discussion above that overreliance on social media by journalists in Africa has potential to promote routine elite access to the news media. It places individuals who wield "social hegemony" (Schudson 2000, 184) at a vantage point in terms of defining and pontificating what makes news as they have the appropriate infrastructure to guarantee a reliable and steady supply of the raw materials of news production.

Another clear ethical concern related to the challenges of verifying information sourced from Facebook. A number of journalists highlighted the dangers of relying on distorted information from the platform, especially given its very nature as a 'social setting' which "provides no good way for its users to assess whether what they're getting at any given time is [. . .] intelligent or accurate" (Peters 2011, 155). As one senior reporter at *The Herald* explained, "People shouldn't read too much into Facebook updates because for most people it's a playground where anything goes. So, if we are to judge people by what they write on their walls, we are heading for disaster [. . .]". These concerns led to an ingrained sceptical attitude to Facebook among some senior 'old school' journalists. For example, one veteran editor at *The Zimbabwe Independent* remonstrated thus: "reporters need to understand that *Facebook is not a Factbook;* it can be a hazardous source of information" (emphasis added). For these cautious journalists, the default approach was to take everything sourced from Facebook with a pinch of salt. This demonstrates a reflective awareness of the potential professional threats embedded in using social media as a journalistic tool. It echoes Berger's (2005, 1) observation that Southern African journalists are far from "lacking when it comes to critical perspectives with ICTs and global information networks".

One of the greatest challenges and threats to established practices was also evident in the lack of a structured gatekeeping approach to managing the huge volumes of UGC posted on the newspapers' social media platforms. Although this editorial lacuna was in part hinged on manpower shortages in the newsrooms,[10] some senior editors saw Facebook as a 'playground', not really meriting moderation, albeit useful as a journalistic tool.

This contrasted with their view on the UGC generated from the newspapers' websites. As the Zimpapers' Group Online Editor explained,

> *Comments on Facebook are often considered inconsequential and social,* but on our websites it's different [. . .]. It's easy for readers' comments to be associated with our newspapers, which could result in lawsuits. So, we keep a close eye on our newspaper websites instead.

Some editors were also generally hesitant to consider 'winnowing' (Singer et al. 2011) their social media platforms because of their strategic role in driving traffic to their newspaper websites. Explaining this, AMH's Group Online Editor stated,

> We have given our readers free rein on our social media platforms because we want the numbers they drive to our news websites. As you know, this is important for our advertisers. So, we don't want to be perceived as stifling our loyal online readership.

Although the newspapers' reluctance to moderate UGC on Facebook can be seen as inadvertently providing a corrective balancing act that challenges Zimbabwe's polarised press by giving readers (from across political divides) unfettered space to interact and exchange ideas, the laxity has opened flood gates for abuses and extremist political views which hardly find space in the newspapers' print versions, at least in uncensored terms. This demonstrates the challenges faced by newsrooms in encouraging readers to engage with their news content "while at the same time defending the core of news production [and dissemination] as a preserve of professionals" (Hermida 2011, 180).

CONCLUSION

This study has examined how the integration of social media, Facebook in particular, into the day-to-day newsmaking routines of Zimbabwean print newsrooms is transforming established traditional newsmaking practices and cultures. Although all the newsrooms studied are still broadly in the "era of experimentation" (Newman 2009), it is clear from the data presented in this chapter that Facebook and related interactive digital technologies are increasingly taking centre stage, influencing the strategic direction and practice of print journalism in Zimbabwe. Journalists (and their newsrooms) have adopted and entrenched Facebook into the idiosyncrasies of their professional contexts. The platform is thus providing a useful extra layer of functionality, enabling stories to be generated and disseminated in new ways that corroborate and temper with established cultures, practices and professional norms in both positive and negative ways.

In particular, the interactive and participatory cultures emerging with the appropriation of Facebook across newsrooms are redefining the means by which journalists engage with their readers as well as how readers relate and respond to the news content. The practices are turning the newsrooms "into an open, ongoing [collaborative] social experiment" (Singer et al. 2011, 1) that gives readers unprecedented access to the social production and reception of news. These changes are particularly marked for the traditionally conservative state-controlled newsrooms, which have long cultivated an innate "professional distance from their readers" (7).

From this study, we can surmise that although Facebook (and related social networking sites) present unprecedented professional and ethical dilemmas to traditional journalism in Africa, with much still to be learnt, there is confidence in the role that social media might play in maintaining the underlying values of journalism in the digital age. Critical thinking still needs to be done around the value that should be attached to participatory and interactive cultures and how exactly they should be integrated into everyday journalistic practice. Furthermore, journalists require new skills and training on a range of techniques and skills of engagement surrounding participatory UGC and social media as well as judgment about when and how to use information sourced from these interactive platforms.

NOTES

1. It is important to point out that despite Facebook's position as one of the defining platforms of social media (with over 800 million users worldwide), it has received very limited scholarly attention in the context of journalism (see Sherwood and Nicholson 2012).
2. The surge in the use of web-based digital technologies is broadly attributed to the phenomenal rise in Internet connectivity in the country. For example, the Internet penetration rate rose sharply from about 9.8 percent in March 2008 to 15.7 percent in June 2012, which represents a high figure relative to other sub-Saharan African countries (Internetworldstats.com 2012).
3. The state-controlled press in Zimbabwe is generally perceived to be blatantly partisan in its support for the Zimbabwe African National Union—Patriotic Front (ZANU-PF), which, until the establishment of a power sharing deal with the leading opposition political party, the Movement for Democratic Change (MDC) in 2008, was the ruling party in Zimbabwe since independence in 1980.
4. The space on each user's Facebook profile page that allows friends to post messages for the user and is visible to the user's network of friends on the site.
5. Manheru is an alias purportedly used by an infamous political columnist in the state-controlled *Herald*. He is widely thought to be the press secretary in the president's office and permanent secretary in the Ministry of Information in Zimbabwe. His position makes him the official spokesperson for President Robert Mugabe.
6. For ethical reasons, I have chosen to anonymise all the names of the readers involved in the conversation with the editor-in-chief.
7. The reader is suggesting that the editor should read the story with the neutral lenses of an ordinary reader who is not bound by a partisan editorial policy as is common in Zimbabwe.

8. See, for example, http://www.herald.co.zw/images/Terms_and_Conditions.pdf.
9. *Washington Post*'s Social Media Policy: http://socialmedia.biz/social-media-policies/washington-posts-social-media-policy/.
10. For example, Zimpapers' Group Online Editor was responsible for singlehandedly managing content from all the newspapers' interactive platforms (i.e., updating and editing all the newspapers' websites as well as populating and monitoring various social media platforms across all newspapers).

REFERENCES

Accone, Tanya. 2000. "Digital Dividends for Journalism in Africa." *Nieman Reports* 54(4): 67–69.
Berger, Guy. 2005. "Powering African Newsrooms: Theorising how Southern African Journalists make use of ICTs for Newsgathering". In *Doing Digital Journalism: How Southern African Newsgatherers are using ICTs,* edited by Berger, Guy, 1–14. Grahamstown: High Way Africa.
Bijker, Wiebe E. 1995. *Of Bicycles, Bakelite and Bulbs: Towards a Theory of Sociotechnical Change.* Cambridge, MA: MIT Press.
Bruns, Alex and Highfield, Tim. 2012. "Blogs, Twitter, and Breaking News: The Produsage of Citizen Journalism". In *Producing Theory in a Digital World: The Intersection of Audiences and Production in Contemporary Theory,* edited by Lind, Rebecca A., 15–32. New York: Peter Lang.
Canter, Lily. 2013. "The Misconception of Online Comment Threads: Content and Control on Local Newspaper Websites". *Journalism Practice* 7(5): 604–619.
Domingo, David. 2008. "Inventing Online Journalism: A Constructivist Approach to the Development of Online News". In *Making Online News: The Ethnography of New Media Production,* edited by Paterson, Chris and Domingo, David, 15–28. New York: Peter Lang.
Emmett, Arielle. 2008. "Networking News". *American Journalism Review* 30(6): 40–43.
Esipisu, Isaac and Kariithi, Nixon. 2007. "New Media Development in Africa." *Global Media Journal: Africa Edition.* Accessed February 20, 2009. http://academic.sun.ac.za/ gmja/Academic.htm.
Glasgow University Media Group. 1980. *More Bad News.* London: Routledge.
Gulyas, Agnes. 2013. "The Influence of Professional Variables on Journalists' Uses and Views of Social Media". *Digital Journalism,* 1(2): 270–285 .
Hall, Stuart, Critcher, Chas, Jefferson, Tony, Clarke John N. and Roberts, Brian. 1978. *Policing The Crisis: Mugging, The State, and Law and Order.* London: Routledge & Kegan Paul.
Hermida, Alfred. 2011. "Fluid Spaces, Fluid Journalism: The Role of the 'Active Recipient' in Participatory Journalism". In *Participatory Journalism: Guarding Open Gates at Online Newspapers,* edited by Singer, Jane et al., 177–191. New York: Wiley-Blackwell.
Hermida, Alfred. 2012. "Tweets and Truth: Journalism as a Discipline of Collaborative Verification". *Journalism Practice* 6(5–6): 659–668.
Hine, Christine. 2000. *Virtual Ethnography.* London: Sage.
Ibelema, Minabere. 2008. *The African Press, Civic Cynicism, and Democracy,* New York: Palgrave Macmillan.
Kaplan, Andreas M. and Haenlein, Michael. 2010. "Users of the World, Unite! The Challenges and Opportunities of Social Media". *Business Horizons* 53(1): 59–68.
Kelly, Wilson. 2008. "In Your Facebook: Why More and More Journalists are Signing Up for the Popular Social Networking Site". *American Journalism Review* 30(1): 12–13.

Kupe, Tawana. 2003. "The Untold 21st Century Story". *Rhodes Journalism Review* (23):18.

Lewis, Seth C. 2012. "The Tension Between Professional Control and Open Participation: Jornalism and its Boundaries". *Information, Communication & Society* 15(6): 836–866.

Lowery, Courtney. 2009. "An explosion Prompts Rethinking of Twitter and Facebook". *Nieman Reports* 63(3): 32–34.

Mabweazara, Hayes M. 2010. "'New' Technologies and Journalism Practice in Africa: Towards a Critical Sociological Approach". In *The Citizen in Communication: Re-visiting Traditional, New and Community Media Practices in South Africa*, edited by Hyde-Clarke, Nathalie, 11–30. Capetown: Juta & Co.

———. 2011a. "The Internet in the Print Newsroom: Trends, Practices and Emerging Cultures in Zimbabwe". In *Making Online News: Newsroom Ethnographies in the Second Decade of Internet Journalism*, edited by Domingo, David and Paterson, Chris, 57–69. New York: Peter Lang.

———. 2011b. " 'Wiring African' Newsrooms: The Internet and Mainstream Journalism Practice in Zimbabwe". In *Cultural Identity and New Communication Technologies: Political, Ethnic and Ideological Implications,* edited by Wachanga, Ndirangu D., 144–162. Pennsylvania: IGI Global.

———. 2011c. "Newsmaking Practices and Professionalism in the Zimbabwean Press". *Journalism Practice* 5(1): 100–117.

———. 2013. "Normative Dilemmas and Issues for Zimbabwean Print Journalism in the 'Information Society' Era". *Digital Journalism* 1(1): 135–151.

Meikle, Graham and Young, Sherman. 2012. *Media Convergence: Networked Digital Media in Everyday Life.* New York: Palgrave Macmillan.

Moyo, Dumisani. 2009. "Citizen Journalism and the Parallel Market of Information in Zimbabwe's 2008 Elections". *Journalism Studies* 10(4): 551–567.

Moyo, Last. 2009. "Repression, Propaganda, and Digital Resistance: New Media and Democracy in Zimbabwe". In *African Media and the Digital Public Sphere,* edited by Okoth, Mudhai F., Wisdom, Tettey J. and Fackson, Banda, 57–71. New York: Palgrave Macmillan.

Mudhai, Okoth. F. 2004. "Researching the Impact of ICTs as Change Catalysts in Africa". *Ecquid Novi: South African Journal for Journalism Research* 25(2): 313–335.

Newman, Nic. 2009. "The Rise of Social Media and its Impact on Mainstream Journalism". Reuters Institute for the Study of Journalism Working Paper. Accessed January 20, 2013. http://reutersinstitute.politics.ox.ac.uk/fileadmin/documents/Publications/The_rise_of_social_media_and_its_impact_on_mainstream_journalism.pdf.

Nyamnjoh, Francis. B. 2005. *Africa's Media: Democracy and the Politics of Belonging.* London: Zed Books.

Paterson, Chris. 2008. "Introduction: Why Ethnography?". In *Making Online News: The Ethnography of New Media Production,* edited by Paterson, Chris and Domingo, David, 1–11. New York: Peter Lang.

Pavlik, John V. 2000 "The Impact of Technology on Journalism". *Journalism Studies* 1(2): 229–237.

Pavlik, John V. 2005. "Running the Technological Gauntlet: Journalism and New Media". In *Making Journalists,* edited by De Burgh, Hugo, 245–263. London: Routledge.

Peters, Justin. 2011. "On Facebook and Freedom: Why Journalists Should Not Surrender to the Walmarts of the Web". *Columbia Journalism Review* 50(4): 155–160.

Picard, Robert G. 2009. "Blogs, Tweets, Social Media, and the News Business". *Nieman Reports* 63(3): 10–12.

Robinson, Sue. 2011. "Convergence Crises: News Work and News Space in the Digitally Transforming Newsroom". *Journal of Communication* 61(6): 1122–1141.

Schudson, Michael. 2000. "The Sociology of News Revisited". In *Mass Media and Society*, edited by Curran, James and Gurevitch, Michael, 175–200. London: Arnold.

Sherwood, Merryn and Nicholson, Matthew. 2012. "Web 2.0 Platforms and the Work of Newspaper Sport Journalists". *Journalism: Theory, Practice & Criticism* 1–18.

Singer, Jane et al. 2011. "Introduction: Sharing the Road". In *Participatory Journalism: Guarding Open Gates at Online Newspapers,* edited by Singer, Jane, et al., 1–9. New York: Wiley-Blackwell.

van Dijk, Jan G. M. 2006. "Digital Divide Research, Achievements and Short-comings". *Poetics* 34(4–5): 221–235.

Part II
Ethics and Regulations

5 Online Journalism Under Pressure

An Ethiopian Account

Terje S. Skjerdal

INTRODUCTION

Online journalism[1] in Ethiopia has shown little improvement since the mid-2000s. The immediacy of the Internet is poorly exploited, with news sites appearing mostly as replicas of their parent print or broadcasting outlet. Even though there has been some improvement in technological features, the sites only to a very limited extent incorporate interactivity. In terms of total volume, most media content in Ethiopia is still produced for traditional radio, television and newspapers. The number of local news blogs has actually decreased since 2007;[2] this is despite the fact that more and more citizens are regular Internet users. Overall, the development in Ethiopian online reporting is in many ways contrary to expectations of steady growth in the new media sector in developing societies. There are combined reasons for this situation. One is limitations in technological infrastructure, leaving Ethiopia as one of the most poorly connected countries in the world. Another is lack of profit related to the online media. A third reason for the missing progress in online journalism, perhaps more pervasive than the other two, is government policy and strategy. In recent years, the authorities have instituted numerous measures that serve to restrict rather than encourage a vibrant online sphere. This has in turn had an impact on the private media houses, which only exhibit modest interest in the online media as an opportunity for journalistic achievements.

The main purpose of this contribution is to shed light on Internet governance in a semi-authoritarian regime and discuss how it affects journalistic production. The case of Ethiopia carries particular interest in this regard because the country has emerged as a frontrunner in African online surveillance. For several years, Ethiopia was the only nation in Sub-Saharan Africa known to filter Internet content (Faris and Zittrain 2009). Specific websites are routinely blocked in the country, especially those promoting the political opposition. Bloggers and online journalists are subject to intimidation and face sporadic legal persecution. The first signs of coercion against online reporting came in 2006 when certain critical websites suddenly became inaccessible through the state-owned Internet service provider (ISP). The coercion mounted in 2011 when a new anti-terrorism law began to be used against journalistic activity, particularly targeting online reporting.

This study builds on analyses of regulation as well as interviews with stakeholders and journalists locally and in the Ethiopian diaspora. In terms of theory, the analysis draws on general literature pertaining to online regulation, with particular emphasis on research conducted in transitional societies. The study finds that the emphasis in the main research literature, which typically focuses on societies in the Middle East and East Asia where formal regulation and provisions play a significant role, is deficient for describing Internet governance in Ethiopia. In the case of Ethiopia and perhaps in other African countries, the analysis should instead pay more attention to informal forms of control. In the lack of formal directives for the online media, improvised control measures, ad hoc directives and pragmatic application of general legislation all play a role in exerting control over online reporting.

INTERNET CONNECTIVITY AND ONLINE JOURNALISM IN ETHIOPIA

Ethiopia is frequently quoted as one of the least online connected countries in the world. This despite the fact that the nation was once considered a pioneer in African telecommunication, with the first long distance telephone line set up between the cities of Addis Ababa (Central Ethiopia) and Harar (Eastern Ethiopia) as early as 1894 (Abii and Girma 1999). Today, Ethiopia has one of the least efficient telecom networks on the continent. The International Telecommunication Union lists Ethiopia as the country with the second lowest proportion of Internet users in the world (ITU 2011). In a population of nearly 90 million people, only 96,000 persons (1.1 percent) can be described as Internet users, according to Internet World Stats (Miniwatts 2012). This would make Ethiopia the least connected of all African countries. However, there is reason to believe that the actual figure of Internet users is somewhat higher. This is indicated by the number of Ethiopian citizens who have signed up for a personal profile on Facebook, which reached 980,000 in September 2013 (there are obviously more Internet users in total than those who have an account on Facebook). Moreover, a nationwide media consumption survey among 4,000 households found that 4.9 percent of the respondents are regular users of the Internet (Ward 2011a). Internet use is understandably much higher in the cities than in the rural areas. Active use of online communication is often combined with exposure to other media types. Thus, for Ethiopia, there is little evidence to suggest that high Internet consumption leads to less use of newspapers, which is often assumed to be the case in western societies. To the contrary, a survey among university students in the capital city Addis Ababa found a correlation between high exposure to online news and heavy newspaper reading (Sophia 2006).

The Internet is not yet a prioritized area for Ethiopian media houses. All larger media organizations have invested in a news site on the Internet, but the content is mostly replicated from respective print editions or radio/television programmes. This mirrors the findings of an earlier study of Ethiopian newspapers on the web, which concluded that the sites fall in replicated and variant genres (Kibnesh 2006). There is accordingly modest use of interactive features on the sites, and updates may only occur once or twice a week according to the frequency of the printed edition. Only a few of the sites contain options to post reader comments, and none of the sites of state-owned media houses or that of the private pro-government news agency Walta Information Center contain such features. Inviting reader comments on the websites of the state-owned media could be risky because it would mean an opportunity for the public, particularly the Ethiopian diaspora living abroad, to load the sites with critical comments against the incumbent. Pro-government sites in the diaspora, however, such as Aigaforum.com, do encourage reader interaction.

There are only a few private media ventures in Ethiopia which rely solely on online editions. One is New Business Ethiopia (www.newbusinessethiopia .com), focusing on business and general news, although updates are infrequent. Another example is *Jimma Times* (www.jimmatimes.com), a news site which opened in 2008 with particular focus on issues related to the Oromo ethnic group. Both sites have tried to rely on local and international advertisements as a means of income. The profit generated from advertisements is nonetheless insufficient to sustain the websites as professional media outlets because the reading public is too small. Even so, the Internet represents a potential for groups which are short of finances to start a traditional media outlet. In the case of *Jimma Times*, an attempt to publish a printed newspaper (Yeroo) lasted for only a few weeks and was abandoned primarily for economic reasons. The online edition continued in its place, although illustratively, the site ceased in 2012 after four years of existence. Thus, despite low production-related costs, very few media ventures in Ethiopia have seized the opportunity of exploiting the online potential.

The chances for journalists in traditional media outlets to use the Internet in their daily work are somewhat limited, although the situation has certainly improved over the past decade. In a pan-African study on ICT reporting conducted in 2003, the researchers found that the largest news organization in Ethiopia, Ethiopian Television (ETV), only had one computer connected to the Internet for all its reporters (Stanbridge and Ljunggren 2003, 93). The same study discovered that the state-owned newspaper *The Ethiopian Herald* had neither an Internet connection nor a fax machine at the time. Indeed, the lack of access to new technology was not necessarily regarded as a disadvantage for the reporters in the news organizations. The acting head of the English section of ETV expressed that the journalistic focus ought to be elsewhere: "The majority of our people live in rural areas and they don't enjoy the information the world provides through ICTs.

And we have so many more important issues to debate on than information society" (Tefera Ghedamu cited in Stanbridge and Ljunggren 2003, 93). A decade later, the situation has certainly changed, and reporters of *The Ethiopian Herald* emphasize that one of the good things about their work environment is outstanding Internet access in the newsroom. The condition is less favourable in state-owned radio and television, where only 18 percent of the journalists have Internet access in their own office (Gebeyehu 2011; cf. Feyisa 2011). The Internet is primarily used by the journalists to get an overview of local and international news stories and is much less employed as a tool in the news research process. This is a direct consequence of the scarcity of information provided by public offices in Ethiopia on the World Wide Web. To gather facts and information, journalists as a general rule still have to show up at the appropriate office and post a query orally or in writing. Few government offices have a tradition for online communication, and many officials still only rely on personal Hotmail or Yahoo email addresses, if they can at all be reached via email.

These limitations notwithstanding, the online media should not be regarded as unimportant for Ethiopian journalism. On the contrary, reporters pick up story ideas and gather information through the Internet, especially in relation to international news. There is also a mirroring effect in the local media, meaning that reporters develop further Ethiopia-related stories from the global media, which then come back to the local media with international perspectives embedded. Thus, stories in the local media frequently contain comments and views from the international society, even though the topic itself may only concern domestic affairs. This is made possible through active use of the Internet by reporters in the newsgathering process. Thus, a comprehensive survey querying about the operations of Ethiopian media houses found that a number of the media outlets, both print and broadcasting, regard the Internet as one of their main sources of information (Ward 2011b). Global exchanges therefore play an important role in contemporary Ethiopian journalism despite the government's attempt to restrict the news flow in and out of the country. This requires a consideration of the impact of the Ethiopian diaspora in the news production routines.

THE ETHIOPIAN DIGITAL DIASPORA

It has been suggested that more online content concerning Africa is being produced overseas than within the continent itself (Ya'u 2008). The claim may very well hold water for Ethiopia, which boasts a highly active digital diaspora, mainly residing in Europe and North America. The diaspora runs numerous news sites on the Internet, many of which are updated on a daily basis. The most popular site, Nazret.com (based in Washington DC), has close to 10,000 visitors a day on average (Quantcast 2012). The discussion forums on the diaspora sites are among the most vibrant places for debating

Ethiopia issues today. In the case of Nazret.com, it is not uncommon that hot news items provoke more than 100 reader comments. In contrast to the editing style of Nazret.com, which emphasizes objectivity and impartiality, most sites run by the 'conflict-generated diaspora' (Lyons 2007) advocate a political stance—usually in opposition to the Ethiopian leadership. This is a reflection of the political profile of the Ethiopian diaspora media milieu, which comprises mainly actors who previously played an active role in politics and media back home (Hafkin 2006; Lyons 2006; Skjerdal 2011).

The diaspora news sites are of uneven journalistic quality. Politically motivated, the sites do not always care to check facts and background information before posting news. To mention but one example, several diaspora sites declared that President Girma Wolde-Giorgis had died when he was in hospital for medical treatment in March 2012. Nonetheless, some days later, he was back in his office. Because of this and similar slips, it was difficult to trust the information when in July 2012, the same diaspora sites began to speculate that Prime Minister Meles Zenawi had passed away after failing to appear at public conventions. This time, however, the websites in a way forecasted the destiny of the Prime Minister when he actually did pass away a month later on 20 August 2012.

Among the most speculative sites is Ethiopianreview.com, which is also one of the most popular websites with the global Ethiopian diaspora. The site has a trivial relationship with defamatory speech and consistently referred to the late Prime Minister Meles Zenawi as 'tyrant', 'Nazi', 'the butcher of the Horn of Africa' and so forth (Skjerdal 2009, 337). Not only Ethiopians but also foreign authorities have scorned the content on Ethiopianreview. com. In July 2011, a British high court sentenced the site's editor Elias Kifle to pay GBP 175,000 in libel damages to an Ethiopian businessman after the site had falsely accused the man of murdering his daughter's alleged lover in Iraq. The editor has also been found guilty on various charges by Ethiopian courts throughout the years. In January 2012, Elias[3] was sentenced to life imprisonment in absentia by the Ethiopian Federal High Court, which found him guilty of supporting terrorist activities. Nonetheless, residing in exile in the US, the *Ethiopian Review's* editor ridiculed the verdict and made it clear that he had no intention of paying the fine, thereby joining several other Ethiopian online editors who have been tried and found guilty in absentia.

There are, however, Ethiopian diaspora sites which stand for a more serious journalistic reporting style. One case is Addisnegeronline.com, the online edition of a former critical weekly in Ethiopia, *Addis Neger*, which ceased publication in December 2009 following government pressure. After the editors fled abroad (Mesfin 2010), the outlet continued as an online channel with editorial bases in Sweden and the US. The site has maintained the sharp commentary profile that the previous print edition was known for. In a similar vein, the critical weekly *Awramba Times* folded in November 2011 after government pressure and was resurrected as a diaspora site in May 2012, operating from Washington DC. Interestingly, both *Addis Neger* and *Awramba Times*, which used to publish only in the Amharic language in Ethiopia, use a combination of Amharic and English in their new online editions. As a result, their audience base has expanded significantly. Combined with effective use of social media channels (particularly Facebook and Twitter), diaspora sites such as Addisnegeronline.com and Awrambatimes. com represent a notable extension of the Ethiopian media sphere.

To some extent, news exchanges in the diaspora media have an impact on the local Ethiopian media as well. Diaspora channels even manage to break local news ahead of the domestic media on some occasions. This was the case in January 2009 when Ethiomedia.com reported that prominent judge and party leader Birtukan Mideksa went on a hunger strike after she was detained by the police. The website had local stringers in Addis Ababa who fed the editors in Everett, WA, USA with information. Within hours, the news made its way from Ethiomedia.com to the international media and back to the local Ethiopian media. This demonstrates the extent to which local Ethiopian journalists must follow online diaspora media channels not only to keep informed about international news but also to stay informed about local developments.

INTERNET CONTROL IN ETHIOPIA

It is somewhat troublesome for local journalists, nonetheless, to follow diaspora websites on a regular basis. This is due to the frequent blocking of critical sites in Ethiopia. The number of blocked websites has increased over the last few years. As of November 2012, about 70 news sites are subject to blocking, in addition to approximately 40 blogs and 15 political party websites, all managed by Ethiopians in the diaspora. A few websites for international rights groups, such as that of the Committee to Protect Journalists (www.cpj.org), are occasionally blocked as well.

When the obstruction of websites first began to occur in May 2006, the authorities blamed it on technical problems with the national Internet service provider. However, as the obstruction started to become more systematic, it left little doubt that the government was behind it. The official confession came in March 2010 (two months before the national elections), when the Prime Minister announced that the regime was ready to jam foreign radio broadcasts if they brought 'destabilising propaganda' (BBC News 19 March 2010). In terms of Internet blocking, it is commonly assumed in research circles that Ethiopian authorities make use of Chinese technology (Gagliardone, Repnikova and Stremlau 2010, 15; Gagliardone and Stremlau 2012, 20). That there exist ties between Ethiopia and China in digital media strategy became evident at a workshop held in Addis Ababa in June 2012 when the Ethiopian Peoples' Revolutionary Democratic Front (EPRDF; the government coalition) and the International Department of the Chinese Communist Party discussed "mass media capacity building, mass media institution management and Internet management" (EPRDF 3 June 2012).

Control of online activity is further exerted through intimidation of bloggers and reporters. Individual journalists have been detained and questioned by the local police on several occasions. The intimidation was brought to a new level in late 2011 and 2012 when the Anti-Terrorism Proclamation of 2009 began to be used against members of the political opposition as well as media workers. At the time of writing (August 2012), three local journalists have been charged under the anti-terrorism law, one of whom is an online reporter. Additionally, six journalists in the Ethiopian diaspora have been charged in absentia under the same law, all of whom work for online media outlets. Thus, a pattern emerges where the online media are increasingly targeted in the government's communication strategy.

In the global literature, Internet governance is debated both in regard to western and non-western societies. A tension between two types of regulatory regimes emerges from the literature: one emphasizing self-regulation and one giving emphasis to formal regulation. Whereas the self-regulatory approach calls particular attention to the power of the industry and the audience, the model of formal regulation primarily emphasizes the role of the authorities in the control scheme. The prime example of formal regulation is China, which has passed more than 80 laws and directives aimed at Internet regulation (Calingaert 2010, 69). The argument in the following discussion, nevertheless, is that neither of these governance models quite fits the situation in Ethiopia. I will suggest that in the place of self-regulation and formal regulation, a more suitable model for describing online governance in Ethiopia instead ought to put the main emphasis on informal control. This model will be described more closely in the following section after discussing the general relevance of the two contrasting models of self-regulation and formal regulation.

SELF-REGULATION

Self-regulation is commonly portrayed as the regulation principle par excellence for the online media, both from a market and a free speech point of view. In the early days of the World Wide Web, i.e., the so-called 'open Internet' phase before the year 2000, self-regulation was regarded as something close to a natural standard for online technology (Palfrey 2010). It was argued that the free flow of ideas could best be secured if the online media were regulated outside of the political domain. From 1997 onwards, various self-regulatory bodies were set up in Europe and North America (Price and Verhulst 2005, 19). The idea that the ultimate control with Internet communication should rest with the market and the users remains a fundamental principle in online regulation in many societies throughout the world, particularly in the West. That said, self-regulation does not imply the total abandonment of official directives. There are, for example, central directives delimiting ISP establishments and the registration of IP addresses. Furthermore, online activity is not beyond the reach of general legislation. To illustrate, illegal publicizing, such as sharing classified information, remains just as unlawful on the Internet as in traditional media channels. It has therefore been suggested that self-regulatory principles of the online media could more aptly be described as regulated self-regulation (Schulz and Held 2004), entailing a compromise between centrally controlled regulation and genuine self-regulation.

Successful implementation of self-regulatory principles requires both a central authority willing to entrust the civil society with the responsibility of regulation and a civil society prepared to take up the duty. Neither condition is entirely met in Ethiopia. On the one hand, the government has not displayed readiness to hand over control to the media industry or to independent agencies. This is demonstrated by the persisting monopoly of Ethio Telecom (which has been dubbed the last remaining telecommunication monopoly in Africa; see Gagliardone and Stremlau 2012, 12) as well as the centralized control of the Ethiopian Broadcasting Authority. To be fair, the government has been open to some delegation of authority by encouraging the media industry itself to erect an independent media council which could handle complaints from the public, but for all practical purposes, the risk of losing de facto control over communication policy through a media council would be miniscule. Additionally, the media industry has not exhibited any strong potential to exert self-regulation. After about ten years of planning, a media council bringing together the state media and the private media industry was established in July 2012, but the impact of the authorities is still noticeable in its operation, and it remains to be seen whether the council will achieve genuine power.

There are certain areas of Ethiopian digital communication which are outside of regulatory mechanisms and could thus qualify as a form of self-regulation. This includes the right to open and run websites on local servers. Thus, in contrast to print and broadcasting media, which historically have been subject to various licencing and registration requirements in Ethiopia, the Internet represents an opportunity to establish a media outlet quickly, cheaply and beyond licencing procedures. However, only a limited number of journalists have seized this opportunity, and the established media houses mostly limit web production to duplication of content from their parent media channels. These challenges regarding the lack of a self-regulatory tradition in the Ethiopian media resonate with experiences elsewhere in Sub-Saharan Africa (Krüger 2009; M'membe 2011), but the Ethiopian situation is additionally strained by a government reluctant to accept loss of control with any media channel that could potentially be used to spread oppositional ideas.

FORMAL REGULATION

In regimes with tight control over the Internet, formal regulation usually plays an important role as a conduit for rationalizing the governance strategy. China alone has more than 80 laws and directives aimed at Internet regulation (Calingaert 2010, 69). Legal directives in Asian Internet governance range from mandatory registration systems to prohibition of specific online content, including libellous speech, blasphemy and political provocations (Deibert et al. 2012). African media governance, however, is generally far less pervasive in terms of provisions related to online communication, according to research conducted by the OpenNet Initiative (see regional reports on www.opennet.net; cf. Warf 2011). Ethiopia is a case in point, where there are no proclamations specifically regulating content in online media channels. Interestingly, despite its recent date, the media law of 2008 makes no mention of online communication at all but limits 'mass media' to 'periodicals and broadcasters' (proclamation no. 590/2008, clause 2(1)). Accordingly, restrictive clauses in the media law concerning publicizing of various types of media content do not apply to websites unless a court induces an extended interpretation of the legislation.

Notwithstanding the lack of proclamations regulating online content at the federal level, there are a few examples of restrictions introduced and executed at lower levels in the state administration. For example, in December 2006, the Ethiopian Telecommunications Corporation (now Ethio Telecom) ordered Internet cafés to register their users with the intention of identifying the use of voice over IP, which at the time could be interpreted as illegal according to Telecommunication Proclamation no. 49/1996, clause 24(2). In actuality, the registration has not been much used. Despite suspicion that the authorities—together with the federal police—introduced the registration of Internet users as a means of surveillance of dissidents, in actuality, IP telephony, such as Skype, represents a threat of clogging the local bandwidth as Ethiopia is not yet connected to the EASSy high-speed submarine cable located outside the coast of East Africa. Measures which restrict the use of IP telephony could therefore in one way be regarded as beneficial for the majority of Internet users in Ethiopia. However, in July 2012, the Parliament passed new legislation, the Telecom Fraud Offences Proclamation no. 761/2012, explicitly legalizing the use of IP telephony in the country (contrary to reports by international rights organizations claiming IP telephony was prohibited), although it simultaneously introduced licensing requirements on such operations as a means to protect the local telecommunication industry financially. This proclamation remains the only legislation directly regulating online operations in Ethiopia. The nation can therefore not quite be juxtaposed with China, Iran and other heavily Internet regulated regimes when it comes to online media policy. At the same time, the government is clearly eager to control online communication in the country. This leads us to consider informal control as a third approach to Internet governance.

INFORMAL CONTROL

A major part of Ethiopian Internet governance with relevance for journalistic activity does not fall in either of the categories of self-regulation or formal regulation. Instead, the authorities are found to apply a range of informal and largely disorganized mechanisms to control information flow in digital media channels. Filtering of online content is one such measure. According to the Internet watchdog OpenNet Initiative, Ethiopia was the first country in Sub-Saharan Africa to apply IP filtering (Faris and Zittrain 2009; www.opennet.net). It is still one of very few countries in the region to filter online content, although analysts suspect certain other regimes are considering similar technology, notably Eritrea (RSF, 2012). As mentioned above, the filtering represents a challenge for journalists who try to stay informed about current events and debates. However, Ethiopian Internet blocking appears less systematic than archetypical Asian filtering, which targets content and software in a highly organized manner (Deibert et al. 2012). In Ethiopia, a controversial website may be blocked one day and open the next, making it more difficult to see a pattern in the filtering strategies. For example, the author of this paper has observed how critical diaspora sites such as Ethiomedia.com and Addisvoice.com have been switched on and off throughout the week on the national ISP Ethio Telecom. There is nevertheless enough evidence to conclude that the blocking of websites in Ethiopia is politically motivated, whereas filtering based on social interests is not a phenomenon in the nation's Internet control strategy (cf. Deibert et al. 2008).

Intimidation of individual journalists and bloggers has become another means of informal control with online practices in Ethiopia. The number of local journalists subject to direct intimidation is still low but significant, with veteran journalist Eskinder Nega having received the most attention from international press freedom groups. A staunch critic of the EPRDF government through regular columns on various global news sites, Eskinder was detained and arrested numerous times in Addis Ababa before he eventually faced a harsh 18-year prison sentence for encouraging terrorist acts in July 2012. Among the charges he faced were claims that he used the Internet in an attempt to bring Egyptian and Tunisian-like protests to Ethiopia. Similar charges of terrorist attempts were brought against the previously mentioned six online journalists in the diaspora who were sentenced in absentia in a parallel court process. The growing confrontations between the authorities and web reporters are testimony of the increasingly influential role of the online media in the public debate in Ethiopia.

The government itself is also seen to take part in online discussion as a means to counter online criticism. It uses specific outlets, notably the diaspora site Aigaforum.com, to spread pro-government messages, although rarely signed. Illustratively, in November 2009, the site published an opinion article that eventually forced the editors of the previously mentioned critical publication *Addis Neger* into exile. The article, which was initially printed in the government daily *Addis Zemen*, contained threats which could only be interpreted as a warning that the authorities were preparing legal prosecution against *Addis Neger*. The article did not carry any signature, but it clearly originated from the central government. This strategy of using the official local media in conjunction with certain online channels has a watershed effect on the Ethiopian media in that the government draws a dividing line between media outlets it regards as acceptable channels and those which are not. Channels which are not recognized by the government risk repercussions of various kinds, such as Internet blockage and denial of access to public information. The campaign against *Addis Neger* is also characteristic of the tacit nature of Ethiopian media governance. In typical vein, the authorities did not apply formal directives or open actions against the publication but posted an implicit warning that could be described as a means of informal control. For Ethiopian media workers, the risk that similar pressure could materialize in their own situation is always imminent. The indeterminate nature of the controlling mechanisms has a chilling effect on journalists, who resort to self-censorship to avoid possible negative repercussions (cf. Skjerdal 2010).

CONCLUDING REMARKS

Ethiopian online journalism has in many ways been at a standstill since the mid-2000s. Few achievements have been made in terms of content and style, although the online public has grown considerably. The tendency to vibrancy in the blogosphere observed during the 2005 elections has shrunk to a rather small community of sporadic contributors. In terms of breaking news, local online channels are habitually beaten by international news sites, which are much better equipped to bring speedy and confident reports. At the same time, much online production concerning Ethiopia has been relocated from the local media houses to independent diaspora channels edited from Europe and North America. The present discussion has concentrated on one important explanation for these developments, specifically the protracted media strategy of the Ethiopian government. Whereas there have been noticeable achievements in terms of improved media (2008) and broadcasting (2007) legislation, the informal means of control are all the more important for understanding day-to-day developments in Ethiopian media governance. The online media are targeted in a particular way as they carry potential for rebellion much more forceful than classic media channels do.

As demonstrated above, informal control of online media in Ethiopia consists of filtering of websites, random registration of Internet users and intimidation of reporters. Surveillance technology has also been detected, including the use of so-called Deep Packet Inspection, which makes it more difficult for online users to escape filtering by means of circumvention software (Al-Saqaf 2010). Ethiopian security is also susceptible to tap personal email communication, demonstrated by the court case against *Feteh* reporter Reeyot Alemu where email messages from opposition groups located abroad were used as evidence. Similar instances of tapping of email content have been reported from mainstream newsrooms in Zimbabwe (Mabweazara 2011).

Additionally, slow development in telecom infrastructure must be mentioned as an important reason for the lack of progress in the Ethiopian online sphere. With nearly all other countries along the east coast of Africa connected to the East Africa Submarine Cable System (EASSy), it is puzzling that Ethiopia has not yet managed to make a connection despite recurrent assurances that the country will soon activate the land cables that have already been prepared for the purpose. On the other hand, in order to maintain a degree of control with the Internet, better connectivity may not be regarded as urgent. Nevertheless, a dual attitude is evident in the Ethiopian approach to governance strategy in the digital media sector. On the one hand, as long as new technology is defined as an instrument for social and economic development, it is embraced by the government and included in official plans and strategies. However, if defined as a conduit for political expression, the online technology becomes counterproductive to the government's strategies and therefore must be restricted.

With these control mechanisms in mind, there is nevertheless a risk of underestimating the impact of online communication in local journalism. Despite the restrictions that exist, the journalistic environment in Ethiopia is increasingly reliant on online exchanges. The Internet is both a source of information and a channel for global connectivity. Despite frequent blocking, the journalists gain access to censored diaspora sites through alternative channels. Social media, particularly Facebook, play an important role in this regard. On many occasions, illustrated by the media coverage of the passing of Prime Minister Meles Zenawi in August 2012, social media function as a journalistic draft where reporters can discuss rumours before publishing the news in a 'proper' media channel. This discussion therefore concludes that Ethiopian Internet control is only partially effective, and certainly, the rapidly growing online public will make it increasingly difficult for the authorities to tame the online media by means of informal control alone.

NOTES

1. 'Online journalism' in this chapter refers to journalistic content production aimed for mass distribution through a variety of interactive media channels, such as computers, mobile telephones and tablets, although for all practical purposes, traditional computers represent the only channel which online journalism in Ethiopia is currently focusing on.
2. In a study of political blogs in Ethiopia, Helen Yosef (2011) presents a survey which shows that the most popular local blogs in the period 2003–10 came on the scene before 2007. Of the 40 supposedly most prominent political blogs created since 2003, as many as 33 (83%) appeared in 2007 or earlier, with 2005 as the peak year. Many of these blogs are now inactive and have not been replaced.
3. Ethiopian tradition always refers to persons by their first name.

ACKNOWLEDGEMENT

The author wishes to thank Endalkachew Hailemichael, lecturer at Arba Minch University, for valuable comments.

REFERENCES

Note: Ethiopian authors are listed according to the local name tradition, i.e., by first name.

Abii Tsigie and Feyissa Girma. 1999. "Telecommunications in Ethiopia: Past, Present, and Future". Report. Accessed 17 November 2012. http://www.vii.org/papers/ethiopia.htm.

Al-Saqaf, Walid. 2010. "Internet Censorship Challenged: How Circumvention Technologies can Effectively Outwit Governments Attempts to Filter Content". In *Increasing Transparency and Fighting Corruption Through ICT: Empowering People and Communities,* edited by Strand, Cecilia, 71–93. Stockholm: Spider. Accessed 17 November 2012. http://www.spidercenter.org/sites/default/files/Increasing%20transparency%20and%20fighting%20corruption%20through%20ICT.pdf.

Anyefru, Emmanuel. 2008. "Cyber-Nationalism: The Imagined Anglophone Cameroon Community in Cyberspace". *African Identities* 6(3): 253–274.

BBC News. 9 March 2010. "Ethiopia Admits Jamming VOA Broadcasts in Amharic". Accessed 17 November 2012. http://news.bbc.co.uk/2/hi/8575749.stm.

Calingaert, Daniel. 2010. "Authoritarianism vs. the Internet". *Policy Review* 160: 63–75.

Deibert, Ronald, Palfrey, John, Rohozinski, Rafal and Zittrain, Jonathan, eds. 2008. *Access Denied: The Practice and Policy of Global Internet Filtering.* Cambridge, MA: MIT Press.

———. 2012. *Access Contested: Security, Identity, and Resistance in Asian Cyberspace.* Cambridge, MA: MIT Press.

EPRDF (Ethiopian Peoples' Revolutionary Democratic Front). 3 June 2012. "Workshop conducted". Accessed 17 November 2012. http://www.eprdf.org.et/web/guest/news/-/asset_publisher/c0F7/content/3-june-2012–26–2004.

Faris, Robert, and Zittrain, Jonathan. 2009. "Web Tactics". *Index on Censorship* 38(4): 90–96.

Feyisa Girma Bedanie. 2011. "New Media Technology as a Source of Foreign News in Oromiya Mass Media Organization: Challenges and Opportunities". MA thesis, Addis Ababa University.

Gagliardone, Iginio, Repnikova, Maria and Stremlau, Nicole. 2010. "China in Africa: A New Approach to Media Development?" Report. Oxford: Centre for Socio-Legal Studies, University of Oxford. Accessed 17 November 2012. http://pcmlp.socleg.ox.ac.uk/sites/pcmlp.socleg.ox.ac.uk/files/China%20in%20Africa_2010.pdf.

Gagliardone, Iginio and Stremlau, Nicole. 2012. "Digital Media, Conflict and Diasporas in the Horn of Africa". Report. Open Society Foundations. Accessed 17 November 2012. http://www.soros.org/initiatives/media/articles_publications/publications/mapping-digital-media-digital-media-conflict-horn-of-africa-20120221.

Gebeyehu Bekele. 2011. "Media and New Technology in Ethiopia—A Study of an Interface: A Case Study of the ERTA/ETV newsroom". MA thesis, Addis Ababa University.

Hafkin, Nancy J. 2006 [actual year of publication: 2011]. "'Whatsupoch' on the Net: The Role of Information and Communication Technology in the Shaping of Transnational Ethiopian Identity". *Diaspora* 15(2–3): 221–245.

Helen Yosef. 2011. "Backfiring Repressions: The Polarization of Ethiopian Blogs". MA thesis, University for Peace, Costa Rica.

ITU (International Telecommunication Union). 2011. "World Telecommunication/ICT Indicators Database 2011". Accessed 17 November 2012. http://www.itu.int/ITU-D/ict/statistics/.

Kibnesh Chala. 2006. "Use of Internet as a Medium of Disseminating Information by Ethiopian Newspapers". MA thesis, Addis Ababa University.

Krüger, Franz. 2009. "Media courts of honour: self-regulatory councils in Southern Africa and elsewhere". Report. Friedrich-Ebert-Stiftung. Accessed 17 November 2012. http://library.fes.de/pdf-files/bueros/africa-media/07368.pdf.

Lyons, Terrence. 2006 [actual year of publication: 2011]. "Transnational Politics in Ethiopia: Diasporas and the 2005 Elections". *Diaspora* 15(2–3): 265–284.

———. 2007. "Conflict-Generated Diasporas and Transnational Politics in Ethiopia". *Conflict, Security and Development* 7(4): 529–549.

Mabweazara, Hayes M. 2011. "The Internet in the Print Newsroom: Trends, Practices and Emerging Cultures in Zimbabwe." In *Making Online News: Newsroom Ethnography in the Second Decade of Internet Journalism,* edited by Domingo, David and Paterson, Chris, 57–72. New York: Peter Lang.

Mesfin Negash. 2010. "Welcome to Addis: What it Means Being a Journalist in Ethiopia". In *Harnessing Africa's Digital Future,* edited by Mdlongwa, Francis and Letlhaku, Moagisi, 64–73. Johannesburg: Konrad Adenauer Stiftung.

Miniwatts Marketing Group. 2012. "Internet World Stats." Accessed 17 November 2012. http://www.internetworldstats.com.

M'membe, Fred. 2011. "Self-Regulation Isn't Perfect, but Statutory Regulation Is Much Worse". In *Media in Africa: Twenty Years after the Windhoek Declaration on Press Freedom,* edited by Berger, Guy, 74–75. Windhoek: Media Institute of Southern Africa. Palfrey, John. 2010. "Four Phases of Internet Regulation". *Social Research* 77(3): 287–296.

Price, Monroe E. and Verhulst, Stefaan G. 2005. *Self-regulation and the Internet.* The Hague: Kluwer Law International.

Quantcast Corporation. 2012. "Audience Report, www.nazret.com." Accessed 17 November 2012. http://www.quantcast.com/www.nazret.com?country=GLOBAL.

RSF (Reporters sans frontières/Reporters Without Borders). 2012. "Internet Enemies Report 2012". Accessed 17 November 2012. http://en.rsf.org/IMG/pdf/rapport-internet2012_ang.pdf.

Schulz, Wolfgang and Held, Thorsten. 2004. *Regulated Self-Regulation as a Form of Government: An Analysis of Case Studies From Media and Communications Law.* Luton: University of Luton Press.

Skjerdal, Terje S. 2009. "A critical look at the digital diaspora: perspectives from Ethiopia". In *The power of communication: changes and challenges in African media,* edited by Orgeret, Kristin S. and Rønning, Helge, 311–348. Oslo: Unipub.

———. 2010. "Justifying Self-Censorship: A Perspective from Ethiopia". *Westminster Papers in Communication and Culture* 7(2): 98–121.

———. 2011. "Journalists or activists? Self-identity in the Ethiopian diaspora online community". *Journalism, Theory, Practice & Criticism* 12(6): 727–744.

Sophia Nesri. 2006. "Patterns of Internet and Newspaper use in Ethiopia: The Case of Graduate Students in Addis Ababa University". MA thesis, Addis Ababa University.

Stanbridge, Roland and Ljunggren, Maria. 2003. "African Media and ICT4D: Documentary Evidence". Report, Economic Commission for Africa. Accessed 17 November 2012. http://www.uneca.org/aisi/docs/mediastudy.pdf.

Ward, David. 2011a. "Audience Survey: Ethiopia 2011". Report. Electoral Reform International Services (ERIS). Accessed 17 November 2012. http://ukinethiopia. fco.gov.uk/resources/en/pdf/ethiopia-audience-surve.

———. 2011b. "Ethiopia Media Mapping". Report. Electoral Reform International Services (ERIS). Accessed 17 November 2012. http://www.eris.org.uk/images/ userfiles/File/Ethiopia%20Media%20Mapping%202011%20-%20Final%20 Report.pdf.

Warf, Barney. 2011. "Geographies of Global Internet Censorship." *GeoJournal* 76(1): 1–23.

Ya'u, Yunusa. 2008. "Ambivalence and Activism: Towards a Typology of the African Virtual Publics". Paper Presented at the 12th CODESRIA general assembly, Yaoundé, Cameroon, December 7–11. Accessed 17 November 2012. http:// www.codesria.org/IMG/pdf/Y-Z-_Ya_u.pdf.

6 The Use of Social Media as News Sources by South African Political Journalists

Ylva Rodny-Gumede and
Nathalie Hyde-Clarke

INTRODUCTION

The advent of new media technologies and the proliferation of social media networks has certainly had an impact on traditional news routines and practices. The Internet and more readily accessible mobile technology mean that larger numbers of the public are able to participate in online forums and share opinions and experiences. This has fundamentally changed the way in which news media interact with their audiences and gather information and the role that the news media play in a democracy.

Social media and networking sites challenge standard modes of reporting and interpretations of events (Lazaroiu 2010). Although there were hopes that such advances would create a better informed citizenry, it appears that these forums often serve merely as platforms to disseminate personal opinions, to discuss events of a more private nature or as ways to expand one's social circle. Ryfe (2012) argues it may be that new media and new forms of journalism cannot fill all the gaps left by the loss of traditional journalism; however, journalists have only just begun to figure out how to best use these new media platforms to enhance journalism and public debate. Currently, however, there are sites for more nuanced debates about world issues and political arguments, but overall, more emphasis seems to be placed on the social aspect (Hyde-Clarke and Van Tonder 2011). The most popular social networks include Twitter and Facebook, and it is not unusual to find news agencies, political figures and organisations hosting sites or posting comments on these. News media organisations and individual journalists also use new media such as Twitter and Facebook to connect with their audience, reach new audiences, practice their craft and even sometimes change notions of who practices journalism through citizen journalism and user generated content (Bosch 2010). However, Herrera and Requejo (2012) argue that news media organizations have yet to realise the potential of social media platforms, especially Twitter, for re-energizing traditional journalism by listening to and talking with their audiences and by linking to external content that enriches discussions. Similarly, Ludtke (2009) argues that social media can bring greater depth and breadth to journalists' work. This article will focus on one aspect of journalists' work, albeit a very important one, namely, that of sources and the usage of social media sources in mainstream journalism.

In terms of the practices of journalism, the Internet contains a wealth of information that helps journalists to identify stories and sources, and the sheer accessibility of public information provides news organisations and individual journalists with very cheap and quick access to information. One's immediate impression is that such a rich and diverse pool of data would enhance news stories, and much has been said of the rise of citizen journalism and the opportunity this presents for better informed articles. However, digital news gathering is not without its own problems. The anonymity that is afforded by this technology complicates the issue significantly. The traditional value of verifying authenticity of information through multiple sources is more important than ever. Hermida (2010) argues that the traditional model of journalism in which facts are defined as information and quotes from official sources is in flux. With the instant dissemination of information via social media from a wide array of official as well as unofficial sources, norms and practices of journalism are changing. Hermida, therefore, talks of new forms of journalism that he refers to as "ambient journalism", a form of journalism exemplified by Twitter and the way in which this kind of information distribution "[. . .] goes beyond being just a network for the rapid dissemination of breaking news from individuals. Rather it can be seen as a system that alerts journalists to trends or issues hovering under the news radar" (Hermida 2010, 302). The greatest challenge that journalists thus face in this information era is not necessarily the need to negotiate and navigate the thousands of sites and comments posted but rather the need to distinguish between a legitimate piece of information and those that are less valid. Huckerby argues that

> The web is not some orderly library, tended with care by diligent scholars; sometimes it's more akin to a garbage heap. As a reporter, you need to be expert a sifting out the rubbish, and at detecting the dubious claims and biased presentations that abound. (Huckerby 2005, 56)

This was illustrated in November 2010 when a BBC reporter asked the African National Congress[1] Youth League (ANCYL) leader, Julius Malema, about comments made on a Twitter account in his name. Malema claimed not to have an account and threatened to close Twitter down should his impersonator not desist from posting comments (SAPA 2010). This resulted in a flurry of activity on Twitter, and within a week, 22 fake Julius Malema accounts had been created (Daniel 2010). Whereas the ANC Youth League's threats were treated with hilarity and disbelief, the case does emphasise the difficulty in validating and authenticating these sources. As *The Washington Post's* senior editor, Milton Coleman, noted, "Social networks [. . .] can be valuable tools in gathering and disseminating news and information. They also create some potential hazards we need to recognise" (cited in Grensing-Pophal 2010).

Whereas it is possible to find research articles and studies on how journalists should engage with and "harness" (Gleason 2010, 6) social media with a view to capturing a larger, more media savvy audience, there is very little available about how precisely they should cite information found on these networks. In some instances, newsrooms may have teams that scour social media, identifying trends and breaking stories that are then shared with journalists, who are expected to incorporate elements of these in their reports (ibid). Yet, it is often left to the journalists themselves to navigate this space and to decide to what extent such comments may or may not be useful. This may be particularly challenging for more experienced journalists who may not necessarily have the same training as their multimedia-platform younger contemporaries (Powers 2012). Regardless, studies on the use of social media as a source as opposed to a channel are scarce—and in Africa, even more so. As Mabweazara (2010, 12) notes, "Research on the use of 'new' technologies such as the Internet, email and mobile phones by journalists is Africa is limited, [and] fragmented [. . .]". Research is also scarce on journalistic sourcing practices with regards to social media. This chapter thus seeks to address this scarcity of information by examining reporting practices in the South African news media with regards to the use of social media. It explores responses from political journalists and media monitors as to what extent journalists use them and to what extent they think they should rely on these sources. Notions of bias and credibility are also examined in light of concerns raised.

The data that forms the basis for this chapter has been collected from a series of telephonic and electronic qualitative surveys. The sample includes responses from 11 journalists with experience in the newsroom ranging from six to 20 years. Four work for the public service broadcaster, the South African Broadcasting Corporation (SABC) in radio and television, and one works for e-tv, the only South African terrestrial commercial broadcaster. The remaining six work for regional and national newspapers, including *The Sunday Times, City Press, Mail & Guardian, The Star* and *Business Day.* The political journalists were asked questions about whether they rely on social media sources, if they consider these legitimate and how they attribute/cite social media sources in their news stories. The political journalists were also asked whether they believed social media sources to be more biased than more traditional sources. An additional six responses were received from media monitors from Media Monitoring Africa, Media Tenor South Africa, the Open Society Institute for Southern Africa and SOS: Support Public Broadcasting Coalition, who were asked about their own observations of how South African journalists use social media sources in political news reports and whether they believed these sources were more biased than other more traditional news sources.

This chapter will start by examining traditional sourcing practices and then consider how these relate to and are challenged by social media networks. Do journalists believe that social media sources are more biased than traditional sources, and what new practices do they or have they adopted to make provision for these less verifiable sources? By considering these questions, the chapter is able to present a general argument for what is currently considered 'best practice' and how it may be improved going forward.

NEWS SOURCES AND ROUTINIZATION OF PRACTICES IN JOURNALISM

Sources of information are the lifeblood of journalists (Rudin and Ibbotson 2002). They provide the essential basic information for news stories across media industries and platforms (ibid). Journalism relies on accurate information and, as such, cannot function without a steady provision of news from a wide range of sources. Therefore, there is a routinization of journalistic practices that speaks directly to sources. Tuchman (1978) states that

> The routines inherent in journalistic practice (which structure journalists' relationship with their sources, audiences and their adoption of and interpretation of impartiality requirements) enable journalists to retain their professionalism (and integrity) while meeting many of the needs of the organization. (Tuchman cited in Harrison 2006,141)

Hence, routine practices in journalism help journalists balance organisational/structural pressures with more traditional roles of journalism (Harrison 2006).

As part of their routine practices, journalists build up a network of trusted sources as well as a network of often quoted sources, in particular official sources. As Schudson (2000, 184) puts it, "The bureaucrat provides a reliable and steady supply of raw material for news production". The so-called 'news net' is intended for the 'big fish', and therefore, news media place reporters at legitimated institutions where stories can be expected to be found (Tuchman 1995). With regards to journalists' relationship to their sources, a common critique is that not all sources are equal, and therefore, there is a bias towards official sources in journalism.

Journalists are often criticised for relying too heavily on official sources, and researchers see the choice of sources in the production process with regards to who gets to be quoted or not as an exercise of power (Harrison 2006). This can give some sources, apt at gaining access to the media, the power to set the news agenda and can lead to some sources being labelled as either insiders or outsiders (ibid). Other scholars query this power and ask who actually holds the power in the relationship between journalists and their sources (see Harrison 2006; Schudson 2003, 2000). There seems to be an agreement among scholars, however, that official sources often have the upper hand not only in relation to non-official sources but also in the relationship between journalists themselves and their sources (Schudson

2003). Journalists tend to be highly attuned to the bureaucratic organization of government (ibid). Safe to say is that the relationship that journalists have with their sources is complex and constantly changing (Harrison 2006). Reporter-source studies tend to be twofold in the sense that they evaluate the power of the media institution as such, and they detail the dynamics of news production (Schudson 2003). In this sense, these studies evaluate the ever-changing nature of news production.

In journalism, it is important to distinguish between primary and secondary sources. Primary sources can be defined as a source that is "personally researched by the journalist in terms of face-to face interviews, visits, observation and first-hand experience" (Rudin and Ibbotson 2002, 32). Secondary sources, on the other hand, may be defined as "any existing material, whether it is written, stored on electronic data bases, audio/video recorded on different formats or indeed found on the Internet" (ibid). It might sometimes be difficult to distinguish between the two different categories, particularly when it comes to social media sources as there is sometimes an overlap between what people say in a personal capacity vis-à-vis an official statement. This is emphasised by almost all interviewees in the study. For example, Rudin and Ibbotson (2002) define any personal conversation as a primary source; however, a letter, they argue, is to be considered a secondary source. Hence, it might be difficult to classify an email as either a primary or a secondary source; the same could be said of comments on an online chat forum. Of course, sources go beyond just interviewees as sources can refer to a whole range of contacts and references. First-hand sources, however, tend to be interviewees. In general, primary sources or first-hand sources are considered more reliable than secondary sources—of course, this is not always the case. Journalism, however, tends to put primary sources first and only use secondary sources as background information for stories. Hence, a primary source can be referred to in a story or even quoted. Both categories of sources must, of course, be verified for accuracy and reliability in a way that conforms to general journalistic principles of ethics and good practice. How then do journalists use social media sources, and are these considered as primary or secondary sources in news stories? Moreover, what are the implications for this for journalism in terms of accuracy and legitimacy.

SOCIAL MEDIA SOURCES IN NEWSMAKING PRACTICES

The use of social media by journalists is controversial. Meintjies (4 September 2011, 5) says,

> Ever wondered why the journalists who break really BIG stories aren't spending 24/7 on Twitter? Well, it's because they're busy working on those stories [. . .] it's easy to be an expert on the web. It's quite another thing to prove yourself in the newsroom.

This view is supported by one of the political journalists interviewed, who states that he does not use social media such as Facebook or Twitter as he feels that "part and parcel" of being a good reporter is to not allow your stories or ideas to be dictated by tweets and other social media: "News is the current state of things and nothing less, unless we talk history, so I analyse current events and develop my own story ideas" (SABC respondent 1). This view is also shared by some of the South African media monitors interviewed, who argue that journalists should express extreme caution when using these sources, warning that social media tends to consist of "a very small, and very opinionated group of people, who speak to other, very opinionated people" (Media Monitor 1). This talks to the idea that those who are expressing an opinion through social media networks do not necessarily represent the wider population or even a specific group of people. Instead, the media monitor argues that journalists might use comments found through social media networks to "spice up their articles" (ibid), which might give the impression that this view is representative of a specific group without having to qualify whether this is in fact the official view of that particular group.

There is also the idea that social media sites need to be verified for authenticity in terms of who is behind them. With regards to the story about ANC Youth League President Julius Malema recounted at the beginning of the chapter, one of the political journalists interviewed raises this as a good example of how journalists can be fooled. She says that whereas most South African journalists were aware that the particular tweet supposedly made by the Youth Leagues President was fake, a BBC reporter took the tweet at face value and asked questions about the contents of the tweet during a news conference. What then happened was that Malema simply stated that he was not on Twitter and that the question was therefore invalid (e-tv respondent). The way around this, she says, is to ask politicians in person when given a chance for their legitimate Twitter, blog and Facebook accounts (ibid). She also emphasises that she always checks the information gained thorough social media networks: "It is almost always possible to make a quick call and get someone to either confirm or deny the information. If that doesn't work, I simply don't use the information until I can get it confirmed. For me, news is about more than one source, so relying on just one online source is not done" (e-tv respondent). Most of the political journalists interviewed would agree that source verification is the most important aspect of a journalist's job and that you do not rely on rumours and gossip spread via social media sites. This is exemplified by one interviewee who says, "[. . .] I don't rely on hearsay. I rely on reputable people and organisations" (*City Press* respondent 1).

Amongst the interviewees, there was a range of approaches being employed when considering social media sources and their information. Almost all of the political journalists admitted to using social media sources regularly, but they were very discerning about which ones they accessed.

Some only frequented official online sites such as news agency websites, recognized research institutes, political party website and/or blogs. Others stated that they monitor political parties and politicians, for example, "I monitor every action/stories from political parties and politicians. It helps me to stay informed" (SABC respondent 2). Others valued certain social media networks over others and were more specific on the nature of the social media used: "Twitter in particular is fast becoming a formidable source of information" (e-tv respondent).

Facebook and Twitter seem to top the preferred list. Blogs were, however, cited as well. Respondents overwhelmingly admitted that they were increasingly relying on social media sources to receive tips, follow breaking stories and conduct follow-ups. Most journalists cited ease of access and the fact that social media provide additional information on stories currently in the media or under way as the main reason for using social media sites. This is where "breaking stories come from" (SABC respondent 3), and "these online sources provide the tip-off for story" (e-tv respondent). Another political journalist mentioned using these sources to monitor the rival media outlets and to keep abreast of other stories currently in the media that might be worth covering to "[. . .] stay informed of what is happening even if you are not going to do a story on that issue" (SABC respondent 2).

The political journalists interviewed cite source verification as paramount to all journalistic practices, and there is agreement that primary sources are considered more reliable. So, what do they think happens to these traditional values and practices of journalism if journalists tend to rely more on social media sources in their daily practice? Also, if journalists can be said to rely too heavily on official, more traditional sources, can social media sources provide an alternative?

SOCIAL MEDIA SOURCES AS A CHALLENGE TO TRADITIONAL AND/OR OFFICIAL SOURCES

A consistent criticism of the news media is that if they are to fulfil their democratic role, they should draw upon a wider variety of news sources (Schudson 2003). The social and democratic functions of journalism speak to the idea that journalism should utilise a diversity of sources and include 'the voiceless' as preferred sources. It becomes a call for going beyond solely official sources and instead looking at alternative sources. Lynch (2008) argues that journalists need to go beyond official sources; however, relying on non-official and non-traditional sources would mean a radical departure from the conventional idea that the use of official sources is a cornerstone of objective reporting.

Ordinary people are often neglected as sources in journalistic texts (Lederach cited in Lynch 2008). Often, they do not represent official power, whether on the side of an official government or as part of a militia (in a

conflict zone), because they are perceived as being too biased or too personally entrenched in their situations to be neutral. It is also more difficult to
verify the authenticity of ordinary, non-official sources (Lynch 2008). This
is confirmed by the interview data, where all interviewees testify to the fact
that all sources need to be verified and that this can be more difficult when it
comes to social media. This is discussed in more depth in the following section. Access to alternative sources is of course one of the major obstacles to
going beyond official sources. Once again, official sources win over ordinary
people who could speak to lived experiences and give a different perspective
on an issue or a situation. Official sources also typically favour journalists
from leading news outlets over journalists from smaller and maybe less prestigious media (Schudson 2003).

Good practice requires that journalists verify their sources and the information they provide by seeking out counterarguments. If these counterarguments cannot be found from more traditional sources, then journalists
need to seek out alternative sources (Lynch 2008). To this could be added
the crucial role of the alternative media, grassroots media and community
media in supplying alternative views to those traditionally associated with
sources who wield "social hegemony" (Schudson 2000, 184).

Online social media sources can constitute a break with the over reliance
on official sources. Given that potential, South African political journalists
seem to consider social media sources such as tweets, blogs, and Facebook
when researching stories. Many, however, were careful to distinguish between reading social media to get an idea of public opinion about an issue
or policy and actually using that comment as a source in a news story. This
is also emphasized by Mabweazara (2011, 64), who argues that "Overreliance on the Internet also seems to cement established relations between elite
forces and newsmakers". However, social media sources could provide a
dimension that more traditional sources do not in terms of gauging public
opinion and staying abreast with what ordinary people are thinking. As respondents in this study put it, "[. . .] social media often reflects public opinion" (SABC respondent 4), "Social media is where people interact" (*City
Press* respondent 1) and "I use Facebook to gauge people's reaction and
Twitter to track a developing story" (*City Press* respondent 2).

The idea that social media is used to track and follow breaking stories
was mentioned in many of the interviews. The frequency of reliance on
social media seems to be directly related to the importance of the event.
National elections and big political events seem to be particular triggers of
activity on social media sites. There is also a sense that political parties as
well as individual public officials have become more social media conscious,
and their presence is felt on various social media platforms. One political
journalist explained:

> There was a period during national election campaigns for 2009 when
> political parties modernised their campaign methods and COPE[2] and

the DA[3] in particular were very active on Facebook (*Mail & Guardian* respondent).

A number of breaking stories around political events in South Africa were cited as having triggered a lot of activity through different social media networks. It would therefore seem that social media sources are used predominantly for quickly accessing information around big news events. However, if these are being relied upon more and more, particularly for the ease of access and the speed of which information can be accessed, what happens to source verification and issues of reliability and legitimacy?

SOCIAL MEDIA SOURCES AND CONCERNS OF LEGITIMACY AND BIAS

There are problems with regards to using alternative sources, particularly when it comes to social media sources. The way in which journalists use their sources is closely related to the concept of objectivity. Objectivity is seen as a professional ideology of journalism (Tuchman 1978). It is by invoking objectivity that journalism can claim to be truthful and accurate (McNair 1998). Whereas scholars have often maintained that objectivity in journalism is unattainable (cf. Calcutt and Hammond 2011), routines of journalism such as fact checking and relying on more than one source have developed as ways for journalists to obtain some sort of objectivity in their reporting, "as ways to help the reporter rise above his or her individual dispositions or biases" (Calcutt and Hammond 2011, 99).

Critics argue that objectivity in journalism is unattainable for reasons of human fallibility, i.e., as humans, we are biased by our backgrounds and interest and, as such, cannot be objective. Also, selection processes within journalism further distort ideals of objectivity (Calcutt and Hammond 2011). Calcutt and Hammond (2011) also argue that there is a further objection to the realisation of objectivity in journalism that springs from the idea that objectivity is achieved solely from relying on official sources, an idea that they argue undermines journalism's democratic role.

The notion that there is a bias towards using official sources in journalism (Lynch 2008) springs from the idea that official sources seemingly come with a disclaimer of already having been verified and of being trustworthy through their official status/offices (ibid). There are also normative expectations on journalism from its audience. Journalism worldwide is suffering a crisis of credibility in the sense that people believe less and less that the information they get from the news media is trustworthy (Kurtz 1998). Reese (2001) argues that the audience thinks it benefits society that journalists adhere to certain roles and ethical conduct and that the journalists observe certain standards that do not violate expectations of social order. For the news media to be credible, audiences need to perceive the news media as objective and truthful and as reporting only the facts. Thus, it is conceivable that the audience also thinks that the media only use the best, most reliable sources.

The question is whether or not electronic sources can be relied upon and whether the journalists are supposed to rely upon these kinds of sources in their reporting. There is also the question, especially with regards to conflict, that social media sources have a tendency to be more biased and that people feel more at ease expressing their political beliefs in these networks, even if these beliefs could be seen as less politically correct and/or even amount to hate speech. When asked about the legitimacy and credibility of social media sources, respondents agreed that all sources (whether traditional or online) need to be verified:

> All information needs to be verified with the people mentioned in that matter and more people who are close to the action. Relying on Online information only is dangerous because rumours are spread every minute and many of them remain rumours (*Mail & Guardian* respondent).

This is reiterated throughout the interviews and is applied to social media sources as well as more traditional sources. The political journalists all testify to the fact that the news tip-offs received come from direct phone calls, faxes, e-mails, SMS or via Facebook/Twitter and other social networks. However, as one political journalist put it,

> Regardless of the way the information reaches us, it still has to be subjected to a rigorous process of verification and confirmation—and that would be to interview the source of the information personally. Ideally, we try to get three independent sources for each story. (SABC respondent 4)

Even though all sources need to be verified, there are examples of sources that are being used despite being difficult to verify, Wikileaks being one such source: "The information on Wikileaks cannot generally be confirmed, and so it comes with an automatic disclaimer" (SABC respondent 4).

However, some of the political journalists emphasise that they would only use social media emanating from official sources, such as other news outlets, government sources or known organisations such as "[. . .] research institutes, universities, government websites" (*Star* respondent 1). One political journalist explained:

> If I am to quote from an online source, I make sure that the website is a legitimate website of that source, e.g., I will never use *Financial Times* (FT) in an article unless it is from the FT website . . . I only rely on Twitter for breaking news if the news originates from credible and known news agencies and outlets. The same applies for Facebook. (*City Press* respondent 2)

When quoting official sources, however, respondents point out that it is important to identify whether sources are saying things in their own capacity vis-à-vis what they paraphrase or copy from other sources. Re-tweeting of comments made by others is one area where most journalists felt they needed to exercise extra vigilance. It was important to establish what sources are first-hand comments made by an original author and what is merely re-tweeted: "[. . .] credibility of source is paramount, and differentiating between what they are saying and what they are merely repeating/retweeting" (*Business Day* respondent 1).

Although most respondents stated that they had not experienced any major problems or fallouts when using or quoting social media sources, one political journalist mentioned one minor incident and the steps taken to correct it. He explains, "I had one instance recently when I quoted an author as a she (because that's what the web source I looked at described the author) and a reader pointed out the error, which I corrected in my next column" (*Star* respondent 1).

In order to get around these types of problems, the media monitors interviewed for this study agreed that possibly the best method of using social media sources was to adopt a 'mixed method approach' that incorporated both traditional and new media comments. This would make for a more comprehensive and credible report: "Journalists have to tap every source they can on a story, and the internet is a rich resource if used properly. Whether it is a problem to rely too much on online sources really depends a great deal on the story" (Media monitor 6). There was also a clear sense that it would be "[. . .] inadequate to rely solely on online material, as this would preclude first-hand reportage and one very real criticism of current trends in journalism is the decline in first-hand observational reporting" (ibid). Social media sources should really only be used as supplementary information to what has been originally uncovered. As one media monitor put it,

> Internet sources should help provide background information to the story and provide more nuances in cases where the story involves something novel (e.g., the tsunami). In other words, journalists should not use Internet sources as primary sources. They could also use online sources to tip them on stories—for example, most media now get their tips from Twitter. (Media monitor 5)

When asked whether they felt that social media sources are more biased than traditional sources and whether they thought that people feel more at ease expressing their political beliefs through social media networks, even if these beliefs could be seen as less politically correct and/or even amount to hate speech, the journalists' responses were slightly more divided. In this regard, most political journalists stated that it was possible that comments made through social media networks were more biased: "There's still a feeling of informality about online media that may put some people more at ease than if they thought their words were going into a newspaper or out on air" (*Business Day* respondent).

The majority of the sample of media monitors were more stringent in their response, believing that political bias was more apparent when considering social media and general online sources: "Internet sources are less bound by the conventional professional ideologies of journalism, and therefore would be less likely to comply with notions of 'objectivity', 'balance', 'neutrality' etc." (Media monitor 4). Another media monitor spoke of social media as used more for stating opinions than for news dissemination:

> The Internet as a platform is for those who have an opinion expressing it to those who want one, while the traditional media is (more) for the dissemination of news and information (hence neutral). Internet is more emotional, traditional media more rational. Logically, Internet sources hence are more biased, politically and otherwise (biased to be seen rather as a polarisation). (Media monitor 1)

Other media monitors confirm this and argue that social media provides a platform for outspokenness, where people feel free to express their opinions in frank and straightforward ways "and to have more indemnity from direct and immediate verification. Being frank is often also seen by others as being biased" (Media monitor 5). There is also a sense that social media sources often have established themselves for a specific purpose, which makes them more 'biased' from the start:

> Internet is pre-packaged (mostly by established and often 'positioned' institutional sources) meaning that there is greater chance for such information to carry the preferred views of its sponsors. The danger in this era of lazy, copy-and-paste journalism is that not many journalists would seek to interrogate this information to eliminate the biases that it is likely to carry. (Media monitor 2)

However, other media monitors felt it was unnecessary to separate one type of source from another. For example, one stated that "All sources are biased, have motives and agenda, and all sources need to be treated with caution and scepticism. I'm not certain there is much difference whether one accesses such sources online or directly" (Media monitor 5). Another goes on to elaborate:

> I would need to understand why people suggest Internet sources are more biased. Subject to other insights, I would not immediately say there is anything about the Internet as such which breeds greater bias. After all, practically everybody is there: from World Bank to anarchists, from Helen Zille to my 15-year-old son. And it would include blogs, mainstream news sites, twitter, organisational sites and much else.

> I think one has to unpack what kinds of sources one means: certainly, journalists make a mistake if they see the Internet as a single, undifferentiated thing. Each site or blog needs separate consideration to check for bias. (Media monitor 6)

On the one hand, there is a sense that all sources are or can be biased and that agendas need to be cleared. On the other hand, there is also a sense that not all sources are the same, that official sources are often distinguished from newer social media platforms, which tend to be considered more biased or polarised in terms of their views. It is clear that most journalists use social media as sources and, within limits, do consider these as legitimate provided they have been verified in accordance with journalistic practices. How then do journalists introduce and quote these in their texts?

THE CITATION OF SOCIAL MEDIA SOURCES

The fact that journalists are increasingly using social media as sources prompted questions on how these are being cited and introduced in news text. How sources are cited relates directly to questions of journalistic accountability. Most political journalists interviewed emphasised that they would quote a social media source by directly stating that it was sourced from Facebook, Twitter or pointing out that something was said on a social network site:

> I cite sources of the reports archived online, e.g., "The *Financial Times* reported last week that [. . .]" I cite Facebook to quote people, for example, " Mosiuoa Lekota, president of COPE, said on Facebook that he would fire Shilowa [. . .]"; the same applies for Twitter. (*City Press* respondent 2)
>
> Toward the bottom of the story I would quote the tweet or Facebook update and describe it as such. In broadcast, tweets are quoted verbatim but broadcast has the added advantage of being able to show the actual tweet on screen. (e-tv respondent)

This practice seems compatible with the expectations of those monitoring and observing the practices of the news media in South Africa:

> As with all sources, Internet sources should be verified and not taken only on face value. Internet sources should also be contextualised, i.e., when online sources are used, journalists should explain who produced these sources, where they were found, whether they should be considered as authoritative, factual information or as opinion and debate. (Media monitor 4)

However, a few political journalists mentioned that they would do their best to contact the sources directly and preferred not to rely on the actual comments posted. This meant that social media sources could then be considered as traditional or primary sources, and so some journalists state that "I quote them as individuals only" (*City Press* respondent 1) and "directly where possible, i.e., direct attribution of quotes" (*Business Day* respondent 1). This approach was also supported by one of the media monitors interviewed, who said that quotes from social media sites "should always be followed up with interpersonal communication and verification" (Media monitor 5). Thus, most journalists would agree that social media sources need to be acknowledged in the same way as any other source in accordance with standard journalistic practices.

CONCLUDING REMARKS

This chapter has looked at reporting practices in the South African news media with regards to the use of social media sources. It has explored responses from journalists, media scholars and media monitoring groups as to what extent journalists use these sources and to what extent they consider them reliable and credible. The chapter has also looked at whether or not such sources can be considered more biased than other more traditional sources.

Almost all respondents state that they do indeed rely on and use social media sources mainly for breaking stories, background research and as a useful tool for gauging public opinion. This is also the view of Ansell (2011), who says that to ask useful questions to official sources, you need to be well informed and hence might have to go to alternative non-official sources to get the initial background information to a story. The idea is to be broad enough in your approach to a story, and in your research, this applies to both lengthier investigations as well as assignments with shorter deadlines (ibid). Ansell (2011) also argues that for a shorter deadline, journalists might have to settle for one Internet—sourced overview; however, the same rule still applies for verifying the facts of your story. Overall, however, it would seem that South African journalists still rely more on traditional sources. This is a similar finding to research conducted with Iranian journalists and their use of social media as a newsgathering tool during the Iranian elections in 2009 (Knight 2012). This study showed that despite rhetoric around the importance of social media in alerting the global community to events in the country, Iranian journalists did not turn to social media to gather information but instead relied mainly on traditional sources of information (Knight 2012).

Almost all respondents indicated that in general, Internet sources are indeed more politically biased than traditional sources, and it is important for one to specify the types of Internet sources that are biased. Also, it is very important that journalists and all media practitioners treat every source with caution and scepticism. In other words, a journalist should not just use any source without questioning whether it is reliable or not. Another major finding is that such sources should be verified before being used, and the decision about how much one should rely on these sources depends on the story/assignment covered. Also, too much reliance on social media sources by journalists is causing a decline in observational reporting.

Notably, one aspect of using social media that the South African journalists did not mention was the "ability to identify and make connections with sources" (Grensing-Pophal 2010). A study in the United States showed that many journalists were using social media to contact previously inaccessible or unknown sources and set up appointments or interviews (ibid).

Of course, much more research is needed in this field, and there should be greater monitoring of the use of social media as sources to determine whether any new patterns or routines emerge. It seems safe to say that the usage of social media sources is increasing in the mainstream news media in South Africa, and although these kinds of sources might be more difficult to verify, the same journalistic practices of verifying and cross-checking information apply. The challenge lies in developing skills for assessing these kinds of sources and for not falling prey to lowering professional standards when deadlines are tight and financial bottom lines dictate the timeframe for how news stories are produced. Furthermore, emphasis needs to be placed on editorial control and editorial oversight mechanisms in the news media with regards to the usage of social media as well as the incorporation of user-generated content in the mainstream news media.

NOTES

1. The African National Congress (ANC) is the majority political party in South Africa.
2. Congress of the People: an opposition party.
3. Democratic Alliance: the largest opposition party in South Africa.

REFERENCES

Ansell, Gwenda. 2011. *Introduction to journalism*. Third edition. Johannesburg: Jacana.
Bosch, Tanja. 2010. "Digital Journalism and Online Public Spheres in South Africa". *Communicatio: South African Journal for Communication Theory & Research* 36(2): 265–275.
Calcutt, Andrew and Hammond, Philip. 2011. *Journalism Studies: A Critical Introduction*. London: Routledge.
Daniel, Jeremy. 2010. *The Julius Malema Twitter Guide*. Accessed 31 October 2011. http://memeburn.com/2010/11/will-the-real-fake-julius-malema-please-tweet-up.
Galtung, Johan. 2000. "The Task of Peace Journalism". *Ethical Perspectives* 7(2&3): 162–167.
Gleason, Stephanie. 2010. "Harnessing Social Media". *American Journalism Review* 32(1): 6–7.

Grensing-Pophal, Lin. 2010. "Social Media: Journalism's Friend or Foe?" *EContent* Jan/Feb: 25–28.

Harrison, Jackie. 2006. *News.* London: Routledge

Hermida, Alfred. 2010. "Twittering the News: The Emergence of Ambient Journalism". *Journalism Practice* 4(3): 297–308.

Hermida, Alfred and Thurman, Neil. 2008. "A Clash of Cultures: The Integration of User-Generated Content within Professional Journalistic Frameworks at British Newspaper Websites". *Journalism Practice* 2(3): 343–356.

Herrera, Susana and Requejo, Jose Louis. 2012. "10 Good Practices for News Organizations Using Twitter". *Journal of Applied Journalism and Media Studies* 1(1): 79–95.

Huckerby, Martin. 2005. *The Net for journalists: A practical guide to the Internet for journalists in developing countries.* Paris: UNESCO.

Hyde-Clarke, Nathalie and Van Tonder, Tamsin. 2011. "Trends of Mobile Phone Internet Usage in the Greater Johannesburg area, South Africa". *Journal of African Media Studies* 3(2): 263–276.

Knight, Megan. 2012. "Journalism as Usual: The Use of Social Media as a Newsgathering Tool in the Coverage of the Iranian Elections in 2009". *Journal of Media Practice* 13(1): 61–74.

Kurz, Howard. 1998. "The Erosion of Values". *Columbia Journalism Review* Mar/Apr: 44–47.

Lazarouio, George. 2010. "The World-Changing Potential of Crowdsourced Journalism in a Corporate-Dominated Mass-Communications Environment". *Geopolitics, History, and International Relations* 2(2): 248–255.

Lynch, Jake. 2008. *Debates in peace journalism.* Sydney: Sydney University Press.

Lynch, Jake and Galtung, Johan. 2010. *Reporting conflict: new directions in peace journalism.* St Lucia: University of Queensland Press.

Mabweazara, Hayes. M. 2010. "'New' Technologies and Journalism Practice in Africa: Towards a Critical Sociological Approach". In *The Citizen in Communication: Revisiting traditional, new and community media practices in South Africa,* edited by Hyde-Clarke, Nathalie, 11–29. Cape Town: Juta & Co.

———. 2011. "The Internet in the Print Newsroom: Trends, Practices and Emerging Cultures in Zimbabwe". In *Making Online News: Newsroom Ethnographies in the Second Decade of Internet Journalism,* edited by Domingo, David and Paterson, Chris, 57–69. Oxford: Peter Lang.

Meintjies, Marvin. 2011. "Twitterati Have Broken Story . . . Can u Fix It?" *Sunday Times* 4 September, 5.

Powers, Elia. 2012. "Learning to Do it All". *American Journalism Review* 34(1): 10–13.

Reese, Stephen D. 2001. "Understanding the Global Journalist: A Hierarchy-of-Influences Approach". *Journalism Studies* 2(2): 173–187.

Rudin, Richard and Ibbotson, Trevor. 2002. *An Introduction to Journalism: Essential Techniques and Background Knowledge.* Oxford: Focal Press.

Ryfe, David M. 2012. *Can Journalism survive? An Inside Look at American Newsrooms.* Cambridge: Polity Press.

SAPA. 2010. "Twitter Users Laugh at Malema". News24.com. Accessed 10 January 2012. http://www.news24.com/SciTech/News/Twitter-users-laugh-at-Malema -20101104.

Schudson, Michael. 2000. "The Sociology of News Production Revisited (again)". In *Mass media and society, 3rd Edition,* edited by Curran, James and Gurevitch, Michael, 175–200. London: Arnold.

———. 2003. *The Sociology of News.* London: W.W. Norton & Company.

Tuchman, Gaye. 1978. *Making News: A Study in the Construction of the Reality.* New York: Free Press.

————. 1995. "The News Net". In *Approaches to the Media: A Reader,* edited by Boyd-Barett, Oliver and Newbold, Chris, 294–299. London: Arnold.

Vujnovic, Marina, Singer, Jane B, Paulussen, Steve, Heinonen, Ari, Reich, Zvi, Quandt, Thorsten, Hermida, Alfred and Domingo, David. 2010. "Exploring the Political-Economic Factors of Participatory Journalism: Views of Online Journalists in 10 Countries". *Journalism Practice* 4(3): 285–296.

Part III

Online Journalism and Politics

7 Immediacy and Openness in a Digital Africa

Networked-Convergent Journalisms in Kenya*

Okoth Fred Mudhai

INTRODUCTION

Before the US crackdown on the WikiLeaks website mainly in 2010–2011, the narrative of freedom dominating discourses on uneasy deployment of new information and communication technologies (ICTs) in journalism was more prevalent in Africa—and developing regions—than in advanced democracies. Little wonder WikiLeaks did not include African media partners in their potent 2010 'cablegate' exposés.

Many African countries have made progress with regard to civil liberties and freedom of expression[1] following post-colonial adjustments, but the sensitive data held by WikiLeaks would have been at higher risk if hosted on the continent's servers—although the US government's reaction to the website's exposés show that the danger would be as great anywhere else. Despite progress that Kenya had made away from extreme media repression, masked gunmen under instructions from internal security minister raided the headquarters of the country's oldest media house, the Standard Group (SG), in early 2006—disrupting newspaper and TV operations. Their crime had been to "rattle a snake", so they had "to be bitten" (Ogola 2010, 123). Ironically, WikiLeaks founder Julian Assange said that their first exposé on corruption was "the holy grail of Kenyan journalism"[2] as local media were initially reluctant to publish the content.

From the 1996 Zambian government ban of the *Post* online to the recent onslaughts on bloggers in parts of the continent, ICT uses in journalism in Africa have reflected national contexts, with restrictions often resulting in self-censorship as well as innovations that borrow from and build on global developments. This 'glocal' context perspective defines the examination here of the new media use in journalism in Africa, particularly Kenyan news media coverage of selected issues or stories—mainly between constitutional referenda in 2005 and 2010. The focus is on coverage by two leading newspapers in their striving to keep up with emerging alternative spaces of networked online expression. The aim is to explore the extent to which the coverage reflects immediacy and openness in a networked and converged environment, with implications for democracy. The chapter employs a limited comparative approach and qualitative content-genre analysis.

METHODOLOGICAL APPROACH

In examining the changing nature of journalistic practices in Africa with a focus on Kenya, this chapter links what is happening on the continent with larger conceptual and contextual developments. It is in this sense that a limited comparative approach is adopted. The chapter also uses qualitative content analysis and genre analysis to examine news and information output. This is based on the assumption that "news registers, on the one hand, the organizational constraints under which journalists labour [and] on the other hand, the literary forms and narrative devices journalists regularly use" (Carey cited in Fenton 2010, 11). A group of researchers used as one of their methods "qualitative analysis of news content" to track "a range of story types across" mainly online platforms (Fenton 2010, 12). This approach is especially used here to examine digital-era coverage of recent developments in Kenya—especially between constitutional referenda in 2005 and 2010, during which the disputed December 2007 general election was held and resulted in unprecedented violence. The happenings selected were sampled purposively due to their political significance locally and globally.

Focus on text has its weaknesses, but if done qualitatively, it gives some insight into journalistic trends and culture: "research on online journalism could benefit from a greater recognition of and reflection on *the text as a unit*. . . . Genre theory and discourse analysis could for instance be valuable tools" (Steensen 2010, 12, emphasis in original). Lüders et al. (2010, 949) point out the need to take into account the "textual practice" of both production and reception—considering "both changing social expectations and textual conventions". For Lüders et al. (2010), four elements of this approach are text, genre, media and platform, whereas for Bhatia (2008), the four levels are text, genre, professional practices and professional culture.

NETWORKED-CONVERGENT JOURNALISM AND DEMOCRACY

The WikiLeaks mode of operation shows how networking in a converged digital media environment has become crucial to journalistic practice around the world—with influence in Africa. To Becket (2010, 1), it is "clear that networked journalism has arrived" in the form of "a remarkable combination of online and mainstream, professional and citizen media [. . .] news media that has audience interactivity, participation and connectivity". Pointing out that the Internet not only adds to news coverage, especially during dramatic moments such as elections, but also changes the reporting, Becket (2010, 1) goes on to define this concept:

> By 'Networked Journalism' I mean a synthesis of traditional news journalism and the emerging forms of participatory media enabled by Web 2.0 technologies such as mobile phones, email, websites, blogs, micro-blogging,

and social networks [. . .]. It changes the creation of news from being linear and top-down to a collaborative process.

This kind of journalism adds value through editorial diversity, connectivity–interactivity and relevance, besides offering 'free' content, curation of premium content and journalism as a public service (Becket 2010, 17), and in the process, it helps by "saving journalism so it can save the world" (Becket 2008, subtitle). This kind of journalism is catching on in Kenya and other parts of Africa—driven more by alternative practitioners such as bloggers than by conventional media houses. Noting that "all media are local media, so we need to pay attention to the special circumstances of African journalism", Beckett (2008, 116) identifies the nature of the state (fragile, liberation, complex and poor) and the diffusion of technology—especially mobile phone explosion in spite of obvious digital divide issues—as characterising "African Networked Journalism" (120), which is "shifting power around" and "reflecting a deep urge among citizens for a more direct and open form of political communication" (126).

Becket's conceptualisation is not new, especially given its borrowing from other scholars such as Castells (2000), whose idea of the network society values technology-enabled networks more than hierarchies as it is shared by others such as Fenton (2010), and it builds on the convergence concept which has mainly been used in reference to professional journalism. Although there are multiple conceptualisations of convergence, Larry Pryor's working definition is "work together to produce multiple products for multiple platforms to reach a mass audience with interactive content, often on a 24/7 timescale" (cited in Quinn and Filak 2005, 4). It is "a revolutionary and evolutionary form . . . varies from country to country and from culture to culture both within countries and individual companies" (Quinn and Filak 2005, 3). This variation is apparent even in Africa, where there are differences within countries and between countries due to various forms of obstacles.

Obstacles include "cultural factors", such as the "intergroup bias dynamic" of journalists valuing their medium-career more than others do (Quinn and Filak 2005, 15). For instance, for a long time, staff at the newspaper division of SG Ltd and its Kenya Television Network (KTN) operated from different buildings in Nairobi. Although this was partly to do with previous ownership history, staff from both companies hardly shared newsrooms, offices and resources even in recent years when they shared a building, although the situation is changing. "Angels will not work with people they perceive as devils . . . print journalists who look down on television people, labelling them as dimwit poor spellers, are less likely to welcome broadcast people into their newsrooms" (Quinn and Filak 2005, 15). All the same, SG management has in some cases deployed journalists across the two outfits—mainly from the newspaper to KTN.

Although in the UK, the *Guardian* and the BBC have enhanced their newsroom convergence to avoid a medium-based approach, the SG scenario is not unique even in the developed world. In the US, Juan Antonio Giner argues "that most forms of newspaper and television convergence were more like multiple independent operations than pure collaboration . . . different family circuses with different cultures shared the same tent but in each ring they still were acting as a single circus" (Quinn and Filak 2005, 7). Although the situation is beginning to change in some of Africa's bigger media houses, including the leading one in East Africa, the Nation Media Group (NMG), separate teams still tend to go out to cover an event for different media for the same company. It is, all the same, a matter for the editors to consider on a case-by-case basis.

Rich Gordon has identified at least five forms of convergence common in the US (cited in Quinn and Filak 2005): ownership convergence (cross-promotion and content sharing in the same company), tactical convergence (content-sharing and partnership between companies), structural convergence (changes in newsgathering and distribution, such as creating teams to repackage content), information-gathering convergence (multi-skill reporting) and storytelling or presentation convergence (needing appropriate equipment for the working journalist). In Kenya, both SG and NMG adopted structural convergence by creating special web teams—mostly repurposing print material for the web. NMG even created a senior post of managing editor in charge of media convergence. Nairobi's Capital FM also launched its Digital Media Division to distribute content via their website and mobile phone.

In Kenya, there have been some concerns—especially by the trade union—that information gathering and story-telling convergence results in exploitation and poorer quality news content and packaging, but this has somewhat been reduced by the changing environment where citizen journalists happily operate in such a manner for no pay. As Gordon notes, such concerns include not just remuneration but also quality of work of the multimedia reporting, also known as *platypus* or *Inspector Gadget* or *backpack* journalism: "[. . .] this presents the most controversial form of convergence as people debate whether one person can successfully produce quality content in all forms of media" (cited in Quinn and Filak 2005, 6).

Convergence has become necessary due to increasing ease of access to different forms of technology, as a result of social and legal structural factors and due to audience considerations. In Kenya, the media have concentrated more on computer-based convergence, but they are increasingly aware that the mobile phone has become an important platform. Despite perceptions that in Africa, time is not as important as it is in the developed world (BBC, 2003), a new generation of content 'prosumers' (producer-consumers) want to be able to access information on the move and at their convenience quickly. Unlike in some parts of the US where the battle is more for convenience-hungry time-poor asset-rich people's "disposable time" rather than their "disposable income" (Quinn and Filak 2005, 9), most media houses in Africa would want to see evidence of income first before investing resources in the battle for time. Unfortunately for the media houses, cell phone networks until recently took a huge percentage of revenue from content distribution. This is what a City University of New York student entrepreneur discovered when she won a share of US $43,000 seed money[3] to disseminate news via cell phone in Nigeria: "It would be more expensive for me to broadcast through phone companies" (personal interview 2009).

All the same, the democratic significance of networked and convergent journalism is the potential of "reshaping the relationship between media producers and consumers" (Jenkins, cited in Liu et al. 2009, 44) in a participatory culture. Two characteristics, immediacy and openness, are particularly of significance. Although it is not correct for Anderson (2009, 5) to argue that "[. . .] electronic journalism is still in its infancy", there is validity in the argument that the Internet "does provide entirely new ways of accessing recent and breaking news 24 hours a day", and this can result in "news provision . . . [being] . . . truly democratized". The new digital environment has "accelerated greatly the speed at which news can be transmitted and affected significantly the range of issues that can be covered" (Anderson 2009, 5–6). Although this immediacy enabled Kenyans to instantly watch developments at crucial moments such as the 2007 general election, it unsettled the government so much that it ordered a ban on live broadcasts. With immediacy comes some bias and errors, but the same could also be challenged or corrected: "It is a world where a certain new bias has developed, one which turns around technology [. . .]" (McGregor1997, 2). The ban on mainstream media (especially local TV) coverage did not prevent some live reporting, in particular by alternative reporters—for instance via mobile phone and blogs. In an open media environment, it is more difficult to control immediacy, as the Kenyan government realised. "Networked journalism proposes to take advantage of the new opportunities for collaboration [. . .] to gather and share more news in more ways to more people than was ever possible before" (Jeff Jarvis in Beckett 2008, vii).

Some of the alternative journalists are activist journalists. For activist digital journalism, "the promise lies in the ability of activist news outfits and the social movements they support to create an alternative information sphere that provide news, reports, and mobilizing information" (Wall 2003, 121). For this crop of journalists, objectivity is a myth, as the Kenyan case showed. "In this new digital activist sphere, objectivity in the news is seen as impossible to achieve; instead reporters are often movement members who share movement values [. . .] this sphere anticipates an active audience that will not only make sense of complicated events, but act [. . .]" (Melissa 2003, 121–122). And act they did in Kenya during the 2007–2008 post-election violence. Some of the networks came up with practical solutions, such as the Ushahidi (witness) crowdsourcing website, in the subcategory of crisis reporting. "Various information technologies play an increasingly important role in the dissemination of news and information during a crisis. These technologies are increasingly digital, wireless, and mobile and provide Internet connectivity" (Pavlik 2003, 75). Openness that results in ordinary people reporting and engaging with the news raises "the potential for mis-information" (Pavlik 2003, 76). Yet, in their study of Flickr use in *crisis informatics,* Liu et al. (2009, 43) note that "sharing photos in such [crisis] situations can be informative, newsworthy and even therapeutic".

The media environment in most of Africa is increasingly becoming open more dramatically than has happened in the developed democracies. A more closed environment restricts the *range* of issues and sources for news (Anderson and Weymouth 2009, 34). Tightening control of information flow is becoming increasingly difficult for governments compared to when Hilliard (in Robins and Hilliard 2002, 15–16) wrote that "with few exceptions, all governments in Africa retain tight control of content, mostly through direct censorship". News is no longer largely under the control of senior news executives, who now recognise "the digital universe opening up before them" (Allan 2006, 169) as "digital devices [. . .] are as powerful as they are transportable, opening up new possibilities in first-person reporting, fact-checking and 'watch-dogging' [. . .]" (Allan 2006, 171). With a more open communication space, African journalists (some of whom are correspondents for foreign outlets, especially following under-resourcing of foreign bureaus) are better placed to counter dominant images of hopelessness and desperation projected by global media companies. It is in this regard that the former editor of *The Namibian* newspaper, Jean Sutherland, argued that "at a time in Africa when the widespread view is predominantly one of disease, suffering, war, famine, and poverty", Africans "now have the opportunity to provide a more complete picture of the people and events in our countries" (Hilliard in Robins and Hilliard 2002, 20). The annual Highway Africa new media conference and publications by the events initiator Guy Berger (2005 and 2007) highlight the great interest in the use of new media in gathering, packaging and disseminating news and information.

All is not rosy in the differentiated local African contexts, which should be borne in mind. Some parts of the continent still have an unfavourable legal and political environment for digital media even though Ogundimu (2002, 221) argues that "[. . .] unlike the older forms of mass communication, African governments have generally stayed away from attempts to control the Internet". An ordinary 'down to earth' Egyptian Law student Abdelkarim Nabil Suleiman, aka Kareem Amer, was expelled from university and jailed by the state for four years as well as beaten and detained on account of his critical blog entries (Reporters Sans Frontières 2010a; Suleiman 2004). He is one of hundreds of the country's resilient blogosphere members repeatedly harassed by Egyptian authorities, whose actions have earned the country a place on the list of 'Internet enemies' (Reporters Sans Frontières 2010c). For posting online at an Alexandria Internet café a video of police officers sharing proceeds of a drug deal, citizen journalist-activist Mohammed Khaled Said was killed by two policemen outside the open access facility (Reporters Sans Frontières 2010b). These cases helped build up anger that exploded in the 2011 'revolution'.

Other examples include Sudan's temporary blockage of the UN-sponsored Miraya FM radio in November 2010, Rwanda's ban of the independent newspaper *Umuvugizi* online in June 2010, Algeria's blockage of the website of independent Radio Kalima-Algérie (www.kalimadz.com) for a few days in March 2010 and Mauritania's jailing of *Taqadoumy* website editor Hanevy Ould Dehah in 2009.[4] All the same, the situation in Africa is not as bad as it is in some countries in the Middle East and Asia. No sub-Saharan African country was on the radar of Reporters without Borders' top list of Internet enemies, but two from North Africa—Egypt and Tunisia—which were (Reporters Sans Frontières 2010c) bore the brunt of the 2011 'revolutions'. However, the situation could easily change, especially with China's closeness to a number of African regimes.

There is also the problem of access to digital networks by journalists and audiences: "I have been struck repeatedly by the miracle of reporters working with erratic (or no) computer connections and electricity [. . .]" (Ansell n.d., 6). Although there is hope that competition and regulation will bring prices down with new fibre-optic cable projects, access will remain a problem—although no worse than barriers to accessing conventional media.

A more complex problem is access to high-level research and interactivity that is truly democratic—also not unique to Africa but could be worse there. "There are serious doubts as to just how many people within the advanced democracies are likely to use the Internet in such a sophisticated way or even use it for following hard news at all" (Anderson and Weymouth 2009, 33). Not even users in the US and the UK exhibit high-level engagement with the Internet (Anderson and Weymouth 2009, 33). A 2008 Harvard Berkman Center for Internet and Society report points out the limitations of "participatory and online" newsgathering and dissemination even though they "supplement and expand" coverage (Miel and Faris, cited in Goggin 2011, 107). Goggin (2011, 107) points out that "this critique . . . underestimates the scope and depth of the shift underway"—especially in relation to mobile in news, a key platform particularly in Africa.

One aspect of access is sourcing, linked to gatekeeping. Wider sourcing and greater interactivity are key to diversification of voices and representation in news, so it is in this context that in the next section, we examine Kenya's mainstream and alternative media coverage of selected events and happenings, well known and obscure. African journalists, having been among early adopters of the Internet and mobile phones, are increasingly "doing it digitally" and are "breaking the dependence on gatekeepers and secretaries to get access to key sources" (Berger 2005, 9, 12). However, Forbes et al. (2005, 35) argue that "in reality, the use of the Internet for electronic investigative journalism in Africa still has a long way to go". Developments in this area may be hampered by the fact that in the wake of intensified terrorist threats, legislation in Kenya, South Africa and Zimbabwe, among others, imply that sourcing information from the Internet is either monitored or requires obligation to report suspicions of threats (Forbes et al. 2005, 89). It is for this reason that a WikiLeaks approach would meet great difficulty but would help foster a more open society.

All the same, African journalists have not shied away from exploiting digital technology in sourcing news and information, including sensitive ones. South Africa's *Mail & Guardian* team of Sam Sole, Stefaans Brümmer and Adriaan Bassonusing were commended by judges for winning a R200,000 Kuiper Award for Investigative Journalism for, among others, "using the internet to track down individuals in obscure places" (M&G 2009). Namibian investigative journalist John Grobler makes use of websites like Global Witness and an extensive network of colleagues, sources and fellow travellers. Of course, he also uses the Internet but cautions,

> Public sources, including the Internet, only take you halfway there. But it makes it enormously easy . . . The newspapers here are small, no huge budgets, but the Internet has certainly leveled the playing fields in this regard . . . (T. Kenichi Serino, contribution[5] in Ansell n.d., 2)

In Nigeria, Obijiofor (2009) analyses how four newspapers—*Daily Sun, Punch, The Guardian* and *This Day* in early 2008—relied on email and web-based sources to cover especially the rebel side of the country's Niger Delta conflict.

EMERGING NEWS GENRE-PLATFORMS: AFRICA AND GLOBAL CONTEXTS

Various forms of journalistic practices are emerging in the networked and converged digital environment, which expand the range of producers and sources and enable greater interaction than before. One is mobile journalism (Mojo) or mobile news (Goggin 2011). Like the convergence concept, one definition puts more emphasis on conventional rather than alternative journalism: "Mobile journalism [. . .] is a concept aimed at professional journalists, their identity, changing practices, conditions and processes of work [. . .] 'Mojo' is the use of mobile phones by journalists for reporting" (Goggin 2011, 107).

Those who view 'mojo' as a revolutionary concept in news include journalists such as Norwegian Frank Barth-Nilsen (mojoevolution.com) and Australian Stephen Quinn (globalmojo.org) as well as video share broadcasting sites such as Qik (qik.com), Bambuser (bambuser.blogspotcom) and Mogulus (Goggin 2011, 108). Leading newspapers around the world, including in Africa, now offer a mobile phone channel or service. Goggin (2011, 100) notes that "[. . .] mobile news is a very important and potent facet of contemporary news and journalism, as it is, in particular situations, of the larger forces of culture and politics". Certain African governments (Nigeria and Kenya) have attempted or threatened to shut down mobile phone networks. Of particular significance to the developing world is the use of the short messaging service, or SMS (Goggin 2011), as the application has less technical demands on the higher number of low-cost handsets. While text messaging and alerts build on from the pager, the Internet via "mobiles offer a conjunct but distinct form of online news" using "convergent media applications . . . [making mobiles] . . . culturally significant" for professional journalists as well the public (Goggin 2011, 100–101). The SMS in particular has been used innovatively by Sri-Lanka-based JasmineNews (Goggin 2011). In Kenya, SMS was partly used for rumours that caused some panic during the 2008 post-election violence.

Another feature that makes the mobile phone significant for reporting and consuming news and information is the camera. The camera-enabled mobile phone in particular allows any user to capture images otherwise "out of the range of the professional photographer's lens" (Beckett, cited in Goggin 2011, 106). Posting such images online or sending them to news outlets locally and abroad democratises the gathering and dispersal of news with minimal or no journalistic or official gatekeeping and censorship. This makes "opportunistic eyewitness photography easier than it has ever been" (Liu et al. 2009, 43). An example is the mid-2009 Iranian Green Revolution coverage on YouTube of the shooting and death of Iranian student protester Neda Agha-Soltan (Goggin 2011, 99).

Activist journalists have found mobile phones particularly useful. The use of mobiles for human rights activism has been highlighted in Burma (Goggin 2011, 105) and a number of African countries (Mudhai 2006). One specific example is "the *Voices of Africa* project, launched in May 2007" with a strong feature being "the use of mobiles for newsgathering" (Goggin 2011, 106). The project's "contribution to media and democracy" (106) is evident in the open nature of contributions of articles and still-moving images "without a computer and without having traditional Internet connection" (Nyirubugara, cited in Goggin 2011, 106).

Not particularly subversive and routine is the use of mobile phones by conventional journalists. Following interviews with several Kenyan journalists and other media actors in January-February 2010, Karlsen (2010, 1) had the following to report:

> Kenyan news journalists use mobile technology in several ways . . . set up interview appointments [. . .]; conduct telephone interviews; they record interviews [. . .] which is particularly useful in conflict-sensitive reporting; they send Internet links to their sources whom can read the online news from their mobile phone's browser.

As a result, the author argues, the mobile phone has given journalists greater access to sources, and the public have better access to the media, especially radio call-in shows, and this "can help to promote democracy in the country" (Karlsen 2010, 1). The concept of 'Mojo', for instance in the

2008 Nokia Research Centre and Reuters partnership with University of Witwatersrand in South Africa, is perceived to be more sophisticated than such routine usage.

Other platforms for news creation, distribution and consumption are Social Networking Sites (SNS), especially Facebook and Twitter, by ordinary people and mainstream media (Crawford 2011, 116–117). It is worth noting that major news broadcasters such as CNN "treat Twitter like another broadcast outlet [. . .] another pipe to push down news feeds" (Crawford 2011, 118), but not for responding to feedback and virtually not following users or anyone. The situation is not any different for African media outlets. However, Twitter has become very useful for alternative news coverage; for instance, in the mid-2009 Iranian post-election protests and brutality, it exposed the slowness and failure of mainstream media such as CNN (cnnfail.com) (Goggin 2011, 99–100, 122). In certain cases, such as the bombing of Jakarta in mid 2009 and the ditching of US Airways Flight 1549 into the Hudson River, news breaking can be truly via Twitter, but "describing these moments as journalism is retrofitting an established mode of practice onto something that is materially different" (Crawford 2011, 120). In Africa, a well-known great Twitter-Facebook or social media moment came in the coverage of the Tunisian unrest that peaked in January 2011 with the exit of President Zine El Abidine Ben Ali (Howard 2011; Ingram 2011; Martin 2011; Zuckerman 2011).

A more common form in Africa is blogging by ordinary people as well as blogging by journalists, dubbed 'j-blogging' (Robinson 2006). Most blogs are personal and have limited audiences, and 2006 US surveys indicated that "among blogs only 5 per cent of postings matched the criteria" of serious news reporting (Anderson and Weymouth 2009, 34). Although blogs were hyped in the UK around elections, they hardly played any significant role— with hardly any difference between the 2001 and 2005 elections (Deacon et al., cited in Anderson and Weymouth 2009, 34). Blogs have all the same been a significant platform for coverage or dissemination of alternative news and views that would otherwise hardly appear in the mainstream media— especially in Africa where self-censorship is prevalent among conventional journalists. "It was on the Internet that one of the biggest scandals of the decade was exposed: following blogger Wael Abbas' posting of torture videos filmed in police stations, the implicated police officials were arrested and indicted" (Reporters Sans Frontières 2010c). Good blogs tend to be focused and are based on a culture of dissent (Allan 2006). For detained Egyptian blogger Suleiman and his partners, the focus is on human rights: "Our main goal is to defend the rights of Muslim and Arabic women against all form of discrimination and to stop violent crimes" (Suleiman 2004, home page). Like in other parts of the world, certain bloggers, such as those publicly persecuted in North Africa and parts of West Africa as well as some 'celebrity' ones in less restrictive environments such as Kenya and South Africa, are so well known that others seek audiences through links with them. "An emergent hierarchy is forming between a small number of celebrity bloggers and the vast majority" (Allan 2006, 173). In the case of Kenya, Zuckerman (2009) singles out a network of well-known Kenyan bloggers, such as Ory Okolloh (www.kenyanpundit.com) and White African (www.whiteafrican.com), and details their discourses around the 2007–2008 electoral crisis.

Another common and even older form of journalistic platform is the conventional website. As early as 1997 alone, at least 50 newspapers were online in Africa (Robins and Hilliard 2002). A key issue for mainstream outlets in Africa is how to improve the features to include the latest aspects of networked and convergent journalism. There are also a number of unconventional news and information websites. They include surveillance ones such as Ushahidi, or Witness (www.ushahidi.com), and Sudan Vote Monitor (www.sudanvotemonitor.com), content aggregators such as Kenya Moja, or One Kenya (www.kenyamoja.com), message board Kenyan List (www.kenyanlist.com), those with a local focus such as Abeingo News (www.abeingo.org) and Diaspora ones such as Semaniseme: Voice of Kenyans (www.semaniseme.com). Nigeria's Jonathan Elendu has a unique website that focuses on investigative reporting (www.elendureports.com). "Elendu Reports demonstrates the potential of diligent no-holds-barred investigative reporting" (Okafor 2005).

NEW MEDIA AND COVERAGE OF SELECTED MILESTONES AND HAPPENINGS IN KENYA

One thing that was discernible in the Kenyan media coverage of the 2005 referendum on a draft constitution following 15 years of agitation and negotiation was the ease with which it was possible for mainstream and alternative journalists to interview former Chairman of the Constitution of the Kenya Review Commission, Prof Yash Pal Ghai, who resigned a year before the vote which he was opposed to in principle. The results of monitoring mainstream print and broadcast outlets indicated that private media reporting was balanced, whereas state media was 'grossly' biased (Andreassen and Tostensen 2006).

Limited examination of some of the recent reporting by Kenyan media does not reveal revolutionary transformation of access. Instead, one gets the impression that they are still at the mercy of sources, but the positive development is that of openness in that they more clearly express their frustration to the news consumer. One of the stories that kept appearing in the Kenyan news media from 2006 was that of abuse of power by the Armenian Artur brothers, Margaryan and Sargasyan, believed to have been involved in the raid of the SG newsroom and later expelled from the country. From abroad, they fed Kenyan mainstream journalists. In one report,[6] the duo provided journalists with documents claiming that Kenya had in 2008 authorised them to return as investors. In the report, the journalists pointed out to readers a discrepancy in the names and disclosed the mode of access to the sources. "In email interviews with the *Sunday Nation,* one of the brothers said he did not have any issue with the misspelt names". The paper also informed readers that they could not reach the relevant government official: "Immigration minister Otieno Kajwang could not be reached for comment on the document as his phone was switched off". The mere existence of the technology does not necessarily deliver the source and the story.

Apart from abuse of power, a common type of story that Kenyan journalists usually work on relates to corruption, with sources often unwilling to cooperate. One such story touched on tender awards to the relatives of Water and Irrigation Minister Charity Ngilu in her ministry.[7] In apparent transparency, the journalists went into details about attempts to get the story from the minister and her assistant via mobile phone (calls and SMS):

> Mrs Ngilu did not respond to repeated calls from the *Sunday Nation* on Saturday. But people close to the minister called the newsroom trying to find out contents of the story after the *Sunday Nation* sent short text messages to Mrs Ngilu. The SMS message to Mrs Ngilu read: "We are doing a story on procurement issues in your ministry. Specifically, we wish to know if you were aware that some of the firms that won tenders were owned by your relatives. Kindly let us know as we plan to run the story tomorrow (today)." The one to the assistant minister read: "We are doing a story on procurement issues in the Water ministry. Specifically, we wish to know if you are aware that your relative Apaa Dennis is a director of one of the firms that won controversial tenders. Kindly let us know as we plan to run the story tomorrow." But the two had not responded to our enquiries by the time we went to press.

Although some stories in the mainstream press still appear without bylines, there is a trend especially in the two leading dailies (published by NMG and SG) to have the reporter's byline accompanied by the author's email address. For news reports, this tends to appear at the top of the story, but in commentaries, the email address tends to be at the bottom. Stories whose authors are anonymised, especially those that seem sensitive, often appear with the general News Desk email address. The provision of contacts shows that the newspapers expect the readers to engage with the journalists (who hardly engage with readers/users) as well as with the content and each other through the usual provision for comments by those who register.

These developments are partly driven by the thriving alternative reporting that is more open and from which at times Kenyan mainstream journalists plagiarise (Zuckerman 2010, 189). The mainstream media content also gets relayed by alternative media practitioners, including SNS and blogs.

One genre that is thriving in the alternative realms is that of citizen video journalists. They film, package and disseminate online interesting and dramatic footage—mainly of wrongdoing—captured in opportunistic circumstances. One example is a YouTube video of an overloaded pick-up truck with Kenyan registration as it swerves precariously and flips with passengers in back.[8] Another one posted in January 2011 is that of a traffic policeman in a brawl with a lorry driver, watched by members of the public.[9] In the second video, someone is suggesting in Swahili to the cameraman to make sure they film all of the policemen, including their force numbers, for unprofessional conduct against the lorry driver.

One factor is how immediacy has been crucial, especially during a major event such as during a vote. The live coverage of the Kenyan 2007 election and the brief ban on such coverage has been widely known. Although mainstream broadcast media streamed content live online (although mainly via paid-for websites[10]) and websites used the 'breaking news' genre on their websites, the government ban on live coverage resulted in some Kenyan bloggers "redoubling their efforts as citizen reporters" (Zuckerman 2010, 190). A number of these bloggers changed from monitoring and commenting on what was being reported by the mainstream media to actually reporting what was happening on the ground, with account and images "that were hard to find in international media coverage of the confrontations" (Zuckerman 2010, 191, citing blogger Daudi Were). It is through these efforts that the network of Kenyan bloggers linked up with technology specialists to develop the "free and open source software for information collection, visualization and interactive mapping" that is Ushahidi (www.ushahidi. com). Through this "collaborative citizen journalism" (Zuckerman 2010, 192) came crisis reporting and crowdsourcing genres. "Basically, you have an incident—that hopefully someone gets a picture or video of. A report on what happened and who was involved, and a location. That information is submitted and then populated into a map-based view that is easy to search by location and/or category" (Hersman 2008). Immediacy was a vital aspect of this platform. "All events submitted are reported real time to the engine so that they will display immediately" (Andrew in Hersman 2008). Such a form of alternative reporting provided quite a challenge for the mainstream media.

The aftermath of the 2007 election debacle also showed that Kenyan citizen journalists make an effort to engage with ethical issues in sometimes frank and open discourse: "Some bloggers and online forums try to moderate their content, but others appear to have shunned moderation [. . .]. Some bloggers called for responsible writing [. . .]" (Njeri 2008). In the end, new media immediacy and openness was a double-edged sword as 'hate' texts easily found their way online, via SMS and on the air.

In the 2010 Kenyan constitutional referendum, the two leading Kenyan dailies once again displayed a case of mainstream journalism playing catch-up with the alternative—and with journalistic trends around the world. During crises and major events, Kenyan bloggers log their observations and thoughts live, so rather than simply post breaking news every now and then, the *Daily Nation* and the *East African Standard* incorporated live text coverage of the referendum. On 4 August 2010, the day of the referendum, the *Daily Nation* started its live text on its website at 06.50 East African Standard Time, also drawing attention to their Facebook and Twitter presence. Apart from giving background information and providing relevant links, coverage gave updates on observation by their reporters in the field and quoted some of the ordinary users who gave updates via Facebook and Twitter. One of the Tweets quoted on the live text was "15:58: mtotowajirani on Twitter: Most international media focussing on 'voting amid tight security'. They're itching for bloodshed . . . NOT happening!" One of the last live text entries quoted US President Obama commenting at a US town hall meeting with Kenyans on the Kenyan elections. The live text ended at 17.00 at the close of the polls.

The two papers once again used live text to report the promulgation of the new constitution on 27 August 2010 and employed similar strategies of coverage from the beginning to the end of the ceremony. One highlight of these live text reports was breaking news on an unexpected guest. The Nation reported: "09:16am—Surprise as Sudan President Omar al Bashir arrives for the ceremony. He is wanted by the International Criminal Court at The Hague for war crimes in Darfur." This was followed up with a quote by the Foreign Affairs minister on the matter. The Standard live text quoted a known human rights lawyer: '10:00[EAT] - Your Say: "I am seated . . . metres away from the main dais. The mood is, sorry, was great and palpable until the indictee Bashir walked in. How embarrassing for us! Am ashamed to have this man among us on this Day. Haroun Ndubi"'. An interesting entry in the Nation live text related to the Kenyan Prime Minister: "1:07pm—Something interesting to note: Raila is a trending topic worldwide on the social media network Twitter". The Nation live text ended with an invitation to view their gallery of pictures relating to the event and to download President Kibaki's speech. The Standard live text ended with one of the rather loaded last entries: "12:53[EAT] - Kibaki just entered his fuel guzzler". This form of immediacy and networked-convergent reporting had not been routine before 2010.

The online news and commentaries on Kenya by Kenyans and mainstream or alternative journalists reflect the generic characteristics of similar outputs in other parts of Africa and the world. Characteristics include immediate publishing, time stamping, contact for the author and comment by the reader, which could result in transformation of the text (including audio and video formats). One common feature is intertextuality between mainstream and alternative media forums and platforms.

CONCLUSION

In this article, we have employed qualitative content analysis and genre analysis in a bid to integrate discursive and professional practices of journalism, linking intratextual and extratextual aspects as per Bhatia (2008). The global, national, institutional, organisational and professional contexts have been taken into account in analysing the transformation of journalism practice and culture in Africa with a focus on Kenya, especially the two leading newspapers. There remain issues around accuracy and trustworthiness of certain online alternative media, but this affects mainstream media just as much. For this reason, Kenya's two leading dailies have made attempts to enhance openness and accountability by trying to be as forthright as possible about their sourcing. There are also attempts to include less powerful voices, although the usual elite sources still dominate. In addition, there are attempts to adopt live, networked and converged reporting, especially during major events. Finally, the Kenyan mainstream media appear to be playing catch-up in terms of technology use with local alternative practitioners as well as global players.

It is worth noting that the mainstream media journalists or their editors have yet to actively engage with the reader, for instance by responding to some of the comments posted at the end of stories. This is not unique to Kenya or Africa as most journalists and editors simply do not have the time for such dialogue, but it does undermine the logic of such a generic provision. Another matter of interest is the increasing role of and interest in social media, especially Facebook and Twitter—crucial for the 2013 Kenyan elections.

NOTES

*. A version of this work appeared in *Journalism: Theory, Practice & Criticism* 12(6): 674–91, 2011, a SAGE Journals publication. http://jou.sagepub.com/content/12/6/674.abstract. DOI: 10.1177/1464884911405470.
1. While the overall trend of progress is discernible, there are worries—in recent years— of a backslide. See, for instance, Freedom House "Sub-Saharan Africa" assessment (http://www.freedomhouse.org/regions/sub-saharan-africa).
2. "Julian Assange: Why the world needs Wikileaks", Ted Talk, July 2010, accessed 2 August 2013, http://www.ted.com/talks/julian_assange_why_the_world_needs_wikileaks.html.
3. See "Three '08 Students Win Entrepreneurial Journalism Contest", accessed 2 August 2013, http://www.journalism.cuny.edu/2008/12/23/three-08-grads-win-entrepreneurial-journalism-prizes/.
4. Based on various reports from the websites of *Sudan Tribune*, AllAfrica.com and Reporters Sans Frontiéres.
5. Titled "A certain tenacity: Mozambique, Namibia and Kenya".
6. *Sunday Nation* Reporter, "We are Free to Return to Kenya: Artur Brothers", *Sunday Nation*, 20 November 2010, accessed 10 December 2012, www.nation.co.ke/News/We%20are%20free%20to%20return%20to%20Kenya%20say%20Artur%20brothers%20/-/1056/1057428/-/lopofl/-/index.html.
7. Samuel Siringi, "Family Deep in Ngilu's Troubled Waters", *Sunday Nation*, 21 November 2010, accessed 10 December 2012, www.nation.co.ke/News/politics/Family%20deep%20in%20Ngilu%20troubled%20waters/-/1064/1057406/-/tvjccdz/-/index.html.

8. Various posts from mid November 2010 by, among others, Rallycrashes88, accessed 17 November 2010, www.youtube.com/user/rallycrashes88.
9. Various posts from January 2011, accessed 10 December 2012, Capital FM Kenya YouTube Channel, http://www.youtube.com/watch?v=TyzYZQ7m7iI; Kenyan List, http://www.kenyanlist.com/kls-listing-show.php?id=52266; CastTV, www.casttv.com/video/t1hz4fm/traffic-cop-motorist-in-highway-brawl-video.
10. Examples: www.kenyamoto2.com, www.jumptv.com and www.africast.tv.

REFERENCES

Allan, Stuart. 2006. *Online News*. Maidenhead: Open University Press.
Anderson, Peter J. with Ward, Geoff. 2009. "Introduction". In *The Future of Journalism in the Advanced Democracies*, edited by Anderson, Peter J. and Ward, Geoff, 3–16. Aldershot: Ashgate.
Anderson, Peter J. and Weymouth, Anthony with Ward, Geoff Ward. 2009. "The Changing World of Journalism". In *The Future of Journalism in the Advanced Democracies,* edited by Anderson, Peter J. and Ward, Geoff, 17–38. Aldershot: Ashgate.
Andreassen, Bêard-Anders and Tostensen, Arne. 2006. "Of Oranges and Bananas: The 2005 Kenya Referendum on the Constitution". Chr. Michelsen Institute. Accessed 23 January 2011. http://aceproject.org/eroen/regions/africa/KE /http___www-cmi-no_pdf__file-_publications_2006_wp_wp2006–13.pdf/view.
Ansell, Gwen. n.d. "Introduction: Investigative journalism in Africa—Walking through Minefield at Midnight". *Investigative Journalism Manual* 2–6. Konrad-Adenauer-Stiftung. Accessed 7 November 2010. http://investigative-journalism-africa.info/?page_id=42.
BBC. 2003. "Can Africa Keep Time?". 28 October 2003. Accessed 22 January 2011. http://news.bbc.co.uk/1/hi/world/africa/3211923.stm.
Beckett, Charlie. 2008. *Supermedia: Saving Journalism So It Can Save the World.* Oxford: Blackwell Publishing.
———. 2010. *The Value of Networked Journalism.* Conference concept report, POLIS (Journalism and Society). London: The London School of Economics and Political Science.
Berger, Guy, ed. 2005. *Doing Digital Journalism: How Southern African Newsgatherers are Using ICTs.* Grahamstown: Highway Africa. Accessed 21 December 2010. www.highwayafrica.com/media/guyberger/Doing_Digital_ Web.pdf.
———. 2007. "African Journalism Meets ICTs: Whither the Wealth of Networks". Accessed 21 December 2010. nml.ru.ac.za/files/African%20journalism%20 meets%20ICT%20final.doc.
Bhatia, Vijay K. 2008. "Genre Analysis, ESP and Professional Practice". *English for Specific Purposes* 27:161–174. Accessed 17 December 2011. https://shop.elsevier.com/authored . . . /english_specific_purposes1.pdf.
Castells, Manuel. 1996. *The Rise of the Network Society.* Oxford: Blackwell.
Crawford, K. 2011. "News to Me: Twitter and the Personal Networking of News". In *News Online: Transformations and Continuities*, edited by Meikle, Graham and Redden, Guy, 115–131. New York: Palgrave Macmillan.
Fenton, Natalie. 2010. "Drowning or Waving? New Media, Journalism and Democracy". In *New Media, Old News: Journalism and Democracy in the Digital Age*, edited by Fenton, Natalie, 3–16. London: Sage.
Forbes, Derek with Neujahr, G. and Mathurine, J. 2005. "A Watchdog's Guide to Investigative Reporting". Johannesburg: Konrad Adenaur Stiftung. Accessed 21 December 2010. http://www.kasmedia.org/pdf/watchdog-guide.pdf.

Goggin, Gerard. 2011. "The Intimate Turn of Mobile News". In *News Online: Transformations & Continuities*, edited by Meike, Graham and Redden, Guy, 99–114. New York: Palgrave Macmillan.

Gordon, Rich. 2003. "The Meanings and Implications of Convergence". In *Digital Journalism: Emerging Media and the Changing Horizons of Journalism*, edited by Kawamoto, Kevin, 57–74. Oxford: Rowman & Littlefield.

Hersman, Erik. 2008. "Using Technology to Chronicle Incidents of Violence". White African blog, 07 January 2008. Accessed 2 August 2013. http://whiteafrican.com/2008/01/07/using-technology-to-chronicle-incidents-of-violence/.

Howard, Alex. 2011. "A Reader: Tunisia, Twitter Revolutions and the Role of the Internet".gov20.govfresh,18 January2011. Accessed22 January2011.http://gov20.govfresh.com/a-reader-tunisia-twitter-revolutions-and-the-role-of-the-internet/.

Ingram, Matthew. 2011. "Was What Happened in Tunisia a Twitter Revolution?". Gigaom, 14 January 2011. Accessed 22 January 2011. http://gigaom.com/2011/01/14/was-what-happened-in-tunisia-a-twitter revolution/.

Karlsen, Camilla. 2010. "Kenya Connected: Mobile Technology is Linking Journalists to Local Sources". MA thesis, University of Southern Denmark. Mobile Active website. Accessed 17 December 2010. http://mobileactive.org/research/kenya-connected-mobile-technology-linking-journalists-local-sources.

Liu, Sophia B., Palen, Leysia, Sutton, Jeannette, Hughes, Amanda L. and Vieweg, Sarah. 2009. "Citizen Photojournalism during Crisis Events". In *Citizen Journalism: Global Perspectives*, edited by Allan, Stuart and Thorsen, Einar, 43–64. New York: Peter Lang.

Lüders, Marika, Prøitz, Lin, and Rasmussen, Terje. 2010. "Emerging Personal Media Genres". *New Media & Society* 12(6): 947–963.

MacGregor, Brent. 1997. *Live, Direct and Biased? Making Television News in the Satellite Age.* London: Arnold.

Martin, Tim. 2011. "Tunisia's Twitter Revolution?" Radio France Internationale, 22 January 2011. Accessed 23 January 2011. http://www.english.rfi.fr/africa/20110122-tunisias-twitter-revolution.

M&G. 2009. "M&G investigative journalists scoop prestigious award". *Mail & Guardian* Online, 17 April. Accessed 5 November 2010. www.mg.co.za/article/2009–04–17-mg-investigative-journalists-scoop-prestigious-award.

Mudhai, Okoth F. 2002. "The Internet: Triumphs and Trials for Kenyan Journalism". In *Beyond Boundaries: Cyberspace in Africa*, edited by Robins, Melinda B. and Hilliard, Robert L., 89–104. Portsmouth, NH: Heinemann.

———. 2006. "Exploring the Potential for More Strategic Use of Mobile Phones". In *Reformatting Politics: Information Technology and Global Civil Society*, edited by Dean, Jodi, Anderson, Jon and Lovink, Geert, 107–120. New York: Routledge.

Njeri, Juliet. 2008. "Battle of the Blogs in Kenya". BBC Monitoring, 16 January 2008. Accessed 22 January 2011. Available URL http://news.bbc.co.uk/1/hi/world/africa/7189291.stm.

Obijiofor, Levi. 2009. "Journalism in the Digital Age: Nigerian Press Framing of the Niger Delta Conflict". *Ecquid Novi: African Journalism Studies* 30(20): 175–203.

Ogola, George. 2010. " 'If you rattle a snake, be prepared to be bitten': Popular Culture, Politics and the Kenyan News Media". In *Popular Media, Democracy and Development in Africa*, edited by Wasserman, Herman, 123–136. New York: Routledge.

Ogundimu, Folu F. 2002. "Media and Democracy in Twenty-First-Century Africa". In *Media and Democracy in Africa*, edited by Hydén, Goran, Leslie, Michael and Ogundimu, Folu F., 207–238. Uppsala: Nordiska Africaninstitutet.

Okafor, Emeka. 2005. "Investigative Journalism: Elendu Reports". Posting in Africa Unchained, 16 October, 2005. Accessed 2 August 2013. http://africaunchained.blogspot.com/2005/10/investigative-journalism-elendu.html.

Pavlik, John V. 2003. "New Technology and News Flows: Journalism and Crisis Coverage". In *Digital Journalism: Emerging Media and the Changing Horizons of Journalism*, edited by Kawamoto, Kevin, 75–90. Oxford: Rowman & Littlefield.

Powell III, Adam C. 2010. "Reinventing Local News: 2010". Accessed 19 December 2010. http://communicationleadership.usc.edu/publications/reinventing_local _news_2010.html.

Quinn, Stephen and Filak, Vincent F. 2005. *Convergent Journalism: An Introduction – Writing and Producing Across Media*. London: Focal Press.

Robins, Melinda B. and Hilliard, Robert, R., eds. 2002. *Beyond Boundaries: Cyberspace in Africa*. Portsmouth, NH: Heinemann.

Robinson, Susan. 2006. "The Mission of the J-blog: Recapturing Journalistic Authority Online". *Journalism* (7): 65–83.

Reporters Sans Frontières. 2010a. "Blogger Beaten and Kept in Detention after Completing Four-Year Jail Sentence". 10 November 2010. Accessed 11 Novem ber 2010. http://en.rsf.org/egypte-blogger-beaten-and-kept-in-10–11–2010,38799 .html.

———. 2010b. "Two Policemen Go on Trial for Young Activist's Death". 28 July 2010. Accessed 11 November 2010. http://en.rsf.org/egypte-two-policemen-go -on-trial-for-28–07–2010,38045.html.

———. 2010c. "Internet Enemies: Egypt". Accessed 11 November 2010. http:// en.rsf.org/internet-enemie-egypt,36679.html.

Suleiman, Abdelkarim N. 2004. Kareem-Amer.com (Personal blog). Accessed 13 November 2010. www.karam903.blogspot.com.

Wall, Melissa A. 2003. "Social Movements and the Net: Activist Journalism Goes Digital". In *Digital Journalism: Emerging Media and the Changing Horizons of Journalism*, edited by Kawamoto, Kevin, 113–122. Oxford: Rowman & Littlefield.

Zuckerman, Ethan. 2009. "Citizen media and the Kenyan Electoral Crisis". In *Citizen Journalism: Global Perspectives*, edited by Allan, Stuart and Thorsen, Einar, 187–196. New York: Peter Lang.

———. 2011. "The First Twitter Revolution?" *Foreign Policy* 14 January 2011. Accessed 22 January 2011. http://www.foreignpolicy.com/articles/2011/01/14/ the_first_twitter_revolution.

8 Online Journalism, Citizen Participation and Engagement in Egypt

Ahmed El Gody

INTRODUCTION

Journalism online started in Egypt in 1994, giving the country one of the longest-running online traditions in Africa. The utilisation of online technologies in news making has irrevocably changed the nature of news consumption. The expansion to online platforms by several media organisations has provided audiences with ready access to news as well as space to interact amongst themselves and with media organisations. As Egyptians become active online citizens (sometimes journalists), they provide detailed descriptions of Egyptian street politics, posting multimedia material, generating public interest and reinforcing citizen power and democracy. This has engendered a new form of journalism—Network Journalism—consequently creating a conscious sense of how to reach out to citizens and listen to them as well as enabling them to listen and talk back and to each other in ways that paved the road for the January 2011 revolution. Egyptian online journalists and activists evaded government pressure and managed to voice their cause online, leading many to label the Egyptian revolution the 'Facebook' or the 'Twitter' Revolution.

This chapter seeks to explore the introduction and development of online journalism, including citizen participation and engagement in Egypt. It specifically looks at how online media developed from the basics of simply duplicating offline content to a fully digitized interactive networked space in which citizens develop and consume news and information. The digital platforms also provide space for active citizen engagement on matters of the everyday, including politics. This fusion of online information is widely believed to have been the catalyst for the changes in the Egyptian political scene (El Gody 2012).

INTERNET DIFFUSION IN THE EGYPTIAN SOCIETY

Internet services reached Egypt in 1993 through the Egyptian Universities Network and the Supreme Council of Universities (Abdullah 2005a).

Between 1993 and 1996, Egypt was ranked among countries with the lowest Internet penetration in the world, with connectivity reaching only 0.1 per cent of the population. Global trends, however, forced the Egyptian government to recognise the power of Information and Communication Technologies (ICTs) as an important factor in achieving sustainable economic development (Dutta 2002). To promote Internet connectivity and use, the Egyptian government decided to commercialise Internet use, nevertheless keeping tight control over the Internet through effective monitoring and regulations. Internet commercialisation was considered a first step towards the deregulation of telecommunication services (Kamel 2002).

The Egyptian government continued to emphasise the development of ICT infrastructure and launched the National Information Highway Project, inviting the private sector to contribute to this initiative. The success and maturity of this model encouraged further deregulation of other telecom services in Egypt (Abdullah 2005a). Since January 1996, Egypt has led both the African and the Arab world in terms of Internet penetration and access. Indeed, in order to further develop ICT infrastructure, the Egyptian government created a separate ministry for ICT in September 1999 (Information and Decision Support Centre, 2010). The Ministry of Communication and Information Technology (MCIT) coordinated the efforts of various government entities and private interests. The Ministry was headed by Ahmed Nazif, who in July 2004 became Prime Minister of Egypt until 2011. Nazif led a government of technocrats and businessmen who believed that technology could be controlled and managed if steered by the right policies (Abdallah 2005b). The MCIT continued to deregulate and privatise Internet services in Egypt and ensured the growth of the ICT sector. The Ministry created a new Telecommunications Act, which proposed a gradual phasing out of the state's control over communications services and allowed more private-sector participation while keeping government supervision and possible control (ibid).

The techno-business government implemented several projects in this context, such as E-government, where all municipalities, all 35 national ministries, the Office of the Prime Minister, the Parliament and the Office of the President could be accessed through a portal. This was followed by a number of projects including Tele-medicine Network, e-Learning, e-payment and e-signature projects (MCIT 2012).

In a decade, government investment in ICT infrastructure paid off with the number of fixed phone lines increasing to 14.6 million lines with zero waiting time and the number of mobile lines increasing to 91.92 million with 112.7 percent penetration. By 2012, there were over 4,600 IT-based companies generating over US$ 2.5 billion for the Egyptian economy per year. The Egyptian ICT industry has experienced an annual growth rate of 35 percent. Egypt also has a highly technical IT workforce in the private sector, estimated at more than 176,000 professionals (MCIT 2012).

Between 2000 and 2012, Internet users increased sevenfold, reaching 38.7 million users by 2012 with 37.9 percent penetration and a 38 percent annual increase in high-speed Internet subscribers. The mushrooming of the Egyptian online population coincided with a surge in online news content, surpassing the 20 million pages mark in three years (ibid). Soon, news outlets, social networks and blog-rings were at the centre of the Egyptian online experiences (El Gody 2012).

Regionally, Egyptian news websites top the most visited websites in the Middle East, with almost 45 percent of online news media content in the Arab world emerging from Egypt and with nearly 30 percent of Arab bloggers being Egyptians (Pitnak 2011). Over 11 million Egyptians use Facebook (forming nearly 1 percent of all Facebook users worldwide), and another 3 million use YouTube, making Egyptians the 23rd ranked country globally in terms of users (El Gody 2012).

The introduction of private, non-partisan, citizen journalists' news websites not only broke the government's news coverage monopoly but also the citizen's 'politics of silence' such that users became active and indeed interactive participants. The interactivity of new technologies led to a more horizontal and less vertical communication model, enabling citizens to bypass the controlled traditional mass media (Ghareeb 2000; El Gody 2007).

A number of studies have discussed how the rapid introduction and spread of online news websites have "[a]ccelerated the erosion of the state's monopoly over the framing and ratification of identities and loyalties, and the public's perception of public issues" (Hudson 2006, 1; see also Radsch 2007; Hamdy 2012). According to Hafez (2006), transnational satellite channels and alternative news websites have compensated for feeble political parties, facilitating new trends in politics, affecting the dynamics of democratisation by reducing the isolation of movements for political change and circumventing the obstructions created by those currently in power.

The state's tight control over media has made such outlets lose their appeal, thus forcing audiences to migrate to online spaces (Hafez 2006). Studies conducted by the Arab Advisors Group between 2005 and 2007 demonstrate that only 3.9 percent of the Egyptian population turn to the government media, whereas 88.4 percent turn to private and pan-Arab outlets. Similarly, government newspapers like *Al Ahram* lost 80 percent of their circulation to new independent newspapers and to websites. During the past ten years, over 800 news websites have evolved, with more people accessing alternative news sources and resources. There is evidence that the traditional forms of media coverage are losing their audience share, with a huge decrease in viewer numbers, circulation and advertising revenues (Hamdy 2011; El Gody 2012).

TRADITIONAL MEDIA AND THE DEVELOPMENT OF ONLINE JOURNALISM

To understand the development of online journalism, one needs to understand the Egyptian media oeuvre. For the past 60 years, the Egyptian media have been shaped by loyalty to the political regime. William Rugh's 1979 classification of Egyptian media as authoritarian remains valid (Rugh 1979, 2004). By definition, an authoritarian media system is controlled by the government through direct ownership and/or strict laws and regulations. In such an environment, the media serves to promote the political, social and economic programmes of the regime. The government steers the media agenda and the direction of news to filter what receivers hear and see. Egyptian journalists thus do not explore issues beyond the limits of a traditional system governing the nature of the relationship between the political class and the rest of the population (Rugh 2004). Thus, for the Egyptian government, deciding to go online served two purposes: an avenue to continue manipulating the media market and a tool to send political messages to allies, especially the United States (Mahmoud 2000; El Gody 2012).

Internet technology was introduced to Egyptian newsrooms in 1996 as a government-induced aid for media organisations to catch up with global developments and trends. Dar Al Tahrir's publication *Al Gomhuria* was the first Egyptian newspaper to go online with gif/jpg images of clips from the newspaper. Between 1996 and 2000, 18 Egyptian newspapers—including the major dailies—joined the cyber world. By February 2010, 63 publications, representing 40.4 percent of the Egyptian print media industry (see Table 8.1 below), had their own websites.

Between 1996 and 2000, online presence was rather modest. A study conducted on 12 Egyptian newspaper websites showed that whereas the Internet played a role in expanding newspaper circulation, "it is only another form of the printed paper" (El Gody 2003, 47) and not a tool to develop news content or interactivity with an audience. In a previous study entitled *ICT and Journalism in Egypt* (2003), I concluded that the Egyptian media are not providing any services in addition to presenting a free replica of their paper to online readers. The study further showed that 80 percent of news

Table 8.1   Number of electronic publications

Year	Number of Publications
1996	1
1998	4
2000	18
2002	26
2004	29
2006	42
2008	56
2010	63

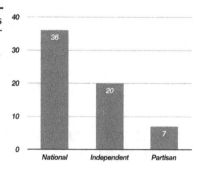

(Source: El Gody 2012)

sites are not regularly updated, with some going for more than four months without being updated.

The study further noted that 75 percent of Egyptian news sites did not offer any real-time news services to readers, 80 percent of the online sites did not provide news archive or database services, and 70 per cent did not provide a news search tool (Ibid). Similar studies note that media organisations see Internet technologies as simply facilitating the digitisation of their offline traditions. Salama (2009), for example, observes that although government journalists pretended to know their audience 'through technologies' and to generate 'institutional knowledge', journalists do not use the technology to address citizens' needs or to be part of their discussions.

Online journalists were thus seen as second-class citizens inside news organisations, their role being to assist 'real' journalists. Terms such as computer-assisted reporting and online journalism were not embraced in newsrooms. Organisations' websites were simply seen as an add-on to the original 'offline' content. Some newspapers, especially opposition newspapers, saw Internet technologies as a failed investment—an economic burden that could not be shouldered given that online revenues were neither high nor particularly promising (Mahmoud 2001; Salama 2009).

Heinonen (1999) contends that net journalism passes through two stages in order to actively participate in the new media system: revolutionary and evolutionary. The revolutionary stage occurs when news organisations introduce ICTs into the workplace, whereas the evolutionary stage occurs when the news management and journalists utilise the technologies and what they represent in terms of digital communication, interactivity and their effect on the news organisation as a professional entity in its relation with their audience (Heinonen 1999; Cardoso 2007). According to Heinonen's rationale, it seems Egyptian media at that point in time were stuck in the first stage. One explanation for this is provided by Ragab (2007), who states that government journalists had been raised in the 'age of fear' and that they sourced their information from government in order to send specific messages to the people.

The introduction of independent and non-partisan opposition newspapers in the Egyptian market by the turn of the century radically altered the media landscape, bringing new topics that had never been discussed to the fore as well as raising the bar of freedom of expression. This new wave of journalism depended on a new generation of techno-savvy journalists. Media organisations saw the utilisation of ICTs in newsrooms as an important way of escaping government pressure and control over sources of information. The Internet and its associated technologies served as a bottomless news hole where journalists could dig for alternative resources (Ragab 2007). The technologies therefore added a new dimension to the production and consumption of news journalism in Egypt. They facilitated the creation of new communication spaces in which diverse voices engage in conversations about matters affecting their daily lives (Murphy 2010).

This discussion stems from the concept of 'network journalism'. Pavlik (2001) stated that journalists who use ICTs acquired "the ability to [. . .] build new communities based on shared interests and concerns, and since [they have] the almost unlimited space to offer levels of reportorial depth, texture, and context that are impossible in any other medium" new media can transform journalism, hence transforming societies (Pavlik 2001, 29).

Bardoel and Deuze (2001) further stated that the journalists cannot work in "splendid isolation" any more but will be a node in a complex social network "between technology and society, news and analysis, annotation and selection, orientation and investigation" (Bardoel and Deuze 2001, 101).

Furthermore, Tambini and Cowling (2002) embraced the role played by 'network journalists' to improve citizens' participation in local democratic processes. The authors explained that ICTs networked a 'third sphere' of free, public deliberation, untainted by the state or by commerce that an audience could access. Through new media, an audience can network according to their interests, using new facilities ranging from using government web pages—as a more efficient means to access political information—to experimenting with electronic voting and organizing interest groups and neighbourhood alliances. Journalists in this 'network sphere' are seen as 'gatewatchers' facilitating discussion, knowledge and information between different audiences/networks (Bardoel 1996; Castells 2007; Murwira 2010; Tambini and Cowling 2002).

In transitional societies moving towards democracy, such as Egypt, political development is a central topic which journalists negotiate with their audience. Castells' (2003) viewed journalism as the core of network society, with journalists working as nodes and among nodes, strengthening the network communication power and counter power by facilitating discussion among and between different audience organizations and networks, especially in democratizing societies such as Egypt. Indeed, journalists inform the audience and facilitate informed choices as 'gatewatchers', not as watchdog 'gatekeepers', in power struggles among audience, media and politics. News websites become the playground for political parties, activists and groups as various ideologies create 'online spaces of flows' to cater to the emerging needs of readers (Rasch 2007). Political actors are invested in creating news portals to attract communities and to enable the communities to interact with each other's ideas, on the one hand, and with the ideas of the news portals, on the other. Building a strong website was seen by independent media as a tool to attract audiences away from government media. Many newspapers initiated collaborations with ICT companies in the training of their journalists on how to appropriate new technologies for newsmaking practices, including interacting with audiences. *Al Masry Al Youm,* for example, built its online portal in collaboration with the UK *Guardian* newspaper and signed a deal with the BBC Arabic service to train their journalists on the use of multimedia elements (El Gody 2012).

Online media journalists thus posed a threat to government-affiliated journalists. They were seen as more appealing to audiences and offering better coverage by providing a quantum information leap away from a stagnant 'silent' system (Radsch 2007). New media journalists echoed and discussed audience voices—and their hopes for change and democratisation.

Consequently, the Egyptian media map changed. Until 2005, the *Al Ahram* and *Al Gomhuria* websites were the most visited news portals. However, independent news websites like *Al Masry Al Youm, Al Dostor,* and *Al Shorouk* now dominate Egypt's electronic website market. In 2012, Al *Masry Online* attracted 1,400,000 unique viewers per day, maintaining an average of 20 percent year-on-year increase. On the other hand, the government *Al Ahram* site's hits dropped from 850,000 in 2005 to 480,000 in 2012 (El Gody, 2012). Independent news portals such as *youm7, masrawy* and *moheet* started providing real-time, updated and interactive features, attracting an average of one million viewers daily. *Masrawy.com,* for example, attracts over 1.3 million visitors surfing nine million pages per day. News portal *Al Youm7* won Forbes website of the year for 2010 and 2011 as the most visited news website in the Middle East (Forbes 2011; El Gody 2012).

NETWORKED JOURNALISM: THE NEW ONLINE JOURNALISTS

ICTs have fostered the flow of information by facilitating a faster and less restricted publication and circulation of news. Many scholars have highlighted the role played by the new wave of 'neo journalists' in facilitating information flow (Pierandrei 2007). One of the journalists' main tasks was to offer a forum for debate in order to create a networked sphere where different opinions are available and can be heard between the nodes and arrows (Kaplan and Haenlein 2010). Pierandrei (2007) states that the impact of ICTs on Egyptian newspapers lies in the 'shaking up' of media organisations, with the new paradigms forcing them to think about the needs of the audience.

The utilisation of online activists and social media actor networks seemed to be the only way to survive. The convergence of ICTs, including information networks, into the newsroom structure and practices has become the 'core function' of the new journalists. Pierandrei (2007) has likened the role of digital platforms such as blogs to a 'second superpower' capable of being used for 'nation motivation'. Similarly, Ito (2004) contends that citizen-driven journalism facilitates an emergent democracy through its ability to support a network of local and global conversations and debates. This network exceeds traditional mass media forms through its ability to allow ideas and opinions to arise from the collective wisdom of the network.

Due to the tight control of the media in Egypt, several journalists operate websites whose sole purpose is to facilitate the expression of their opinions freely. The early ring of citizen journalists included several members from *Al Shaab,* a banned pro-Muslim Brotherhood newspaper which started publishing its stories online to evade government interference (El Gody 2007).

New forms of convergence journalism, such as mixing text with audiovisual material, have developed, and citizen journalists have become sources of information for pan-Egyptian/Arab media. Notable citizen journalists such as Wael Abbas, the author of the *Egyptian Awareness* blog, have raised awareness on police brutality by posting videos depicting police violence. Wael Abbas scooped a story about the harassment of women in Cairo.

Similarly, *Al-Mudawwenoon,* an Egyptian group of citizen journalists and bloggers, has become a powerful tool of democratisation that inspires many citizens. Previously passive consumers of information have become energetic participants or potential editors in a new kind of journalism that places the mainstream media under increasing pressure. Bloggers have become forms of independent news agencies, giving 'grassroots' up-to-the-minute news and other information. The Egyptian blog ring includes over 170,000 closely networked blogs, most of which follow and influence each other as well as create a form of 'agenda cutting' (see Nagwa Abdel Salam Fahmy in this volume). Traditional methods of newsmaking have started to erode as citizens migrate to alternative new media platforms which have successfully added to the widening spectrum of perspectives available, thus allowing for more representation of citizens and less attention to authoritative opinion (Hamdy 2010). Political journalism blog-rings, including the *Kefaya* (Enough!) movement, *Shayfenkom* (we are watching you), *Manalla* and *Baheya,* are considered the best example of how Internet political activities can be taken from the virtual world to the real world, consequently loosening the government's grip on the media.

During the 2005 presidential elections, the online journalists ring opposed a fifth term for President Mubarak or succession by his son Gamal and exposed the falsification of election results as well as sought genuine democratic reforms in Egypt. Tens of thousands of citizens demonstrated in several protests, which were organised through the Internet to support their cause (El Gody 2012). Similarly, during the 2010 Parliamentary elections, online activist organisations such as *Kefaya, U-shahid* and *Shayfenkom* established monitoring committees and online teams during the elections, becoming the main authorities on fraud committed during the election process and gaining international recognition (Hamdy 2010).

New forms of social activities including Facebook, YouTube and Twitter journalism have developed, providing Egyptian citizen journalists with alternative platforms for sociopolitical activism, such as 'tweeting' live demonstrations and 'YouTubing' strikes. In 2008, Esraa Abdel Fattah used Facebook to call for support for strikes by factory workers demanding higher wages, with over 100,000 respondents gathering in just a few days. Following the pressure caused by this Facebook group, the government detained Esraa in mid-April 2008 on charges of helping to organise the April 6 protests. However, Esraa was released on 23 April after a personal plea to President Mubarak. This Facebook group later became the *6 April Youth Movement,* which is one of the main contemporary political movements (Reporters Without Borders 2010).

THE FUSION OF ONLINE 'NETWORKED' GROUPS

With Egyptian society moving into the electronic age, more people are communicating in cyberspace. Since 2005, Egyptians have been utilising news websites to debate current events, criticise the government, public officials and political parties, share personal experiences, propose solutions to current sociopolitical problems as well as construct various visions of the country's future (Parks 2005).

Citizens have harnessed ICTs to create online news sites, blogs, video blogs, YouTube channels, podcasts, SMS text messages and mobile phone web publishing platforms as well as to establish accounts on social networks like Facebook and Twitter. This was mainly to produce and disseminate public journalism and advocacy at a faster pace than that of government control, regulations or censorship (Hamdy 2008). In 2010–2011 during the rise of opposition against the Egyptian government, Lawrence Pintak counted over 13,500 active Egyptian citizen news journalism websites that provided "politically driven reportage on local events [. . .] break[ing] numerous off-limits to the mainstream Egyptian media" (Pitnak 2010, 299) by utilising ICTs and thus clustering citizens around the idea of embracing democratic change (Pitnak 2011).

Online news sites have become a playground for activists, political parties and various interests groups. Egyptians have clustered into groups, each with its own agenda, linked in one form or another to the democratisation process. ICTs were seen as wielding potential for the country's sociopolitical democratisation. Activists saw in the Internet an opportunity to curb government censorship by creating space in which individuals participated in discussions about matters of common concern in an atmosphere free of coercion, dependencies, acquiescence or silence. This led to a more horizontal communication model that enabled citizens to bypass the regime and traditional mass media.

Studying online deliberation in Egypt, one can identify ten online actors in the Egyptian cybersphere: the Extremist, the Liberal, Official, Religious, Young, Women, Elite, Civil e-societies, Egyptian communities in the West and the voices of business organisations (Bakkar 2008; El Gody 2012). Three main online clusters benefited most from new technologies by creating news websites to attract and interact with an audience. The first group were *political activists,* including Liberals, Socialists, Leftists, Islamists, civil society and human rights groups, all historically deprived of their freedom of expression and coerced into silence for decades. The second group were *religious groups,* especially Shiites, Baha'is, Christians and Islamic salafi radicals, who found in the Internet an arena in which they could express their ideologies and concerns. Finally, the *social groups* that challenge Arab social norms and traditions also found the Internet to be a medium where they could meet and create pressure groups to make their voices heard (Bakkar 2008; Radsch 2008). I discuss these online groups in turn below.

POLITICAL NETWORKS

Opposition parties, banned political groups and organisations such as the Muslim Brotherhood, the Communist Party and human rights groups such as the Ibn Khaldoun Centre for Developmental Studies, deprived of their freedom of expression, used the Internet as a tool to engage users through newsgroups and chatrooms in discussions about political reform. As the Muslim Brotherhood leader Mahdi Akef pointed out in an interview with *Al Masry Al Youm* in response to the movement's winning of over 25 percent of the 2005 Egyptian Parliamentary elections, "Gaining access to the Internet was a great triumph to voice our opinion and gain political ground" (El Gallad 2005, 1).

According to Akef, as the Egyptian authorities restricted traditional forms of campaigning, the Muslim Brotherhood created websites to showcase their candidates' programme as well as to interact with local electorates. *Ikhwan Online,* the brotherhood's official news website, further developed an online newsletter because of the lack of independent sources of information offering news and analysis of the Egyptian situation. Other opposition groups, such as the Salfi opposition, used Internet technologies to send emails through specialised mailing lists to express their opposition to government practices. Through the use of emails and websites, they created intimacy with their audience and gained political support (El Gody 2008).

RELIGIOUS NETWORKS

Several studies noted that between 35 and 65 percent of the total number of Arabic websites were either about Islam or preaching for Islam. This observation indicates the exceedingly large number of web pages with Islamic content that multiplied in the 2000s, especially after 9/11 in response to the growing hate campaign against Islam (Andersson 2003; El Gody 2008). Some of these websites, such as Islam.net, became internationally acknowledged in cultural dialogues.

In 2005, the Alexa website announced that the Egyptian Islamic preacher Amr Khalid's website (amrkhaled.net) was the second most popular individual website after Oprah Winfrey's. It is noticeable, however, that a growing number of the religious websites prioritise a fundamental (*Salafi*) interpretation of religion. Meanwhile, there has also been a rise in cyber-terrorism sites and blogs promoting xenophobia and hate speech. In the confessions of an Iraqi suicide bomber, he stated that he adopted his ideologies from the Internet and that he learned how to make explosives through the same website. Moreover, for religious minorities, the Internet became a tool used by Shiite Muslims and Al Quraanieen to unite their voice and appear as powerful movements across Egypt. Egyptian Copts launched several websites to outline Christians' problems, whereas Baha'is used Internet technology to create awareness about their beliefs and to seek international recognition (El Gody 2008).

SOCIAL CHANGE NETWORKS

As more and more citizens joined the digital public sphere, many started to address social rigidness in the region. Issues like identity of the state, women rights and culture tolerance were initiated online. They expanded their social networks and gained confidence in their ability to transform some traditions. Thus, a parallel community of activists emerged, and individuals who would otherwise not be involved in activism saw the Internet as an alternative space for expressing themselves (Badran 2011). For example, women took to the Internet in their quest to gain political representation in the parliament. Several online campaigns pressured the Egyptian government to submit to a mandatory female percentage quota in the parliament. These efforts resulted in a presidential decree allocating 64 new seats on top of the 444 in the legislature to women (Badran 2011; El Gody 2007; Information and Decision Support Centre 2010).

Focusing on citizen activism through blogs, Radsch (2008) observes that the appropriation of blogging news sites as catalysts for social change followed three stages: the experimental stage, the activist stage and the diversification and fragmentation stage. In the experimental stage, a few media organisations, individual bloggers and journalists discovered the Internet as a platform for publishing news that challenges the mainstream media. A study conducted by Quinn and Walters (2004) on the new media's role during the Third Persian Gulf War (the Iraq War) showed that many Egyptians relied primarily on alternative media websites to obtain news about the war. Similarly, several journalists published news that could not find space in the mainstream media online. A number of them established their own online services, blogs, activist websites and the like, all publishing news that could not otherwise be published in their newspapers.

These developments were followed by the activist stage during which online media shifted towards the audience agenda and aligned themselves with civil movements such as Kifaya and the Muslim Brotherhood. Since 2004, the activist movement in Egypt has been growing, with over 3,000 political groups active online, and the movement is responsible for organising more than 3,000 demonstrations to express their opposition to government reforms, policies and corruption (Radsch 2008).

The foregoing developments were followed by the diversification and fragmentation stage, which witnessed an expansion in the number of alternative media outlets pushing themselves into the Egyptian public realm. These included activists, Leftists, the Muslim Brotherhood, cultural and personal bloggers, Copts, Baha'is, homosexuals, Salafis and social commentators (Hamdy 2009). The groups used the Internet to create posts that were considered a weapon against the restricted flow of information enforced by the Egyptian government. This demonstrates a shift in the media's influence in society, with citizens empowered to take information from alternative sources rather than traditional ones (Fahmi 2009).

CONCLUSION

This chapter surveyed the development of online journalism and the growth of social networks in Egypt. Though there is a mixture of opinion as to how influential online media outlets and networks have been in the Egyptian uprisings, it is argued that their main role was to provide organizational infrastructure for online media websites as well as generate awareness among citizens on the Egyptian government's corruption thus fostering the necessary requirements for collective action.

In Egypt's democratisation initiative, the fusion of independent media and social media perhaps perform the most critical function by combining to play the role of a mediator in information transactions within the society. Independent media use social media as an alternative source of information and a platform to bridge events on the streets and the Internet. This convergence has developed the role of journalism in Egypt, altering it from simply reporting on the political process to actively shaping and influencing the political process. The media plays a role in deeply engaging with the public in regard to arguments about politics and their effect on the audience's daily lives (Radsch 2008; Fahmi 2010). Given that social media tools can be leveraged to spread information, Shirkey (2009) argued that social media may have the potential to provoke and sustain political uprisings by amplifying particular news and information produced by independent media. Citizen and independent journalists' utilisation of social media (Deuze 2008) has created a new professional who works as a node in the complex environment between technology and society, news and analysis, annotation and selection, and orientation and investigation. As journalists cannot work in 'isolation' anymore, particularly with the abundance of information and the facts that first, the public are perfectly capable of accessing news and information for themselves and, second, the institutional players (profit, governmental, non-profit, activist, etc.) are increasingly geared towards addressing their constituencies directly instead of using the news media as a go-between (Bardoel and Deuze 2001).

During the opening months of 2011, the world witnessed a series of demonstrations that ended President Hosni Mubarak's 30-year presidency. The Egyptian revolution was, by far, the one most covered by the media during the Arab Spring not only because of Egypt's position as a main political hub in the Middle East and North Africa but also because journalists/activists were using different forms of media to communicate the Egyptian voice to the world. Even with the Egyptian government shutting down Internet connectivity in January 2011, cutting off mobile communications, imprisoning dissenters, blocking media websites, confiscating newspapers and scrambling and disrupting satellite signals in a desperate effort to limit media coverage, Egyptian online dissidents evaded government pressure and voiced their cause on social networking websites. This led many to label the Egyptian revolution the Facebook or Twitter Revolution (El Gody 2012).

Nuns and Ide (2012) see the Tahrir tweets as representing some of the most remarkable real-time reporting ever seen. Twitter was a kind of alternative press, a way of getting the word out to other Egyptians and the outside world and a means of undermining the state-controlled media. However, the uprising was not, as some have called it, a 'Twitter revolution'. Twitter was a tool, not a cause. The revolution had much deeper roots founded by independent media stretching back years. The success of the revolution lay in journalists and citizens' utilisation of new technologies. The rise of participatory culture helped ordinary people create their own content and distribute it via social networks, creating the feeling of "Wow [. . .] I am not alone", as articulated by Wael Ghoneim, moderator of the *We are All Khaled Said* page that sparked the idea of the revolution. This 'user-generated-content' enhanced the traditional logic of political action among ordinary people, showing that the "power of the people is stronger than the people in power" (Ghoneim 2012, III).

REFERENCES

Abdullah, Rasha. 2005a. "Taking the E-train: The development of the Internet in Egypt". *Global Media and Communication* 1(2): 149–165.

———. 2005b. "What They Post: Arabic-Language Message Boards after the September 11 Attacks". In *Online News and the Public*, edited by Salwen, Michael, Garrison, Bruce and Driscoll, Paul, 279–302. Mahwah, New Jersey: Lawrence Erlbaum Associates.

Alexa. 2011. Top Sites in Egypt. Accessed 16 December 2011. http://www.alexa.com/topsites/countries;2/EG.

Badran, Mona. 2011. "Is ICT Empowering Women in Egypt? An Empirical Study". Accessed 4 April 2012. http://mak.ac.ug.

Bakkar, Ammar. 2008. "Who Says What on the Arabic Internet? Notes About Content of Arabic Internet Message". *Journal of Website Promotion* 3(1–2): 2–13.

Bardoel, Jo. 1996. "Beyond Journalism: A Profession Between Information Society and Civil Society". *European Journal of Communication* 11(3): 283–302.Bardoel, Jo and Deuze, Mark. 2001. "'Network Journalism': Converging Competencies of Old and New Media Professionals". *Australian Journalism Review* 23(2): 91–105.

Cardoso, Gustavo. 2007. *The Media in the Network Society: Browsing, News, Filters and Citizenship*. Lisboa: lulu.com and CIES-ISCTE.

Castells, Manuel. 2007. "Communication, Power and Counter-Power in the Network Society". *International Journal of Communication* 1(1): 238–66.

Dutta, Soumitra. 2002. "ICT Challenges for the Arab World". Development gateway. Accessed March 07, 2012. http://topics.developmentgateway.org/knowledge/rc/filedownload.do~item Id = 290684.

El Galad, Magdy. 2005. "The Unorthodox Methods of Campaign proven Success for the Banned Group". *AlMasry AlYoum* Saturday. 17 December 2005.Accessed 19 May 2008. www.almasry.alyoum.com.

El Gody, Ahmed. 2000. "Egyptian based model for the uses and limitations of online journalism applications". Masters Thesis, American University in Cairo.

———. 2003. "Egypt". In *African Media and ICT4D: A Baseline Study on the State of Media Reporting on ICT and Information Society Issues in Africa,* edited by Stanbridge, Roland and Ljuunggren, Maria. London: Economic Commission for Africa.

———. 2007. "New Media New Censorship". In *New Media and the New Middle East,* edited by Seib, Philip, 213–234. New York: Palgrave.

———. 2012. *Journalism in a Network: Role of ICTs inside Egyptian Newsrooms.* Örebro: Örebro University Press.

El Khazen, Jiahd. 2007. "Censorship and State Control in the Arab World". Paper presented to the Arab Media Forum Dubai, United Arab Emirates (UAE).

Fahmi, Wael. 2009. "Blogger's Street Movement and the Right to the City. (Re)claiming Cairo's real and virtual 'spaces of freedom'". *Environment & Urbanization* 21(1): 89–107.

Ghareeb, E. 2000. "New media and the information revolution in the Arab world: An assessment". *Middle East Journal* 54(3): 395–418.

Ghoneim, Wael. 2012. *Revolution 2.0: The Power of the People Is Greater Than the People in Power: A Memoir.* New York: Houghton Mifflin Harcourt.

Hafez, Kai. 2006. "Arab Satellite Broadcasting: Democracy without Political Parties". *Transnational Broadcasting Studies* 15. Accessed 10 January 2012. www.tbsjournal.com/Archives/ Fall05/Hafez.html.

Hamdy, Naila. 2005. "Extreme Makeover: Can the US Public Diplomacy Campaign Enhance America's Image in the Arab World". *Global Media Journal* (Arabic Edition) 1(2). Accessed 11 January 2007. http://www.globalmediajournal.com.

———. 2008. "Arab Citizen Journalism Shaped by Technology: Creates a Challenge to Mainstream Media, Authorities and Media Laws". Paper presented at the International Association for Mass Communication Research—IAMCR, Stockholm, Sweden.

———. 2010. "Arab Media Adopt Citizen Journalism to Change the Dynamics of Conflict Coverage". *Global Media Journal* (Arabian Edition) 1(1): 3–15.

Heinonen, Ari. 1999. *Journalism in the Age of the Net. Changing Society, Changing Profession.* Tampere: Tampere University Press.

Hofheinz, Albrecht. 2005. "The Internet in the Arab world: Playground for political liberalization". *International Politics and Society* 3(16): 78–96.

Hudson, Heather. 2006. *From Rural Village to Global Village: Telecommunications for Development in the Information Age.* London: Routledge.

Information and Decision Support Centre. 2010a. "Electronic Newspapers and Alternative Media" (in Arabic). Accessed 12 February 2011. http://www.idsc .gov.eg/.

———. 2010b. "Profiling Social Media in Egypt" (in Arabic). Accessed 12 December 2011. http://www.idsc.gov.eg/.

Ingraham, Patricia and Donahue, Amy. 2000. "Dissecting the Black Box Revisited: Characterizing Government Management Capacity". In *Governance and Performance: New Perspectives,* edited by Heinrich, Carolyn and Laurence, Lynn, 292–312. Washington D.C.: Georgetown University Press.

Ito, Joi. 2004. "Weblogs and Emergent Democracy (version 3.2)". Accessed 27 May 2009. http://joi.ito.com/static/emergentdemocracy.html.

Kamel, Sherif and Hussein, Maha. 2002. "The emergence of e-commerce in a developing nation Case of Egypt". *Benchmarking: An International Journal* 9(2): 146–153.

Kaplan, Anders, and Haenlein, Michael. 2010. "Users of the World, Unite! The Challenges and Opportunities of Social Media". *Business Horizons* 53(1): 59–68.

Livingstone, Sonia, Bober, Magdalenaand Helsper, Ellen. 2005. "Active Participation or Just More Information? Young People's Take up of Opportunities to act and Interact on the Internet". *Information, Communication and Society* 8(3): 287–314.

Ministry of Communication and Information Technology, Egypt. 2012. "Quarterly Statistics". Accessed 4 June 2012. http://www.mcit.gov.eg.

Murwira, Vincent. 2010. "The Open Newsroom: The Broadcast News Ecosystem in an Era of Online Media Migration and Audience Participation". MA Thesis, University of Auckland.

Parks, Lisa. 2005. *Cultures in Orbit: Satellites and the Televisual.* Durham: Duke University Press.

Pavlik, John. 2001. *Journalism and New Media.* New York: Columbia University Press.

Pierandrei, Elisa. 2007. "Impact of covering New Media in Journalism: A New Tool to Foster Information in Egypt". Masters Thesis, The American University in Cairo.

Pintak, Lawrence. 2010. "Arab media and Al Jazeera Effect". In *Global Communication: Theories, Stakeholders, and Trends,* edited by McPhail, Thomas, L., 290–304. London: Wiley-Blackwell.

———. 2011. *The New Arab Journalist: Mission and Identity In Time of Turmoil.* London: IB Tauris.

Quinn, Stephen and Walters, Tim. 2004. "Al-Jazeera: Ripples in a Stagnant Media Pool". In *Global Media Go to War,* edited by Berenger, Ralph, 57–73. Cairo: American University in Cairo Press.

Radsch, Courtney. 2007. "How Al Jazeera is Challenging and Improving Egyptian Journalism". *Reset: Dialogue on Civilizations.* Accessed 14 June 2012. http://www.resetdoc.org/EN/Radsch-Ucsb.php.

Ragab, Hassan. 2007. "Egyptian Press: What do we Miss?" *Al Akhbar Newspaper,* 2 January, 8.

Rugh, William. 1979. *The Arab Press: News Media and Political Process in the Arab world.* New York: Syracuse University Press.

———. 2004. *Arab Mass Media: Newspapers, Radio, and Television in Arab Politics.* Westport: Praeger.

Salama, Salama A. 2009. *Al Sahafa Fauf Safeeh Sakhen* [Journalism over Hot Tin Roof]. Cairo: Dar Al Ain.

Tambini, Damian and Cowling, Jamie, eds. 2002. *New News: Impartial Broadcasting in the Digital Age.* London: Institute of Public Policy Research.

Wilson, Samuel and Peterson, Leighton. 2002. "The Anthropology of Online Communities". *Annual Review of Anthropology* 31(1): 449–467.

9 Online Citizen Journalism and Political Transformation in the Tunisian and Egyptian Revolutions
A Critical Analysis

Sahar Khamis and Katherine Vaughn

INTRODUCTION

For many years the Arab world has been witnessing a perplexing paradox, namely, the gap between the vibrant and active media landscape where many resistant and oppositional voices could be heard, on one hand, and the dormant and stagnant political landscape, which did not exhibit any serious signs of active change, popular participation or true democratization, on the other hand. One explanation that some Arab media scholars (Seib 2007; Khamis 2007; 2008) used to account for this puzzling gap was the notion of the 'safety valves', i.e., that Arab media, especially the opposition press, were being exploited by the autocratic ruling regimes as a platform for people to vent their angry feelings and resentment towards their authoritarian governments instead of taking decisive steps in the direction of radical reform and transformation, thus substituting words for action (Seib 2007). It was not until the latest wave of political upheaval, commonly known as the 'Arab spring', swept the Arab region that this phenomenon changed thanks to the utilization of new social media by young political activists.

This chapter demonstrates how new modes of communication in the Arab world, especially online citizen journalism through blogging, tweeting, Facebook posting and YouTube video uploading, changed the function of Arab media from being just 'safety valves' to becoming effective 'mobilization tools', which aided the transition to democratization and political change as evidenced in both the Tunisian and Egyptian revolutions of 2011. The chapter discusses how online citizen journalism can provide effective tools for supporting the capabilities of the democratic activists by allowing forums for free speech and political networking opportunities, providing a virtual space for assembly, and supporting the capability of the protestors to plan, organize and execute peaceful protests. Additionally, the chapter explores how online citizen journalism can provide forums for enabling ordinary citizens to document the protests and government brutality and to disseminate their own words and images to each other and, most importantly, to the outside world through foreign media.

Special attention will be paid to the communication struggle which erupted between the people in both of these countries, on one hand, and their repressive governments, on the other hand, by discussing the measures taken by the dictatorial regimes in both of these countries to block the flow of information and to inhibit mobilization efforts, thus combining the repression of protestors on the streets with the suppression of the truth in the media arena. It will also explore the measures taken by the Tunisian and the Egyptian citizen journalists and activists to resist their governments' persistent efforts to both silence the peoples' voices and to present the states' fabricated versions of the story.

ONLINE CITIZEN JOURNALISM IN THE ARAB WORLD: DEFINITION AND BACKGROUND

Citizen journalism can be defined as ordinary citizens documenting their own version of reality and telling their own side of the story, and specifically, in *online* citizen journalism, "ordinary citizens use digital media tools to report on events on the ground, uploading text and videos directly to the Internet or feeding the information and videos to media outlets" (Khamis and Vaughn 2011). Thus, documentation of events on online platforms such as blogs and social media (e.g., tweets, Facebook posts and YouTube videos) could be construed as acts of citizen journalism. This may be especially true under conditions of state repression and censorship of the press, where the blogosphere could serve "as a powerful alternative [to professional journalism], free at the point of consumption and relatively free at the point of production—if the mighty hand of the state can be avoided" (Khibany and Sreberny 2009, 131). Indeed, Allan and Thorsen (2009, 5) point out that the "normative alignment of citizen journalism with the public interest can be thrown into even sharper relief in countries where the basic principles of press freedom cannot be taken for granted" and where repressive governments around the world have sought to place strict limits "refusing to recognize the right of the citizen—let alone the citizen journalist—to express himself or herself freely, without prior restraint or censorship" (ibid). Similarly, Atton and Hamilton (2008, 135) point to the close relationship between "alternative journalism" and "notions of social responsibility" or even "overt advocacy and oppositional practices" that rely on first-person and eyewitness accounts, a stance that foreshadowed the rise of YouTube citizen journalism as exhibited later in the context of the Arab Spring.

One of the most significant advantages of citizen journalism is that it has the potential to fuel 'public mobilization', or 'public will mobilization', in which 'public will' can be defined as "a social force that can mobilize organically, or with external support and influence, to become a political lever for social change . . . [it] has the potential, if adequately resourced, organized, and mobilized, to serve as the impetus for social change" (Salmon et al.

2010, 159). Public will usually "crystallizes around a social condition that is recognized as problematic; it coalesces into a collective consensus about how the problem can and should be ameliorated; and it can erupt, through coordination of resources and collective resolve, into social action" (Salmon et al. 2010, 159).

Before 1990, the Arab media landscape was highly uniform, monolithic and tightly controlled by authoritarian regimes that controlled most media outlets, especially broadcast media, in an effort to shape, streamline and even monopolize media messages (Khamis and Sisler 2010). After 1990, the Arab media landscape underwent significant transformation largely due to the introduction of satellite television channels and the Internet (Khamis and Sisler 2010). These new media led to a shift from the monolithic, state-controlled and government-owned media pattern to a more pluralistic and diverse media scene (Khamis 2007, 2008; Atia 2006). Then, with the advent of blogs and social media, 'citizen journalism' added a new voice to the media mix, namely, the voice of the Arab people themselves.

The rise in social media usage in the Arab world followed a rise in overall Internet and mobile phone penetration in the region. A study by Philip Howard (2011) encompassing predominantly Muslim countries throughout the world shows that mobile phones and Internet penetration have increased dramatically over the last 10 years, with technology adoption rates in these countries among the highest of all developing nations. The same study indicated that since 2001, the increase in Internet users has outstripped the increase in computers per household, likely reflecting the use of Internet cafes (which can be found in both urban and rural areas), libraries as well as the collective use of computers among family members and circles of friends.

The Internet allows for the dissemination of cultural content in the Arab world (Howard 2011). Much of the user-generated content is transmitted using social media, such as Facebook, the video-sharing portal YouTube, Twitter and short message service (SMS) or text messaging. These media enable peer-to-peer communication between users and can be linked to each other, allowing users to transmit their ideas and images to large numbers of people. Therefore, it is safe to say that one of the most important avenues through which public opinion trends and public spheres are both shaped and reflected in modern Arab societies is the Internet (Zelaky et al. 2006). The significance of the introduction of the Internet stems from the fact that it defies boundaries, challenges governmental media censorship and provides an alternative voice to traditional media outlets, which echo official, governmental policies and views.

The Internet is also a rapidly growing and expanding medium, especially among youth. Recent research studies indicate that Internet use is increasingly more prevalent among younger age groups within the Arab world, especially the 20- to 30-year-old age group, which uses the net more avidly compared to the rest of the population, and those younger than 20 years old are the group growing most rapidly in the Arab world (Abdulla 2007). This can very well explain why and how new media were effectively deployed by young people in the Arab world to trigger political reform.

Howard (2011, 182) notes that through social media, citizen journalists who are dissatisfied with traditional media's version of events are telling their own stories and that "these patterns of political expression and learning are key to developing democratic discourses." He observes that social media not only help start democracies, but they also help entrench existing ones, and the 'networked design' of social media is the key factor threatening authoritarian regimes because "These are the communication tools for the wealthy, urban, educated elites whose loyalties or defection will make or break authoritarian rule" (Howard 2011, 11).

Social media can also serve as channels for expressing collective consciousness and national solidarity. Daron Acemoglu (Freeland 2011) argues that opponents of a dictator need to feel that their views are widely shared and that enough of their fellow citizens are willing to join them. He indicates that "What really stops people who are oppressed by a regime from protesting is the fear that they will be part of an unsuccessful protest. When you are living in these regimes, you have to be extremely afraid of what happens if you participate and the regime doesn't change." He further contends that satellite television and social networking have made it easier to let each individual know that his/her views are shared by enough people to make protesting worthwhile and safe (Freeland 2011).

After providing this brief overview of the concept of online citizen journalism, its introduction in the Arab world and its potential effect on public mobilization, we now turn our attention to the significant role it played in the Tunisian revolution.

ONLINE CITIZEN JOURNALISM IN THE TUNISIAN REVOLUTION

Before the revolution in Tunisia, the Ben Ali regime's 'sanitized' state-controlled national media without real political opposition "meant the persistence of a monolithic discourse which glorified Ben Ali's rule" (Zayani 2011, 2). Tunisia had the harshest media controls in the Arab world, mitigated somewhat by the Internet and satellite television stations, such as the independent Qatar-based Al Jazeera, whose freewheeling journalism and commentary had often led to complaints from the Ben Ali regime over what it claimed was a 'hostile campaign' against it (Lynch 2012, 76). The Tunisian government also aggressively censored the Internet, blocking both political websites and non-political video sharing sites (Zuckerman 2011).

The Tunisian uprising was triggered on Friday, 17 December 2010 when a 26-year-old unemployed man, Mohamed Bouazizi from the town of Sidi Bouzid, immolated himself to protest joblessness and corruption. Bouazizi, who was trying to support his family as an unlicensed fruit vendor, had

had his wares confiscated by corrupt and abusive police just prior to setting himself on fire in front of the provincial headquarters (Noueihed 2011). Protests began the same day spontaneously in the town of Sidi Bouzid and had spread to three other towns by Sunday (Al Jazeera 2010). The police were reported to use tear gas, rubber bullets and live ammunition to counter the protesters, but the casualties only served to increase public anger, and by Tuesday there were massive protests in Tunis and demands that Tunisia's dictator Zine el Abidine Ben Ali steps down (Chrisafis and Black 2011). When Bouazizi, who had been hospitalized for his burns, died on January 4, his funeral fuelled the protests, which continued until January 14 when Ben Ali fled to Saudi Arabia (Reuters 2011).

Bouazizi's self-immolation exposed the Tunisian people's frustration with "living standards, police violence, rampant unemployment, and a lack of human rights" (Rifai 2011). Nejib Chebbi, an opposition member and the head of the *Al Mawkif* newspaper, told Al Jazeera, "There is a huge frustration, with no hope to find a job and [the people] were humiliated by the government" (Al Jazeera 2010). It is this mix of humiliation, corruption and economic distress that triggered the revolution in Tunisia, which later on spread to many other parts of the Arab world.

Digital activism was already part of the landscape in Tunisia before these latest protests. In January 2008, there were protests against the Ben Ali regime in the Tunisian city Gafsa, during which some protesters were killed (Amnesty International 2009). According to Kouraich Jaouahdou, a Tunis-based activist, a video of the killings was posted to the video-sharing website Dailymotion, and although the deaths did not become widely publicized, the Ben Ali regime blocked Dailymotion, YouTube and, temporarily, Facebook (blocking Facebook, which was a popular service, brought more attention to the protests and deaths than there would have been otherwise, and this likely led to the regime lifting the Facebook ban) (Joyce 2011). Tunisian blogger Riadh Guerfali attributes the success of the Tunisian revolution to the successful combination of the Internet (including social networking sites like Twitter and Facebook) with mobile phones and foreign media coverage, such as France 24 (Todd 2011).

Although activists from the Progressive Youth of Tunisia were involved in the uprising, the protests in Sidi Bouzid were spontaneous (Ryan 2011), and they also appeared to be leaderless (Joyce 2011). Protesters used Facebook to communicate because although it was monitored, it was not blocked by the regime (Ryan 2011). Social media also played a key role in gaining momentum for the protests. For example, as people in Tunis posted on their status updates on Facebook that they were heading out to the protests, others in their network decided to go as well (Joyce 2011). Ethan Zuckerman (2011) echoes this observation, noting that "as others followed their updates, it's likely that news of demonstrations in other parts of the country disseminated online helped others conclude that it was time to take to the streets".

Social media also served as a means for protesters to report on conditions on the ground and to advise others who were engaged in activism or protest.

The blog nawaat.org provided practical advice on avoiding identification by authorities when sharing information online (Todd 2011). During the Tunisian protests, social media such as Facebook, Twitter and SMS were used to warn protesters of sniper locations, and a type of 'online-mobile synergy' emerged, where locations initially reported by SMS or a phone call by one person would then be posted to Facebook or tweeted by another person with a computer such that computers and mobile phones became "separate entry points to the same network" (Joyce 2011).

After protests began in Sidi Bouzid, the reports were posted on Facebook and Twitter, and videos were uploaded to YouTube and Dailymotion (Joyce 2011; Al Jazeera 2010). The videos of the first modest protests were exceptional given the level of state repression at the time (Ulrich 2010). Hashtags, which are user-generated tags that mark keywords or topics in a tweet with a '#' symbol, can be used to track the popularity of specific keywords and topics. By 23 December 2010, the hashtag #sidibouzid was trending with Tunisian Twitter users (Ben Mhenni 2010). By 29 December 2010, Al Jazeera reported that "the Twitter website was full of commentary" (Al Jazeera 2010). As the uprising grew from a local phenomenon to a national uprising, Twitter hashtags discussing the protests reflected this, changing from #bouazizi to #sidibouzid and finally #tunisia (Ryan 2011). Besides social media, during the uprising, news of demonstrations spread organically and rapidly through Tunisia's existing online forums and email listservs, such that these "online networks truly served as a digital grapevine through which much news of the revolution spread" (Brisson and Krontiris 2012, 104). Tunisians also used the 'blogosphere' to report on events and express their political opinions. For example, the influential blog nawaat.org covered the unrest in Tunisia (Todd 2011).

This political struggle, which the Tunisian people launched to rid their country and its people of dictatorship, corruption, authoritarian rule and humiliation, was equally paralleled by another struggle between the government and the people in the media arena.

Because there was essentially no press freedom under the Ben Ali regime, the protests—if they were covered at all—were reported as acts of "vandalism or terrorism" (Zuckerman 2011). Although state television ignored the protests, broadcasting music concerts as protests raged (Almiraat 2011a), citizen journalism played a crucial role in disseminating news. Rochdi Horchani, an activist and relative of Bouazizi, stated that the protesters had "a rock in one hand, a cell phone in the other" (Ryan 2011). From the early hours of the protests, these citizen journalists had become an important source of news for the international media, posting videos of the protests and providing updates on the numbers killed, eventually overwhelming state media (Bounenni 2011). The key difference between Sidi Bouzid events and similar protests that took place in the past was the efforts of locals to get the word out. For example, videos of the first protests were posted the same day by some of Bouazizi's relatives and were picked up by Al Jazeera's *Mubasher* (live) channel (Ryan 2011).

On 9 January 2011, Global Voices (Al Hussaini 2011a) reported that nawaat.org posted videos to YouTube and the video sharing site Vimeo and that Tunisian 'netizens' were "working around the clock to show the rest of the world the ongoing carnage in their country": "Despite the fact that protesters on the ground are facing a heavy-handed response from the authorities, and cyber-activists are facing the same dilemma, photographs, testimonies and videos showing the daily mayhem are appearing online [. . .] the Twitterosphere is on fire." Although YouTube had been blocked since 2007, the blog nawaat.org had a YouTube channel, which displayed "streaming videos [. . .] showing scenes of horror, the tears and screams of mothers whose sons were killed and protesters being attacked by tear gas and fired at using live ammunition, as well as scenes from protests and funerals" (Al Hussaini 2011b).

The citizen-captured videos linked events in the poorer areas of Tunisia with the broader population, becoming "the raw material for a much greater online apparatus that could amplify each injury, death, and protest" (Madrigal 2011). Although many Tunisians relied on satellite television channels, such as Al Jazeera, France 24, and Al Arabiya, to follow the news of the uprising (Ryan 2011), by 8 January 2011, those who had Internet access were mostly using Facebook to track events as they were unfolding, and Facebook reported "several hundred thousand more users" than ever before in Tunisia, with users spending twice as much time per visit than they did before the unrest (Madrigal 2011).

A Tunisian blogger, Slim Amamou (Almiraat 2011b), said that some of the anger of the protesters stemmed from feelings that their voices were not being heard, and he said that Internet citizen-journalists were the only ones covering them:

> In a few weeks, people were compulsively following and sharing information in social media and censorship could not keep up with them: they've been overwhelmed and information was getting through and everyday more people were rallying for the cause. You can't do a revolution without a working Information System. And since 'old' media was dysfunctional, Internet Social Networks played this role.

'Netizens' from around the world rallied to the protesters' cause and echoed their calls, with tweets of support coming from such disparate places as India, Egypt, the US, Denmark and Taiwan, using the hashtags #sidibouzid and #tunisia (Al Hussaini 2010). For the diaspora, Facebook became their primary means to learn what was happening in the neighbourhoods of their family and friends (Madrigal 2011). Writing in French from Paris, Tunisian blogger Slim (Almiraat 2011a) praised social media, saying Tunisians "have never been so well informed about what is happening. Instant and viral sharing of photos, videos and witness accounts from protesters on Facebook and Twitter has been intense since the beginning of the movement. The border between the real and virtual worlds has never been so tight".

When the protests began in Tunisia, the regime did not completely block Facebook as it had after Gafsa (for fear of drawing more attention to the protests), but instead it blocked just those pages with content on the protests (Joyce 2011). Then, on 3 January 2011, the regime hacked into activists' email accounts and accessed and disabled their blogs and Facebook pages (Al Hussaini 2011c), and conducted a "systematic, government-organised 'phishing' operation aimed at wiping out their online dissent" (Ryan 2011). The Tunisian government also used less sophisticated tactics during the protests, such as shutting off power and Internet access in Sidi Bouzid and nearby towns, and arresting bloggers, activists and even a rapper who posted a song on YouTube criticizing the regime (Ryan 2011).

However, as the regime attempted to disempower the activists, the activists fought back, asserting their right to political participation and free speech. Tunisia's tech-savvy activists had been circumventing the state's controls for years before the uprising (Zuckerman 2011). Although most Tunisians couldn't access the blocked Facebook pages, some people knew how to use proxy servers to view the pages (Joyce 2011). However, even less technologically adept activists were able to thwart the regime. In the town of Kasserine, where protesters were suffering a deadly police crackdown, activists smuggled memory cards containing video footage of the violence to neighbouring Algeria and then back again to Tunis, where the images were uploaded to the Internet and picked up by international news channels (Joyce 2011).

Marc Lynch (2012, 74–75) posits that because the Ben Ali regime had such a tight grip on the 'public sphere', it became "distinctively vulnerable to a cascade of dissent once those controls faltered". And because of the tight controls on the media, it should come as no surprise that the population turned to Facebook, which was very popular in Tunisia, to disseminate information about the uprising: "Here, social media, which has often been awarded too much importance in the spread of the Arab uprisings, played a genuinely important role" (Lynch 2012, 76).

Egyptians enjoyed a freer media landscape than the Tunisians prior to the uprising, with a more active blogosphere and vibrant political discourse. However, many Egyptians were deeply unhappy with the repressive Mubarak regime and poor economic conditions. Indeed, although the Egyptian revolution gained significant momentum from the Tunisian revolution, the stage had been set in Egypt by existing protest movements and a network of activist groups who had learned from their previous attempts to effect change. One group called the *April 6 Movement* used cell phones, blogs, Twitter, Facebook and YouTube to document Egyptian police excesses, organize meetings and protests, alert each other to police movements and get legal help for those who had been arrested (Nelson 2008; Ishani 2011). Some of the groups' affiliates underwent training by digital journalists through a US nongovernmental organization (Ishani 2011).

A popular Facebook group affiliated with the *April 6 movement*, "We Are All Khaled Said", also existed before the uprising and was famously linked to Wael Ghonim, its (initially) anonymous creator. The Facebook page had over 350,000 members before 14 January 2011, and it was named after Khaled Said, a young Egyptian man who was dragged from a café and beaten to death in the street by police in June 2010 for posting a video on the Internet exposing police corruption (Giglio 2011, 15).

More than six million Egyptians have Internet access, and cell phones are ubiquitous, many of which are sold with the Facebook mobile web application (Nelson 2008). One survey (IBB Office of Research 2011) of 502 Egyptians aged 15 and older living in Cairo and Alexandria reported that during the Egyptian uprising, the Internet was the second most popular medium (television being most popular), with more than 5 percent of respondents overall and 16 percent of those aged 20–29 years stating it was the "most important" news source. Regarding social media, the report states that

> As press reports have suggested, a significant proportion of Cairo and Alexandria residents appear to have used various forms of peer-to-peer communications, in addition to accessing key Internet sites, both to follow the news and to share it with others. Roughly a fifth of those interviewed reported getting information via social networking sites and/or via text messages from friends and family; somewhat smaller numbers claimed to have used these and similar technologies to share information and news they had heard with other people.

As shown above, social media were already being used in previous protests in Egypt, and so it is no surprise that it was put to use again in the run up to the January 25th protest. The National Coalition for Change used Facebook, Twitter and YouTube to get the word out and sent text messages saying, "Tell your friends" and "Look what is happening in Tunisia. This is how people change their country" (Baker 2011). The 'We Are All Khaled Said' Facebook page became an important source of information and advice for protesters (York 2011a). During the protests, activists worked to connect reports from the protesters to international human rights monitors and to feed images taken by activists to the international media (Ishani 2011). Jillian York (2011b) said that as violence escalated on Cairo's streets, journalists found it difficult to report on events on the ground, but young Egyptians "were in the thick of things, mobile phones at the ready, often live-tweeting as skirmishes broke out". She added that

> Others in various parts of the city uploaded photographs and pictures from the day's events, not just from Tahrir Square but from side streets as well, documenting graffiti, ordinary life, and those now-famous leagues of neighborhood protection committees. Still others tweeted

from more remote locations, and from cities without the benefit of dispatched reporters. (York 2011b)

Also, in situations like the protests, the advantage of citizen journalism might outweigh the risk of false information because "Egyptians know their country better than CNN, MSNBC, or even Al Jazeera possibly could" (York 2011b). Therefore, citizen journalists can be the most reliable and credible source of news and information during these significant political events.

As in the case of the Tunisian revolution, the Egyptian revolution also entailed not only a political struggle but also a communication struggle between the government and the activists, many of whom used online citizen journalism as a means of spreading their messages and making their voices heard locally, regionally and globally.

Egyptian protesters had been forced to contend with Internet monitoring before the uprising, but not to the extent seen in Tunisia before its uprising. However, once the protests began to threaten the Mubarak regime's existence, the state used a more aggressive method to impede Internet and mobile phone access: on 28 January 2011, the Egyptian government shut off the Internet and mobile phone services for the entire country, resulting in an Internet blackout that lasted almost one week (Ishani 2011).

Like their Tunisian counterparts, the Egyptian tech-savvy activists were fighting back against state control prior to the 2011 protests. Many increased their capabilities by reaching out to the international community to educate themselves on new technologies for bypassing state controls. Some in the April 6 movement worked with the Kenyan NGO Ushahidi to develop their "capabilities for securely and credibly capturing raw video and reporting on the ground with mobile phones and building online content around it", and yet more received training from a US nongovernmental organization on how to use mapping tools, such as Google Maps and UMapper, to document protests and choose demonstration sites (Ishani 2011).

Whereas professional journalists struggled to get their stories out during the Internet blackout, "street protesters were using land lines to call supporters, who translated and published their accounts on Twitter for an international audience hungry for news of the unfolding events" (Ishani 2011). However, the blackout's long duration forced activists to find more innovative workaround solutions, such as setting up FTP accounts to send videos to international news organizations (Ishani 2011). Another solution they found was using landlines to connect to Internet services in neighbouring countries by calling international numbers with older dial-up modems, a connection that was slow but sufficient for posting tweets about events on the ground (Sigal 2011; Seibt 2011). They even resorted to using Morse code, fax machines and ham radio to get the word out about events on the ground, and the website for the activist group 'We Rebuild' transcribed transmissions from Egyptian amateur radio stations and posted resources for circumventing the blackout (Seibt 2011; *Daily Mail* 2011). They also smuggled satellite phones and satellite modems into Egypt, which did not depend on Egypt's infrastructure to function (*Daily Mail* 2011).

Egyptian citizen journalists also took advantage of international efforts to help them. During the Internet blackout, Google and Twitter scrambled to offer a new 'speak-to-tweet' service wherein users could call an international telephone number to post and hear Twitter messages without the Internet (*BBC* 2011). Some recordings appeared on the Twitter account from Egyptians who learned about the service during the blackout, possibly via phone calls with friends and family outside of Egypt (York 2011c). This last point highlights an interesting 'two-way' phenomenon, whereby Egyptian activists were supported by the flow of information coming to them from abroad while simultaneously influencing international public opinion abroad through their coverage of the Egyptian uprising and the information they provided on it.

CONCLUDING REMARKS

The previous overview of both the Tunisian and Egyptian revolutions revealed a significant role for online citizen journalism in terms of boosting public will mobilization, accelerating the transition to democratization and increasing international awareness.

Howard et al. (2011, 13) found that people around the region Tweeted about local events and that "Stories of success and difficulty spread widely and created a kind of 'freedom meme'. The same meme travelled across the region through Facebook and YouTube, as inspiring images were captured by mobile phone and transmitted". Lynch (2012, 81–82) points to the "rapid diffusion of the Tunisian experience and the immediate crystallization of a shared narrative across the region" as "the truly unique contributions of the new media". It was assisted by Al-Jazeera, which "picked up on and carried the framing of the protests developed online, working with rather than against the social media narrative":

> What political scientists and experts from other regions missed was the real significance of the new Arab public sphere in unifying political space. Al-Jazeera, satellite television, Facebook, and Twitter bound together these national struggles into a single, coherent narrative of an Arab Intifada. (Lynch 2012, 124)

Furthermore, because of the Internet and citizen journalism, Arab governments are hindered because images of their actions will be broadcast and seen by "their citizens, their neighbors and their children and grandchildren" (Tufekci 2011) and, one can also add, by the rest of the world at large. In other words, it could be said that the ability of these new forms of communication to expose the wrongdoings of the ruling regimes and to demonstrate their brutality has led to a new era of accountability and responsibility on the part of these governments that did not exist before this information revolution. Today, no government can afford to totally ignore the power of public opinion on its own streets or to completely block its ears to the cries of its own people, thanks to the new media in the protestors' hands.

This signals the fact that this new communication revolution has succeeded in empowering the people in many parts of the Arab world and in providing them with new 'weapons', namely, their cell phones and computers, to engage in their simultaneous political and communication struggles against their authoritarian regimes and long-time dictators. We can contend that citizen journalism "is a promising new breed of news-making that has been championed by various scholars [for] granting ordinary citizens a novel, hands-on role" (Reich 2008, 739).

However, in hailing the role of citizen journalism in boosting the process of democratization and paving the way for political transformation, two important points have to be considered. First, it is important to avoid the simplistic approach of technological determinism, which privileges the tools of communication over the actors who are using them and the contexts within which they are used. This highlights the importance of adopting "'cyberrealist' thought about the prospects for electronic democracy", which "embrace[s] neither the hyperoptimistic technological determinism of the early 1990s nor the doomsday anxieties of the pessimistic backlash" (Shane 2004, xii). This requires adopting a balanced and even-handed approach in thinking about "what . . . democratic revitalization would require of new technologies in principle and what those technologies are likely to offer in practice" (Shane 2004, xii). In other words, this realistic, even-handed and balanced approach compels us to acknowledge the role of new modes of communication, such as citizen journalism, in acting as catalysts and boosters of change, while being fully aware of their limitations in bringing about this change given that they cannot have a magical effect and are not capable of enacting change without offline activism in the real world. Second, this requires acknowledging that "[. . .] digital space and digitization are not exclusive conditions that stand outside the nondigital. Digital space is embedded in the larger societal, cultural, subjective, economic, and imaginary structurations of lived experience and the systems within which we exist and operate" (Sassen 2004, 299).

This 'embedded media perspective', in turn, alerts us to the danger of uncritically borrowing Western theoretical concepts and models and applying them blindly to non-Western contexts, which could invite the dangers of distortion, misunderstanding and confusion, not to mention the privileging of Western cultural norms and standards, which poses the danger of ethnocentrism. This calls for the evaluation of each media system according to its own unique features, indigenous qualities and dynamic transformations, which are closely related to the historical, cultural, social and political contexts prevailing in each country.

Finally, it is safe to conclude that although there are many unpredictable outcomes in today's wave of Arab awakening and even more unanswered questions, one fact remains: The technology race will continue and so will the political and communication struggles in the rapidly changing Arab world. Online citizen journalism will continue to play a significant role in impacting both of these struggles, although the specific form of this process, the pace with which it functions, its positive and negative implications as well as its potentials and limitations will vary significantly based on the uniqueness of each country and the individuality of its media environment.

REFERENCES

Abdulla, Rasha A. 2007. *The Internet in the Arab World: Egypt and Beyond*. New York: Peter Lang Publishing.

Al Hussaini, Amira. 2010. "Tunisia: the Cry of Protestors Echoes around the World". *Global Voices*. Accessed 10 March 2011. <http://globalvoicesonline.org/2010/12/30/tunisia-the-cry-of-protestors-echoes-around-the-world/>.

———. 2011a. "Tunisia: 'Please tell the World Kasserine is Dying!'" *Global Voices*. Accessed 10 March 2011. <http://globalvoicesonline.org/2011/01/09/ tunisia-please-tell-the-world-kasserine-is-dying/>.

———. 2011b. "Tunisia: YouTubing the Uprising". *Global Voices*. Accessed 24 March 2011. <http://globalvoicesonline.org/2011/01/13/tunisia-youtubing-the-uprising/>.

———. 2011c. "Tunisia: Anonymous vs. Ammar—Who Wins the Battle of Censorship?" *Global Voices*. Accessed 10 March 2011. <http://globalvoicesonline.org/2011/01/03/tunisia-anonymous-vs-ammar-who-wins-the-battle-of-censorship/>.

Al Jazeera. 2010. "Tunisia Struggles to End Protests: Demonstrations Over Unemployment and Poor Living Conditions Continue Despite President's Warnings of Reprisals" [Article online]. *Al Jazeera English*. 29 December 2010. Accessed 10 March 2011. <http://english.aljazeera.net/news/africa/2010/12/20101229122733122341.html>.

Allan, Stuart, and Thorsen, Einar. 2009. "Introduction". In *Citizen Journalism: Global Perspectives*, edited by Allan, Stuart and Thorsen, Einar, 1–14. New York: Peter Lang.

Almiraat, Hisham. 2011a. "Tunisia, Algeria: the Revolution Will Not Be Televised". *Global Voice*. Accessed 10 March 2011. <http://globalvoicesonline.org/2011/01/10/tunisia-algeria-the-revolution-will-not-be-televised/>.

———. 2011b. "Tunisia: Slim Amamou Speaks About Tunisia, Egypt and the Arab World". Accessed 10 March 2011. <http://globalvoicesonline.org/2011/02/11/tunisia-slim-amamou-speaks-about-tunisia-egypt-and-the-arab-world/>.

Amnesty International. 2009. "Tunisia: Behind Tunisia's 'Economic Miracle': Inequality and Criminalization of Protest". Accessed 24 March 2009. <http://nawaat.org/portail/2009/06/18/tunisia-behind-tunisias-economic-miracle-inequality-and-criminalization-of-protest/>.

Atia, Tarek. 2006. "Paradox of the Free Press in Egypt". July 31, 2006. USEF (US-Egypt Friendship Society) Expert Panel, Washington D.C.

Atton, Chris and Hamilton, James F. 2008. *Alternative Journalism*. New Delhi: Sage.

Baker, Aryn. 2011. "How Egypt's Opposition Got a More Youthful Mojo". *Time*. Accessed 10 March 2011. <http://www.time.com/time/world/article/0,8599,2045446,00.html>.

BBC. 2011. "Egypt Protesters Use Voice Tweets: Google and Twitter Have Launched a Service Which Circumvents the Ban on Net Services in Egypt". Accessed 24 March 2011. <http://www.bbc.co.uk/news/technology-12332850>

Ben Mhenni, Lina. 2010. "Tunisia: Unemployed Man's Suicide Attempt Sparks Riots". Accessed 10 March 2011. <http://globalvoicesonline.org/2010/12/23/tunisia-unemployed-mans-suicide-attempt-sparks-riots/>.

Bounenni, Bassam. 2011. "The Limits of Silencing Tunisia". *Foreign Policy*. Accessed 10 March 2011. Available<http://mideast.foreignpolicy.com/posts/2011/01/12/the_limits_of_silencing_tunisia>.

Brisson, Zack, and Krontiris, Kate. 2012. *Tunisia: From Revolutions to Institutions*. The World Bank, Washington, D.C. Available from <http://www.infodev.org/en/Publication.1141.html>.

Chrisafis, Angelique, and Black, Ian. 2011. "Zine al-Abidine Ben Ali Forced to Flee Tunisia as Protesters Claim Victory". *The Guardian*. Accessed 10 March 2011. <http://www.guardian.co.uk/world/2011/jan/14/tunisian-president-flees-country-protests>.

Daily Mail. 2011. "How the Internet Refused to Abandon Egypt: Authorities Take Entire Country Offline, But Hackers Rally to Get the Message Out". Accessed 24 March 2011. http://www.dailymail.co.uk/news/article-1351904/Egypt-protests-Internet-shut-hackers-message-out.html.

Freeland, Chrystia. 2011. "The Middle East and the Group on Effect". *AFP*. Accessed 10 March 2011. <http://blogs.reuters.com/chrystia-freeland/2011/02/18/the-middle-east-and-the-groupon-effect/>.

Giglio, Mike. 2011. "The FaceBook Freedom Fighter". *Newsweek*. 21 February: 14–17.

Howard, Philip N. 2011. *The Digital Origins of Dictatorship and Democracy: Information Technology and Political Islam*. Oxford: Oxford University Press.

Howard, Philip N., Duffy, Aiden, Freelon, Deen, Hussain, Muzammil, Mari, Will, and Mazaid, Marwa. 2011. "Opening Closed Regimes: What Was the Role of Social Media During the Arab Spring?" *Project on Information Technology and Political Islam* Research Memo 2011.1. Seattle: University of Washington.

IBB Office of Research. 2011. "Research Memorandum: Media Consumption During the Uprising in Egypt". Broadcasting Board of Governors. Accessed 10 March 2011. <http://media.voanews.com/documents/Egypt_Flash_Final_sans_attitudes_TOC.doc>.

Ishani, Maryam. 2011. "The Hopeful Network." *Foreign Policy*. Accessed 24 March 2011. <http://www.foreignpolicy.com/articles/2011/02/07/the_hopeful_network>.

Joyce, Mary C. 2011. "A Media Narrative of the Tunisian Revolution." Accessed 24 March 2011. <http://www.meta-activism.org/2011/03/a-media-narrative-of-the-tunisian-revolution/>.

Khamis, Sahar. 2007. "The Role of New Arab Satellite Channels in Fostering Intercultural Dialogue: Can Al-Jazeera English Bridge the Gap?" In *New Media and the New Middle East,* edited by Seib, Philip, 39–52. New York: Palgrave Macmillan.

———. 2008. "Modern Egyptian Media: Transformations, Paradoxes, Debates and Comparative Perspectives". *Journal of Arab and Muslim Media Research* 1(3): 259–77.

Khamis, Sahar, and Sisler, Vit. 2010. "The New Arab 'Cyberscape': Redefining Boundaries and Reconstructing Public Spheres". *Communication Yearbook* 34: 277–316.

Khamis, Sahar, and Vaughn, Katherine. 2011. "Cyberactivism in the Egyptian Revolution: How Civic Engagement and Citizen Journalism Tilted the Balance". *Arab Media & Society* 14. Accessed 6 June 2012. <http://www.arabmediasociety.com/?article=769>.

Khibany, Gholam, and Sreberny, Annabelle. 2009. "The Iranian Story: What Citizens? What Journalism?" In *Citizen Journalism: Global Perspectives,* edited by Allan, Stuart and Thorsen, Einar, 121–132. New York: Peter Lang.

Lynch, Marc. 2012. *The Arab Uprising: The Unfinished Revolutions of the New Middle East.* PublicAffairs: Perseus Books Group. Kindle Edition. Retrieved from Amazon.com.

Madrigal, Alexis. 2011. "The Inside Story of How Facebook Responded to Tunisian Hacks". *The Atlantic.* Accessed 10 March 2011. <http://www.theatlantic.com/technology/archive/2011/01/the-inside-story-of-how-facebook-responded-to-tunisian-hacks/70044/>.

Nelson, Anne. 2008. "The Web 2.0 Revolution—Extended Version". *Carnegie Reporter.* Accessed 24 March 2008. <http://carnegie.org/publications/carnegie-reporter/single/view/article/item/71/>.

Noueihed, Lin. 2011. "Peddler's Martyrdom Launched Tunisia's Revolution". *Reuters.* Accessed 10 March 2011. <http://www.reuters.com/article/2011/01/20/us-tunisia-protests-bouazizi-idUSTRE70J1DJ20110120>.

Reich, Zvi. 2008. "How Citizens Create News Stories: The 'News Access' Problem Reversed". *Journalism Studies* 9(5): 739–58.

Reuters. 2011. "Timeline: Ben Ali Arrest Sought as Protests Continue". Accessed 10 March 2011. <http://www.reuters.com/article/2011/01/28/us-tunisia-protests-events-timeline-idUSTRE70P61V20110128>.

Rifai, Ryan. 2011. "Timeline: Tunisia's Civil Unrest: Chronicle of Nationwide Demonstrations Over the Country's Unemployment Crisis". *Al Jazeera.* Accessed 10 March 2011. <http://english.aljazeera.net/indepth/spotlight/tunisia/2011/01/201114142223827361.html>.

Ryan, Yasmine. 2011. "How Tunisia's Revolution Began: From Day One, the People of Sidi Bouzid Broke Through the Media Blackout to Spread Word of Their Uprising". *Al Jazeera.* Accessed 24 March 2011. <http://english.aljazeera.net/indepth/features/2011/01/2011126121815985483.html>.

Salmon, Charles T., Fernandez, Laleah, and Post, Lori A. 2010. "Mobilizing Public Will Across Borders: Roles and Functions of Communication Processes and Technologies". *Journal of Borderlands Studies* 25(3&4): 159–70.

Sassen, Saskia. 2004. "Sited Materialities with Global Span". In *Society Online: The Internet in Context,* edited by Howard, Philip N. and Jones, Steve, 295–306. California: Sage Publications.

Seib, Philip. 2007. "New Media and Prospects for Democratization". In *New Media and the New Middle East,* edited by Seib, Philip, 1–18. New York: Palgrave Macmillan.

Seibt, Sébastian. 2011. "Egyptians Find Loophole to Government Web Blackout". *France 24.* Accessed 24 March 2011. <http://www.france24.com/en/20110201-speak-to-tweet-egypt-twitter-google-join-protesters-internet-blackout-mubarak>.

Shane, Peter M. 2004. "Introduction". In *Democracy Online: The Prospects for Political Renewal through the Internet,* edited by Shane, Peter, xi–xx. New York: Routledge.

Sigal, Ivan. 2011. "Egypt: Information Getting out Despite Information Blackout." *Global Voices.* Accessed 24 March 2011. <http://globalvoicesonline.org/2011/01/28/egypt-information-getting-out-despite-information-blackout/>.

Todd, Tony. 2011. "Blogger Wins Freedom of Speech Prize". *France 24.* Accessed 10 March 2011. <http://www.france24.com/en/20110310-tunisian-blogger-awarded-freedom-speech-prize>.

Tufekci, Zeynep. 2011. "As Egypt Shuts Off the Net: Seven Theses on Dictator's Dilemma". *Technosociology.* Accessed 10 March 2011. <http://technosociology.org/>.

Ulrich, Claire. 2010. "Tunisia: 'We Are Not Afraid Anymore!'" *Global Voices*. Accessed 10 March 2011. <http://globalvoicesonline.org/2010/12/31/tunisia-we-are-not afraid anymore/>.

York, Jillian. 2011a. "How Are Protestors in Egypt Using Social Media?" Accessed 10 March 2011. <http://jilliancyork.com/2011/01/27/how-are-protestors-in-egypt -using-social-media/>.

———. 2011b. "Critique of Media Coverage of Egypt Is a Strong Case for Twit-ter". Accessed 24 March 2011. <http://jilliancyork.com/2011/02/04/critique-of -media-coverage-of-egypt-is-a-strong-case-for-twitter/>.

———. 2011c. "Egypt: a Voice in the Blackout, Thanks to Google and Twitter". *Global Voices*. Accessed 24 March 2011. <http://globalvoicesonline.org/2011/02/01/ egypt-a-voice-in-the-blackout-thanks-to-google-and-twitter/>.

Zayani, Mohamed. 2011. "Social Media and the Reconfiguration of Political Action in Revolutionary Tunisia". *Democracy & Society* 8.2: 2–4.

Zclaky, Ehab, Eid, Gamal, Sami, Sally, and Ziada, Dalia. 2006. *Implacable Adver-saries: Arab Governments and the Internet*. Cairo: The Arabic Network for Hu-man Rights Information.

Zuckerman, Ethan. 2011. Editorial. "The first Twitter revolution? Not so fast. The Internet Can Take Some Credit for Toppling Tunisia's Government, But Not All of It". *Foreign Policy*. 14 January. Accessed 10 March 2011. <http://www.foreignpolicy. com/articles/2011/01/14/the_first_twitter_revolution?page=0,0&wpisrc =obnetwork>.

10 J-Blogging and the 'Agenda Cutting' Phenomenon in Egypt

Nagwa Abdel Salam Fahmy

INTRODUCTION

The speed and complexity of the Web 2.0 evolution has opened the door for Egyptian activists to express their opinions and to be heard by a large number of Internet users despite the low level of democracy in their country. The active Egyptian Internet user is benefiting from this technology in many ways, including blogging. The chapter focuses specifically on the role of blogs in reporting stories that were 'cut' from traditional media outlets.

From a 'technicist' approach, blogging can be defined as frequently updating websites using a personal content management system, with material posted in reverse chronological order that consist of text, photos and other multimedia content, with regular date-stamped entries, links to related materials and an accessible archive to old posts (Harper 2005; Gill 2004). The normative-functional approach, on the other hand, classifies blogs as personal journals that individuals use to write about different topics of interest. They often attract a large or small number of net users allowing them to post their comments and even have conversations with other users (Treem and Thomas 2010; Gil de Zuniga et al. 2011).

In the context of journalism, the phenomenon of blogging has attracted a number of researchers. Singer (2005) observes that blogs written by journalists are more likely to be *news digests:* short and snappy items calling attention to some aspects of politics or civic affairs, often with links to other more detailed media content. Lowrey (2006) similarly observes that most of the content on journalists' blogs is commentary on news stories. Blogging as a phenomenon is thus considered a 'new' genre of journalism and a part of the news ecosystem. An increasing number of professional journalists (especially independent journalists) are participating in this phenomenon, and their blogs are known as j-blogs (Chu 2012).

Gill (2004) further contends that a blog can be considered a form of journalism practice that does not need production or distribution processes or any kind of investment. Bloggers simply need computer access and a hosting service to report their observations and analyse events in a meaningful way (Lasica 2001). The goals and motivations behind blogging and traditional journalism practices are essentially the same. They all seek information, comment on events, participate in a community and document daily life and self-expression. In addition, Lasica (2001) further conceives j-blogs as central to collecting, reporting, sorting, analysing and disseminating news and information. Harper (2005) sheds light on the importance of accuracy in journalism and observes that j-blogs often reject the mainstream media's concern with fairness and objectivity as they usually present the journalist's personal point of view.

In an authoritarian regime—like Egypt during the Mubarak era—professional journalists can be deprived of their right to work in any news platform when state security officers blacklist them, so blogging became an important news platform for attaining their audience as their blogs were not monitored or controlled by state security, and j-blogs became inevitable tools for expressing themselves and communicating news and information.

To gather data for this study, I conducted a qualitative analysis of selected news items that were not reported or were 'cut' from the media agenda in 2009. The 'cut news' resurfaced on one of the most popular Egyptian j-blogs, *El Wa'y el Masry*, or the "Egyptian Conscious", written by a journalist blogger Wael Abbas.

Thus, seven news stories were selected for analysis from the *Al Wa'y Al Masry* blog. The stories were selected using several criteria, including the fact that they were about domestic issues that were spread among Egyptians for their political significance and were posted exclusively on this blog. The aim of this qualitative analysis was to provide a comprehensive analysis of reporting tools, frames, linkage and comments that emerged while covering news stories.

To illuminate the role of journalist blogs in Egypt, we will first create a deep understanding of the blogging phenomenon in Egypt, its role to promote political reform and social movements in Egypt and its impact on spreading an alternative kind of news that was never published in the mainstream news media. The next part of this chapter will focus specifically on several untold news stories that were published on the *Al Wa'y Al Masry* blog to provide evidence of the blog's role in getting those news stories to the surface.

A BRIEF CONTEXTUAL BACKGROUND OF BLOGGING IN EGYPT

The blogging movement in Egypt has been growing since 2004 when active political groups began to express their opposition to government reforms. They organized demonstrations and boycotts as well as criticized governmental policies and corruption and helped to develop civic society in Egypt. The practice can be seen as an evolving phenomenon that can be considered a weapon against the restricted flow of information enforced by the state to control the mass media. This expresses a shift in the media's influence on society as people now take information from alternative sources rather than from the traditional ones. Political blogs reflect what people on the street are saying and suffering.

The first decade of the 21st century was characterized by increased Internet use in Egypt, with Internet access being approximately US $5 per month, which is much cheaper than in any other Arab country (AKR 2009). In Egypt 16 percent of the population accesses the Internet (14.5 million people); this percentage rose in 2010 to about 29.5 percent (23.02 million Internet users in Egypt (Egypt ICT indicator, 2011). As of 2009, there were 160,000 bloggers, which represents 30 percent of blogs in the Arab world. Significantly, according to a *Daily News Egypt Newspaper* report on 31 July 2008, 68 percent of these blogs use Arabic language, and 20 percent use both Arabic and English (Michael 2009). From the 160,000 Egyptian blogs, about 48.3 percent are considered 'active', and most of the bloggers are between the ages of 20 to 35 years old (Etling et al. 2009). This represents a younger, well-educated net generation that use technological tools to spread their influence on Egyptian society. Nowadays, the Egyptian blogging community is more than a news source; it represents an alternative public space and acts as a bridge between events on the streets and the Internet (Fahmi 2009).

On the blogs, Egyptian Internet users can freely express their comments on everyday life and current events in Egypt. Some of these blogs have become well known and influential in the political scene. They create an interactive community by posting news updates and asking for user comments. They also benefit from the fact that there is no law that governs or controls bloggers.

It is in this context that journalist bloggers use their blogs as a tool to break through censorship and the highly conservative pro-government mainstream media in Egypt. They use their blogs to circumvent political obstacles and directly publish their news stories as well as build a direct relationship with their readers.

It is important to note that Egypt has been ruled by emergency law from 1981 until May 2012, a year after President Mubarak stepped down and the Supreme Council of the Armed Forces took power. For three decades since the assassination of former President Sadat in October 1981, emergency law was imposed on Egypt for one year and was renewed annually until May 2012. According to the emergency law, the security forces in Egypt have the power to monitor, arrest and detain suspects for an undefined period of time without trials. It was a green card for all governmental abuses of power and violations of human rights by state security forces. Moreover, in 2010 Egypt was labelled "one of the enemies of Internet" by the Paris-based Press Freedom Watchdog because, among other reasons, many bloggers had been jailed indefinitely (RWB 2009). Given the rapid rise of Egyptian political blogs, it is important to understand their role and explain the motivation of the bloggers. This chapter therefore aims to help us better understand

Egyptian j-bloggers and their role during Mubarak's authoritarian regime. It specifically aims to explore the role of j-blogs in reporting stories that were 'cut' or ignored by traditional media outlets during the late Mubarak period as bloggers were largely motivated by the desire to tell news stories which were overlooked by the mainstream media.

ACTIVE BLOGGING IN THE CONTEXT OF 'AGENDA CUTTING'

The constant growth of literature on agenda-setting research began with a study by McCombs and Shaw for the 1968 US presidential election, which drew a link between the media and the formation of the public agenda (Tai 2009). This approach shows that the news media coverage was beginning to have a significant influence on the public agenda. The agenda-setting process includes aspects from the media agenda, public agenda and policy agenda as well as the interrelationship among these aspects. How the story is covered and reported or not covered at all, the phenomenon of 'agenda cutting', arises from the media's agenda formation or building.

Although agenda-setting research usually accepts the media agenda as a given without considering the process by which the agenda is constructed, a variety of factors, including the individual personalities of those involved in reporting a story, news values, the organizational culture of a media outlet or other external political, economic or social influences affect the decision to publish news stories (Rogers and Dearing 2007). These factors set the news agenda and keep certain issues off the national agenda by ignoring them or cutting them from the news. This connects with the phenomenon of agenda cutting.

Colistra (2008) argues that agenda cutting is not simply the opposite of agenda setting; rather, agenda cutting occurs as a result of more complex forces which have different motives and intentions for keeping an event away from the public eye. According to Wober (2001), there are at least three reasons for omitting news: logistical constraints, journalistic prejudices and internal and external influences (Colistra 2012).

The phenomenon of 'agenda-cutting' was raised for the first time in a Wober (2001) article when he mentioned the variety of ways and instances in which a news topic finds itself low on a news agenda or even out of it. Lately, few scholars were interested in it due to the difficulties inherent in any study that aims to uncover news stories that went unreported despite the fact that they had all the elements that would make them newsworthy (Colistra 2008). In an earlier article, Colistra (2006) observes that "There are difficulties with studying and theorizing the agenda-cutting approach, as it is a challenge to examine and measure instances of agenda-cutting because this means to measure something not presented in the mainstream news media".

It is important to distinguish between agenda cutting and censorship; censorship is a top-down exclusion of news due to strict orders from authorities, and journalists are obliged to omit specific news from their news agenda. Agenda cutting, on the other hand, arises when journalists or key officers overlook specific news stories. This is established by either "placing an item low on the news agenda or removing it from the agenda once it is there or completely ignoring it so it never makes it onto the news agenda in the first place" (Colistra 2006). Writing about the 2004 US Presidential election, Jae Kook Lee (2007) found that political blogs had an influence similar to that of the mainstream media. A similar observation is made by Reese et al. (2007), who describe the relationship between weblogs and traditional journalism as complementary. Other researchers have reported a complex, symbiotic relationship between mainstream media coverage and political blogs as each tends to have an immediate impact on the other (Wallsten 2007). A study by Kulikova and Perlmutter (2007) on Kyrgyzstan's 'Tulip Revolution' found that bloggers were a rich source of information not available from the traditional media outlets. However, this finding could be explained by the political climate in which the bloggers practice. Kulikova and Perlmutter (ibid) further argue that bloggers play a more significant role in a dictatorship.

Moving ignored and devalued information from the margins to the mainstream news media is common in networked information societies (Rutigliano 2008). Rutigliano observes that bloggers could generate widespread attention for information largely ignored by state-related media institutions, thereby helping to create a public sphere. In this sense, blogs can promote digital democracy and defend human rights. As Mckee (2005) argues, everyday access to the Internet for everyone in a society makes it a vital way to communicate information and ideas. The Internet can thus be used as a virtual space where people can be informed and interact.

Cunha (2009) supports some aspects of the Internet's role in postmodern societies, arguing that it can empower political movements and provide a good foundation for a battle of ideas. Correspondingly, Moyo (2011) considers Zimbabwean j-blogs as an alternative online media platform that publishes unfiltered raw stories and news about the hard conditions of their life and politics.

Rong (2009), however, proffers a contradictory finding by considering online discussion in an authoritarian regime as a kind of verbal conflict that does not encourage citizens to actively participate in public issues as they are talking to their peers, so their voice is not heard by policy-makers—the people that really matter. However, applying the Habermasian Public Sphere theory in a networked environment forms sub-systems of communication loops. The characteristics of this new communication ecosystem relate to the fluidity and increasingly greater mutual influence between similar sub-systems of communication. (Friedlang et al. 2006). This concept makes us think about the role of blogs in creating public awareness and involvement in local issues that can mobilize ordinary citizens and therefore push their community towards democratisation.

EGYPTIAN BLOGGERS FOR NEW SOCIAL MOVEMENT

Blogs in Egypt flourished and gained popularity around 2005. Many political and human rights activists started using blogs to express their opinion and opposition to governmental policies that coincide with numerous opposition street movements in Egypt. Hence, since 2005, blogs have been considered a form of digital opposition (Samir 2010).

New social movement theorists argue that activists depending on Information Communication Technology (ICT) are usually early adopters of new technologies, and they use the technologies to share messages and express their opinions (Huang 2009). El Gody (2009) suggests that new media (including blogs) allow ordinary people in Arab countries to actively participate in live discussions and debate issues that concern their daily life, therefore breaking all traditional political taboos. For the Egyptian case, new social movement activists have shifted their opposition online where they focus on politics, economics, human rights and social issues that have been overlooked for decades by Egypt's mainstream media. The issues covered include torture in police stations and the harassment of women in the streets. Bloggers provide detailed descriptions of street protests and even post video footage of incidents.

They have initiated a new Egyptian battle for democracy and political reform, using blogs as a way to engage a new generation of Internet users who are active in social movements. The blogs are used to generate public interest and to reinforce citizen power and democracy. This interactive, electronic citizen-journalism is considered by Internet users to be more truthful, reliable and revealing than the mainstream media. Nowadays, the Egyptian blogosphere is more than a news resource. Fahmi (2009) agrees with this view and argues that the Egyptian blogosphere is an alternative urban hub that acts as an interface between events in the streets and the Internet, thereby facilitating a sense of community. This active blogging wave interacts with other social networks like Facebook and Twitter and makes it possible for many voiceless activists to express their opinion and mobilize supporters.

In her early study about blogs interested in current events, Gill (2004) examines the social influence of blogs by tracing how their discourses influence and shape the news agenda and news stories of major news outlets. Other researchers suggest that blogs portray the social and psychological characteristics of their authors as they tend to express their identity, share their own experiences and voice their thoughts while they interact with others and create an online community by using 21st century digital communication technology (Guark and Antonijevic 2008).

In their study, Kahn and Kellner (2004) suggest that online activists use blogs to promote their own agenda and interests. They report stories reflecting their community on a wide variety of topics although usually focused on local events. They post photographs of their community, links to survey polls and other outside content (Carpenter 2007). Hagan (2009) reports that the positive impact of the blogosphere as a movement is that it transforms passive readers into active users. He further contends that the blogosphere movement organized itself in response to what Internet users saw as a credibility crisis among mainstream media, whether state or privately owned.

On the other hand, political blogs in Egypt demonstrate the power they have to affect the news agenda and even events as at times, bloggers act as freelance, grassroots reporters and fact-checkers. Egyptian blogs are sometimes used to feed stories to the mainstream media (the 2006 case of Emad el Kabir is one well-known example). Bloggers usually reveal alternative views of news stories and events presented by mainstream media. They are no longer simply observers of events; rather, they shape how these stories are reported and perceived by the public.

In a number of recent studies about Arab bloggers, researchers note that bloggers are able to contribute to shaping public opinion during politically charged moments. As a result, many were subject to retaliation from state police, and by the end of 2008, three bloggers had been jailed for their blog activities (Hamdy 2009; Etling et al. 2009). Otterman's (2007) research on the Egyptian blogosphere notes that bloggers are spreading a culture of disobedience by raising awareness of the difficulties the Egyptian society faces. They also adapt to newer Internet technologies such as Facebook, Flickr and Twitter, using them to promote their ideas for political change and reform.

Activist-bloggers consider their blogs a virtual extension of 'the street' as they use their blogs to mobilize supporters and to demonstrate their opposition and anger towards authorities. They are considered role models for a generation of young Egyptians, who are so impressed with their courage that they have become folk heroes to other young activists. Levinson reports in a *Christian Science Monitor* article on 24 August 2005 that Internet activists in Egypt used to merely rely on blogs to find out the time and place of demonstrations and to debate the effectiveness of opposition strategies. Lately, they benefit from a multiplatform of Social Media Networks (SMN) to express their opposition. They extend their communities by linking to and from other networks using Facebook, Twitter, YouTube and Flicker, among others. This allows them to empower their collective action and reach out for more supporters.

As noted earlier, easy and inexpensive Internet access in Egypt facilitates the development of social movements by reaching people everywhere, making people aware of what is happening and helping them to make informed decisions. Blogs fit into this context by discussing and disseminating information on political, economic and social issues. Egyptian bloggers form a well-organized community whose members often meet offline, forming friendships and networks that go beyond the virtual world. According to Otterman's (2007) study, some have been subjected to police harassment and detention. A Human Rights Watch report described the systematic arrest and harassment of peaceful political activism (HRWR 2008, 2009).

A good example of this is the arrest of a group of political activist-bloggers who travelled to Nag Hamadi in Upper Egypt to give condolences to the family of a Christian Copt who was killed on Christmas Eve in January 2010. Other examples of such harassment include when activist-blogger Wael Abbas was sentenced to six months in prison after he was accused of damaging his neighbour's (a police officer) Internet cable (ANHRI 2010). Also, Ahmed Doma was imprisoned for a year after visiting Gaza in 2009 without permission from the authorities and was released in February 2010 (ANHRI 2010). Another example is that of Karim Amer, who was jailed for four years on 7 November 2006 for criticizing Egypt's President Hosni Mubarak and the Al-Azhar religious institution (CPJ 2010). Similarly, blogger Massad abu Fagr was imprisoned in October 2008 for criticizing both Christianity and Islam and was denied visitation. As noted in *Egypt News* on 17 February 2010, Mohamed Khalaf, a blogger, was also sentenced to one year of hard labour in December 2009 for criticizing the Egyptian court system.

Another incident in this crackdown on Internet activism was the arrest of an activist who created a Facebook group ('6th of April') calling all workers to go on strike on 6 April 2008 and for a demonstration on Mubarak's birthday in May 2008. Tens of thousands of people joined the group, and the woman who set it up, Esraa Abd al Fattah, was arrested. These incidents collectively demonstrate how Internet activists transform into street activists in Egypt. It is obvious that state security and intelligence officials during Mubarak's tenure began to monitor Internet activism, seeking to prevent any potential form of mobilizing people or manifesting opposition online. From the above, a question arises: to what extent can j-blogs facilitate and expose the 'agenda cutting' phenomenon? To address this question, the next section focuses on a sample of stories carried on *Al Wa'y Al Masry's* Blog. The stories provide good examples of 'agenda cutting' in news.

REVEALING AGENDA CUTTING CASES IN *AL WA'Y AL MASRY'S* BLOG

From the *Al Wa'y Al Masry* blog, we can provide a comprehensive analysis of the reporting tools, frames, linkages and comments that emerged in the coverage of particular news stories. The stories were selected using several criteria: they were all focused on domestic issues and posted exclusively on Abbas's blog, *Al Wa'y El Masry.*

Abbas is an independent blogger and journalist who started his journalistic career at one of the opposition party newspapers, *El Ahaly,* and as a freelancer for international magazines. He started blogging in 2004 in an attempt to give his readers information about what really happens in Egypt, especially issues about government repression, political protests and sexual harassment in Egypt. At first he published his articles in Modern Standard Arabic, but now he writes in the Egyptian dialect, often using very vulgar and insulting words, especially when referring to the police. Abbas's blog became one of the most well known Egyptian blogs after he published images of alleged attacks on demonstrators during the 2005 referendum on the constitutional amendment. In 2006, he also published videos of the mass sexual harassment of women in central Cairo during an Islamic holiday.

The most important scandal he disclosed was in 2006 when he posted videos of a bus driver, Emad El Kabir, being sexually abused at a police station. The video spread all over the national and international news media (Abbas 2006).

The overall posts on the *Al Wa'y El Masry* blog during 2009 totalled 35. The number of posts varied from one month to another. These posts received 1189 comments, most of which were pseudonymous. The primary focus of most comments is on political news stories that reveal scandalous remarks on the Egyptian political scene.

The case studies included in this chapter were of exclusive news stories published in 2009 on Abbas's blog. The stories are examples of how particular news stories were 'cut' from the agenda of the mainstream media. Torture and police abuse were the main exclusive stories published on *Al Wa'y Al Masri*. On 23 January 2009, footage was posted showing a police officer violently attacking and arresting a citizen, who was then taken away to the police station. The blog posting recorded the day and time of this incident and prompted 36 user comments on this story. Some comments on this story were excusing the police for the brutality and even suggested that the victim could have been a thief who deserved to be beaten. Other comments considered it as proof of systematic police violence (Abbas 2009).

Another news story which was framed as a torture incident, published on 8 February 2009, was entitled "Another Emad El Kabir tragedy in Ain Shams police station". The 40-second footage portrays a sexual assault on a man and is preceded by a warning that the footage is graphic. The story cites the time and place of the incident, the names of the police officers who ordered the attack as well as the source of the footage, activist-blogger Sameh El Arousy. There were 81 comments on this story, including one which stated that the story was picked up and published on February 9th by the Egyptian newspaper *7th Day*. Another comment considered this story to be an unbelievable act of violence, suggesting that activists should organize a demonstration against this kind of violence. This quote was an example of those comments: "To be honest, i dont know should we be with that victim or against him yes he must be there for a reason, but no matter what the reason is, they cant deal with him that way" (Abbas 2009).

On 26 May 2009, Wael Abbas reported on his blog that Sameh El Arousy had to flee the country as the police were threatening him and his wife for publishing and distributing the video (Abbas 2009). Wael Abbas published another video clip framed as police torture, on 12 August 2009, taking place in a police station in Port-Said (Abbas 2009). On 9 March 2009, Abbas published a story about the Egyptian army cadets who organized an attack on a police station, seeking revenge for alleged abuse by the police on one of their colleagues. The story was accompanied by seven video clips which ranged from 26 seconds to six minutes in which the cadets pelted with stones and electric guns a police station and a car deemed to belong to the district police chief.

Through this story, Abbas reveals the state of chaos that dominates the relationship between the Egyptian Army and Police. The blog also posted links to other news agencies reporting this story (bbc.com, bbc.arabic, Associated Press, euronews.com, a Spanish news agency and others). Abbas's story also included a statement by an anonymous Egyptian news editor who said he received an order not to publish any details of this incident. More than 70 comments from blog readers show their credibility and clear appreciation for the disclosure of this news story (Abbas 2009).

On 24 December 2009, Abbas further posted a story and copies of Interior Ministry documents ordering the tapping of a key Egyptian political figure's phone as there was speculation that this person intended to participate in the 2011 presidential elections. The Interior Ministry officially denied the story and initiated an investigation into the documents that ordered the phone tapping, but the findings of the investigation were never reported. This story attracted 33 comments on the blog and spurred a national discussion on who ordered the tapping of key Egyptian figures' phones. Some of the comments on the news story appreciated the publication of the documents but questioned the ability of a blogger to penetrate the highly secured Interior Minister's offices and to photocopy documents (Abbas 2009).

Another exclusive news story published on Abbas's blog (17 August 2009) came from an ex-policeman and Egyptian writer living in the United States, Omar Afifi. He wrote that during President Mubarak's 2009 visit to Washington, his son, Gamal and his wife took a shopping trip to a famous jewelry store while two Egyptian ministers waited for them outside. This story attracted many comments that reflected belief in the story's credibility. For example, one comment read as follows:

> The most important issue is that Egyptian tax victims will not pay his hotel costs. To shop at Chanel is okay as long as he is rich man ya Wael, but to keep two ministers waiting outside is kind of shameless. The newspapers in Egypt will never dare to publish a single word about him. Do you remember what happened to our friend in Dostoor newspaper :). (Abbas 2009)

CONCLUDING REFLECTIONS

This chapter has focused on the role played by blogs in the publication of news ignored by the mainstream Egyptian media under the strict dictatorial Mubarak regime. The chapter examines Wael Abbas's 2009 j-blog posts to demonstrate how blogs work in opposition to expose the 'agenda-cutting' of mainstream media by reporting on stories not reported elsewhere. These stories include human rights violations, torture and corruption. In addition, j-blogs reveal and criticize top government personnel such as the military and the president's family. They help prompt public discussion and awareness on the news 'cut' from the public domain, thus performing a watchdog role of sorts. The blogs represent an independent voice that does not need governmental permission to express opinion and to break all political taboos in Egyptian society.

J-Bloggers thus use their blogs to represent news that is deliberately avoided by traditional media. They use their own news sources, documents, photos, footage and hyperlinks to other blogs and news sites that support their news, giving evidence of their credibility, accuracy and news exclusivity. The comments on the blog *Al Wa'y Al Masri* could be seen as some form of a debate. The first party believes the blogs' news is accurate, reliable and trustworthy, whereas the second party could be considered pro-government citizens who tend to view this blog as inaccurate. The pro-government party sometimes goes far in insulting the blogger and other commentators considered as anti-government. This finding supports Etling at al. (2009), who conclude that blogs engage the public sphere and give significance to debates between the blogs' commentators.

We can conclude that Egyptian j-blogs contribute positively to the disclosure of news stories that are 'cut' from the mainstream media. Although there is no clear censorship on journalism practices in Egypt, Egyptian journalists are trained to manage a self-censorship that controls the reporting of anti-governmental issues. Not only do j-blogs bring public attention by reporting the 'hidden' news stories, but they also add diversity to the voices and present another view of the Egyptian political scene. J-blogs thus help enlarge the margin of freedom of expression for the new and traditional media in Egypt. They further support public concern for domestic issues.

Unfiltered Egyptian blogs during the last period of the Mubarak regime in 2005–2011 could be considered a platform for free discussion about internal issues. They also facilitate the spread of information and contribute to the promotion of political reform. The study finds that bloggers use many strategies to vouch for the credibility of the news they publish. They provide documents, use video clips sometimes recorded on mobile phones and provide links to other sources that confirm their stories.

Activists or political bloggers are a powerful and effective medium that raises awareness, spreads information and organizes discussion. The Egyptian blogosphere plays an effective role in reporting news stories not reported elsewhere. They influence public opinion framing of issues related to government abuse as the blogs are considered the main source of such information. This study provides evidence that supports the perceived role of the blogosphere as a primary actor in investigating news events.

The new media not only enable ordinary people to set their own media agendas but also help them to connect with other people who care about similar issues. Nevertheless, blogs seem to hold an uncertain level of credibility among their readers as reflected in their comments. Blogs can often turn into a battlefield where bloggers and blog users utilize vulgar language when arguing and defending their ideas.

Despite methodological problems of studying 'agenda-cutting', this study shows that blogs play an important role in the communication systems of authoritarian states by counteracting the 'cutting' of news stories considered sensitive from the mainstream media. In this way, blogs represent an alternative media that blog users rely on for information about real life in their communities.

REFERENCES

Abbas, Wael. 2006. "New Video for Police Crossing the Line". Accessed 20 January 2010. http://misrdigital.blogspirit.com/archive/2006/11/index.html [In Arabic].
———. 2009a. New Video for Police Attack to Citizen in Street. [Web log message]. Available http://misrdigital.blogspirit.com/archive/2009/01/index.html [In Arabic] (Accessed November 17, 2009).
———. 2009b. "Another Emad El Kabir tragedy in Ain Shams Police Station". Accessed 20 November 2009. http://misrdigital.blogspirit.com/archive/2009/02/index.html.
———. 2009c. "Jimmy Buy Jewelry to Doja". Accessed 20 November 2009. http://misrdigital.blogspirit.com/archive/2009/08/index.html [In Arabic].
———. 2009d. "Noor, Sabahy, El Baradey Without Comment". Accessed 28 December 2009. http://misrdigital.blogspirit.com/archive/2009/12/index.html [In Arabic].
———. 2009e. Scandal of Cadets Attack to Mayo Police station. Accessed 12 November 2009. http://misrdigital.blogspirit.com/archive/2009/03/index.html [In Arabic].
———. 2009f. "Video for Torture at Port-Said". Accessed 20 November 2009. http://misrdigital.blogspirit.com/archive/2009/08/index.html [In Arabic].
———. 2009g. "What Sameh El Arousy?" Accessed 17 November 2009. http://misrdigital.blogspirit.com/archive/2009/05/index.html [In Arabic].
ANHRI (The Arabic Network for Human Right Information). 2010. "Arab Bloggers Union Welcome Doma Release". Accessed 10 December 2010. http://wwwanhri.net/egypt/makal/2010/pr0223–2.shtml [In Arabic].
AKR (Arab Knowledge Report). 2009. "Towards Productive Intercommunication for Knowledge". Accessed 10 February 2010. http://www.mbrfoundation.ae/English/Pages/AKR2009.aspx.
Armstrong, Cory L. and Collins, Steve J. 2009. "Reaching Out: Newspaper Credibility Among Young Adult Readers". *Mass Communication and Society* 12(1): 97–114.
Carpenter, Serena. 2007. "US Online Citizen Journalism and Online Newspaper stories: A content Analyses of their Quality and Value". Doctoral Dissertation, Michigan State University.
Chaffee, Steven and Metzger, Miriam. 2001. "The End of Mass Communication?" *Mass Communication & Society* 4(4): 365–379.

Chu, Donna. 2012. "Interpreting News Values in J-blogs: Case Studies of Journalist Bloggers in Post-1997 Hong Kong". *Journalism: Theory, Practice & Criticism* 13(3): 371–387.

Colistra, Rita F. 2006. "Agenda Cutting: New Theoretical Developments In The Agenda-Building And Agenda-Setting Processes". Paper presented at The 4th International Symposium Communication in the Millennium. Accessed 10 April 2010. cim.anadolu.edu.tr/Archives/2006.

———. 2008. "Reporter Perceptions of Influences on Media Content : A Structural Equation Model of the Agenda—and Frame-Building and Agenda-Cutting Processes in the Television Industry". Doctoral Dissertation, University of North Carolina at Chapel Hill.

———. 2012. "Shaping and Cutting the Media Agenda: Television Reporters' Perceptions of Agenda-and Frame- Building and Agenda-Cutting Influence". *Journalism & Communication Monographs* 14(2): 85–146.

Committee to Protect Journalists. 2010. "Attacks on the Press 2009. A World Wide Survey by the Committee to Protect Journalists". Accessed 10 December 2010. http://cpj.org/AOP09.pdf. Pp:207–210

Cunha, M. Jonathan, 2009. "Deliberating Public Spheres: How Does Net Neutrality Enable Democracy?" Masters Thesis, Northeastern University.

Dearing, James W. and Rogers, Everett M. 1996. *Communication Concepts 6: Agenda-Setting*. Thousand Oaks: Sage.

Egypt ICT Indicator. 2011. "The future of the Internet Economy in Egypt. A statistical profile". Accessed 10 June 2012. http://www.egyptictindicators.gov.eg/ar/Pages/default_ar.aspx.

El Gody, Ahmed. 2009. "The Image of the United States in the Arab Blogosphere". Paper presented at the annual meeting of the International Communication Association. Accessed 10 March 2010. http://www.allacademic.com/meta/p301249_index.html.

Etling, Bruce, Kelly, John, Faris, Rob and Palfrey, John. 2009. "Mapping the Arabic Blogosphere: Politics, Culture, and Dissent". Internet & Democracy Case Study Series, Berkman Center Research Publication No. 2009–06. Accessed 10 March 2010. http://cyber.law.harvard.edu/sites/cyber.law.harvard.edu/files/Mapping_the_Arabic_Blogosphere_0.pdf.

Fahmi, Wael S. 2009. "Blogger's Street Movement and the Right to the City. (Re)claiming Cairo's real and virtual spaces of freedom". *Environment & Urbanization* 21(1): 89–107.

Friedland, Lewis A., Hove, Thomas and Rojas, Hernando, 2006. "The Networked Public Sphere". *The public* 13(4): 5–26.

Gil de Zuniga, Homero et al. 2011. "Blogging as a journalistic practice: A model linking perception, motivation, and behavior". *Journalism: Theory, Practice & Criticism* 12(5): 586–606.

Gill, Kathy E. 2004. "How can we Measure the Influence of the Blogosphere". In WWW 2004 Workshop on the Weblogging Ecosystem: Aggregation, Analysis and Dynamics. Accessed10 December 2010. http://faculty.washington.edu/kegill/pub/gill_blogosphere_www2004.pdf.

Guark, Laura J. and Antonijevic, Smiljana. 2008. "The Psychology of Blogging: You, Me, and Everyone in Between". *American Behavioral Scientist* 52(1): 60–68.

Hagan, Stephen P. 2009. "The Progressive Blogosphere as E-Movement: Identity, Mobilization and The User-Based-Model". Doctoral Dissertation, Southern Illinois University Carbondale.

Hamdy, Naila. 2009. "Arab Citizen Journalism in Action: Challenging Mainstream Media, Authorities and Media Laws". *Westminster Paper in Communication and Culture* 6(1): 92–112.

Harper, Christopher, 2005. "Blogging and Journalistic Practice". Paper presented at the Fourth Media in Transition Conference. Cambridge: Massachusetts Institute of Technology. Accessed 10 March 2010. http://web.mit.edu/commforum/mit4/papers/harper.pdf.

Huang, Bi Y. 2009. "Analyzing a Social Movement's use of Internet: Resource Mobilization, New Social Movement Theories and the Case of Falun Gong". Doctoral Dissertation, Indiana University.

HRWR (Human Rights Watch Report). World Report 2008. Accessed 10 March 2010. http://www.hrw.org/legacy/wr2k8/pdfs/egypt.pdf. Pp. 265–271

———. World Report 2009. Accessed 10 March 2010. http://www.hrw.org/sites/default/files/related_material/egypt.pdf. Pp. 454–459.

Kahn, Richard and Kellner, Douglas. 2004. "New Media and Internet Activism". *New Media & Society* 6(1): 87–95.

Kenix, Linda J. 2009. "Blogs as Alternative". *Journal of Computer-Mediated Communication* 11(1): 790–822.

Khamis, Sahar. 2011. "The transformative Egyptian Media landscape: Changes, challenges and comparative perspectives". *International Journal of Communication* 5:1159–1177.

Kulikova, Svetlana V. and Perlmutter, David D. 2007. "Blogging Down The Dictator? The Kyrgyz Revolution and Samizdat Websites". *International Communication Gazette* 69(1): 29–50.

Lasica, Joseph D. 2001. "Blogging as a Form of Journalism". *Online Journalism Review.* Accessed 10 March 2009. http://www.ojr.org/ojr/workplace/1017958873.php.

———. 2003. "Blogs and Journalism Need Each Other". *Nieman Reports.* Accessed 10 February 2010. http://www.nieman.harvard.edu/reportsitem.aspx?id=101042.

Lee, Jae Kook. 2007. "The Effect of the Internet on Homogeneity of the Media Agenda. A Test of the Fragmentation Thesis". *Journalism & Mass Communication Quarterly* 84(4): 745–760.

Lee, Yang-Hwan. 2008. "Individual Media Dependency (IMD) and Social Networking Website: Exploring Relations between Motivational Dimensions of IMD and SNW Use". Paper presented at the annual meeting of the International Communication Association. Accessed 10 March 2010. http://www.allacademic.com/meta/p234838_index.html.

Lowrey, Wilson. 2006. "Mapping the journalism-blogging relationship". *Journalism* 7(4): 477–500.

Mckee, Alan. 2005. *The public Sphere: An Introduction.* Cambridge: Cambridge University Press.

Moyo, Last. 2011. "Blogging Down a Dictatorship: Human Rights, Citizen Journalists and the Right to Communicate in Zimbabwe". *Journalism* 12(6): 745–760.

Otterman, Sharon. 2007. "Publicizing the Private: Egyptian Women Blogger Speak out". *Arab Media & Society.* Accessed 10 April 2010. http://www.arabmediasociety.com/?article=13.

Patwardhan, Padmini, and Ramaprasad, Jyotika. 2005. "Internet Dependency Relations and Online Activity Exposure, Involvement and Satisfaction: A Study of American and Indian Internet Users". Paper presented at the annual meeting of the International Communication Association. Accessed 10 March 2010. http://www.allacademic.com/meta/p12774_index.html.

Reese, D. Stephen, Rutigliano, Lou, Hyun, Kideuk and Jeong, Jaekwan. 2007. "Mapping the Blogosphere. Professional and Citizen-Based Media in the Global News Arena". *Journalism: Theory, Practice & Criticism* 8(3): 235–261.

Reporters Without Borders. 2009. "Internet: A Weapon of Mass Revolution?" Accessed 10 March 2009. http://preprod.reporters-sans-frontieres.org/Internet-a-weapon-of-mass.

Rogers, Everett M. and Dearing, James W. 2007. "Agenda-Setting Research: Where has it Been? Where is it Going?" In *Media Power in Politics*, edited by Graber, Doris, 80–97. Washington: CQ Press.

Wang, Rong. 2009. "Research on Public Sphere in cyberspace: Dominance, verbal conflict and interaction processes of China's online forum". Paper presented at the 4th Communication Policy Research, South Conference, Negombo, Sri Lanka. Available at Social Science Research Network. Accessed 10 March 2009. http://papers.ssrn.com/sol3/papers.cfm?abstract_id = 1554222.

Rostovtseva, Nataliya. 2009. "Inter-Media Agenda Setting role of the blogosphere: A content analysis of the Reuters photo controversy coverage during the Israel-Lebanon conflict in 2006". Masters Thesis, University of North Carolina at Chapel Hill.

Rutigliano, Louis W. 2008. "Covering the Unknown City: Citizen Journalism and Marginalized Communities". Doctoral Dissertation, University of Texas, Austin.

Samir, Ibrahim. 2010. "Survey of Egyptian Youth Uses of Blogs". Masters Thesis, AinShams University [In Arabic].

Singer, Jane B. 2005. "The Political J-blogger: 'Normalizing' a New Media Form to Fit Old Norms and Practices". *Journalism: Theory, Practice & Criticism* 6(2): 173–198.

Siveetser, Kaye D., Porter, Lance V., Chung, Deborah S., and Kim, Eunseong. 2008. "Credibility And The Use Of Blogs Among Professionals In The Communication Industry". *Journalism & Mass Communication Quarterly* 85(1): 169–185.

Tai, Zixue. 2009. "The Structure of Knowledge and Dynamics of Scholarly Communication in Agenda Setting Research, 1996–2005". *Journal of Communication* 59(3): 481–513.

Treem, Jeffery and Thomas, Kristin. 2010. "What Makes a Blog a Blog? Exploring User Conceptualizations of an Old 'New' Online Medium". Proceedings of the Fourth International AAAI Conference on Weblogs and Social Media, 23–26 May, 347–350, Washington, D.C.

Wallsten, Kevin. 2007. "Agenda Setting and the Blogosphere: An Analysis of the Relationship between Mainstream Media and Political Blogs". *Review of Policy Research* 24(6): 567–585.

Wober, Mallory J. 2001. "Agenda Cutting: Some Remarks on the Phenomenon and its Importance". Paper Presented at Media Tenor's Agenda-Setting Conference, Bonn, Germany.

Part IV

Consumption and Networking

11 Online News Media Consumption Cultures among Zimbabwean Citizens
'Home and Away'

Tendai Chari

INTRODUCTION

The online newspaper is transforming the way in which people consume news globally, not least in Africa. The artificial boundaries imposed by geography have broken down thanks to the online newspaper's ability to reconnect readers with their homelands and friends in far-flung places. Its virtual news delivery mode has not only changed perceptions of what is news and where, when and by whom it can be consumed but also the way in which spatially disconnected citizens obtain news about their homeland. As a result, some scholars are speculating on the future impact of the online newspaper on journalism and society (Lee and Carpini 2010). Although many sub-Saharan African countries are grappling with a myriad of challenges that militate against the widespread diffusion of new media technologies (Banda 2010), online newspapers are becoming an integral component of the African media culture (Mano and Willems 2010; Sey 2011).

This chapter seeks to advance the objectives of this book by examining the online newspaper consumption practices of local and diaspora Zimbabwean citizens in order to open new pathways for theorizing how spatially disconnected citizens deploy the online media to renegotiate their citizenship. What motivates citizens to consume online newspapers, the kind of news and information they look for and the different practices they engage in are questions that lie at the centre of this study. The chapter provides additional data necessary for understanding media audiences and the future prospects of the online newspaper in the context of media convergence.

Zimbabwe shares a number of similarities with other sub-Saharan countries in terms of a weak economy and low penetration rates of new media technologies. However, the country is unique in that it has experienced unprecedented and multifaceted crises (Mlambo and Raftopoulos 2010), which have rolled back efforts to fulfil the government's objective of transforming the country into an "information society by the year 2015" (GOZ, 2005). Despite the economic crisis, the country has registered growth in the mobile telephony sector (Kabweza 2012), and its highly literate population (UNDP Statistical Digest cited by ZIMDIASPORA 2010) is an asset for the mass adoption of the online newspaper in future.

Spurred by the digital revolution media of the late 1990s, media organizations in the country sought to increase their market share by introducing online versions of their newspapers, with the first online newspaper being started in 1998 (Chari 2011). The adversarial approach of the privately-owned media in mediating the economic and political crises of the 2000s prompted the government to introduce stringent media laws that resulted in the closure of several newspapers between 2003 and 2005, thus forcing hundreds of journalists to migrate to countries in the SADC region and European countries, where they started online newspapers and websites. The restrictive media environment, which is dominated by state-controlled media, has also contributed to online newspapers being perceived as sources of information alternative to state propaganda (Freedom House 2012). Economic hardships also made newspapers a luxury that the majority of people could not afford. With an estimate of over three million[1] Zimbabwean citizens living outside the country (UNDP 2010), online newspapers took the mantle left by privately owned newspapers as they became critical conduits for the diaspora population to symbolically reconnect with their motherland.

Whereas the production practices and the political economy of online newspapers have received some academic attention (D. Moyo 2007, 2009; L. Moyo 2011; Mabweazara 2010, 2011), research on the consumption practices of online newspapers in Africa is scant. Understanding the consumption cultures of their audiences is imperative in order to determine their possible impact on society.

METHODOLOGICAL DISCUSSION AND DATA COLLECTION

The aim of this study was to generate empirical knowledge of online newspaper consumption practices among the Zimbabwean citizenry in order to broaden understanding of the impact of the online newspaper on society. The comparative approach of the study necessitated harnessing qualitative methods to map out the online newspaper consumption cultures of subjects in different localities by using their lived experiences, perspectives and feelings as entry points. Quantitative data collection and analysis methods were used to validate, elaborate, corroborate and enhance clarity of those experiences and perspectives rather than addressing separate questions (Bryman 2006).

Some scholars argue that blending qualitative and quantitative methods may help achieve rigor in research in the sense that the weakness of one method will be offset by the strengths of another (Bryman 2006). To this extent, data were collected using a 26-item survey questionnaire, eight of which were open-ended, whereas 18 were closed-ended. Respondents were required to identify the online newspapers they read, when they read them, the time they read them and their motives for reading them. Open-ended questions were meant to collect qualitative data to corroborate the quantitative data. One hundred and twenty (120) printed questionnaires were distributed in

Harare, the capital city of Zimbabwe, between 29 October and 3 December 2011. An online version of the questionnaire was emailed to acquaintances in the diaspora, who were requested to forward the same to their email contacts, thus making the sampling procedure essentially snowball-cum purposive.

The questionnaire was distributed to people who had the experience of reading online newspapers. The selection of respondents was made with the objective of ensuring equal representation in terms of class, age group and gender. However, the rural-urban, class and age divide which characterizes online Internet access in the country made it impossible to achieve a representative sample. Other considerations such as ethnicity were deliberately ignored because the main aim of the study was to generate theoretical insights rather than making generalizations based on populations. The same reasons also informed the choice of Harare, the capital city of the country, as the location for the study.

Although the respondents were mixed in terms of age and gender, the majority were working and well educated (minimum Ordinary Level, and the highest level was PhD). Seventy-nine percent of the respondents were male, and 21 percent were female. Thirty-seven percent fell in the 26–35 age group, and 70 percent had some tertiary education. The fact that more young people than elderly people have computer skills and are predisposed to new media technologies also accounts for the dominance of this age group in the sample. The difficulty of determining who had or had not read an online newspaper and the inaccessibility of the diaspora population justified the use of the snowball sampling procedure.

Of the 120 questionnaires distributed, 86 were returned, hence, a return rate of 72 percent. Diaspora respondents were from the United Kingdom, Australia, Canada, South Africa, Botswana, Iran, Saudi Arabia, United States of America, Lesotho, Namibia, New Zealand, Germany and France. Quantitative data were analyzed using SPSS v 19, whereas the qualitative component was extrapolated, coded thematically and interpreted using the hermeneutic approach whereby the meaning of social phenomena is revealed through interpretation rather than observation.

Although snowball and purposive sampling procedures have been criticized for being biased and unrepresentative primarily because the choice of subjects depends on the opinions of respondents first accessed (Atkinson and Flint 2001), the procedure has been found to be a valuable tool for studying the habits of social groups that are difficult to access (Atkinson and Flint 2001).

INTERNET ACCESS AND ONLINE NEWSPAPERS

Zimbabwe is a latecomer to the information superhighway, but Internet access is expanding, with the penetration rate growing from 0.3 percent in 2000 to 15.7 percent by the end of 2011 (Freedom House 2012). The mobile telephony sector has been growing, particularly after the dollarization of the economy, increasing from 6.8 percent in 2006 to 72.1 percent at the end of 2011. In 2012 the number of Internet Service Providers stood at 128, up from six in 2003 (Internetworldstats 2010. As a result of the relative economic and political stability experienced during the past three years, Internet use has also been growing steadily. As of June 2010, the country had 1,422,000 Internet users, translating to a penetration rate of 11.8 percent, which is relatively higher than the continental average of 5.6 percent (Banda 2010). In spite of this huge growth, the Internet is still a preserve of the urban elite, whereas rural communities remain in the margins of the information superhighway. A 2011 All Media Products Survey (ZAMPS) found that 24 percent of adults in urban areas use the Internet, with 83 percent of the users accessing the web at least once a month (Freedom House 2011). Infrastructural challenges, such as poor connectivity and the unavailability of electricity as well as high costs and economic decline, have acted as obstacles against the widespread diffusion of the Internet. As of May 2012, Internet cafes in the capital city Harare were charging US $1 for 30 minutes, which is unaffordable considering the fact that the average civil servant earns about US $253 (Share 2012). Home Internet packages cost US $50 per month, excluding installation fees, and a modem costs US $60, whereas the average computer is priced at US$ 600 (Freedom House 2012).

Online newspapers have become key sources of information for the country's technologically savvy urban elite in the diaspora and at home. Foreign-based news websites such as *NewZimbabwe.com, The Zimbabwesituation. com, The Zimbabwemail.com* and others have become critical sources of news and information alternative to the state-controlled media. Editorially, most of these publications and websites are anti-government and rely on stringers based in the country to source sensitive news about events in the country. Because of the repressive legislative media environment, most of these correspondents use pseudonyms to circumvent punishment.

Apart from foreign-based online newspapers, Zimbabweans abroad and in the country also read mainstream newspapers online. All mainstream newspapers in the country have open access Web editions, which are mirror images of the printed editions. The digital editions carry display and classified adverts that differ significantly from the printed editions. Digital editions do not carry all the stories contained in the printed editions but selected 'main' stories. The high costs of maintaining websites means that the web editions are not updated regularly (unless there is major breaking news).

Recent studies show that the online newspaper in Zimbabwe is, among other reasons, valued for its affordability, convenience, accessibility and timeliness, although it is still considered an elite medium, and there are no indications that it will necessarily replace the print newspaper (Chari 2011). There is also considerable interdependence between mainstream and 'online only' publications and websites published by Zimbabweans in the diaspora in terms of stories, thus resulting in some kind of intra-media agenda setting.

Thus, it is common to find stories originating from some websites being published in mainstream newspapers and vice-versa. This shows that the online newspaper, whether as a 'stand alone' phenomenon or an extension of the printed newspaper, is making an impact on journalism and society. With the gradual expansion of mobile technology in the country, the influence of the online newspaper is expected to grow significantly.

MEDIA CONSUMPTION PRACTICES: AN OVERVIEW

The issue of media consumption has been explored using different approaches, the dominant one being the Uses and Gratifications approach. The Uses and Gratifications theory examines how audiences use different media in different contexts (Papacharissi 2008). The theory dates back to the 1940s when some scholars discredited the hypodermic media theory, arguing that media effects were a complex process. Unlike the powerful effects tradition, which assumed immense media power and a passive audience, the Uses and Gratification theory accentuates the limited power of the media and an active audience.

The functionalist/instrumentalist approach of the theory has invited criticism from some scholars who argue that it views media use as being linked to individual needs and uses (Chandler 1994; Morely 1992). Chandler (1994) has labelled the theory 'vulgar gratification' because of its emphasis on individual psychological and personality factors and negation of the socio-cultural context in which media consumption takes place. Scholars like Chandler argue that the Uses and Gratification theory's functionalist approach is politically conservative because it is hinged on the assumption that people always find some content gratifications from the media, thus reflecting an uncritical attitude towards the mass media.

Morely (1992, 52) criticizes the Uses and Gratification approach for being "insufficiently sociological" because the individual psychological attributes which influence media consumption are absolved from the broader social context of the audience. He argues that if the audience is "abstracted from the social groups and sub-cultures which provide a framework of meaning for their activities, it means that the audience is still being conceived as atomized masses", the same way they were viewed in the stimulus-response model (ibid).

Some scholars have argued that media use is essentially 'sociable', meaning that media content provides a significant basis for self-identification or supporting subcultural identities. This sociability of audience behavior takes several dimensions, such as consuming certain media in order to maintain certain peer group relationships (Riley, Rosengren and Windahl cited in McQuail 1994). Ruggierro (2000, 5) has criticized the earliest researchers for failing to "explore the links between the gratifications detected and the psychological or sociological origins of the needs satisfied" and for the research's inability to identify the "interrelationships among the various media functions, either quantitatively or conceptually, in a manner that might have led to the detection of the latent structure of media gratifications".

As a response to some of the alleged weaknesses of the theory, there have been some revisions to the Uses and Gratification Theory (McQuail 1994; Blumler and Katz cited in Chandler 1994; Palmgreen cited in Papacharissi 2008). Instead of focusing on 'gratifications sought' only, it is now possible to talk about 'gratifications obtained', leading to the expectancy-value theory (Palmgreen cited in Papacharissi 2009). Essentially, the expectancy-value theory views media use behaviour as depending on a belief that a particular type of media content has attributes which are perceived to carry a positive or negative value. The revised version of the Uses and Gratification approach views media consumption as a process circumscribed by an interplay of forces that implicate the broader context in which the media consumption takes place.

Although the bulk of research on Uses and Gratifications focuses on traditional media, attention is shifting to new media such as the Internet (Papacharissi and Rubin 2000), the cellular phone (Leung and Wei 2000), online newspapers (Schoneville 2007; Van Heekeren 2005; Ihlstrom, Lunberg and Pedrix 2003; Ihlstrom and Lunberg 2002) and social media (Johnson and Roy 2009).

Schoneville (2007) used the survey method to investigate factors that influence online newspaper-reading behaviour in the Netherlands. The study concluded that habit was the most influential determinant on intention and behaviour. In addition, people who have a habit of reading the printed newspaper are also more inclined to read the online edition, meaning that online and print newspapers are complementary. Van Heekeren (2005) has investigated story preferences of readers in *The Sydney Morning Herald* and the gratifications that readers derive from online news. The study concluded that the web news reader wants entertainment first and foremost and prefers event-based stories to analytical pieces.

A comparative study of online newspaper audiences in Sweden, Slovakia and Spain found significant differences among these countries in terms of the place where the online newspaper is read, the content read and the audience's attitude towards the content (Ihlstrom, Lunberg and Pedrix 2003). These differences were attributed to cultural and/or infrastructural factors. This study shares a number of concerns with the present study in terms of the focus on audience consumption habits and motivations for such consumption patterns. Ihlstrom, Lunberg and Pedrix's study has a broader scope because of its cross-cultural comparison. The main limitation of this study is that reasons for the differences and similarities across the three countries were not fully accounted for.

Ihlstrom and Lundberg (2002,1) conducted a longitudinal study of the audience of Swedish online newspapers using survey questionnaires to determine the "user expectations of current and future issues" among readers of online newspaper editions. The study tackled issues such as how often people expose themselves to online newspapers, the type of content they read, why they read them and where they read online newspapers.

Unlike Ihlstrom and Lundberg, whose study compared reading habits of the same readers over a long period of time, the present study compares audiences in different localities. The present study follows Bennett's assumption that online newspapers have the potential to reconfigure notions of citizenship (2007) in that the interactive nature of online newspapers has changed the notion of the audience from being passive consumers to "produsers" (Akerberg et al. cited in Dockney et al. 2010, 77). Thus, examining how spatially separated audiences interact with the new medium is important in order to gain insights on the potential of online newspapers to act as a site for negotiating citizenship.

Based on the reviewed literature and conceptual framework discussed above, this chapter addresses two principal questions: How do Zimbabwean citizens in the country and the diaspora consume online newspapers? What factors motivate them to consume these online newspapers? The chapter further discusses the implications of the online newspaper consumption cultures for "citizenship" in the context of digitization.

ONLINE NEWSPAPER CONSUMPTION HABITS AND PRACTICES

The main online publications read by diaspora citizens are *The Zimbabwesituation.com*[2], read by 65 percent of the respondents, *NewZimbabwe.com* (62 percent), *The Herald* (58 percent), *The Sunday Mail* (27 percent), *Daily News* (19 percent), *News Day* (19 percent), *The Zimbabwe Independent* (19 percent), *ZimDaily.com* (15 percent) and *The Zimbabwe Mail* (15 percent). Local citizens mostly read those newspapers that have printed editions and are circulated within the country, such as the state-owned daily *The Herald* (52 percent), the privately owned daily *News Day* (40 percent), the state-owned tabloid *H-Metro* (23 percent), *The Sunday Mail* (20 percent), *Daily News* (20 percent), *NewZimbabwe.com* (13 percent), *The Zimbabwesituation.com* (12 percent), *The Zimbabwe Independent* (9 percent), *The Standard* (9 percent) and *Google News.com* (9 percent).

The consumption of online newspapers is mainly influenced by accessibility and familiarity with the printed version of the newspaper. Local citizens who have more access to printed newspapers read a wider range of online publications, with a combined total of 40 online publications compared to 20 for diaspora citizens. The influence of familiarity on the use and selection of online newspapers is evidenced by the fact that some publications which are popular with citizens in the country were hardly mentioned by the diaspora. An example is *H-Metro*[3] newspaper, which was the third most popular with respondents living in the country. The newspaper was never mentioned by a single respondent from the diaspora.

As will be demonstrated below, this shows that the online media consumption culture of the audience resembles the offline one. The inability by the diaspora to access print versions of some newspapers which they used to read while they were in Zimbabwe discourages them from reading certain newspapers whose print versions they are not familiar with, such as *H-Metro* mentioned above.

Studies have shown that there is a correlation between the readership of the print and digital editions of a newspaper (Lee and Carpini 2010). Thus, locals who have access to more printed newspapers are more likely than their diaspora counterparts to read their online versions because they relate easily to their content. This supports findings of earlier studies that concluded that there is a complementary relationship between the printed newspaper and its web version (Bergstrom 2006; Ahlers 2006; Chari 2011). As observed by Lee and Carpini (2010, 1), "people's online news consumption behavior largely mirrors their offline news consumption habits". This conforms to the attendance theory, which states that "most news consumers proactively seek news coverage from the same sources that they consume in traditional media" (Lee and Carpini 2010, 5). Thus, the habitual dependency on the media has a self-reinforcing effect (Rosenstein and Grant cited in Lee and Carpini 2010, 5). Flint has also noted the "duality of reader interest" in print and online reading habits, whereby readers of printed newspapers are more likely to read their online versions (cited in Van Heekeren 2005, 3).

Moreover, the inclination of the diaspora citizens towards political stories predisposes them to information-seeking behaviours that accentuate discrimination of both media and content. The diaspora, more than the locals, has a greater preference for anti-government publications than for state-controlled publications, which they consider conduits of state propaganda. For instance, one respondent based in the United Kingdom accused the state daily *The Herald* for being 'anti-MDC', implying that the paper was biased against the former opposition party the Movement for Democratic Change. Another one from Australia accused *The Herald* of peddling unreliable information and praised foreign-based online newspapers for being sources of information alternative to state views, stating thus:

> Thanks to these online publications, we can easily get informed on everything we want to know. What is sad is that reading through *The Herald* would give an impression that the paper is being used to weaken the MDC by advancing and portraying (sic) the party in an unfavorable light. It is for this reason that I do not consider it a reliable source of information on Zimbabwe.

This shows that the selection and readership of online newspapers by Zimbabwean citizens reflects contours of political affiliation in a politically bifurcated society. Appandurai (cited in Vertovec 1999, 5) argues that the process of deterritorialization creates "exaggerated senses of criticism or attachment to politics in the homestate" among the diaspora, which borders on fundamentalism. This 'fundamentalism' does not only manifest itself through hyper-political activism (Baser and Swain 2010) but also through media practices that magnify the tension between living in one place and longing for another (Kvasny and Hales 2009).

FREQUENCY, PLACE AND TIME

The frequency with which a person has contact with media matters a great deal, and so do the time spent and the place in which they consume the particular media. There is a trade-off between reading an online newspaper and reading a book. How much time people commit to reading a newspaper shows how seriously they take its content and their degree of access to the medium, which in turn may affect the degree to which they are influenced by the medium. The consumption of online newspapers reflects contours of the digital divide, with 85 percent of the diaspora respondents reporting that they read online newspapers everyday compared to 57 percent for local citizens. The 'developed' status of most countries in which the diaspora lives makes access to online newspapers easier than back home, where a plethora of factors make it difficult to access the Internet regularly. Thus, 65 percent of the diaspora read the online newspaper in the morning, 23 percent in the afternoon, whereas 19 percent read in the evening. The large number of the diaspora who read online newspapers at home (85 percent) compared to 41 percent of the locals who do so also underscores the differences in Internet access between the diaspora and locals. The diaspora is prone to more habitual and ritualistic online media tendencies than the locals are because they have more access to the Internet than those living in the country.

None of the diaspora respondents read online newspapers at Internet cafes because they can access them from home and work. The antiquated state of Zimbabwe's telecommunications infrastructure, frequent electricity cuts and a small bandwidth worsen the already wide gap in Internet access between the diaspora and the locals. More access to the Internet by the diaspora implies that the reading of online newspapers becomes intricately interwoven with work and entertainment activities, whereas locals regard them as a luxury.

Whereas the consumption of online newspapers by the diaspora is embedded in their everyday practices, locals access them opportunistically. As will be discussed in the subsequent sections, the digital divide is a plausible explanation for the different online newspaper consumption cultures between the diaspora and locals. Their existence in separate spaces shapes different information-seeking habits. Personal preferences relating to how often one reads an online newspaper, where, when and why are moulded by geography.

MOTIVATIONS FOR READING ONLINE NEWSPAPERS

One objective of this study was to investigate the motives for reading online newspapers by diaspora and local Zimbabwean citizens. Respondents were asked to rank some statements about the type of news they read in online newspapers using a four-point Likert scale. Table 11.1 below shows the factors that motivate Zimbabwean citizens to read news online.[4]

Table 11.1 below shows that information about the general 'happenings in the country' was the most sought after, with a mean of rank of 2.28, followed by political developments (2.86), business issues (2.88), sports news (3.22) and entertainment news being the least important (3.75).

The findings are contrary to Van Heekeren' study of the top five accessed stories in the online edition of the *Sydney Morning Herald,* which concluded that online newspaper readers were moving from serious to less serious issues like entertainment and sports (2006). The view that the audience's interest in serious stories is waning needs to be moderated in the contemporary context where the online newspaper has become a tool for political activism. As indicated in Table 11.1 below, many people use the online newspaper to get information about what is happening around them because of its immediacy. With the online newspaper, one can quickly navigate from one website to another without leaving one's office or home.

Thus, online newspapers are better positioned to give a 'bird's eye' rather than an in-depth analysis of events. Readers get 'snapshots' or 'slices' instead of a detailed analysis of events, meaning that online newspapers are better suited to act as reference sources for breaking news.

The dominance of political news is corroborated by the qualitative data. Respondents mentioned 'politics', 'political news', 'political developments' and news about 'eminent politicians' as the most sought-after news in online newspapers. Table 11.2 below is an excerpt of some statements that substantiate this view.

Table 11.1   Motivations for reading online newspapers: push factors.

Statement	Mean Rank
I read online publications/websites because I would like to know what is happening in my country.	2.28
I read online publications/websites mainly to get information about political developments in Zimbabwe.	2.86
I read online publications/websites mainly to get information on business issues in Zimbabwe.	2.88
I read online publications/websites mainly to get information on sports.	3.22
I read online publications/websites to get information on entertainment and showbiz in Zimbabwe.	3.75

Table 11.2   Most sought-after news in online newspapers

- "To have a rough idea of the general political and socioeconomic situation in my country" (D1, Canada).
- "To keep abreast with developments at home-Zimbabwe will always be home for me" (D2, UK).
- "To remain in touch with the socioeconomic [and] political developments in Zimbabwe" (D4, Iran).
- "To know the political position of the country" (H1, Harare).
- To get updated about the political state of Zimbabwe" (H2, Harare).

The provision of information which makes the citizen aware of what is happening in the country, what Huxford refers to as the "surveillance function" (2004, 3), is the most important function served by the online newspaper, and immediacy makes it better suited to fulfil this function. The surveillance function positions journalism in a watchdog or monitor role, what Schudson (cited in Barabas and Jerit 2005, 2) refers to as "Burglar and Alarm Journalism", whereby the media alert citizens about problems and issues in the political sphere.

The citizens, therefore, affirm their citizenship by surveying political news so that they can make informed decisions (ibid). Through online newspapers, citizens become more proactive than they would be when using traditional media. The online newspaper has, therefore, given citizens agency to monitor political developments in their home country by availing information that enables the citizenry to make informed choices. Whereas online newspapers in politically and economically stable environments of the West may serve entertainment functions, as was shown in Van Heekeren's study mentioned above, the political function appears to be dominant in contexts where politics permeate all facets of the citizen's life, such as Zimbabwe.

The country's crises, spanning more than a decade, have been a source of great anxiety for the citizenry, who seek information that satisfies their curiosity and sustains their hope for a brighter future. The online newspaper becomes the site for the affirmation of citizenship and belonging for both the diaspora and the locals. The diaspora affirms that citizenship by exercising transnational loyalty through seeking information about their country in the same way they claim citizenship through remittances of funds and other goods, which are now a significant component of the country's Gross Domestic Product (UNDP 2010; Bloch 2012). The online newspaper becomes a location for citizenship enactment and identity production by enabling people to project their desire for belonging.

Tables 11.3 and 11.4 below highlight the difference between the locals and the diaspora with regards to the level of concern about the situation in the country.

Table 11.3 Level of citizen interest in general happenings

I read online news to know what is happening in the country.	n	Mean Rank
Diaspora	26	41.88
Local	86	57.37
P		0.026

Table 11.4 Level of citizen interest in political developments

I read online news to get information about political developments in the country.	n	Mean Rank
Diaspora	26	39.13
Local	86	56.26
P		0.015

In Table 11.3 above, the lower mean rank of 41.88 shows that diaspora respondents are more anxious about general happenings in the country than the locals, whose mean rank is 57.37. When the level of significance is set at 0.05, the small p value (0.02) indicates a significant difference in perception. The lower mean rank shows a higher preference for news about 'general happenings'. This means diaspora respondents are more concerned than locals about the situation in their motherland. Distance creates uncertainty among the diaspora because they have little knowledge about what is happening in distant locations. Social and spatial alienation predisposes people who are living far away from home to seek information so that they are kept abreast about the general happenings in the homeland. Unlike the locals, who have personal experience with the situation, are exposed to a variety of media and, therefore, have concrete information about what is happening in the country, diaspora citizens have abstract knowledge of events happening in the country because of their distanced perspectives (Handerson and Wakslak 2010). This implies that they are prone to over-dependence on mediated reality compared to local citizens who personally experience economic hardships in the country.

As shown in Table 11.4 above, diaspora respondents give more attention than locals to political developments in the country. This is shown by the smaller mean rank of 39.13 compared to 56.26 for citizens living in the country. The small p value (0.015) indicates that there is a significant difference between the diaspora and locals in terms of their preference for political news. This shows that the diaspora is more sentimental than locals about the situation in the country. Because of distance, the diaspora has a tendency to view events in the homeland through the prism of nostalgia.

The fact that local citizens show less preference for news about political developments also shows that the changed political and economic conditions occasioned by the formation of a coalition government between the two main political parties in 2009 has different impacts on the diaspora and the locals. The continued political impasse between the coalition partners (Bratton and Masunungure 2011) and the persistence of poverty in a dollarized economy have a demobilizing effect on the local citizenry. This apathetic view about the country's seemingly endless crises is not peculiar to the locals, as testified by a respondent from South Africa who complained thus: "I used to read online newspapers daily but now less frequently, probably monthly. I guess you realize nothing will change in Zimbabwe and one realizes that the news just depresses you instead of encouraging or updating you". This shows that although separated by distance, the diaspora shares the same identifications with locals and constructs similar discourses outside space and time boundaries (Kvasny and Hales 2008).

The diaspora's strong sentimental attachments towards the homeland reveal that online newspapers have become tools for remembering and fantasizing about the homeland in a globalizing world. Their physical separation from the home country creates a sense of "double consciousness" (Kvasny and Hales 2008, 9) which manifests itself through stronger attachments towards the home country, what Baser and Swain (2010, 37) refer to as "long-distance-nationalism". The diaspora has a tendency to leave a trail of collective memory about the home whose manifestations are maps of desire about the host country (Braakman and Schlenkhoff 2007). Kvasny and Hales (2008, 4) argue that "The collective identity of diasporic Africans and other displaced people and transnational communities is defined by their hybrid relationship to the homeland and the host society".

The longing to belong somewhere by the diaspora is projected through the use of online newspapers to connect with their home country, politically, socially and culturally. Such information-seeking behaviour conforms to Palmgreen's observation that people's expectations, beliefs and judgments can influence their gratification-seeking behaviour and concomitantly the media that they expose themselves to (Palmgreen 1984). Because the circumstances of both the home and host countries are bound to change with the passage of time, it implies that media consumption practices will also change in tandem with the country's sociopolitical and economic idiosyncrasies.

GRATIFICATIONS SOUGHT OR GRATIFICATIONS OBTAINED?

The motives for reading online newspapers are structured by certain intrinsic attributes of the online newspaper which distinguish it from the printed newspaper and by citizens' judgments and expectations about their country. Respondents were asked to rank given statements on a four-point Likert scale. Table 11.5 below displays the results of the factors that motivate Zimbabwean citizens to read online newspapers.

Table 11.5   Motivations for reading online newspapers: pull factors.

Statement	Mean Rank
I read online publications/websites mainly because they update their news regularly.	6.62
I read online publications/websites mainly because they are always first with the news.	7.04
I read online publications/websites because they do not hold back any information.	8.62
I read online publications because they provide accurate reports on Zimbabwe.	8.74
I read online publications/websites because they are sensational.	8.95
I read online publications/websites because they provide complete information.	9.01
I read online publications/websites because they tell it like it is.	9.33
Online publications/websites provide better quality news than the printed newspaper.	9.54
I read online publications/websites because I have no other sources of news and information.	9.76
I read online publications/websites when I do not have anything to do.	10.90

As observed in Table 11.5 above, the audiences of online newspapers are attracted by attributes that differentiate these versions from the printed newspaper, attributes which enhance the quality of information, such as the ability to give "regular updates" (mean rank of 6.2), perceptions that the online newspaper is "always the first with the news" (7.04) and that "they do not hold back information" (8.62). Escapism was given as the least important reason for reading online newspapers (10.90). Thus, the intrinsic characteristics of the online newspaper are more critical than gratifications sought by the audience for determining the future of the online newspaper.

Table 11. 5 above shows that the main attractions to online newspapers are linked to the internal logic of the medium, namely, its immediacy and interactivity. These attractions are graphically represented in Figure 11.1 below. This was corroborated by the qualitative data in which respondents emphatically pointed out immediacy and interactivity as some of the advantages of reading newspapers online. Phrases such as "real time", "current news", "current affairs", "quick updates", "faster", "continuous updates" and "recent news" were used to characterize online newspapers by both the diaspora and local respondents. A respondent from Harare commented that "After reading you can either make comments or seek more

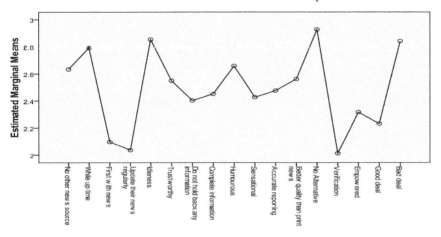

Figure 11.1   Motivations for reading online newspapers: pull factors

clarification from the publishers. There can be direct links with the publisher" (sic).

Locals used these phrases in the same breath with statements that accentuated the affordability of online newspapers, whereas the diaspora emphasized speed. This underscores the influence of the digital divide and economic factors on shaping online consumption habits. A respondent from New Zealand commented that "Online publications have all the information and they deliver it very fast. You can access anything you want and find all the types of news, sports, music etc.". Another one from Harare said, "Online newspapers give you the highlights of a story as it unfolds and no costs are incurred for that". Thus, locals and the diaspora have different expectations of the online newspaper that are shaped by geography, politics and economics.

CONCLUSION

This chapter discussed the online newspaper consumption cultures of local and diaspora Zimbabwean citizens. Significant differences exist between the online newspaper consumption practices of the diaspora and local citizens. These differences are mainly linked to their individual expectations about the political situation in the country and polarities occasioned by geography, economics, politics, infrastructural disparities and the broader context in which the consumption of online newspapers takes place. The chapter argues that the online newspaper is a site upon which spatially disconnected individuals share memories and identifications and sustain social, cultural and political connections to common spaces and localities. The online newspaper has become a locus for the enactment of new forms of citizenship in the context of digitization and globalization.

The study complements existing studies on Uses and Gratifications and related theories by broadening our understanding of the way in which new media are restructuring notions of citizenship in a globalizing context. However, one limitation of this study is the small sample size and the weaknesses linked to self-reported data. Future studies could utilize ethnography in order to have a deeper understanding of online newspaper consumption cultures and practices.

REFERENCES

Ahlers, Douglas. 2006. "News Consumption and the New Electronic Media". *Harvard Journal of Press/Politics* 11(1): 29–52.

Atkinson, Rowland and Flint, John. 2001. "Accessing Hidden and Hard to Reach Populations: Snowball Research Strategies". *Social Research Update* 28(1): 93–108.

Banda, Fackson. 2010. *Citizen Journalism and Democracy in Africa: An Exploratory Study.* Grahamstown: Highway Africa.

Barabus, Jason and Jerit, Jennifer. 2005. "Surveillance Knowledge and the Mass Media". Paper Presented at the annual Meeting of the American Political Science Association, Washington DC, September 1–4, 2005. Accessed 13 May 2012. *http://people.rw.harvard.edu/barabas/working%20papers/Barabas_jerit_surveil -lanceandknowlesge_8–31–05.pdf.*

Baser, Bahar and Swain, Ashok. 2010. "Stateless Diaspora Groups and their Repertoires of Nationalist Activism in Host Countries". *Journal of International Relations* 8(1) 37–60.

Bennet, Lance W. 2007. "Changing Citizenship in the Digital Age". In *Civic Life Online: Learning How Digital Media can Engage Youth*, edited by Bennet, Lance W. The John D. and Catherine T. MacArthur Foundation Series on Digital Media and Learning, 1–24. Cambridge, MA: MIT Press.

Bloch, Eric. 2012. "Diaspora Mainstay of Zimbabwe's Economy". *The Zimbabwe Independent,* 27 April, 2012.

Braakman, Marije and Schlenkoff, Angela. 2007. "Between Two Worlds: Feelings of Belonging While in Exile and the Question of Return". *ASIEN* 104: 9–22.

Bryman, Alan. 2006. "Integrating Quantitative and Qualitative Research: How it is done?" *Qualitative Research* 6(1): 97–113.

Chandler, Daniel. 1994. "Why do People Watch Television?" Accessed 5 May 2012. *http://www.aber.ac.uk/media/Documents/short/usergrat.html.*

Chari, Tendai. 2011. "Future Prospects of the Printed Newspaper in Zimbabwe". *Journal of African Media Studies* 3(3): 367–386.

Dockney, Jonathan, Tomasselli, Keyan, G. and Hart, T. Bongani. 2010. "Cellphilms, Mobile Platforms and Prosumers; Hyper-Individuality and Film". In The *Citizen in Communication: Revisiting Traditional, New and Community Media practices in South Africa*, edited by Hyde- Clarke, Natalie, 75–96. Cape Town: Juta & Co.

Freedom House. 2012. "Freedom on the Net 2012-Zimbabwe". 25 September 2012. Accessed 13 November 2012. *http://www.freedomhouse.org/report/freedom-net/ freedom-net-2012.*

Government of Zimbabwe. 2005. "Information and Communication Technology Policy". Harare: Ministry of Information and Communication Technology.

Handerson, Malorne D. and Wakslak, Cheryl J. 2010. "Psychological Distance and Priming: When do Semantic Primes Impact Social Evaluations?" *Personality and Social Psychology Bulletin* 36(7): 975–985.

Huxford, John. 2004. "Surveillance, Witnessing and Spectatorship: The News and the 'War of Images'". In *Proceedings of the Media Ecology Association 5*, 2004, edited by Hunt, Arthur W., 1–21. Accessed 13 May 2012. *http://www.mediaecol -ogy.org/publications/MEA_proceedings/v5/Huxford/05.pdf Accessed*.

Ihlstrom, Carina and Lunberg, Jonas. 2002. "The Audience of Sweden Local Online Newspapers: A Longitudinal Study". In *Elpup 2002 Proceedings*, edited by Carvalho, J.A. et al. Accessed 14 July 2011. Available *http://elpub.scix.net/data/ works/att/02–09.content.pdf*.

Ihlstrom, Carina, Lunberg, Jonas and Pedrix, Ferran. 2003. "Audience of Online Newspaper in Sweden, Slovakia and Spain: A Comparative Study". In *Proceedings of HCI International Conference*, 22–27 June. Accessed 15 January 2012. *http:// webstaff.itn.liu.se/~jonlu41/publications/permalink-204.htm*.

Internetworldstats.com. 2011. "Internet Usage, Population and Statistics". Accessed 15 January 2012. *http://www.internetworldstats.com/africa.htm#zw*.

Johnson, Phillip, and Yang, Sung Un. 2009. "Uses and Gratifications of Twitter: An Examination of User Motives and Satisfaction of Twitter". Paper presented at the Communication Technology Division of the Association for Education in Journalism and Mass Communication, Sheraton Boston, Boston, Massachusetts, 5–8 August 2009. Accessed 15 June 2012. *https://umdrive.memphis.edu/cbrown14/ public/Mass%20Comm%20Theory/Week207%20Uses%20and%20 Gratifications/Johnson%20and%20Yang%202009%20Twitter%20uses%20 and%20grats.pdf*.

Kabweza, Limbikani. 2012. "The Internet and the Declining Newspaper Readership in Zimbabwe". Techzim, 22 March. Accessed 15 June 2012. *http://www.techzim .co.zw/2012/09/unsurprisingly-newspaper-readership-in-zimbabwe-keeps-declining/*.

Kvasny, Lynette and Hales, Kayla. 2009. "The Internet, Black Identity and the Evolving Discourse of the Digital Divide". In *Overcoming Digital Divides: Constructing an Equitable and Competitive Information Society*, edited by Ferro, Enrico, Dwivedi, Yogesh, Gil-Garcia, Roman and William, Michael D., 260–276. Pennsylvania: IGI Global Publishing.

Lee, Angela M. and Carpini, Dell M. 2010. "News Consumption Revisited: Examining the Power of Habits in the 21st Century". Paper Presented at the 11th International Symposium on Online Journalism. Austin TX. April 23–24 2010. Accessed 24 June 2011. *http://online.journalism.utexas.edu/2010/papers/ LeeCarpini10.pdf*.

Leung, Louis and Wei, Ran. 1999. "Seeking News from the Pager: A value-Expec-tancy Study". *Journal of Broadcasting and Electronic Media* 43(3): 299–315.

Mabweazara, Hayes M. 2010. "New Technologies and Journalism Practice in Africa: Towards a Critical Sociological Approach". In *The Citizen in Communication: Re-visiting Traditional, New and Community Media Practices in South Africa*, edited by Hyde-Clarke, Natalie, 31–50. Cape Town: Juta & Co.

———. 2011. "Newsmaking Practices and Professionalism in the Zimbabwean Press". *Journalism Practice* 5(1): 100–117.

Mano, Winston and Willems, Wendy. 2010. "Debating 'Zimbabweanness' in Diasporic Internet Forums: Technologies of Freedom". In *Diaspora Identities and Transnational Media*, edited by McGregor, John and Primorac, Ranka, 183–197. Berghahn: New York.

McQuail, Denis. 1994. *Mass Communication Theory: An Introduction*. London: Sage Publications.

Meldrum, Andrew. 2005. "Paper for Zimbabwe Expats". *The Guardian,* 12 February 2005.

Mlambo, Alois and Raftopoulos, Brian. 2010. "The Regional Dimensions of Zimbabwe's multi-layered crisis". Paper presented at Election Processes, Liberation Movements and Democratic Change in Africa Conference (CMI and IESE), Maputo, 8–11 April 2010.

Moyo, Dumisani. 2007. "Alternative Media, Diasporas and the Mediation of the Zimbabwean Crisis". *Ecquid Novi: African Journalism Studies* 28(12/2): 81–105.

———. 2009. "Citizen Journalism and the Parallel Market of Information in Zimbabwe's 2008 Election". *Journalism Studies* 10(4): 1–17.

Moyo, Last. 2011. "Blogging Down a Dictatorship: Human Rights, Citizen Journalists and the Right to Communicate in Zimbabwe Journalism". *Journalism: Theory, Practice & Criticism* 12(6): 1–16.

Palmgreen, Philip and Rayburn, J.D. 1985. "An Expectancy-Value Approach to Media

Gratifications". In *Media Gratification Research: Current Perspectives,* edited by Rosengren, Karl E., Wenner, Lawrence A., Palmgren, Philip, 61–72. London: Sage Publications.

Papacharissi, Zizi. 2009. "Uses and Gratification". In *An integrated Approach to Communication Theory and Research,* edited by Stacks, Don W. and Salwen, Michael B., 137–152. New York: Routledge.

Papacharissi, Zizi and Rubin, Alan M. 2000. "Predictors of Internet Use". *Journal of Broadcasting and Electronic Media* 44(2): 175–196.

Ruggiero, Thomas. 2000. "Uses and Gratifications Theory in the 21st Century Mass". *Communication & Society* 3(1): 3–37.

Schoneville, Sander. 2007. "This Just in: Factors Influencing Online Newspaper Reading Behaviour". Masters Thesis, University of Twente. Accessed 14 May 2012. *http://essay.utwente.nl/58916/.*

Sey, Araba. 2011. "New Media Practices in Ghana". *International Journal of Communication* 5: 380–405.

Share, Felix. 2012a. "Civil Servants Fume Over Salaries". *The Herald,* 4 January 2012.

———. 2012b. "New Pay Structure for Civil Servants". *The Herald,* 1 February 2012.

United Nations Development Programme. 2010. "The Potential Contribution of the Zimbabwe Diaspora to Economic Recovery: Working Paper Series II". Accessed 12 May 2012. *http://www.zimbabwesituation.com/WP11.pdf.*

Van Heekeren, Margaret. 2005. "What the Web Reader Wants: An Analysis of Smh. com.au Readership Story Preference". Paper Presented at the Annual Meeting of the Australian and New Zealand Communication Association, 4–7 July 2005. Accessed 13 December 2011. http://www.mang.canterbury.ac.nz/anzca/FullPapers/05MedSocNewmediaFINAL.pdf.

Vertovec, Steven. 1999. "Three Meanings of 'Diaspora', Exemplified Among South Asian Religions". *Diaspora* 7(2): 2–37.

12 The Internet, Diasporic Media and Online Journalism in West Africa

Muhammad Jameel Yusha'u

INTRODUCTION

This chapter examines the nature of online journalism in the West African subregion, including those managed from the diaspora. The West African subregion is one of the most complex and plural parts of Africa, comprising of countries like Nigeria, Niger, Ghana, Cameroon, Senegal, Togo, Benin, Cape Verde, Gambia, Mauritania, Mali, Liberia, Sierra Leone, Guinea, Guinea-Bissau and Burkina Faso.

The countries of this region have diverse histories from pre-colonial times under various kingdoms and emirates to colonial times under the British, French, Portuguese, etc. The chapter is divided into six sections. Following the introduction, the next section will focus on the media landscape in West Africa. What were the forces behind journalism practice, where did it start and what is the nature of ownership in the sub region?

The third part of the article will focus on deregulation of the media environment, which enabled the establishment of private media organisations. This is important because after political independence, media were under government monopoly, and it was the liberalisation policy that opened the way for diverse ownership of the media. As discussed by Camara (2008), the private ownership of the media contributed greatly to the media in West Africa having an online presence. As a result, key media organisations in the region are now available on the Internet, thereby facilitating the growth of online journalism in the region.

The fourth section will focus on specific examples from different media organisations that are available online and will analyse the type of journalism being practiced and the challenges as well as the opportunities they provide. An important issue in online journalism in West Africa is the emergence of the diasporic media through citizen journalism (Kperogi 2011). These are media organisations managed by Africans, particularly those living in Europe and North America. These types of online media serve different functions. They provide uninterrupted news to Africans in the diaspora; they also serve as watchdogs that educate the people about corruption, human rights abuses and other violations perpetrated by various West African governments. Examples of this diasporic media include www.saharareport-ers.com and www.gamji.com serving Nigerian audiences and www.expo-timesonline.net targeting Sierra Leoneans at home and in the diaspora. The last section concludes the chapter by synthesising the issues discussed in the article as well as offering recommendations on the way forward for online journalism in West Africa.

THE MEDIA LANDSCAPE IN WEST AFRICA

Prior to the emergence of newspapers, radio, television and now the Internet, there has always been a method of traditional communication in Africa. According to Wilson (1987), these methods of traditional communication in Africa were neglected with the intervention of colonial rule, and researchers interested in the nature of communication in Africa seldom pay attention to this significant area of study.

The media landscape as it is today in West Africa was a colonial creation traceable to 1801 in Gold Coast—now Ghana—and Sierra Leone (Mano 2008). This is the reason why a lot of the media are in foreign languages like English, French and Portuguese. According to Mano (2008, 130),

> Factors that led to a viable early newspaper sector in West Africa included the presence of a large population that was western-educated and the absence of a colonial settler population that could undermine the development of the press in West Africa, as it did in other regions of Africa.

Newspapers had an earlier start in Anglophone West Africa before they were established in Francophone West Africa. As suggested by Camara (2008, 213),

> Francophone Africa did not have a press prior to the Berlin Conference (1884–1885) and the subsequent establishment of full-fledged colonial rule. Even then, by colonial law, only Frenchmen were allowed to own the press in the colonies. This explains why between 1885 and 1933 all of the few newspapers published in French West Africa were based in Dakar.

Soon after the establishment of newspapers in various countries in the region, radio (1930s) and television (1950s) followed in territories such as the Gold Coast and Nigeria. An important point in this period was that services included Africans working in the stations and broadcasting programmes in local languages like Eve, Twi and Hausa. In French West Africa, radio promoted French colonial policy from 1939 beginning in Dakar, Senegal. Countries like Sierra Leone, Burkina Faso, Cote d'Ivoire, Niger, Senegal and

Ghana also established their television stations but not until after independence (Mano 2008).

Although political power exchanged hands between colonialists and African nationalists, the media landscape in West Africa, as in most African countries, continued to be managed under the same atmosphere as it was under colonial regimes. This picture was further complicated by successive military interventions in the region from the late 1970s to the early 1990s. This is further illustrated by Nyamnjoh in his view that "Postcolonial states in Africa have had much more in common with their colonial counterparts than is often acknowledged by those eager to present Africa as a reluctant student of western achievements in democracy" (2005, 35). However, this picture began to change with the deregulation policies of the 1990s and the emergence of the Internet, which counteracted government monopoly and tried to bypass censorship.

DEREGULATION AND THE EMERGENCE OF THE INTERNET

Discussion of online journalism has to pay attention to the issue of deregulation because it plays an important role in utilising the Internet as a platform managed by private businesses and individuals. The beginning of the 1990s saw a transformation in the nature of journalism in many African countries due to the deregulation of media ownership. Independent media organisations began to emerge. This created a competitive media environment in both the print and electronic media and a platform for political pluralism flourished gradually. This was happening at a time when there was serious economic decline in many African countries. But many of the media organisations managed to survive, and those that could not succeed were replaced by new ones. These privately owned newspapers played a significant role in the political development of African countries by questioning government policies believed to be detrimental to the stability of these countries, and the process of reversing the old trend where many African governments thought that their decisions were beyond any form of scrutiny was set (Hyden and Leslie 2002).

It is important to note that prior to the deregulation of the media industry, the government-owned media had been affected by challenges faced by other sectors of the economy such as the civil service and other public sector works. In terms of resources, the government has more access to funds that can be utilised for social services in many African countries; however, inefficiency and corruption have become a stumbling block. What deregulation did was to create a sense of competition and promote innovation. This is the area where deregulation contributed to enhancing online journalism in West Africa. This process is nearly similar to what happened in the United States and other European countries when the Internet became available for public use in the 1990s. Businesses which include the news media saw it as an opportunity to advertise their products.

Equally important, another factor that contributed to the emergence of private and to some extent independent press in Africa was facilitated by new technologies; more sophisticated printing machines and computers have become available, and the spread of satellite communication has made access to information much easier. This access to information showcases happenings around the world, a factor that might have contributed to accelerating the growth of more private media institutions in many African countries (Yusha'u 2010b, 88). This is a point that Hyden and Leslie (2002) have further illustrated.

Camara (2008) studied how liberalisation and private ownership changed the media landscape in West Africa and brought about more diversity in the nature of ownership of media organisations. To him, the establishment of newspapers like the *Guardian* in Nigeria in the 1980s, *Wal Fadjri* in Senegal and *L'Observateur* in Burkina Faso was a new era. These changes influenced the broadcast sector, consequently leading to a massive spread of private radio stations in the 1990s.

As discussed by Bustamante (2004), one of the key effects of deregulation is the diminishing role of the state. Deregulation has also resulted in the concentration of capital and the merger of large organisations. This is facilitated further by the spread of information and communication technologies, which promotes more diversity in terms of ownership, and the dissemination of information (Bustamante 2004). The outcome of this in West Africa is the emergence of business owners who also decided to invest in the media. And with the Internet available, having an online presence for their products, including news services, is key to their business strategy.

One of the key changes brought by deregulation as discussed by Mano (2008, 134) is that "African media became central to the new struggle for greater political and economic independence . . . before 1990, only a few African countries allowed commercial or nonstate radios". It is not surprising, therefore, that the private media led the way in countries like Nigeria by adopting and appropriating the Internet before the government media did. And to date, the private media seem to do better than government media outfits in online journalism. However, as McChesney (2003) puts it, we should not over celebrate the deregulation of the media industry because deregulation is partly about the debate between public interests and private interests. He contends that "[d]eregulation is better thought of, in most instances and certainly in the case of media, as a misleading term for unabashed and unacknowledged regulation on behalf of powerful self-interested private parties" (McChesney 2003, 126).

THE MEDIA GOES ONLINE IN WEST AFRICA

Despite the economic and political challenges that African countries are facing, adapting to the new technologies has been progressing. The emergence of smartphones and business centres has connected the people much better with the Internet. This is indeed good news for journalism practice in West Africa. In countries like Ghana, Nigeria, Senegal and Sierra Leone, the youth, just like in other parts of the world, have made the Internet part and parcel of their lives. In Cameroon, as discussed by Bruijn et al. (2010), the Internet is changing the lives of the people in different ways, especially because of mobile. Therefore, this accessibility promotes access to news which both the broadcast and print media are capitalising on. In fact, recently, some of the newspapers, like the *Punch* and *Daily Trust* in Nigeria, are testing on-line news provision by subscription, a step that even in countries that have advanced Internet connectivity is still at the experimental level. Journalists are also using blogging to articulate their personal views on some of the stories that have been published or abandoned by the editors. The fact that these media organisations are considering making money from their online content says a lot about the future of online journalism in West Africa. First of all, it strengthens the points discussed in the preceding section about the role of deregulation in the emergence of online journalism, which sees news production as a business. Secondly, it also reiterates the dilemma that news media organisations are facing because they need money and expertise in order to provide online content, yet whereas they make a profit from hard-copies which carry advertising, the online content is normally accessed free. This attempt, however, comes with a big challenge. People can easily go to other news sources to get the same news free, which makes the subscription effort unsustainable for now. For example, the *Punch* newspaper faced this problem, and it had to be abandoned midway.

But before delving deeper into discussions about online journalism in West Africa, it is important to define as well as contextualise online journal-ism as used in the present chapter. From the "ideal-typical" definition of-fered by Deuze (2003, 206), we can differentiate three key features of online journalism. One is multimediality, that is, the ability of the website to carry multimedia functions such as YouTube, audio content such as mp3 players etc. and enough places for text which can form either the main story or analysis of the story, thereby giving the reader a choice on how to consume the message. The second feature is interactivity, which gives the user the op-portunity to be an active participant in the news story, by expressing his/her view and in some instances providing additional context or input into the story. This is common in the websites of key media organisations that have strong online content, like the BBC, where the user is allowed to comment and in some instances is asked if he/she is present where there is a developing story in order to share his eyewitness account. The editors then cross check the content to ensure its veracity and then make it available to the public.

The third aspect is hypertextuality, one of the innovations that make on-line journalism distinct from traditional journalism. The user is given access to links important to the story. These links could be the story that preceded the one the user is reading in order to have a clearer picture of the events that gave birth to the current story. It could be an explanation of the key characters in the story. For instance, an audience living in the United States may not have known anything about Tunisia until the beginning of the Arab awakening in late 2010. A story about the Tunisian uprising can contain a hyperlink about the history of Tunisia, its economy, political system and the socio-economic conditions that triggered the uprising. Basically, hyper-textuality creates the intellectual dimension for understanding a news story which is not easily available in the traditional media of radio, television and newspapers. So in summary, online journalism is a type of journalism that fuses traditional formats of journalism with multimedia features into a single platform that is user friendly.

Beginning in the 1990s after the emergence of the Internet for commercial purposes, the media in Africa also joined the trail—but with a challenge. Africa, according to Banda et al. (2009, 2), "defies many of the technological innovations said to be reconfiguring the structures and process of commu-nication globally. Of significance are poor telecommunication networks in most parts of Africa, resulting in low internet usage".

In West Africa years after the emergence of the Internet, the capacity of the Internet remained very weak, although the arrival of mobile phones has changed the nature of access to the Internet and empowered different communities like the Bamenda village in Cameroon (Frere and Kiyindou 2009; Bruijin et al. 2010). As of 2008, there were only 6.62 Internet users in Senegal, whereas Burkina Faso, Chad, Mali and the Niger Republic did not have up to one user per 100 inhabitants (Frere and Kiyindou 2009). The adoption of online platforms by West African media has facilitated "alterna-tive forms of communication" (Downey and Fenton 2003, 188). Dahlberg suggests that

> Three dominant 'camps' have emerged. First, a communitarian camp, which stresses the possibility of the Internet enhancing communal spirit and values. Second, a liberal individualist camp, which sees the Internet as assisting the expression of individual interests. Third, a deliberative camp, which promotes the Internet as the means for an expansion of the public sphere. (2001, 616)

Although Dahlberg is writing in a context different from that of West Africa, some of the issues identified could be relevant. The third category in which the Internet provides an avenue for the extension of the public sphere is important in West Africa. The West African subregion was among the key regions that were bedevilled by military rule in the decades after indepen-dence. During these decades, the military ensured a monopoly of informa-tion dissemination. There was little room for citizens to express their views. But with key media organisations having an online presence, especially in English-speaking West Africa like in Nigeria and Ghana, citizens can ex-press their reactions to news stories. Key media organisations in the region now have a multiplatform approach to journalism. Newspapers like the

Daily Trust (www.dailytrust.com) have a YouTube channel which provides video versions of stories; newspapers like *Next* (http://234next.com/), also published in Nigeria, have a strong Facebook and twitter presence. This provides a platform for information sharing and a means to elevate public discourse beyond the control of government. In Francophone West Africa, the newspaper *Fraternite Matin* (www.fratmat.info/) is one of the newspapers in Senegal with a strong online presence. The newspaper carries multimedia features, including YouTube and a variety of content that users can choose from. In the Niger Republic, *Le Republican (www.republicain-niger.com/)* is another newspaper that provides Internet content, which serves the need of Nigerians at home and in the diaspora.

Online presence in West Africa is not restricted to newspapers. The broadcast media (both television and radio) have also joined the trail. Some of them provide live stream programmes, therefore giving access to information to interested viewers anywhere in the world. Nigeria's Channels Television (www.channelstv.com/global/live_video.php) is one such station that has 24-hour transmission on the Internet. In Burkina Faso, *Radiodiffusion du Burkina* (www.rtb.bf) also has a strong online presence, providing live transmission of programmes. During the 2012 African Cup of Nations, the station transmitted different matches live with commentary in French.

The meaning of this for journalism in West Africa is the creation of "access to information" and "opportunity for interaction which the internet facilitates" (Gimmler 2001, 31). Computer-mediated communication has created a space for people to engage in conversation on issues affecting their lives (Schneider 1996). Newspapers in the region can easily update their content in times of breaking news, and the audience does not have to wait for 24 hours before they know what is happening in their neighbourhood.

One of the unique things about the Internet "is the opening of new world" especially in this age "for the citizen consumer" (Scammell 2000, 354). The new world opened by the Internet means that the consumer is not only interested in reading the news, but he also wants to participate and engage in the media. It creates room for interaction so that where the media itself is seen to be moving in the wrong direction, the consumer can have input. According to Cuilinburg (1999, 188), "new, more than old, media are interactive and/or multimedia, with hardly any restrictions on transmission by distance and time. New media often presuppose more active communication involvement of users than old media like television and radio". This uniqueness means people can access information wherever they may be; the media in this case have no territorial distinction with the audience.

It took time before African newspapers responded to this challenge, possibly due to what Mansell (2004) calls scepticism about the potential of new media. But the issue is beyond scepticism; the absence of strong capital and infrastructure contributed to a delay in the adoption of the African media into the world of the Internet, especially in the 1990s. However, at the moment, most of the leading newspapers have a presence on the Internet. But still, there is a need for improvement because sometimes the websites disappear or have accessibility problems. The archive sections still need developing because searching for previous stories is difficult and, in some newspapers, even non-existent. There is also "the risk that the internet will only reinforce the interests of the well-connected literate elite living in the cities, while most of the population turn their back on political participation" (Frere and Kiyindou 2009, 85). Whereas the literate members of the society who rely on newspapers for political information read stories that are products of the challenges discussed earlier, a different community that is virtual in nature has space to evaluate and discuss the same political information due to what Rohle (2005, 404) calls "inexpensive written communication". Whereas the challenges faced by the traditional media are likely to undermine the quality of communication, the new media create a space that upholds the quality of the information through active debates and participatory communication. According to Kluver (2002, 500), "governmental and academic commentators have argued that the deficiencies of traditional media in providing political information would be overcome, particularly because of the ways in which new information technologies would empower the polity".

Although Kluver (2002) suggests that the new media will address the shortcomings of the old or traditional media by empowering the polity with political information, the challenge is how does the new media empower the polity especially in countries where only a small fraction of the society have access to the Internet, and political leaders use state resources to establish newspapers?

The presence of newspapers on the Internet provides the opportunity to access information about the country without concern for distance. In particular, Africans in the diaspora are among those who consume information from online versions of newspapers. As discussed by Lievrouw (2001), diasporic communities take advantage of the new media and form virtual communities. The newspapers that are available online have sections for comments where people engage in debate about a particular news story, and many of the commentators live in the diaspora, especially in Europe, North America and Asia, where access to the Internet is easy.

ONLINE JOURNALISM AND THE WEST AFRICAN DIASPORA

A discussion of online journalism in West Africa would be incomplete without understanding the role of West Africans in the diaspora in the growth of online journalism. We can distinguish at least three reasons for the role of West Africans in the diaspora in the development of online journalism. First is access to information and communication technology. A large number of Nigerians, Senegalese, Ghanaians and Cameroonians live in Europe and North America. In Britain alone there are about two million Africans, many of whom are from the West African subregion (Cultural Diplomacy 2012).

A lot of them are also professionals with specialisation in information and communication technology. Therefore, they have the ability, the expertise and a conducive environment to develop a web presence for online discussion groups or even newspapers that are based online.

The second reason is the desire for news. No matter how far away these Africans live, they have a thirst for news about what is happening in their home countries; they want to remain connected with happenings at home to the extent that they put pressure on newspaper publishers to have an online presence in order to serve the needs of the diasporic community (Ndangam 2008). The third reason is the state of governance in African countries. This creates a lot of concern among Africans in the diaspora, and a feeling develops among them that one of the best ways to contribute to abating the state of bad governance in their countries of origin is through an online media which cannot be censored by their governments. Living in foreign countries also gives them some form of immunity from persecution. Developing online media provides an opportunity to Africans in the diaspora to "articulate a more radical communitarian view, drawing on idealisations of the internet as a democratic space in which all social actors' voices may be heard, and where audiences can become active publics" (Matheson 2004, 452).

An important example of how online journalism can contribute to the lives of people is from Sierra Leone. In the 1990s, Sierra Leone faced one of the biggest challenges in its history; it was affected by a civil war that left many people homeless, and a large percentage of the population had to live outside the country. The country almost disintegrated because like most African nations, Sierra Leone was also a colonial creation. Different ethnic groups and regions were forced into nationhood for colonial convenience. Yet according to Tyne (2007), Sierra Leone became a country that survived virtually through newspapers like *Expo Times* (www.expotimesonline.net), which maintained an online presence during the civil war, thereby giving a sense of nationhood to the people. Added to that is the role of Internet discussion groups that brought people from different parts of the world to discuss and think of how to develop their country. One of these discussion groups is *Leonenet*. Tyne suggests that

> Leonenet is a communicative space whose members have created a virtual nation. Because Sierra Leone's geopolitical territory is metaphorically 'hollow', some members of its society have chosen to fill that emptiness through discourse about the country. A virtual nation is defined as any community that communicates in cyberspace, whose collective discourse and/or actions are aimed towards the building, binding, maintenance, rebuilding or rebinding of a nation. Some portion of the community must be members of the diaspora of the nation. Leonenet has the potential to be a virtual nation because its geographically-based state has disintegrated. The symbolic 'nation' has no material referent, such as the state and its institutions, no physical or geographical container.

Leonenet can be viewed as a space where Sierra Leone's state-related symbols are generated and then held in conceptual escrow, waiting for the moment when the state returns to Sierra Leone. (2007, 501)

Although discussions of African diasporic media sites can sometimes be chaotic due to the diversity of opinions expressed, and *Leonenet* was not an exception as discussed by Tyne (2007), in this case, online journalism has become a tool for nation building. It was possible to do so partly because of the three reasons mentioned earlier, namely, the presence of technology, the thirst for news about home countries and the state of bad governance in some African countries, which in the case of Sierra Leone resulted in a bloody civil war.

In Cameroon, a country with multiple colonial histories with both France and Britain, online journalism is one of the ways in which the complex nature of the country is articulated by its citizens. Some of the active online discussion groups which people use to digest news from the happenings in the country is *Camnetwork* and through online versions of newspapers like the *Post*. In Ghana, online news websites like www.ghanaweb.com provide uninterrupted news service to Ghanaians in the diaspora (Sikanku 2011) and at home to the extent that there is a competition for who sets the news agenda between newspapers on the ground and news sites from the diaspora (Ndangam 2008). In Niger Republic, *Niger Diaspora* (http://nigerdiaspora. info/) has become a key media tool that presents news to the French-speaking West African country on almost every issue of national concern.

Nigeria, Africa's most populous country and the largest economy in West Africa, has one of the highest concentrations of diaspora news outlets that are present online. The diasporic media, although not managed by professional journalists, has created fierce competition with the media within Nigeria. Although almost all the key newspapers in Nigeria like *Guardian, Daily Trust, Punch* and *Vanguard* have an online presence, they sometimes have to rely on the diasporic news websites for news. Kperogi (2011) has studied the Nigerian diasporic media, most of them managed from the United States. These diasporic news sites include *Elendu Reports* (www. elendureports.com) and the *Will* (www.thewillnigeria.com), but by far, the most effective and controversial website which even Nigerian authorities cannot ignore is *Sahara Reporters* (www.saharareporters.com). According to Kperogi (2011), *Sahara Reporters* is continuously attracting the attention of the world so that global media organisations like CNN, BBC and other international news agencies even refer to them for some news items on Nigeria. An example of this was in December 2009, when news organisations referred to the website in order to find out the background of the Detroit bomber. In fact, some of these news organisations obtained the first picture of the alleged bomber from *Sahara Reporters*.

Beyond websites that specialise in news reporting from the West African subregion, an interesting development is the individual effort to utilise free blogging facilities provided by Google and WordPress to express views and provide analysis on issues affecting the continent. The Cameroonian blogger Enoh Meyomesse (http://enoh-meyomesse.blogspot.co.uk/), who was imprisoned by the Cameroonian authorities for his criticism of the government on issues of governance, is an example of this sort of journalism. Zainab Usman (http://zainabusman.wordpress.com/), a Nigerian PhD student at Oxford, is another example of how to utilise blogs to expose corruption and governmental inefficiency.

Although there is another argument about this kind of contribution, these bloggers are not trained journalists; they are simply people who have passion for writing and commenting on news analysis. But given the situation in some African countries where dictatorial regimes can pounce on journalists who work within their own countries, the analysis of news provided by bloggers, especially those in the diaspora, could provide strong input to public debate, which can be accessed by members of the public since the Internet does not have borders. In fact, these bloggers also make another contribution; some of their writings are syndicated in various local newspapers both online and in print, which helps to promote healthy debate in West Africa.

Compared to more advanced countries in Europe, North America and Asia, online journalism in Africa still requires more strengthening. But it is certainly an alternative to the mainstream media. Gone are the days when either newspapers or television stations monopolise public opinion. At least the youth and the urban elite who have access to the Internet have alternative sources of news and analysis, and this is a major contribution of online journalism in West Africa.

CONCLUSION

This chapter has explored the role of the Internet and diasporic media in the practice of online journalism. The chapter started by providing historical context for the media landscape in West Africa, in which it was stated that the media as it is today was a colonial creation. And as discussed in a later section of this chapter, although online journalism developed in the latter part of the 20th and the beginning of the 21st century, in a way, the development of online journalism in West Africa is not completely divorced from the colonial heritage of the region because as discussed in the section on the African diaspora, some of the online media are based in the former colonial countries in the West.

The chapter has also explored the notion of deregulation of the media in the 1990s. This is crucial because the development of online journalism is linked with private ownership of the media, which saw the Internet as a platform for commercial activities. The chapter has equally discussed the development of online journalism in West Africa by looking at specific country case studies in both English-speaking and French-speaking West Africa and, finally, how Africans living in the diaspora, particularly in Europe and North America, have become custodians of online journalism because of their thirst for news and the availability of technology.

When viewed within the context of the classification provided by Deuze (2003) about features of online journalism like interactivity, multimediality and hypertextuality, a visit to the web pages of the media organisations studied reveals that there is a degree of interactivity in them. People can make comments and express their views, and for many users, the interactive nature of the websites is an essential feature of online journalism. There is also a degree of multimediality in that the websites carry a lot of multimedia features such as pictures, videos and commentary. But there is still a huge challenge when it comes to hypertextuality. The websites hardly present this feature; the archive sections as discussed by Kperogi (2011) are poorly developed. Although this represents a major shortcoming, it is understandable in the sense that a lot of these websites are managed by individuals out of personal interest rather than as commercial ventures. This is an issue that requires critical thinking and more investment because if individuals run websites that provide news, without a strong means of livelihood, either of the following could happen: When they get an alternative job, they may likely abandon the work and take different opportunities. The other problem could be that they produce low-quality journalism. Neither situation is a good option for online journalism. Another challenge could be the issue of corruption. As discussed by Yusha'u (2009; 2010a), corruption is a big issue in In Africa, and his study on Nigeria suggests that all that journalists require is a platform, and they can use it to seek bribes and other favours in the name of journalism. Once this kind of allegation becomes public knowledge, readers are likely to become sceptical about the truth of the news content. Some of these challenges could also explain why some news websites start actively, but after a few years, they disappear because there are no incentives to carry on with the production of news.

Despite the contribution and gradual growth of online journalism in West Africa, Internet connectivity is still not strong in the region, and despite recent growth, there is a huge population in rural areas where people have never heard the term 'Internet', and where people have access, reading news online is not their priority. In terms of practice, especially for the newspapers that are managed within the region, technical expertise remains a huge challenge. A number of the newspapers can only update their websites once a day because they cannot afford the services of 24-hour personnel to run their online versions, like the more established mainstream sites such as the *Guardian, Washington Post* and the *New York Times*. Therefore, online journalism is not fully developed as a profession.

Lack of electricity is a huge challenge in the practice of online journalism because where newspapers, radio and television stations have the personnel to work on the online versions of the media, there could be logistical problems because they have to dedicate a large percentage of their resources to acquire generators that will provide the electricity to manage the computers as well as monitor the development of news. In summary, four key issues can be identified from the issues covered in this chapter:

1. Online journalism in West Africa is a product of the development of information and communication technology, a development facilitated further by the deregulation of the media industry in the 1990s.
2. So far, private organisations and interested individuals have managed to produce online journalism, whereas government media are behind in developing an online presence or in making effective contributions to the growth of online journalism despite the criticisms of governments about the content of the online media outlets.
3. Africans in the diaspora play a key role in the development of online journalism despite the absence of professional journalism training.
4. Online journalism is still elitist because it is accessed by the literate members of society.

A key question to be asked is, How can online journalism be developed in the West African region given that it is growing and becoming an alternative source of news? The following recommendations will be useful:

1. Introducing online journalism degrees in African universities so that students can be trained in professional aspects so that they can work as real journalists with online skills.
2. Africans in the diaspora interested in online journalism should be encouraged to take journalism courses offered by different universities to acquire the journalistic skills needed so that their journalism practice can go beyond political activism.
3. Citizen journalists who contribute to online journalism should utilise the services of mainstream media organisation like the *BBC* College of Journalism, which offers free online courses and materials for journalists in the UK; so this provides an opportunity especially for West Africans residing in the UK. Another alternative is the *Guardian* Foundation, which provides training and interactive courses for journalists from developing countries.
4. Africans in the diaspora who have IT skills should provide training to media personnel in their home countries in order to improve their web management skills so that they can translate it into practice.
5. Journalists' unions in African countries can establish centres of online journalism training with the specific aim of developing the online skills of journalists who need multimedia capability.

REFERENCES

Banda, Fackson, Mudhai, Okoth F., and Tettey, Wisdom. 2009. "Introduction: New media and Democracy in Africa-A Critical Interjection". In *African Media and the Digital Public Sphere*, edited by Mudhai, Okoth F., Tettey, Wisdom J. and Banda, Fackson, 1–20. New York. Palgrave MacMillan.

220 *Muhammad Jameel Yusha'u*

Bruijn, Mirjam, Nyamnjoh, Francis and Angwafo, Tseghama. 2010. "Mobile Interconnections: Reinterpreting Distance and Relating in the Cameroonian Grassfields". *Journal of African Media Studies* 2(3): 267–285.

Burstamante, Enrique. 2004. "Cultural Industries in the Digital Age: Some Provisional Conclusions". *Media, Culture & Society.* 26(6): 803–820.

Camara, Mohamed Saliou. 2008. "Media, Civil Society, and Political Culture in West Africa". *Ecquid Novi: African Journalism Studies* 29(2): 210–229.

Cuilinburg, Jan Van. 1999. "On Competition, Access and Diversity in Media, Old and New". *New Media & Society* 1(2): 183–207.

Cultural Diplomacy. 2012. "The African Diaspora in Europe". Accessed 25 May 2012. http://www.culturaldiplomacy.org/index.php?en_programs_diaspora_eu.

Dahlberg, Lincoln. 2001. "The Internet and Democratic Discourse: Exploring the Prospects of Online Deliberative Forums Extending the Public Sphere". *Information, Communication and Society* 4(4): 615–633.

Deuze, Mark. 2003. "The Web and its Journalisms: Considering the Consequences of Different Types of Newmedia Online". *New Media & Society* 5(2): 203–230.

Downey, John, and Fenton, Natalie. 2003. "New Media, Counter Publicity and the Public Sphere". *New Media and Society* 5(2): 185–202.

Frere, Marie Soeil and Kiyindou, Alain. 2009. "Democratic Process, Civic Consciousness and the Internet in Francophone Africa". In *African Media and the Digital Public Sphere*, edited by Mudhai, Fred O., Tettey, Wisdom J. and Banda, Fackson, 73–88. New York: Palgrave MacMillan.

Gimmler, Antje. 2001. "Deliberative Democracy, the Public Sphere and the Internet". *Philosophy of Social Criticism* 27(4): 21–39.

Hyden, Goran and Michael, Leslie. 2002. "Communications and Democratisation in Africa". In *Media and Democracy in Africa*, edited by Hyden, Goran, Leslie, Michael and Ogundimu, Folu F., 1–27. New Brunswick, NJ: Transaction Publishers.

Kluver, Alan R. 2002. "The Logic of New Media in International Affairs". *New Media & Society* 4(4): 499–517.

Kperogi, Farooq A. 2011. "Webs of Resistance: The Citizen Online Journalism of the Nigerian Digital Diaspora". Doctoral dissertation, Georgia State University.

Lievrouw, Leah A. 2001. "New Media and the 'Pluralization of Life-Worlds': A Role for Information in Social Differentiation". *New Media & Society* 3(1): 7–28.

Mano, Winston. 2008. "Africa: Media Systems". In *The International Encyclopaedia of Communication*, edited by Donsbach, Wolfgang, 129–136. Malden, MA: Blackwell Publishing.

Mansell, Robin. 2004. "Political Economy, Power and New Media". *New Media & Society* 6(1): 74–83.

Matheson, Donald. 2004. "Weblogs and the Epistemology of the News: Some Trends in Online Journalism". *New Media & Society* 6(4): 443–468.

McChesney, Robert W. 2003. "Theses on Media Deregulation". *Media Culture & Society* 25(1): 125–133.

Ndangam, Lilian N. 2008. "Free Lunch? Cameroon's Diaspora and Online News Publishing". *New Media & Society* 10(4): 585–604.

Nyamnjoh, Francis. 2005. "Media and the State in Africa: Continuities and Discontinuities". In *Untold Stories: Economics and Business Journalism in African Media,* edited by Kareithi, Peter and Kariithi, Nixon, 32–48. Johannesburg: Wits University Press.

Rohle, Theo. 2005. "Power, Reason, Closure: Critical Perspectives on New Media Theory". *New Media & Society* 7(3): 403–422.

Scammell, Margret. 2000 "The Internet and Civic Engagement: The Age of the Citizen-Consumer". *Political Communication* 17(4): 351–355.

Schneider, Steven M. 1996. "Creating a Democratic Public Sphere Through Political Discussion: A Case Study of Abortion Conversation on the Internet". *Social Science Computer Review* 14(4): 373–393.

Sikanku, Etse G. 2011. "Intermedia Influences among Ghanaian Online Print News Media: Explicating Salience Transfer of Media Agendas". *New Media & Society* 42(8): 1320–1335.

Tynes, Robert. 2007. "Nation-Building and the Diaspora on Leonenet: A Case of Sierra Leone in Cyberspace". *New Media & Society* 9(3): 497–518.

Wilson, Des. 1987. "Traditional Systems of Communication in Modern African Development: An Analytical Viewpoint". *Africa Media Review* 1(2): 87–104.

Yusha'u, Muhammad Jameel. 2009. "Investigative Journalism and Scandal Reporting in the Nigerian Press". *Ecquid Novi: African Journalism Studies* 30(2): 155–174.

———. 2010a. "Regional Parallelism and Reporting of Corruption in the Nigerian Press". *Journal of African Media Studies* 2(3): 353–369.

———. 2010b. "Press Coverage of Corruption Scandals in the Nigeria Press: A Comparative Analysis of the Northern and Southern Newspapers". Doctoral dissertation, University of Sheffield.

13 "Our Listeners Would Rather Call than Post Messages on Facebook"[1]
New Media and Community Radio in Kenya

George Ogola

INTRODUCTION

Scholarship on the liberalization of the media sector in Africa continues to paint a mixed picture. Although the media landscape has been radically transformed, with the continent now host to numerous radio and TV stations, newspapers and online media since the early 1990s, a number of challenges continue to frustrate further development of the sector (Nyamjoh 2005; Curran and Park 2000). Debates still abound over the routine enactment of a raft of legal and policy measures which remain inimical to media freedom (Ayittey 1999; Maina 2006). Meanwhile, the acquisition of broadcast licences in Kenya, for example, has often been influenced by one's relationship with the state. Such practices undermine the media liberalization project (Ogola 2011).

As a consequence, policy makers, media players and audiences around the continent are increasingly investing in the various possibilities enabled by new media. Equally, there has been renewed interest in the potential of community media and more specifically radio, a sector which, theoretically at least, seeks to represent voices which largely occupy the 'margins' and which both the private and public media tend to either underrepresent or ignore altogether. This chapter seeks to explore the ways in which new media are adopted and adapted by community radio. Do new media, for instance, radically change the ethos and practices of community radio journalism? Are they enabling a centering or decentering of the margins?

My focus is primarily on two community radio stations in Kenya—Pamoja FM and Koch FM. The former is based in the Ayany estate in Kibera, a sprawling slum in southwest Nairobi, whereas Koch FM operates from two converted disused containers in the Korogocho slums to the east of the city.[2] I hope to use these two stations as illustrative examples to provide us a broad overview of the community radio sector and how it has responded to and has in turn been shaped by new media in Kenya. This study is broadly exploratory, with data gathered from interviews with staff from the two radio stations and through newsroom observation.

LOCATING COMMUNITY RADIO IN AFRICA

It is pertinent to historicise the development of community media more broadly for this enables one to locate the changes but also the continuities of some of the journalistic traditions and practices in community radio in Africa. Community radio is arguably the oldest and most discussed form of community media in Africa. Across the continent, it has largely positioned itself as the *de facto* communication platform for disenfranchised voices. This sector has in many cases emerged as a response to cultural, economic and political marginalisation and in some cases repression. In South Africa, for example, the sector grew as part of the broader response to the apartheid regime's refusal to provide the non-white populations adequate representation in the mainstream and mainly white-owned media. Elsewhere, community radio has especially developed as a result of attempts by communication activists, NGOs and in some cases governments to enable local communities to access information and to participate in a range of development programmes.

Understood in its current form, the first community radio station in Africa was set up in Homa Bay, Kenya in 1982.[3] Funded by the Kenya government and UNESCO, the station was "not only an experiment in decentralisation of structures and programming but was also an effort to gain experience in the utilization of low-cost technology for broadcasting" (AMARC 1998, 12). Across the continent however, the development and status of community media in general and community radio in particular remain varied. Indeed, community media had existed in many forms in the continent many years before the Homa Bay experiment. Community media had operated in the form of radio forums where villagers and farmers came together to discuss communal issues. In South Africa, 'briefcase' radio, a process whereby cassette tapes were carried in briefcases and then distributed on the streets, marked the beginnings of some key community radio stations such as Bush Radio. The station emerged from "a community-based project [. . .] the Cassette Education Trust (CASET), which produced and distributed cassette tapes containing speeches from banned activists, local music and revolutionary poetry in Cape Town" (Chiumbu 2010, 125). Other community radio, especially those in the rural areas, were established mainly through funding from organizations such as UNESCO (AMARC 1998).

However, although community media has a long and fairly chequered history in the continent, it is only in South Africa and Namibia where the sector is explicitly acknowledged in law and provisions made for its development. The South African media sector, for example, provides for a three-tier broadcasting system—public, commercial and community. In Namibia, the 1992 Communications Commission Act prioritizes the allocation of frequencies to those "transmitting the maximum number of hours per day and to community-based broadcasters" (AMARC 1998, 10). In many other countries in the continent, support is patchy. In Zambia, for example, "community media is not mentioned in the ZNBC (Licensing) Regulations Act of 1993 which liberalised the airwaves" (ibid.). In Botswana, an NGO was once denied licence to operate in the Kalahari district "on the grounds that community broadcasting was already being offered by the state-owned Radio-Botswana" (ibid.). In other countries such as Kenya, community media has often been confused with vernacular or local-language media. The latter sector is generally viewed with suspicion as most of the local-language radio stations are owned by politicians who actively use them as political platforms. This was the case before and after the 2007–2008 election crisis when they were used to articulate and animate political and ethnic loyalties and tensions.[4]

In several other countries, however, the trend is slowly changing, with governments gradually acknowledging the need to support the sector. In Benin, for example, community radio is now officially recognized, and "through the Haute Autorité de l'Audiovisuel et de la Communication (HAAC) specific licensing arrangements that guarantee fair access to the radio spectrum are provided" (Myers 2008: 15). Countries such as Mali, Burkina Faso, Benin and Senegal are also developing policies to help grow the community media sector (AMARC 1998). In fact, Mali has been described by Buckley et al. as having "one of the most democratic broadcast laws in Africa" (Buckley et al. 2008, 209) since the fall of the Traoré regime in 1991.

A number of lobby groups and associations have also been vocal in their calls for the creation of a supportive legal and policy regime for the sector. In Kenya, for example, the Kenya Community Media Network (KCOMNET) was formed to, among other things, "lobby for the establishment of a dynamic communication regime [in Kenya] that includes community media as a third sector after public and private media" (KCOMNET 2010). Meanwhile, the Church, UNESCO and a number of international NGOs have continued to support the sector either through sponsorship, training of journalists or the provision of media equipment. The Roman Catholic Church, for example, has a long tradition of establishing radio stations in Zambia, Burkina Faso, Mozambique and the DRC, among other countries (AMARC 1998, 11).

UNDERSTANDING 'COMMUNITY' IN COMMUNITY MEDIA

Although community media have indeed grown variously around the continent, often, questions are asked about what it actually is. In countries such as Kenya, community media are often conflated with regional or local-language media. The lack of a useful policy framework in part arises from the failure to define and understand the media. It is therefore important that we attempt to reflect on its meaning, particularly the 'community' in community media.

The very idea of community media presupposes a set of agreed assumptions on what 'community' stands for. Yet that assumption is problematic.

Indeed, some scholars regard it as a fundamental conceptual error with broader practical implications. Accordingly, scholars such as Opubor have called for an urgent need to "understand the nature of community which underlies media practice, access and ownership" (2000, 14) in community media. He notes that whereas the notion of community today has "a strong non-physical connotation, it still retains a strong physical reference to people in geographical proximity, with frequent, if not continuous contact. People who share certain cultural attributes have access to certain resources of social organization and common institutions, resulting in common beliefs" (12). But we must also acknowledge that those 'communities' are themselves internally diverse and therefore can, as they often do, have just as varied interests. To imagine them as homogenous and therefore structure models around an imagined coherence is to make a fundamental mistake.[5] Opubor, therefore, redirects the discussion and focuses not so much on the notion of community but rather on the communication system that interpellates a community in community media. He argues that a community "creates and is created by a community communication system, which includes the various communication roles (and their actors/performers), needs, and resources available to the individuals and groups which make the community" (13). He suggests that the focus on community media should mainly be on the "elements of a community communication system", a point often ignored by policy makers and theorists of community media. The community communication system is constitutive of but is also partly constituted by the community. Opubor observes that approaches to community media development "have been dominated by exogenous definitions of communities and the imposition of narrow media-based solutions to the cultural, communication and survival problems which communities face" (ibid.). Therefore, a number of community media projects are "driven by noble intentions to promote indigenous development . . . [but] not based on a conceptual or practical foundation arising from a community communication system point of view" (ibid.). He suggests that a communication media system should proceed from a basic understanding of the nature and needs of the community in communication terms.

The conceptual difficulty in defining or indeed in understanding community media is further illustrated by AMARC's definition. The organisation refers to 'community' as a term denoting "a collective or group of people sharing common characters and /or interests and can be defined as "a geographically based group of persons and/or a social group or sector of the public who have common or specific interests such as a community of women in a particular area (e.g., community of women in Dassa-Zoume), community of workers in Karutura township; or a community of youth of Dakar" (AMARC 2008, 13). This definition is useful but also risks simplifying a rather complicated concept. For example, it seems to ignore particularly the ways in which people now move within and across collective formations traditionally referred to as 'communities'. The women in Dassa-Zoume may live in a common geographical space but may also belong to very different 'communities' defined perhaps on the basis of ethnicity, religion or, indeed, social class. They may therefore be part of the community of women in Dassa-zoume and not. The same applies to a 'community' of workers and to a 'community' of youth. Indeed, even the collective nouns 'workers' and 'youth' are themselves ambiguous as they are invested with sets of unqualified assumptions.

Howley, on the other hand, emphasises the idea of 'knowable communities' in his extrapolation of the idea of community in community media. Borrowing from the work of Raymond Williams (1973), he speaks of the role that communication plays "in shaping individual and collective consciousness of the relations of significance and solidarity that we call community" (Howley 2010, 9). He further argues that whereas mainstream media "conceal the interconnected and mutually dependent character of social relations, community media work to reveal this fundamental aspect of human communities" (ibid)—the collective solidarities.

The adoption of new media by community media and audiences introduces a new dynamic to our understanding of 'community'. Communities are now defined by much more than just geographical location. Some 'communities' are now constructed online, at once reifying the geographical locatedness of a group of people and creating new solidarities with affinities revolving around singular and multiple interests that make both visible and invisible location a factor definitive of a community. It is, however, arguable that this has yet to radically redefine the general conception of 'community' as it is understood by community journalists, their audiences or, indeed, policy makers. Community is still largely imagined as a function of geography, a factor seen, for example, in the allocation of broadcast spectrum and in existing funding models and policy regimes.

PROBLEMATIZING THE 'NEW' IN NEW MEDIA AND COMMUNITY RADIO IN AFRICA

The impact of new media on radio in Africa has now received considerable scholarly attention (e.g., Vatikiotis 2010; Ndlela 2010). Unlike the 'exaggerated celebration', to use Winston's (1998) phrase, that has accompanied discussions on new media's impact on journalistic practices in newspaper newsrooms, such praise has been more measured in regard to radio. Even then, discussions still oscillate between utopian and dystopian views of technology (Moyo 2013, 211), positions which "lack the sophistication in grappling with the complex question of the dialectical relationship between technology, agency and structure" (ibid.).

Without substantive qualification, new media has therefore been variously called transformational, revolutionary and even irrepressible in Africa. There is a need to caution against this sort of populism. This is not to undermine the significance or, indeed, ignore the changes that have taken place in African newsrooms as a result of new media; rather, it is to avoid closing down space for more nuanced discussions on new media in the continent. More usefully, perhaps, the focus should not only be on the impact of these emergent technologies but on the manner in which they have been appropriated, domesticated or even ignored by local media. Such an approach insulates us from making claims of impact that cannot be sufficiently qualified.

More fundamentally, in discussions of new media's impact on radio, researchers tend to use the term 'new media' as if it requires no disambiguation. Suffice to say, new media is a highly loaded term. It is neither homogenous nor obvious. Further, its temporality is contextual. Some scholars like Pavlik (2011) attempt a fairly useful disaggregation of the term by providing a five-part conceptual framework which teases out some of its constitutive elements. Pavlik observes that in new media are implied acquisition devices, storage facilities, processing technology, distribution technology and display or access devices. Such disaggregation is important as it allows one to not only understand the range of elements the idea encapsulates but also to investigate fairly precisely their role(s) in journalism. Pavlik notes how acquisition devices such as the mobile phone now enable journalists to conduct interviews and how, in turn, this has helped shrink the spatial distance between journalists and their sources. Meanwhile, media content is now produced and distributed through multiple platforms, including the mobile phone. This is a good example of a new media tool that integrates various technologies. Such tools have had a discernible impact on news production process as well as on recalibrating relationships between audiences and the media. As a consequence, we now even have media audiences being referred to as 'prosumers',[6] or as Rosen (2006) calls them, the people formerly known as the audience, for they not only consume but also produce news.

The debate on and about new media also often centres on the ambiguity that the 'new' in new media seems to either denote or conjure. Whereas some scholars such as McNair trace its etymology to the 1960s when it was used "to encompass an expanding and diversifying set of applied communication technologies" (2005, 38), others such as Mabweazara (2010) argue that the term is best understood when located within specific contexts. In Africa, for example, Mabweazara (2010) rightly describes the notion of new technology as particularly 'convoluted'. Citing Flew, he notes that "it prevents an understanding of what may be different degrees of 'newness' among and across various media" (13). Similarly, Lister et al. (2003) insist on a definition that acknowledges the idea as being "historically relative" (11). They also argue that the genealogy of the term may very well be part of a broader ideological narrative that attaches progress to Western inventions (ibid). Nyamjoh (2005) extends this argument with a definition he claims is rooted in African experiences by problematizing the 'new' in new media. He cites the difficulties in divorcing the old from the new in Africa, a place where technologies are appropriated but simultaneously domesticated to become local. Nyamjoh talks of how Africans are "daily modernising the indigenous and indigenising the modern with novel outcomes. No technology seems too used to be used, just as nothing is too new to be blended with the old for even newer results" (2005, 4). The way in which technologies are adopted and adapted in Africa is fundamentally irreducible to such neat categories as old and new. The 'new' in new media is therefore only useful in so far as it establishes an analytical category.

The debate above notwithstanding, many scholars broadly agree that there are emergent and emerging technologies that have only recently been appropriated in Africa, perhaps as elsewhere, by local media and audiences (see Mudhai 2011; Mudhai, Tettey and Banda 2009; Wasserman 2010). Their impact can be seen in what are evolving journalistic practices and media consumption habits on the continent, even if such impact must always be understood as part of much larger processes of change. Journalists across the continent have integrated a range of new technologies in their newsrooms and journalistic practices and so have local consumers of these media. African news organizations now generally have some online presence, with the platform variously used as the main media outlet, as complementary to print editions of newspapers or radio and TV stations or as a way through which news is generated and feedback received. On occasion, African audiences have also used these new platforms and technologies to assert their influence on news products.

As an illustrative example, in March 2012, the Atlanta-based international news channel CNN was forced to pull a video from its website following online protests criticizing the organization's coverage of a story in Nairobi, Kenya. CNN's Nairobi correspondent David McKenzie had filed a story following an incident in downtown Nairobi where suspected Al-Shabaab militants threw grenades into a bus terminus, killing and injuring several Kenyans. Although factually accurate, the channel carried the story with the banner "Violence in Kenya" superimposed on a graphic of the Kenyan flag. Kenyan online community condemned the use of the banner and encouraged others on Twitter, Facebook and other social networking websites to call for McKenzie and CNN to apologise for what they termed 'poor reporting.'[7] Although itself a novel response to a perceived 'problem' over (mis)representation, what was especially significant was the fact that a reporter from a local newspaper, the *Daily Nation,* used this online 'Twitter storm' to write a story for both the online and print editions of the newspaper.

Although the story may have gone through the usual editorial processes, it is notable that the story idea was generated online, whereas the sources for the story were Tweets and Facebook messages. This 'virtual story' demonstrates how new technologies have become part of the 'news' and the news-making processes in Africa.[8]

Discussing the use of new media specifically in radio, Myers (2008) argues that there seems to have been "a rediscovery of radio in the context of

ICTs, a realisation that technology has made it a two way medium that can help bridge the digital divide by providing a powerful tool for information dissemination and access for 'hard-to-reach rural audiences'". She further notes that "while the adoption and use of some technologies remain constrained by poor technical infrastructure which inhibit, for example, access to the Internet, a number of radio stations—community, commercial and public/state—have nonetheless been able to adopt some of the emerging new media technologies and are now streamed online" (ibid). The same argument is made by Moyo (2013, 211) who talks about the transformation of radio as a medium by the Internet and mobile phones "through multiple platforms such as webcasting, mobile streaming, blogging, podcasts, and indeed social media". Others such as Chiumbu and Ligaga (2013) argue that new media have expanded the "communicative radio spaces" and transformed the "nature of audience engagement" (p. 229).

The most radical appropriations of these new media technologies have, however, largely taken place in commercial radio. Yet as Willems (2013) observes, their transformative potential in so far as they allow for broader and more inclusive public participation is compromised by the various stations' commercial orientation. Despite the growth of community media over the last decade, there is still little to suggest that there is an emergent community media digital culture. In her study of the impact of new media on community radio in Mali, Uganda and Mozambique, Nassanga et al. (2013) argue that there are a number of explanatory mitigating factors, including access to the new media platforms, adequate digital skills and poor infrastructure, and the cost of both set-up and maintenance have constrained the integration of new media into the daily operations of community radio. Although she talks of some new media impact on community radio in her sample case studies, she notes that it has not been dramatic. Therefore, she warns against assumptions about universal access and usage, a tendency which has become notably seductive in various discussions on the impact of new media on African media in general.

GOING LOCAL WITH NEW MEDIA AT PAMOJA FM AND KOCH FM

Pamoja FM and Koch FM were both started by Kibera and Korogocho residents and initially aimed at the local youth. Pamoja FM, for example, has a 'mission statement' which privileges its role as a tool to be used to "empower the youth in Kibera and its environs through education, information and entertainment" (www.pamojafm.com). Koch FM also talks about its focus on the local youth, calling them their 'target audience'. It also outlines its roles as a station meant to "entertain and educate—and teach—the people in the slums" (kochfm.blogspot.co.uk). Both stations are funded by donor agencies. Koch FM is funded by the Norwegian Church Aid, which also donated the containers and equipment used by the station. Pamoja FM, on the other hand, receives financial support primarily from USAID, with organizations such as the BBC and Internews offering occasional training and technical support.

Started in 2007 just prior to that year's fiercely contested general elections, Pamoja FM was also started as a platform for "promoting peaceful co-existence in Kibera"(www.pamojafm.com). Indeed, the name Pamoja means "together" in Kiswahili, and the station still describes itself as "an instrument of peace and a medium for community development" (ibid.) It is a role the station manager Adam Hussein says the station actively played at the height of Kenya's 2007–2008 post-election crisis. Local youth were invited to talk to their peers to shun violence in the area (Abdi and Dean 2008; Mercier 2009)

There is a fairly loose understanding of new media at both Pamoja FM and Koch FM. Although the two stations have an online presence, their usage of the platform is varied but also limited. Pamoja FM has a website which streams the station's programmes live. The station also posts local and international news stories on the site, but these are not regularly updated. The site has a few interactive features, including a discussion forum, a Facebook page and an unused Twitter account. Koch FM, on the other hand, does not have a dedicated website. Instead, it runs a simple blog written by some of the station's editors. In an interview with the author, a manager at the station emphasized their commitment to creating a website for the station. However, this was meant for "people around the world to know about our station and what we are doing" (Interview with author on 8 June 2012). Using the platform for content provision for local residents was not a priority.

During my interviews with staff members from the two radio stations, there was a general acknowledgement of the importance of new media in the news production process. However, what these roles were in local community newsrooms remained unclear. Questions about new media were broadly redacted to mean the use of social media. Even then, at Pamoja FM, for example, some of the editors noted that the use of social media within their newsroom and by their listeners was fairly tentative. At the time of the interview, they admitted to having just over 300 followers on Facebook. They also noted that Twitter was not used by most of their listeners as it was still a relatively new technology to most of them. However, the editors use Twitter to follow other media organizations and journalists "to know about what events are happening and therefore which places to send our reporters" (Interview with author in June 2012). Koch FM's editors said the same of their use of Facebook and Twitter but blamed the limited use of social media by the station on the lack of Internet access in the Korogocho area for most residents.

Although the editors from the two stations noted that they occasionally get some story ideas from Facebook and Twitter, they acknowledged that they still relied almost entirely on established sources living in Kibera and Korogocho. At Pamoja FM, the station relies mainly on a group of volunteer stringers who live in Kibera. The stringers call the station on their mobile phones to alert the editors of potential news stories. Most of these stringers also belong to welfare groups in the slums. These welfare groups have regular meetings where they discuss various issues affecting their community, and through these meetings, the stringers are able to relay to the station the residents' concerns and interests. These then form the basis of the station's programming. The station also occasionally sends out questionnaires to these meetings to get feedback on their programmes. The same approach is used by Koch FM, which also has volunteer reporters living across Korogocho's nine villages. But the station also gets story ideas from the local administration, particularly the local chief. They also make use of local elders residing across the villages that make up the settlement.

It is notable that whereas Pamoja FM's editors seemed to acknowledge the importance of social media in newsgathering and in the distribution of content, they also seemed wary of their potential impact on the station's content; hence, their limited use by the station. For example, one editor observed that most of their 'Facebook friends' were based in Europe and the United States where access to the Internet was much cheaper and easier. Their interests and needs, he observed, were not necessarily similar to those of people living in Kibera. Thus, they feared that disproportionate reliance on story ideas generated online would alienate the station from the local population who, he insisted, remained their primary audience. But the editor also observed that whereas some of their listeners based in Kibera also used their Facebook page to interact with the station, "most listeners would rather call than post messages on Facebook" (Interview with author in Nairobi on 3 March 2012).

One of the most popular technologies used at Pamoja FM is the FrontlineSMS for radio software. Its popularity seemed to stem from the fact that it integrated 'new' technologies with familiar and relatively traditional communication habits. FrontlineSMS for radio is an open-source software that runs on both PCs and Macs and enables users to send and receive text messages with groups of people through mobile phones. The software has an interface which allows a radio station's presenter to interact with listeners live but also to archive contacts. According to the software's developers, this technology can be used for a number of things, including "creating and managing SMS-related contact groups, viewing incoming and outgoing message history, collecting data via SMS, and exporting data for easy analysis. It also enables the user to run their own SMS information service using auto-replies" (www.frontlinesms.com). However, one of its most useful features is that it can work on any GSM network through a PC or laptop without necessarily requiring the user to be online. This makes it particularly convenient for users in areas where Internet connection is either too expensive or unreliable.

According to Pamoja FM's editors, this technology is now well integrated into the operations of the station and has further concretized the relationship between the station and the local community. It enables interaction between the radio station's reporters and their listeners, who send text messages and participate in live programmes. Listeners are also able to text in with possible news items, which can then be followed up by the station's reporters. The station manager also indicated that they use the technology to create a database of their listeners to whom they would then send breaking news or information about their programmes. The use of text messages and call-ins remain by far the most popular method of interaction between the radio station and their listeners. Staff at both stations attributed this popularity to listeners' familiarity with the technology, the ubiquity of the mobile phone, the cost involved in sending text messages or calling and, more importantly, the fact that their "listeners are happiest when they listen to their own voices on radio" (Interview with author on 3 March 2012).

'IMAGINING' COMMUNITIES IN KIBERA AND KOROGOCHO

The frequency restrictions for Pamoja FM and Koch FM mean that they can only broadcast within a 2km radius. Their target audience is therefore largely geographically defined. Perhaps as a consequence of that, the two stations also seem to construct their audiences as homogenous with various internal fissures only underscored in so far as they help to confirm this homogeneity. Kibera and Korogocho are inhabited by relatively poor Kenyans from various ethnic groups. Poverty and ethnicity form a potent mix that often informs the political tensions that intermittently morph into violence in the two settlements.[9] Those tensions are acknowledged and used to inform the dominant discursive practices that ensure that residents are imagined as 'a people'. It is important to note that the funding regimes that sustain these organizations also ensure both consciously and subtly that the 'communities' they serve or target are constructed by the stations as these funders imagine them. The focus on local education and local development are in fact narratives used to legitimize the construction and making of the Kibera and Korogocho 'communities'.

The funding profiles and the silent political roles these stations subconsciously or consciously play impose a very specific ethos on how they operate. Although new media can destabilize, reify and construct new 'communities', this does not seem to be the case at either Pamoja FM or Koch FM. In a fairly broad sense, new media have been appropriated not to challenge but to further legitimize the existing operational ethos that ensures the two organizations continue to serve the same 'communities' and receive donor funding. Although the influence of various new media is perceptible in the ways in which the stations' journalists now gather their news and engage with their audiences, there is no notable reimagining or reconstruction of the target audiences. Indeed, as noted by one of Pamoja FM's managers, their use of Facebook comments by 'friends' to influence story ideas was seen as potentially destabilizing to the station's focus on the Kibera community's interests.

In both stations, this attachment to geography is also reflected in the programming. According to an editor at Koch FM, the station's programming is currently based on a two-year survey they conducted in Korogocho. Local residents told them what they liked and which programmes to take off the air. At Pamoja FM, the programme bouquet has also been developed from similar surveys and remains relatively flexible depending on what the Kibera residents want (Interview with author on 3 March 2012). Typically, they have morning talk shows, programmes on health and social issues, current affairs, politics and music. Examples include "Vijana na Siasa" ("Youth and Politics"), "Tuangamize Ufisadi" ("Let's fight corruption") and music programmes featuring various genres including Reggae, Rhumba, Bongo Flava and Taarab. Meanwhile, international news is streamed from the BBC World Service. These programmes reflect a fairly inclusive, developmental but also conservative approach to programming, one that does not seem particularly interested or indeed capable of challenging the established constructs of the 'communities' that should be served.

CONCLUSION

Various forms of new media have had some impact at both Pamoja FM and Koch FM. This impact should, however, neither be overstated nor understated. The two stations have incorporated some new media technologies to improve their newsgathering, programming, distribution as well as their relationship with their audiences. The mobile phone, for example, has been appropriated and domesticated, becoming by far the most used technology by the stations' reporters and their listeners. At Pamoja FM, the potential of the mobile phone as a journalistic tool is further enhanced by the station's use of the FrontlineSMS for radio software. The mobile phone's ubiquity, relative low cost and openness to adaptation has made it particularly useful for these stations and their audiences. It enables community stringers and general listeners to get in touch with the stations while allowing the latter to send text messages and call in during live broadcasts. The mobile phone transcends, at least in relative terms, some of the major obstacles that make other forms of media necessarily exclusionary to communities living in such informal settlements. Cost, availability and ease of use are some of the notable factors that make it particularly convenient.

Yet it is important to underscore the fact that the mobile phone and the FrontlineSMS radio software are popular in part because they work within an existing communication system. One could argue that some of these technologies in fact strengthen older models of communication and newsgathering practices. For example, although the mobile phone enables 'stringers' to communicate much faster with the radio stations, they still work within fairly traditional communication, organizational and social networks within Kibera and Korogocho. The stations' reporters and editors still have to rely on the local welfare groups to which most are members, local administration and village elders. It would therefore be questionable to privilege the mobile phone and ignore these local networks and/or how they help in the generation of story ideas and programmes for the radio stations. This particularly reifies Opubor's (2000) argument that new media technologies often succeed mainly when adopted around existing 'community systems'.

It is also evident that although the potential of the online platform and social media are acknowledged by the community radio journalists, they are only slowly being integrated into the radio stations' daily operations. For example, although editors are aware of the advantages the online platform brings to a news organization, they are also anxious about the various challenges it poses. First, investment in the platform is constrained by the lack of Internet access for most local residents, who are their primary audience. Second, there is fear that some new technologies, such as social media, could lead to the formation of new powerful 'communities' outside of both Kibera and Korogocho that influence local content. Due to their relative advantage in accessing new media technologies, these emergent online constituencies could end up influencing content and hence dominating local community voices. The strength and relevance of community radio inheres primarily in its locatedness. This means that unless local residents are able to access new media technologies and integrate them to become part of their media consumption habits, the appropriation and use of some new media technologies by community radio will remain patchy. Indeed, in so far as community radio in Kenya is concerned, it is perhaps too early to talk about a digital radio culture.

NOTES

1. Author interview with a radio programme manager. Nairobi, 3 March 2012.
2. Kibera and Korogocho are two of Nairobi's biggest slums. Informal settlements in Nairobi constitute nearly half the city's population (UN-HABITAT 2003).
3. The Homa Bay community radio did not, however, last long and shut down in 1984 (AMARC 1998)
4. For a substantive reading of how these stations were appropriated by the political class to frame the election debate and crisis, see Ogola (2011) and Abdi and Dean (2008).
5. This argument is also made by Myers (2000)
6. This neologism was originally coined by Toffler (1980).
7. See Shiundu, Alphonce. "*Kenyans incensed over CNN reporting gaffe*". 11 March 2012. http://www.africareview.com/News/Kenyans+incensed+over+CNN+gaffe/-/979180/1364190/-/3nr63h/-/index.html.

8. A similar point can be made of the Kony 2012 video that went viral. The stories on and about the video were mainly generated online with Facebook comments and Tweets forming the bulk of the sources used in stories about the video.
9. Kibera was one of the flashpoints during the country's post-election crises. It is within the Lang'ata constituency, represented in parliament by RailaOdinga, the key presidential candidate who contested the outcome of the elections.

REFERENCES

Abdi, Jamal and Dean, James. 2008. "The 2007 General Election in Kenya and its Aftermath: The Role of Local Language Media". *The International Journal of Press/Politics* 13(3): 319–327.

AMARC. 2008. *What is Community Radio*. Braamfontein, South Africa: AMARC Africa and Panos South Africa.

Ayittey, George. 1999. *Africa in Chaos: A Comparative History*. London: Palgrave-Macmillan.

Buckley, Steve, Duer, Kreszentia, Mendel, Toby and O Siochru, Sean. 2008. *Broadcasting, Voice and Accountability: A Public Interest Approach to Policy, Law, and Regulation*. Washington D.C.: World Bank Institute.

Chiumbu, Sarah. 2010. "Media, Alternativism and Power: the Political Economy of Community Media in South Africa". In *The citizen in communication: Re-visiting traditional, new and community media practices in South Africa*, edited by Hyde-Clark, Natalie, 115–137. Claremont: Juta & Co.

Chiumbu, Sarah and Ligaga, Dina. 2013. "Communities of Strangerhoods?: Internet, Mobile Phones and the Changing Nature of Radio Cultures in South Africa". *Telematics and Informatics* 30(3): 242–251.

Curran, James and Myung-Jin, Park. 2000. *De-Westernizing Media Studies*. London: Routledge.

Flew, Terry. 2002. *New Media: An Introduction*. Oxford: Oxford University Press.

Howley, Kevin. 2010. *Understanding Community Media*. London: Sage.

Lister, Martin, Dovey, Jon, Giddings, Seth, Grant, Iain and Kelly, Kieran. 2003. *New Media: A Critical Introduction*. London: Routledge.

Mabweazara, Hayes M. 2010. "'New' Technologies and Journalism Practice in Africa: Towards a Critical Sociological Approach". In *The citizen in communication: Re-visiting Traditional, New and Community Media Practices in South Africa*, edited by Hyde-Clarke, Natalie, 11–29. Claremont: Juta and Company.

Maina, Lucy. 2006. *African Media Development Initiative. Kenya: Research Findings and Conclusions*. London: BBC World Service Trust.

McNair, Brian. 1998. *The Sociology of Journalism*. London: Arnold.

Mercier, Helen. 2009. "Media Culpa? Nairobi Community Radio Stations and the Post-Election Violence". Masters thesis, Lund University.

Moyo, Last. 2013. "Introduction: Critical Reflections on Technological Convergence on Radio and the Emerging Digital Cultures and Practices". *Telematics and Informatics* 30(3): 211–213.

Mudhai, Fred. 2011. "Immediacy and Openness in a Digital Africa: Networked-Convergent Journalisms in Kenya". *Journalism: Theory, practice & criticism* 12(6): 674–691.

Mudhai, Okoth F., Tettey, Wisdom and Banda, Fackson, eds. 2009. *African Media and Digital Public Sphere*. Basingtoke: Palgrave Macmillan.

Myers, Mary. 2000. "Community Radio and Development". *In African Broadcast Cultures: Radio in Transition*, edited by Fardon, Richard and Furniss, Graham, 90–101. London: James Currey.

————. 2008. "Radio and Development in Africa. A Concept Paper Prepared for the IDRC". Accessed 16 November 2012. http://www.dfid.gov.uk/r4d/PDF/outputs/ICTED/Radio_and_Development_Africa_concept_paper.pdf.

Nassanga, Goretti L., Manyozo, Linje and Lopes, Claudia. 2013. "ICTs and Radio in Africa: How the Uptake of ICT has influenced the Newsroom Culture Among Community Radio Journalists". *Telematics and Informatics* 30(3): 258–266.

Ndlela, Nkosi. 2010. "Alternative Media and the Public Sphere in Zimbabwe". In *Understanding Community Media*, edited by Howley, Kevin, 87–95. London: Sage.

Nyamjoh, Francis. 2005. *Africa's Media: Democracy and the Politics of Belonging*. London and Pretoria: Zed Press and Unisa.

Ogola, George. 2011. "The Political Economy of the Media in Kenya: From Kenyatta's 'Nation Building' Press to Kibaki's Fragmented Nation". *Africa Today* 55(3): 77–95.

Opubor, Alfred. 2000. "If Community Media is the Answer, what is the Question?". In *Promoting Community Media in Africa*, edited by Boafo, Kwame, 11–24. Paris: UNESCO.

Pavlik, John V. 2001. *Journalism and New Media*. New York: Columbia University Press.

Poster, Mark. 2006. *Information Please: Culture and Politics in the Age of Digital Machines*. Durham: Duke University Press.

Reporters Without Borders. 2012. "Gap Widens Between Good and Bad Performers in Africa". Accessed 13 June 2012. http://en.rsf.org/press-freedom-index-2011–2012,1043.html.

Rosen, Jay. 2006. "The People Formerly Known as the Audience". Accessed 13 June 2012. http://archive.pressthink.org/2006/06/27/ppl_frmr.html.

Toffler, Alvin. 1980. *The Third Wave*. New York: Bantam Books.

UN-HABITAT. 2003. *The Challenge of Slums: Global Report on Human Settlements*. London: Earthscan Publications.

Vatikiosis, Pantelis. 2010. "Democratic Potentials of Citizen's Media". In *Understanding community media*, edited by Howley, Kevin, 32–14. London: Sage.

Wasserman, Herman, ed. 2010. *Taking it to the Streets: Popular Media, Democracy and Development in Africa*. London: Routledge.

Willems, Wendy. 2013. "Participation—In What? Radio, Convergence and the Corporate Logic of Audience input Through New Media in Zambia". *Telematics and Informatics* 30(3): 223–231.

Williams, Raymond. 1973. *The Country and the City*. London: The Hogarth 200 Press.

Winston, Brian. 1998. *Media Technology and Society: From the Telegraph to the Internet*. London: Routledge.

www.amarc.org

www.frontlinesms.com

www. kochfm.blogspot.co.uk

www.pamojafm.com

14 Online Forums

How the Voices of Readers Are Reshaping the Sphere of Public Debate in Burkina Faso

Marie-Soleil Frere

ONLINE JOURNALISM IN BURKINA FASO

Online journalism is a recent development in Burkina Faso, a landlocked and relatively unconnected country in the Sahel.[1] The first online journalism initiatives were the websites of the main national newspapers. The private daily *L'Observateur Paalga* first launched its website (www.lobservateur.bf) in 2000,[2] followed by its rival *Le Pays* (www.lepays.bf) and the public daily *Sidwaya* (www.sidwaya.bf) (Pare 2008).

In a country where, as of 2011, barely 1.4 percent of the 16 million inhabitants had access to the Internet,[3] where IT equipment remains limited and where the electricity grid, far from being widespread, is often defective, news websites are rather underdeveloped. Most are content with publishing the very same contents from their print edition and have neither a strategy nor a specific newsroom devoted to the web. The periodical press—some titles of which have focused on the practice of investigative journalism that is lacking in the daily press—still prefers to privilege the paper editions.[4] The bimonthly *L'Evénement,* which probably boasts the highest print-run in the country with 7,000 copies, only puts its print edition online after the subsequent print edition has hit the stalls, thereby ensuring that the web does not compete with the print edition, which remains its primary outlet.

The first actor to operate exclusively online emerged in 2003, i.e., the portal *lefaso.net,* which republished articles from the country's main papers, which were supplemented, marginally at first, with its own output. A summary of some 15 articles, comprising the title and first lines of all articles presented on the platform, is sent daily to 29,000 subscribers (24,783 email addresses and 3,995 Facebook users as of 19 July 2012): with a simple click, subscribers can access the site and read the rest of the articles. Subscription to the mailing list is free, as is access to the website and to the discussion forums accessible at the bottom of each article by clicking on the "add a comment" button. From the outset, such portals, which are widespread in West Africa—e.g., *abidjan.net* for Côte d'Ivoire, *seneweb.com* for Senegal, *maliweb.net* for Mali—have been very popular with the diaspora, which often enjoys easier and cheaper access to the Internet than the locals (Pare

2010). Visiting portals enables users to avoid browsing newspaper websites directly, which are often difficult to access and out of date. However, these portals often materialise in a 'lawless' context, with no actual agreement with the newspapers whose contents they collect and publish online.

It is in fact due to the growing discontent of the country's press, which was reluctant to sit by and watch portals continue to publish the entirety of their output outside any contractual framework, but also due to growing competition from other online news providers that *lefaso.net* has put more emphasis in recent years on the development of its own newsroom (which is manned by four reporters). Competition mainly consists of two online news websites that operate from Ouagadougou: *fasozine,* created in 2006 (and which also publishes a magazine), and *Burkina24,* created in 2011 by young members of the diaspora and which, besides articles written by its own journalists, produces both audio and video content (web radio and TV).

Besides the work of professional journalists, the Internet also enables the circulation of what scholars call 'amateur' or 'lay' discourses, or what in more technical terms is called 'user-generated content', created by citizens who do not claim to be journalists. In 2011, when the presidency of Blaise Compaore was rocked by an unprecedented wave of protests (Hilgers 2012), several social networks became particularly animated. Lively political discussions ignored by the country's traditional media took place on Facebook groups such as *Blaise Compaore Dégage*[5] (Blaise Compaore, get out), *Blaise Compaore DOIT Partir*[6] (Blaise Compaore MUST leave), or *Mouvement Blaise Compaore Doit Partir Groupe ouvert*[7] (Movement for the departure of Blaise Compaore—open group), which was by far the largest with over 3,000 friends (Ouédraogo 2011).

But the most influential form of citizen participation on the web in Burkina Faso today is probably to be found in the comments posted by Internet users on news websites. There are three reasons for observing and examining this phenomenon. First, the number of contributions keeps growing: in July 2012, *lefaso.net* recorded over 500 comments per day, and some articles could generate over 150 comments within a few hours.[8] Second, a recent development appears to contradict earlier analyses given that contributions now come mostly from within the country and no longer from the diaspora: over 80 percent of comments on *lefaso.net* or on *lobservateur.bf* now find their origin in the country. Last, exchanges between Internet users on news websites result increasingly in public debates: they are regularly evoked in formal or informal social venues (at symposia, on radio or television programmes but also at social gatherings), feed rumours and trigger the reaction, and sometimes the direct intervention, of the public authorities.

This article rests on a survey of a press corpus and monitoring of online forums on news websites as well as on 15 interviews conducted in July and August 2012 with actors of the media sector in Ouagadougou (journalists, publishers, bloggers, regulatory authority members and experts). It attempts to show how the contributions of Internet users from Burkina Faso, although very small in number, have challenged journalistic practices, upset the sector's regulatory practices and aroused the vigilance of the authorities. As is often the case when dealing with French-language sub-Saharan media, the analytical tools and models developed to study similar phenomena in Europe or the US provide precious indicators to shed light on local practices but do not account for the specificities of the phenomenon anchored in its own particular context. In the case of Burkina Faso, the particular situation of the freedom of the press as well as the attitude of professional journalists help to explain certain particularities of the use of an online space of debate by the 'forumists'.[9]

NEW TECHNOLOGIES AND CITIZEN PARTICIPATION

For several decades, the country's media did not prioritise interactivity with their audiences. Following the liberalisation of the media in 1990, the private press, which bloomed at this time, often devoted a column for the 'letters to the editor'. But in a country where the postal system is fairly underdeveloped, this section was rather underfed and reserved for figures from trade unions, education or civil society who were present in the capital city and were particularly fond of 'opinion columns'.

It is through the "comments" areas of the websites *lefaso.net* and *fasozine.com* that interactivity spread to the online press before permeating the websites of traditional media. In 2007, the private daily *L'Observateur Paalga* was the first paper to allow users to comment on online articles. It was followed by *Le Pays* and *Sidwaya*. This move created interactive spaces for discussion that were initially largely used by members of the diaspora before being gradually occupied by local users.

Online 'Forums' and 'Platforms'

In November 2008, a year after the launch of the interactive features on its website, realising the importance of giving attention to the contributions of Internet users in the print edition, *L'Observateur Paalga* decided to devote a page of its paper edition to the *Forum des internautes* (online forum). It gathers a daily selection of a dozen contributions posted by Internet users on a topic evoked in the previous day's edition. "The editorial board initially wasn't keen on the idea. They didn't think it was pertinent to reproduce the 'wild imaginings' of readers", claims San Evariste Barro, who takes care of the newspaper's forum.[10] But the initiative ultimately managed to impose itself given the growing success encountered by this page. Contrary to the traditional letters to the editor, the 'online forum' page made it possible to present within the same edition the reactions of readers who respond to and question one another. Within a single page, contributions selected from those posted online at times present contradictory views of citizens expressing themselves on a general topic, after the fashion of an interactive vox pop. The newspaper's management soon realised that this page was among the favourite of the readers of the print edition. Counting on this popularity, *L'Observateur Paalga* has gotten into the habit since 2010 of printing on its front page at least three times a week a headline drawn from a user's online comment. The 'online forum' thus grew in prestige by working its way to the front page, even if it is still looked down on by some journalists, who see in this key position a mere matter of demagogy and lucre.

This initiative was soon emulated, and *Le Pays* in turn rapidly created *La Tribune des Internautes* (online platform), whose extracts also make the paper's front page. Reproducing online comments seems to make it possible to raise issues on the front page, which journalists would certainly hesitate to produce under their own name. On 23 July 2012, for instance, following the liberation negotiated by Burkina Faso's mediators of three Spanish hostages detained by AQIM Islamists (Al-Qaeda in the Islamic Maghreb) in northern Mali, *L'Observateur Paalga* ran the following headline: "Burkina Faso and the release of hostages: 'What does the man in the street gain from this operation?'". The question was drawn from an online comment printed in the newspaper and one which, in cabarets and other social venues, many of the country's citizens were asking themselves, but no journalist had seemed willing to evoke such terms. That same day, *Le Pays* ran the headline, "Hostages released by Burkina Faso. 'Who benefits from this PR stunt?'", extracted from a web user contribution published on the 'online platform' page (*Le Pays* no. 5160, 23 July 2012).

A Typology of Contributors

Internet users express themselves under cover of anonymity as no website requires the prior registration of potential contributors. It is thus no easy matter to draw a sociological profile of the average user. It is most likely, however, that the community consists of a small urban elite that is both connected (i.e., with access to IT equipment and electricity) and French-speaking. Contributions are indeed overwhelmingly in French (although it is a minority language in Burkina Faso even if the only official one). The pseudonyms and expressions used (indicative of the first person masculine) suggest that the large majority of contributors are men. As the moderator of the forum on *Le Pays* explains, "we don't see any female pseudonyms when the subject is politics. They intervene rather on social issues or family questions".[11] These active Internet users most likely take advantage of an Internet connection at work as their comments are mostly posted during working hours, with far fewer comments in the evenings or on weekends.[12]

On *lefaso.net,* which features the most comments by far (some articles gathering close to 200 comments within 24 hours), various profiles emerged over the course of the three-week survey.

- The "diaspo" (a citizen of Burkina Faso that is a member of the diaspora): this is the only contributor who often uses his real name and reveals his place of residence. Other clues make it possible for the moderators to identify him as living abroad (keyboard with no accents or the time at which the message was posted). According to the moderators, the "diaspos" are interesting contributors because they often provide a comparative perspective. However, "they have a tendency to look down on native citizens, to reproach them for their lack of reactivity and engagement, to boast about the advantages of living elsewhere, where life is so different".[13]
- The bitter citizen: as elsewhere, forums are outlets for various frustrations, the "meeting point of the discontented" according to Edouard Ouedraogo, managing editor of *L'Observateur Paalga:* "Ninety percent of the comments we receive are hostile to the current government".[14] The general manager of *Editions Sidwaya*, Abou Bakhr Ziza, adds, "People can here voice the anger they can express nowhere else".[15] The pseudonyms used by the contributors are in themselves symbolic of this anger: *Burkinafaché* (angry citizen of Burkina Faso), *Savapa* (all is not well), etc. Some openly present themselves as average citizens who have been forgotten by the authorities: *uncitoyen* (a citizen), *unboncitoyen* (a good citizen), *uninconnu* (an unknown), *unouagalais* (a resident of Ouagadougou), etc. Others still opt for pseudonyms that reflect the ideals they believe to have been violated: *L'intègre* (the upright), *La justice* (justice), *La vérité* (the truth), *Sacksida* (accept the truth), *Au nom de la démocratie* (in the name of democracy), *Indigné* (indignant), etc. Who are these particularly vindictive Internet users? For moderators close to the regime, "the forums are the exclusive domain of the political opposition. They have no print outlet, so they make their voices heard on the forums".[16] But for other moderators and observers of the online press, this bitterness and frustration are in fact the result of "schizophrenic" civil servants. Several moderators believe that the forumists are mostly zealous civil servants, cardholders of the ruling party CDP (Congress for Democracy and Progress) who pledge their allegiance to the system in real life but who take advantage of the web's anonymity to say things and reveal information they could not divulge openly. "If you work as a civil servant or in the corporate world, it doesn't look good if you're not a member of the CDP, so people enrol officially, but they express themselves differently on the net".[17] The belief, therefore, is that the most virulent contributions do not come from the organised opposition, but from individuals within the state apparatus who are perfectly familiar with its ins and outs.
- The professional contributor: he is ubiquitous, present on all forums, day in and day out, commenting on all topics and sometimes even becoming a reference in the small online community. This is, for instance, the case with *Kôrô Yamyêlé*,[18] who expresses himself almost

daily on the forums and whose contributions are often taken up by the dailies in their page devoted to Internet users.[19]

- The political activist: lying in ambush in the forums, he intervenes the moment he believes it is time to defend the interests of his party, whether he is a member of the president's party or the opposition. The number of these activist contributions increases as the elections approach. This is the case, for instance, for an Internet user called *le riche* (the rich man), an ardent defender of the ruling party. According to the moderators interviewed, these political activists do not make up a majority among contributors. The large majority of those who express themselves are not part of a structured group defending a common cause: they are in fact isolated individuals who, in general, are simply voicing their personal discontent.
- The theoretician: a philosopher or jurist, he develops long and detailed arguments.
- The muddler: his interventions lack sense and he is often rebuffed or ignored by the other users.

A separate category deserves to be mentioned because it partly emerged during our field survey: journalists acknowledge that they often express themselves anonymously on the forums of their own papers. Whereas some do so openly, others "settle scores with fellow journalists, sometimes from the same newsroom, in a context where open confrontations are not culturally accepted", claims a journalist with the print media. It is sometimes also a matter of expressing one's disagreement with the paper's editorial line on a specific topic: "Not all the paper's reporters shared the same interpretation of the crisis in Côte d'Ivoire", recalls a former journalist with *Le Pays*. "Some used to post comments on the newspaper's forum, under cover of a pseudonym, to be able to express another point of view than that defended by colleagues covering the event and which had been published".[20] Some journalists also use the forums to disseminate news items they believe are true but for which they don't have any formal proof. "Journalists post information on the forums which they can't publish in their articles because they don't have the necessary sources to support it in case of a judicial procedure, but they still want the public to be aware of the information".[21]

The unbridled expression of critical opinions seems to be related to the guarantee of anonymity. Following a series of abuses we shall return to, the High Communication Council (CSC) had considered asking the website managers to set up a technical device for the prior recording of the identity of contributors, following the method used by several French media.[22] But the regulator ultimately abandoned this project, assuming that this prior constraint would kill off the forums and would be seen as a violation of the freedom of expression, a fact acknowledged by the president of the CSC, Beatrice Damiba: "People would not express themselves as they do if they had to reveal their identity". Abdoul Karim Sango, an expert on media law, goes even further: "The popularity of this anonymous channel proves that there is no genuine freedom of expression in Burkina Faso. People would be too scared to express themselves if they had to reveal their identity".[23]

Hot Subjects

The subjects that drew the most reactions in my survey are domestic and foreign politics (in particular relations between African countries and former metropolises), religion and sex-related issues.

Religion, an unproblematic topic until recently in a country with a high level of interdenominational tolerance and profound syncretism, has become a particularly sensitive topic since war broke out in northern Mali in February 2012 leading to the occupation of the region by the fundamentalist movements Ansar Dine and MUJAO (Movement for Unity and Jihad in West Africa), close to AQIM. Many Internet users have voiced their fear of seeing radical Islamism spread, whereas others take aim at the religious extremism of the Pentecostal movements. "The sensitivity of these questions is making itself felt in a context where, in Burkina Faso itself, Muslim and Christian fundamentalism is progressing", believes Cyriaque Pare, the founder of *lefaso.net*.[24] As an example, on 1 August 2012, an article on a fundamentalist Muslim sect called *Les pieds nus* (The barefoot ones) was published on *lefaso.net,* drawing 187 online comments within 24 hours.[25] Many of them reveal the fear of seeing radical Islam spread to Burkina Faso and called on the state to reinforce measures guaranteeing the country's secularism.

Domestic politics constitutes another favourite subject of online users. On 20 July 2012, for instance, the country's Ministry of Foreign Affairs published an official communiqué on *lefaso.net* following comments made at a symposium in Paris by a civil servant with the French Ministry of Foreign Affairs, Laurent Bigot, on the situation in the Sahel.[26] The speaker's comments were posted on YouTube and taken up by several local papers. He had claimed that the situation in Burkina Faso presented as many sources of concern as those in Mali on the eve of the coup and that Burkina Faso could be "next on the list". Following the Ministry's offended reaction, the online community responded vigorously: there were 73 comments within 24 hours. Some claimed Mr Bigot was "an idiot diplomat" (*Papy* 19 July, 20:58), a "small-time technocrat" (*Quid* 19 July, 19:32). Most, however, approved Bigot's comments: "This is part of the problem with Burkina Faso. No one is free to tell the truth. Instead of seizing certain opportunities to lift up the country, we always prefer to go after those who want to open our eyes or warn us" (*Anawim* 19 July, 20:48).

Last, sex matters, in particular homosexuality and prostitution, are also the subject of much commentary. Thus, whether dealing with political or social taboos, "the forums allow users to express out loud what everyone is thinking in silence, to voice their true thoughts", observes Cyriaque Pare, "in a context where people are always afraid and do not have the courage to express themselves openly, even though the tone and analyses of the papers are often quite daring".[27]

The Risk of Abuse, Involvement of the Regulator and Moderation Tools

As the work of "non-professionals", comments by Internet users do not have to meet the criteria of professional journalism, and yet these comments circulate widely in the public sphere and now also within traditional media, thus falling under the latter's editorial responsibility.

When the first forums were launched, moderation tools were left to the appreciation of the website's administrators, and the comments could either be posted online automatically or not. But after 2008, the public regulatory authority, the CSC, started monitoring the contents of the users' contributions and questioning the media whose forums were home to comments that seemed to violate legal, regulatory or even ethical principles.

It should be noted that the French-language tradition of regulation led the public regulator to examine the media output and report violations of the professional code of conduct, whereas regulators in English-speaking countries generally leave this matter to self-regulation. Indeed, the CSC's organic law specifies that the latter's attributions include (1) monitoring the enforcement of communication laws and regulations in Burkina Faso; (2) contributing to the enforcement of the professional code of ethics by private and public audio and TV broadcasting corporations and companies as well as by private and public newspapers and periodicals distributed or published nationwide.

Although it is true that the CSC's mandate includes the regulation of the written press, the legal basis it relies on to question website managers for what it believes to be online abuse remains fragile. The press code, which dates from 1993, makes no mention of the Internet.

The number of reprimands issued by the regulator increased substantially in 2009, aimed in particular at *L'Observateur Paalga,* whose forum had no a priori moderation. In March 2009, the CSC invited the news media to a symposium on the topic: "Online newspaper forums: what code of conduct should be adopted?". The CSC reminded the managing editors that "the publication by a newspaper of a news item drawn from the web implies its responsibility" (Yaro 2009, 5).

In 2010, following a complaint lodged by a deputy member of the presidential party, Mahama Sawadogo, who was violently taken to task by a user on the website of *L'Observateur Paalga,* the CSC demanded that all online forums be subject to a priori moderation. *L'Observateur Paalga* was compelled to comply with this injunction, forcing users to take responsibility.

> If we think about it, Internet users only have themselves to blame, observed the newspaper in its print edition. We had offered them a

forum for democratic debate which functioned, in a sense, as a form of collective catharsis, a regulator of socio-political tensions. Unfortunately, some users soon turned it into a free-for-all, a space for hurling invectives, libellous and defamatory denunciations, not to mention the settling of scores, sometimes at a personal level. [. . .] But that is too easy, since there can be no freedom without responsibility. One is almost led to believe that some of our fellow citizens do not deserve this freedom we offered them.[28]

All websites with participatory spaces were thus required to set up a mechanism that only allows comments to be posted on the site once they have been approved by a moderator able to verify whether the comment complies with the law and the code of ethics. However, because the CSC's recommendation has no legal basis, its value is primarily pedagogical. Moreover, the CSC has neither the human nor the technical resources necessary to supervise all comments constantly. Since then, the public regulatory authority has continued to react occasionally to comments made by Internet users, either on its own initiative or after it received a complaint from a member of the audience.

Cherif Sy, the managing editor of the newspaper *Bendre,* has so far refused the principle of a priori moderation for his website: "Whether or not a comment is virulent, it is better for it to be expressed like that, in a dialogue with other Internet users who can refute the argument or add some nuance, rather than finding an outlet in the street in another form".[29]

Moderation Criteria and Divergent Appreciations

The obligation to set up an a priori moderation system could have generated a reflection in each newsroom on the criteria that online comments must meet and an explicit formalisation of the guidelines to be communicated to the users (Degand and Simonson 2011, 59). This failed to happen, however; none of the sites with a forum presents an in-house charter or code of conduct to their Internet users, and they do not detail the principles guiding the moderators' choices.

All the moderators surveyed claim to regulate spontaneously and referred only vaguely to any legislation or code of ethics. The moderators are all journalists who follow their "professional sense",[30] their "individual sensitivity"[31] or their "individual experience".[32] Moderators claim to be particularly vigilant with regard to incitements to hatred or crime and abuse or defamation punishable under penal law. The newspaper *Le Reporter* claims to follow the Journalism Code by eliminating "incitements to murder, human rights violations, the dissemination of private information, etc.".[33] Two limits have been posed at *Sidwaya:* defamation and abuse.[34] The only limits evoked at *Burkina24* are that of "abuse" and "attacks against public figures", which often crop up in debates on domestic politics. At *L'Observateur Paalga,* the moderator claims to be particularly vigilant with regard to "individual accusations".[35] It is the only newspaper which once planned "to draw up a code inspired by the charter of Rue 89, but nothing ever came of it".

Although balanced out by the professional experience of the journalists who act as moderators, the lack of any clear moderation criteria constitutes a shortcoming as regards the "education" of the online community. As a result, it is often the Internet users themselves who do their own moderating, reminding one another of the rules of online etiquette ("Everyone has the right to protest", explained a user called *Bouglas* on 20 July at 6:22, "but one must use it with care") or questioning the moderator ("I believe the webmaster of *lefaso.net* should censor some comments which are entirely out of order. One must assume one's responsibilities!", claimed *Hy'da* on 20 July at 8:33).[36]

The lack of clear and explicit criteria might also accentuate the differences of appreciation between the moderators and the regulator. Indeed, on many occasions, it became apparent that the CSC and the rebuked papers or sites did not share the same understanding of the limits posed by the law to the freedom of expression of web users.

For instance, the various reprimands issued by the CSC show that it uses a broad definition of what constitutes an "incitement to violence". Thus, in March 2011, the CSC reprimanded *L'Observateur Paalga* following the publication in its column "Online forum"[37] of a comment in the wake of demonstrations by soldiers which had ended in acts of vandalism (Hilgers and Loada 2012). The user had written, "Long live the soldiers! At least you will have made us think". For the CSC, these words were "like a reward for the acts of vandalism perpetrated by the soldiers against the civilian population's businesses" and "such as to aggravate the legitimate indignation of the victims" (CSC Report 2011). The CSC also held that such comments comprised a "risk of aggravating the social crisis resulting from this situation. Thus, this naturally highlights the paper's social responsibility, which is to promote cohesion and harmony among the people". The moderator of *L'Observateur Paalga* did not share this opinion, of course, neither as to the categorisation of the message posted online nor as to the need to silence certain voices in the name of promoting harmony among the people.

Likewise, the notion of "offence against the Head of Government" was given a broad definition by the CSC, once more in a case involving *L'Observateur Paalga,* in whose pages a user had commented on the Prime Minister's general policy declaration in these terms:

> Mr. Zongo, you talk too much without either saying anything or doing anything: promises, more promises and yet more promises, forever and ever and evermore! You should set up a church where you can preach, and resign from your position as Prime Minister . . .[38]

A few weeks earlier, the same daily was likewise condemned for having posted, following the death of two French citizens kidnapped in Niamey in Niger, a comment by a user accusing President Compaore of "having contacts with those lunatics of AQIM".[39] For the CSC, "such an allegation, unfounded moreover, constitutes an offence against the Head of State".

The reprimands sometimes concern issues where the regulator's competence is unfounded. "The CSC often accuses us of not being balanced on the forum", remarks the managing editor of *L'Observateur Paalga*. "But they can't expect us to invent positive reactions. Sometimes all comments are negative".[40] A balance between positive and negative opinions is not a legal obligation for private media, and the regulator thus has no legal basis on which to rebuke a paper.

Practising Moderation: a Challenge for Newspapers

Moderation, which requires both technical and human resources, is a substantial task for newspapers that are already largely understaffed: they are forced either to assign a journalist to this task or to resign themselves not to be able to treat all the comments they receive. At *lefaso.net,* this is a source of regret: "In February 2012, we had to delete 14,000 comments pending approval. It was impossible to catch up our backlog".[41] At *Le Pays,* where three journalists assume this task alternately, they observed that "Some Internet users believe we are censoring them, when in fact the truth is that there is often simply no one to approve the comments".[42] This lack of reactivity is seen otherwise by Internet users who believe they are subject to censorship.

> When some of your readers, in a desire to contribute constructive criticism, express ideas that go against your editorial line, the comment is systematically censored", wrote a user on *lefaso.net.* "Thus, some are even led to precede their messages with a plea addressed to the moderator, begging him to let them post their message. (*Intégrité* 22 July, 22:28)

The site's administrator denies making a selection based on editorial closeness and advances rather the constraint of human resources.

In such a context, meta-moderation—which consists of contacting the user to ask him to clarify, develop or nuance his thoughts or even to explain to him why his comment cannot be published (Degand and Simonson 2011, 65)—is virtually non-existent. When no reason is given as to why their contribution has not been posted, users often accuse the Webmaster of making unfounded decisions and address moderators directly. In a discussion thread on a trivial subject, a user called *Le Fer* (iron) rebuked the Webmaster with these words: "YOU HAVE CENSORED MY MESSAGE. GOD IS WATCHING YOU".[43] Taking advantage of another discussion thread, some Internet users take the opportunity to reinsert an earlier comment on another issue, which had not been seen or posted online.

Besides the lack of time, the moderators evoke their lack of motivation tied to the lack of interest of their colleagues and sometimes of their superiors for the job they have to perform. At *L'Observateur Paalga*, the journalist in charge of the website feels somewhat "apart from the newsroom", with a less prestigious job to perform.

THE IMPACT OF ONLINE CONTRIBUTIONS

Drawing on the interviews conducted in Burkina Faso, the study attempts to identify the possible impact areas of these diverse daily contributions. The research survey reveals three areas where changes linked to the existence of these forums have been observed: journalistic practices, the reactivity of public authorities and citizen participation.

The Impact on Journalistic Practices

We have already evoked the importance now given to the online community's contributions, not only through a page devoted to them but also through extracts quoted daily on the front page. These highlighted extracts often make waves in a way that journalists themselves would not dare do.

Online discussion forums thus challenge journalistic practices both indirectly by undertaking what journalists do not dare and directly by criticising the work of news professionals. A recurrent critique bears on shortcomings in the treatment of information. "One or more users will sometimes tell us that an article is poorly written or that it is too superficial", observes a journalist with *Le Pays*. "It's true that we are often in a rush and don't have the time to dig deeper or reflect more".[44] In a context where the daily press is full of articles that have been commissioned and bought, forumists challenge journalists on the blandness of their prose. "One user even suggested that the journalists of *Le Pays* take a holiday, since there was nothing interesting in the newspaper anyway", observes a journalist.[45]

The second critique is that the newspapers are too deferential towards the authorities. This was the case, for instance, with the editorials penned by the former general manager of *Editions Sidwaya*, Ibrahiman Sakandé, who was systematically taught a lesson in journalism by online users. In 2010, for example, an editorial he wrote defending the possibility of revising article 37 of the Constitution to allow President Compaore, in charge since 1987, to run for another term ended with these words: "Alternation for the sake of alternation can be anti-democratic if it ends up perverting the finality of democracy, i.e., in this case, muddying the waters and cancelling out the efforts that the sub-region has done for its prosperity and the integration of its people". Dozens of Internet users reacted promptly, taking direct aim at the general manager of *Sidwaya:* "Mister Sakande, I invite you to reread your articles dating from before your appointment. (. . .) The newspaper which readers vaguely trusted is gradually adopting the same editorial line as the newspaper *L'Opinion*.[46] This is regrettable since *Sidwaya* is meant to be a source of information, not communication" (*Le Picqué* 12 July 2010). "Mister General Manager of *Sidwaya,* you are supporting the worst dictatorship this country will ever have known. (. . .) All I'm asking for is an effort and some intellectual honesty" (*Anonymous* 12 July 2010). "Above all, your newspaper does not serve the ruling party, but the whole people!" (*Naabrollé* 12 July 2010).

The appreciation of these online comments varies from one paper to the next. Some journalists are very sensitive, especially when the comments frequently question their professional integrity. "Some journalists ask the web department not to publish their articles online, because they fear negative online reactions".[47] It thus happens that an article on the front page of the print edition is never published online, at the request of the author himself. Journalists who praised the authorities have received so many comments accusing them of compromising that they try to be more circumspect in their appreciation of the ruling party's achievements. Other journalists claim to be indifferent to the comments, rarely consulting online reactions. Last, it (sometimes) happens that the critical online contribution is taken seriously collectively and that the suggestions made are discussed in newsrooms.[48]

In the absence of a formal structure whose vocation would be to criticise the media, the forums end up playing the role of MARS (Means to ensure the social responsibility of the media).[49] They can also lead to the reinforcement of internal self-regulation mechanisms. At *fasozine,* user comments helped in particular to strengthen the board's editorial work. "Those in charge now pay more attention to the articles of the journalists before tossing them online".[50]

Besides this critical appreciation of the journalists' work, a second contribution by Internet users consists of providing additional information, accounts that complement the topics covered. "Internet users know more than journalists since they are more numerous and more dispersed. They can add new information", observes San Evariste Barro.[51] At *Le Pays,* it is thanks to a message posted online that the newspaper learned about the fraudulent birth-certificates scheme in Ouahigouya. The local correspondent was then asked by the paper to verify the information, which proved to be true, and *Le Pays* published the facts.[52]

In early July 2012, user comments enabled the newspaper *Bendre* to denounce the publication of false information by the Paris-based pan-African magazine *Jeune Afrique,* relayed locally by *L'Observateur Paalga.*[53] These two publications had covered an interview conducted with a young artist living in the United States who claimed to be the son of Thomas Sankara. The publication by *L'Observateur Paalga* of extracts from this interview had led to a series of disbelieving comments which led *Bendre* to check the artist's exact date of birth with the administration. Online testimonies and official documents showed that the latter was born in 1989, i.e., two years after the assassination of Thomas Sankara. As the managing editor Cherif Sy acknowledged, it is the Internet users who suggested the path of refutation to *Bendre.*

The contribution of Internet users is thus limited to factual additions: to this day, there has been no structured collaboration aiming to associate the Internet users of Burkina Faso with the production of information by the existing media. The governing principle is thus that of a participative practice that is both juxtaposed (presented beside the journalistic articles) and non-integrated (Noblet and Pignard-Cheyel 2010, 275). Journalism remains the stronghold of professionals who are uncertain as to whether they should enter into a new type of relationship with their public. However, the success of the forums should provide some food for thought, on the one hand, because the quality of some contributions reflects the weakness of their own work: "The day I saw *lefaso.net* publish the post of an internet user in the form of an article, I started thinking about my added value as a journalist",[54] observes a reporter with *Le Pays*. "Today, journalism is no longer a privilege as such: ordinary citizens can show the world that they are better informed than us on a topic we are covering. We must be careful", adds Abdoulaye Tao. "Journalists often become arrogant, and don't want to listen to their audience, but online comments force us to be more humble, aware of the fact that there are other people who sometimes know things better than us".[55]

Journalists should also pay attention because Internet users, over the course of the discussions, grow more interested in the contributions of other users than in the initial article published by the paper. The initial article becomes a mere pretext, a thematic suggestion, and the users claim to set the real terms of the debate. "If political discussion has shifted to the forums, it is because there is not sufficient debate in the media", believes the president of the CSC, Beatrice Damiba.[56] "People are tired of reading about seminars and press conferences. They are after something else", *Le Pays* claims. "It has to be said. Readers are turning to the forums for real news, because they offer alternative information compared to the contents proposed by newspapers".[57] In a context where the daily press has been gangrened by the practice of "commissioned journalism", "sometimes users can be explicit in the comments space beneath an article: guys, drop these useless topics and tackle genuine subjects. What you need to talk about today is this or that".

The Impact on the Public Authorities: An Instrument of 'Good Governance'?

The second area of impact of the online forums can be measured through the reaction of the public authorities, which have become sensitive to the online "buzz". Online monitoring by several executive agencies seems quite certain given the tendency of spokesmen and communications directors to intervene in online debates to set the record straight or express an opinion. The Prime Minister's director of communications intervened directly serveral times on the forum of *Le Pays* to correct information posted by online users. "In the current context, no ministry wishes to be gibed by the online community".[58] Most ministers make sure they have staff members who monitor these forums.

> Each council of ministers is followed by reactions from online users who analyse the different decisions that have been taken. The users comment for instance on the allocation of certain markets on unclear grounds, or the appointments of certain individuals to functions for which they don't have the right profile. It makes one think. . ."[59]

As one Internet user remarked: "The authorities read the forums before they leave home" (*Anonymous* 2 July, 9:47).

Of course, the public authorities know that this online community does not constitute an emanation or a reflection of 'public opinion', but Burkina Faso is a country in which there are no opinion polls: monitoring the reactions of these users thus makes it possible to "take the pulse of what the citizens are thinking".[60] An Internet user expressed the same idea: "Our thanks to *lefaso.net* for this forum which has become a barometer of the state of mind of us simple citizens. Yes, our leaders must know what ordinary citizens think of their behaviour; they ignore us although we went to the same schools as them" (*Dinkous* 2 July 2012, 10:42).

Beyond this function of comments as a "barometer", the question emerges as to whether user comments can in fact change the behaviour of politicians or the political decision-making process. The impact of the public's recriminations on the local authorities, through participation in call-in radio shows, has already been demonstrated on several occasions. Questioned about possible similar effects generated by online debates, journalists and moderators all cited two recent examples. In both cases, decisions seem to have been linked to heated online debates. The link is of course difficult to prove, but the online community's blatant anger was on both occassions evoked by the authority taking the decision.

Thus, on 21 February 2012, *L'Observateur Paalga* published a story about a mechanic who, following an altercation with the driver of a vehicle, was beaten up by soldiers who were aboard the vehicle and dragged back to the police station. It soon appeared that the person on board the vehicle was none other than the Minister of Justice, Jerome Traore. As soon as this information was published, the online community reacted promptly and with great indignation. Within minutes, a user suggested, "We hope that this Minister who takes justice into his own hands will resign" (*Virgil* 21 February, 7:45); "This Minister has abused his authority and should be pursued in court, regardless of whether he is Minister of Justice, as an example of what he was unable to do" (*Marcel ouattara* 8:08); "The Tiao government should not even allow the Minister to take part in the council of ministers tomorrow. He should be relieved of his functions and be prosecuted . . ." (*Zoe wend* 8:25). Within 48 hours of the event, almost 200 comments had been posted, most with a tone of indignation, on the paper's online forum, and hundreds of others had been posted on discussion threads. On 23 February, the President of the Republic, at the suggestion of the Prime Minister, adopted a decree which dismissed the incriminated minister. Whereas the role of the newspaper which revealed this information seems obvious in this affair, many observers believe that the indignation expressed and maintained by the online community probably encouraged the radical sanction imposed on the minister.

A few weeks later, in May 2012, the newspaper *Mutations* revealed another case, this time involving the Ministry of Secondary and Higher Education (MESS): a 14-year-old child, the best pupil at the 2011 BEPC (school certificate taken at about age 14), was prevented from applying for a scholarship at the American School of Ouagadougou following an administrative error made by the Ministry. Contacted by the family, the Ministry only responded after a long interval and with blatant indifference. The online community reacted angrily to the story of this incident. They denounced "the opacity of the scholarship system" (*Anonymous* 11 May, 8:30), "the incompetence, bad will, orchestrated fraud, etc." (*Anonymous* 11 May, 8:32), evoked "an ignoble act", "an attitude of contempt for the poor" (*Emile* 11 May, 11:31) and asked whether all the country's citizens "had the same rights?" (*Touché* 12:32). Seventy-eight messages rebuking the Ministry were posted on *lefaso. net* within a few hours. The Ministry, it seems, was moved. Four days later, it responded with a press release published on *lefaso.net* which refers directly to the online reactions: "The online newspaper *lefaso.net* took up this article on Friday 11 May 2012 and because of the reactions of the Internet users the MESS realized that a number of details were missing, so that many readers were misled". After giving its version of events, the Ministry's press release concluded, "The MESS thanks all the internet users for their contributions to the debate and promises to pursue the modernisation of its administration in order to limit the number of such mistakes". The press release rekindled the discussion among the online community, resulting in two new suggestions: the ministry was asked by Internet users, on the one hand, to publish the names of the ten highest achieving laureates of the BEPC and, on the other, to find a way to compensate the child who was stripped of his chance.

These two incidents show that the authorities are attentive to the reactions of Internet users. However, some journalists see them as isolated events and are circumspect as to the genuine impact of the "buzz" generated online, as they are with regard to their own work, for that matter. "We live in a country where we are free to denounce, but to no effect. We have published dozens of reports denouncing the embezzlement of funds, for instance, but nothing ever comes to trial".[61]

The Impact on Citizens: a Means of Expression and Exchange

Last, the third impact is on the citizens themselves and involves their capacity to communicate together, to share ideas and even to mobilise themselves. These forums have established a genuine dialogue among Internet users, a space for debate which seems unable to take root elsewhere through channels set up for citizen participation (political parties, civil society organisations, etc.). "It's not at all like the letters to the editor we used to publish", claims the moderator of *L'Observateur Paalga*. "Here people can discuss things and answer one another without the paper's interference".[62] This "conversational" character distinguishes the forums from call-in programmes where listeners chat with the host or guest but are not put in contact with one another. The importance of polyphonic exchange transpires in the fact that it is towards these same forums that Internet users have massively turned their attention. It is not just a question of expressing oneself: these users wish to start a debate with others on issues that matter to them.[63]

The impact in terms of collective mobilisation is limited, however: each contributor being anonymous, there is not much chance that this space of dispute will result in organised forms of protest. These are spaces where everyone can express his frustration, but they do so secretly. "We live in an ultra-dominant party system, almost a one-party system. If these forumists are civil servants who are publicly connected to the CDP, they cannot reveal their identity by acting publicly. These are probably people who don't even vote, people who think they can't change things by voting. That is in fact what they often write". The argument, then, is that Internet users express online a frustration which cannot be expressed through the ballot.[64]

For other observers, however, online debates are only the first step in a more complex circuit of information dissemination. "The page devoted to online forums, which is the most popular in newspapers today, feeds conversations in other places of informal discussion, such as tea groups", observes Cherif Sy, the managing editor of the newspaper *Bendre*.[65] It is therefore difficult to assess its actual impact and whether it could lead to any form of collective action.

CONCLUSION

Online discussion forums in Burkina Faso constitute a relatively marginal phenomenon considering the small number of Internet users they mobilise, but the lessons we can learn are nevertheless essential if we wish to understand the role of the media in this country and obtain a better picture of freedom of expression.

First and foremost, this phenomenon forces us to reflect on the situation of journalism as it is practised in Burkina Faso today. Is the tremendous popularity of 'lay' contributions from outside the papers not due to a lack of serious content and analysis or expectations which the current work of journalists is unable to respond to? How is one to interpret the fact that the popularity of the two largest private dailies currently rests on a page devoted to comments made by online users? What is one to make of journalism's credibility in general in a context where citizens need to read user comments to feel they are sufficiently informed? Building on observations made in and about Europe, we can agree that, in the context of Burkina Faso, the journalists "tend to rely heavily on well-known routines and hold on to their core task" and that they distance themselves from the task of moderating forums that are "time consuming, which makes it even more difficult for them to keep on top of the already high workload in the newsrooms" (Paulussen and Ugille 2008, 38). But, these reactions are not linked to their intent to defend the professional quality of their work. In a context characterised by the widespread practice of 'gombo', journalists practise a lucrative activity that is often closer to communication than to news information (Frère 2012). The few periodicals who steer clear of these practices generally struggle to survive and do not invest in their online presence. As regards public media, the fact that they act as the mouthpieces of the ruling party, making room neither for the political opposition nor for citizens with critical views, encourages this search for alternative places for the circulation of balanced information.

The second lesson to be drawn concerns freedom of expression in the country. Although Burkina Faso has a very liberal press law and boasts five dailies, some 20 periodicals, over 100 radio stations and several private television stations, and although it is relatively well ranked in terms of the freedom of the press, the anonymous use of the forums by hundreds of users is proof of the citizens' fear of expressing themselves openly. Are the limits which the Internet users impose on themselves placed higher than those which the sensitivity of the ruling party imposes informally? As the editor of the newspaper *Bendre* writes, "most people only become genuine human beings when they are in their living rooms. In public, they overdo it".[66] Besides the political situation, the public expression of disagreement is also influenced by the cultural context: "In a culture where disagreement is not expressed directly, only anonymity allows one to say things".

Most comments concern the citizens' discontent with the mode of government and the growing inequalities in the country. "It's a kind of catharsis",[67] which sometimes turns into verbal violence. The forums would thus contribute to a form of social regulation, an outlet for frustrations; this might explain a certain ambivalence in the CSC, which keeps reprimanding moderators while ultimately letting things follow their course. If the forums are monitored closely by the authorities to the extent that the latter sometimes feel obliged to justify themselves in front of web users, it is less because of the risks they can engender than because of the extreme sensitivity of a regime which has managed to regain control of most other spaces of expression and finds it difficult to tolerate the fact that another sphere of public debate is not under its control.

Last, one must reflect on the impact of these "meetings of the discontent" in a context qualified as 'semi-authoritarian' (Hilgers and Mazochetti 2010), where political opposition is completely crippled and where independent social bodies (trade unions, civil society organisations) are largely ineffective or have been discredited. It seems unlikely that this discontent will lead to any organised opposition, all the less so given that in Burkina Faso as elsewhere, the question remains as to whether this practice of online contributions by ordinary Internet users will last. It requires time and motivation and could thus rapidly lose steam or be swamped by political activists.

NOTES

1. A semiarid region of North-Central Africa, South of the Sahara Desert.
2. As of July 2012, the website received 12,000 visits a day, i.e., double the print-run (San Evariste Barro, personal interview, Ouagadougou, 25 July 2012).
3. Source: http://www.internetworldstats.com (visited on 19 July 2012).
4. The written press in Burkina Faso includes five dailies, 10 weeklies, four biweeklies, 11 monthlies, one bimonthly (all published in French) as well as two newspapers in national languages (Sango and Diallo 2010, 27).
5. http://www.facebook.com/profile.php?id = 100001959026599.
6. http://www.facebook.com/pages/Blaise-Compaore-DOIT-Partir/193268870716006.
7. http://www.facebook.com/groups/revolutionburkina2011/.
8. Cyriaque Paré, founder of *lefaso.net,* personal interview, Ouagadougou, 3 August 2012.
9. In French, the expression 'forumeur' (forumer) is often used. However, all the people we met in Burkina Faso used the term 'forumiste' (forumist).
10. San Evariste Barro, manager of online content at *L'Observateur Paalga,* interview, Ouagadougou, 25 July 2012.
11. Abdoulaye Tao, moderator of the forum of *Le Pays,* collective interview, Ouagadougou, 6 August 2012.
12. The first reactions once the newspapers have been published online in the evening come from abroad, in particular from regions with different time zones where it is still daytime (United States, Canada). Contributions from Burkina Faso arrive the next morning.
13. San Evariste Barro, manager of online content at *L'Observateur Paalga,* interview, Ouagadougou, 25 July 2012.
14. Edouard Ouedraogo, managing editor of *L'Observateur Paalga,* interview, Ouagadougou, 25 July 2012.
15. Abou Bakhr Zida, general manager of Editions Sidwaya, interview, Ouagadougou, 25 July 2012.
16. Abou Bakhr Zida, general manager of Editions Sidwaya, interview, Ouagadougou, 25 July 2012.
17. Cyriaque Paré, founder of *lefaso.net,* personal interview, Ouagadougou, 3 August 2012.
18. 'Kôrô' means 'big brother' in Jula, and 'yamyêlé' means 'the problem of the destitute problems' in Moore (Mossi language).
19. This Internet user is so familiar to journalists that some of them refer to him explicitly in their articles. See, for instance, http://www.lefaso.net/spip.php?article35713#forum96703.
20. A former journalist with *Le Pays* (anonymously), personal interview, 1 August 2012.
21. Cherif Sy, managing editor of *Bendre,* personal interview, 2 August 2012.
22. Interview with Beatrice Damiba, president of the CSC, Ouagadougou, 25 July 2012.
23. Personal interview, 1 August 2012.
24. Cyriaque Pare, founder of *lefaso.net,* personal interview, Ouagadougou, 3 August 2012.

25. http://www.lefaso.net/spip.php?article49417.
26. See http://www.lefaso.net/spip.php?article49230.
27. Cyriaque Pare, founder of *lefaso.net,* personal interview, 3 August 2012.
28. *L'Observateur Paalga,* Monday 15 February 2010.
29. Cherif Sy, managing editor of *Bendre,* personal interview, Ouagadougou, 2 August
30. *Le Pays,* collective interview., 6 August.
31. Cyriaque Pare, *lefaso.net,* personal interview, 3 August 2012.
32. San Evariste Barro, *L'Observateur Paalga,* personal interview, Ouagadougou, 25 July 2012.
33. Hervé Taoko, *Le Reporter,* personal interview, Ouagadougou, 7 August 2012.
34. Moderator of *Sidwaya,* interview, Ouagadougou, 25 July 2012
35. San Evariste Barro, personal interview, 25 July 2012.
36. http://www.lefaso.net/spip.php?article49238#forum268530.
37. *L'Observateur Paalga* no. 7848, 28 March 2011, p. 28.
38. *L'Observateur Paalga* no. 7843, 21 March 2011, p. 34.
39. *L'Observateur Paalga* no. 7796, 11 January 2011.
40. Edouard Ouedraogo, managing editor of *L'Observateur Paalga.*
41. Cyriaque Pare, founder of *lefaso.net,* personal interview, Ouagadougou, 19 July 2012.
42. Abdoulaye Tao, Dabo Séni and Parfait Silga, collective interview, Ouagadougou, 6 August 2012.
43. See http://www.lefaso.net/spip.php?article49687&rubrique6#forum.
44. *Le Pays,* personal interview, Ouagadougou, 7 August 2012.
45. Abdoulaye Tao, moderator of the website *Le Pays,* personal interview, 7 August 2012.
46. Very committed political pro-government paper.
47. San Evariste Barro, *L'Observateur Paalga,* personal interview, Ouagadougou, 25 July 2012.
48. Abou Bakr Zida, general manager of *Sidwaya,* personal interview, Ouagadougou, 25 July 2012
49. A notion developed by Claude-Jean Bertrand, a French specialist of Media self-regulatory mechanisms.
50. Morin Yamongbe, editor in chief of *fasozine,* personal interview, Ouagadougou, 26 July 2012.
51. San Evariste Barro, *L'Observateur Paalga,* personal interview, Ouagadougou.
52. Abdoulaye Tao, Parfait Silga and Seni Dabo, collective interview, Ouagadougou, 3 August 2012.
53. *Jeune Afrique* no. 26841, 17–23 June 2012 (p. 129) and *L'Observateur Paalga* no. 8155, 22–24 June 2012.
54. Dabo Seni, collective interview, *Le Pays,* Ouagadougou, 6 August 2012.
55. Parfait Silga, collective interview, *Le Pays,* Ouagadougou, 6 August 2012.
56. Interview, Ouagadougou, 25 July 2012.
57. *Le Pays,* collective interview, 6 July 2012.
58. *Le Pays,* collective interview, 6 July 2012.
59. Cyriaque Pare, personal interview, Ouagadougou, 3 August 2012.
60. Abdoul Karim Sango, holder of a PhD in Information and Communication, personal interview, 1 August 2012.
61. Boureïma Ouedraogo, *Le Reporter, personal interview, Ouagadougou,* 7 August 2012.
62. San Evariste Barro, personal interview, Ouagadougou, 25 July 2012
63. Boureima Ouedaaogo and Hervé Taoko, *Le Reporter,* personal interview, Ouagadougou, 7 August 2012.
64. Abdou Zoure, *Burkina24,* personal interview, 6 August 2012.

65. Cherif Sy, managing editor of *Bendre,* personal interview, Ouagadougou, 2 August 2012.
66. Cherif Sy, personal interview, Ouagadougou, 2 August 2012.
67. Edouard Ouedraogo, *L'Observateur Paalga, personal interview, Ouagadougou,* 25 July 2012.

REFERENCES

Conseil Supérieur de la Communication (CSC) (High Communication Council). 2011. *Rapport public 2010* [Public Report 2010]. Ouagadougou.

Degand, Amandine, and Simonson, Mathieu. 2011. "La modération des fils de discussion dans la presse en ligne" [Moderation of debates lists in the online press]. *Les Cahiers du Journalisme* 22/23: 56–73. Accessed 2 July 2012. http://www.cahiersdujournalisme.net/cdj/22_23.htm.

Hilgers, Mathieu. Forthcoming. "Paradoxes of a Semi-Authoritarian Regime: More Protest but Less Opposition. Why Burkina's Spring Fizzled Away?" In *The Arab Revolution of 2011 in Comparative Perspective*, edited by Arjomand, Saïd Amir. New-York : SUNY Press.

Noblet, Arnaud, and Pignard-Cheynel, Nathalie. 2010. "L'encadrement des contributions 'amateurs' au sein des sites d'information, entre impératif participatif et exigences journalistiques" [Framing non-professional contributions to information websites, between necessary participation and journalist requirements]. In *Web social. Mutation de la communication* [Social web. Changes in communication], edited by Millerand, F., Proulx, S. and Rueff, J., 265–282. Québec: Presses universitaires de Québec.

Ouédraogo, Edouard. 2011. "L'influence des réseaux sociaux sur la crise de 2011 au Burkina" [The influence of social network Ouédraogo s on the 2011 crisis in Burkina Faso]. Paper presented at the 8th Symposium on Communication, Ouagadougou, 9 December 2011.

Paré, Cyriaque. 2008. "Médias et société de l'information en Afrique de l'Ouest; Enjeux, discours et appropriations" [Media and information society in West Africa: Stakes, discourses and ownership]. Dissertation, University Bordeaux 3— Michel de Montaigne.

———. 2010. "Médias et société de l'information en Afrique. La difficile révolution du multimédias dans les médias ouest-africains" [Media and information society in Africa: multi platform revolution in the West African media]. *Netsud* 5: 15–37.

Paulussen, Steve, and Ugille, Pieter. 2008. "User-generated content in the Newsroom: Professional and organisational constraints on Participatory Journalism". *Westminster Papers in Communication and Culture* 5(2): 24–41.

Sango, Abdoulaye and Diallo, Boureïma. 2011. *Etat de la Liberté de la Presse au Burkina Faso* [State of press freedom in Burkina Faso.] Ouagadougou: Centre national de Presse Norbert Zongo.

Yaro, Amadou Nebila. 2009. "Le traitement de l'information en ligne: responsabilité juridique des organes de presse" [The treatment of online information: legal responsibility of newspapers]. Paper presented at the conference Journaux en ligne: Quel code de conduite devrait être adopté? [Online newspaper forums: what code of conduct should be adopted?]. Ouagadougou: Conseil Supérieur de la Communication.

Epilogue

As epilogue-author, I will exercise the privilege of evoking the well-worn cliché attributed to the Roman author Pliny the Elder (possibly paraphrasing Aristotle) and affirm once again that *ex Africa semper aliquid novi* (always something new out of Africa). The dictum aptly describes this collection, which captures the spirit of invention and differentiation characteristic of the dramatic and sweeping pace of change in how communications technologies enable and shape public discourse in Africa. Beyond the newsroom, it is clear that new forms of citizenship are emerging around Africa as a result of widespread and innovative popular interactions with new communications technologies, including social media and the adaptation of mainstream media to those trends. There is mounting evidence—including much presented here—that around Africa, blogging and webcasting create popular alternative channels for people to receive and interact with public affairs news. This has been especially the case in countries where mainstream media remain strongly influenced by autocratic regimes, hegemonic political parties and commercially driven media (with the three categories often intertwined). And for many, it seems, the alternative—the informal, the participatory, the crowd-sourced and the 'amateur'—has become the dominant if not the only sources of 'news', forcing the 'mainstream' to adapt, die-away or shun journalism for infotainment.

As the volume's introduction notes, 'online journalism' is a slippery concept, and there is value in asking if it means the same in African as in non-African contexts. If European scholarship on 'online journalism', for example, focuses as much on patterns of online journalism consumption as on the evolving production practices of 'online journalists', should the emergent exploration of 'online journalism' in Africa follow suit given that many citizens of many African countries still lack the practical means to be routine online news consumers? As contributions to this volume suggest, the spotlight for now is on how the 'online' is incorporated into journalistic work in contexts where news production is sometimes strikingly similar to what might be seen in any global news hub—London, New York or Tokyo (as Jordaan's as well as Mavhungu and Mabweazara's descriptions of South African newspapers attest) and, conversely, sometimes distant from Northern norms in terms of its goals and methods. A pressing question remains to what extent the innovation of African journalists will be inclusive of the many that remain on the other side of the digital divide. Moyo's chapter sheds light on the kinds of differences (the 'novi') that make contemporary investigation of the entire communications ecology across countries and regions in Africa vital: the unique intersections between and among communications channels, facilitated by—though rarely limited to—the colossal uptake of mobile telephony around Africa.

Much of this research signals the ongoing tension between an embrace of Western normative theories of journalism when researching non-Western, contextually embedded and rapidly shifting journalistic processes in Africa and their abandonment for possibly more locally pertinent theory. Perhaps what matters most in the end is a relevant and socially valuable journalism which benefits disenfranchised citizens—of whom there are many in Africa. Innovative scholarship has a vital role to play here in conjunction with pioneering and eager public communicators: the journalist, citizen-journalist and 'average' citizen.

The embrace of digital technology in the journalistic sphere has always challenged existing ethical and regulatory frameworks, and the nature of those challenges in Africa is often vastly different from those described by Euro/American-centric scholarly literature. As several chapters observe, the extent of real change within professional journalism, limited to emergent popular communications forms such as Facebook and SMS, is sometimes marginal but also sometimes troubling in its ethical implications. Conversely, as researchers such as Marie-Soleil Frere observe, rapid innovation in journalistic practice often permits a far broader and more open civic discourse, which legal restrictions (often themselves reincarnations of colonial control structures) and resource starvation once prevented. Further investigation of such trends can be found in two special issues: *Ecquid Novi: African Journalism Studies* 34(1) (2013) on "Social Media and Journalism in Africa" (which this author guest edited) and *Journalism: Theory, Practice & Criticism* 12(6) (2011), themed "New Media and Journalism Practice in Africa: An Agenda for Research" (guest edited by Atton and Mabweazara).

This volume unites the work of many scholars based in Africa with others in Europe. It is a fine example of internationalized media research exploiting international networks to bring cutting edge and relevant scholarship about Africa to an African and international audience; it is also a reminder not only of the importance of rigorous data collection at the site of media production and consumption (and the thoughtful integration of the two) but of the crucial role of careful analysis of political context in any examination of journalism. Although it may be premature to declare extinct scholarship considering Africa as one place with one journalism, such a diverse collection of detailed and nuanced research as this is a source of hope.

Whereas north African political transformation and the myriad questions about public communications this inspires currently offer the most visible spur to a burgeoning flow of journalism and media analysis from Africa, for me, the explosion in public engagement within a wider political and cultural sphere, enabled by mobile telephony, raises the most intriguing and pressing questions. It is the impact of that and rapidly increasing Internet access and engagement that is most shaking African journalism. The research presented here should inspire ever more investigation of this period of exciting change.

—Epilogue by *Chris Paterson,*
Senior Lecturer, Institute of Communication Studies,
University of Leeds

Notes on Contributors

Hayes Mawindi Mabweazara (PhD) is a Senior Lecturer in Journalism Studies at Falmouth University, UK. His research on new media and journalism practice in Africa has appeared in the *Journal of African Media Studies; Equid Novi: African Journalism Studies; Digital Journalism; Journalism Practice; Journalism: Theory, Practice & Criticism,* and *Qualitative Research.* He has also contributed to several edited book volumes, including *Making Online News: Newsroom Ethnography in the Second Decade of Internet Journalism* (2011); *Cultural Identity and New Communication Technologies: Political, Ethnic and Ideological Implications* (2011); *The Citizen in Communication: Re-visiting Traditional, New and Community Media Practices in South Africa* (2010). Mabweazara co-edited a special issue of *Journalism: Theory, Practice & Criticism,* 12(6) on "New Media and Journalism Practice in Africa" and is currently guest editing a special issue of *Digital Journalism,* "Digital Technologies and the Evolving African Newsroom". He is the Book Reviews Editor of *Equid Novi: African Journalism Studies* (Routledge/UNISA) and serves on the editorial board of *Digital Journalism* (Routledge).

Okoth Fred Mudhai (PhD), on a 17-month (November 2012 to April 2014) research secondment at the University of Cambridge, is a Senior Lecturer in Journalism and the Course Director of MA Specialist Journalism at Coventry University. His publications include "The Internet: Triumphs and Trials for Kenyan Journalism" in *Beyond Boundaries: Cyberspace in Africa* (2002). He is co-editor of *African Media and the Digital Public Sphere* (2009) and was part of the IT and Civil Society Network at the US Social Science Research Council (2003–2005). His journalism awards include two on ICT at the global level. He was a full-time journalist at The Standard Group (Nairobi) in the 1990s, also contributing to outlets in Africa, the UK and the US. He studied journalism at the University of Nairobi (PgD Mass Communication), worked full time for the *East African Standard* newspaper (Nairobi) and contributed to the *Daily Nation* (Nairobi), *Sunday Times* (Johannesburg), Africa Analysis (London), Voice of America (Nairobi Bureau) and the Kenya Broadcasting

Corporation. He holds an MA in Communication Studies (Leeds) and a PhD in International Relations (Nottingham Trent).

Jason Whittaker is Professor of Blake Studies and Head of the Department of Writing at Falmouth University, UK. He is the author of *William Blake and the Myths of Britain* (Macmillan 1999), *Radical Blake: Influence and Afterlife from 1827* (with Shirley Dent, Palgrave 2002), and *Blake and the Digital Humanities* (with Roger Whitson, Routledge 2012) as well as several books on new technologies, including *The Cyberspace Handbook* (Routledge 2004) and *Producing for Web 2.0* (Routledge 2009). With Steve Clark, he is the editor of *Blake, Modernity and Popular Culture* (Palgrave 2007) and, with Steve and Tristanne Connolly, of *Blake 2.0: William Blake in Twentieth-Century Art, Music and Culture (Palgrave 2012).*

Katherine L. Vaughn is a dual Masters in Public Policy candidate and MBA candidate at the School of Public Policy and R.H. Smith School of Business, respectively, at the University of Maryland, College Park. Katherine has co-authored a series of articles and chapters on social media's role in the Arab Awakening, and she is currently conducting a qualitative study on the constraints of women entrepreneurs in Morocco.

Muhammad Jameel Yusha'u (PhD) is a Senior Lecturer in Media and Politics at Northumbria University, Newcastle upon Tyne. He was a lecturer in Mass Communications at Bayero University, Kano, Nigeria and was also an Associate Lecturer in Global Journalism at the University of Sheffield, UK. He has worked as the British correspondent for the Hausa Service of radio Deutsche Welle and was a former producer at the BBC World Service, London, where he worked in different departments such as the Hausa Service, World Today and BBC news online. His recent articles have been published in *Ecquid Novi: African Journalism Studies, Journal of African Media Studies* and *Global Media and Communication.*

Sahar Khamis (PhD) is an Assistant Professor in the Department of Communication at the University of Maryland, College Park. She is an expert on Arab and Muslim media and the former Head of the Mass Communication and Information Science Department in Qatar University. Dr. Khamis holds a PhD in Mass Media and Cultural Studies from the University of Manchester in England. She is co-author of the book *"Islam Dot Com: Contemporary Islamic Discourses in Cyberspace"* (Palgrave Macmillan, 2009). She has also authored several book chapters and articles in international and regional academic journals on Arab and Muslim media in both English and Arabic.

Last Moyo (PhD)'s research and teaching interests include new media, civic engagement and democracy in Africa; media political economies;

comparative media systems; development communication; and media and peace journalism. His lecturing experience spans Africa, Europe and Asia, where he has taught a wide range of Media Studies subjects at the University of Wales (part time), the University of the Witwatersrand, South Africa (full time), the UN-mandated University for Peace Graduate Programme in East Asia (full time), and at the National University of Science and Technology, Zimbabwe (full time). Moyo has been a recipient of prestigious research funding from Carnegie Mellon, IDRC, Canada (via Carleton University), and others, which have helped him to conduct academic research covering mostly the region of Southern Africa. Apart from his enduring interest in digital cultures and popular resistance, his research has grown and expanded into the broad areas of digitisation and media convergence, where he has focused not only on digital cultures and practices but also on structures, institutions and the political economies of the media.

Marie-Soleil Frère is a Senior Researcher at the National Fund for Scientific Research (Belgium). She teaches and heads the Research Center (ReSIC) at the Department of Communication and Information Sciences at the University of Brussels. Her research focuses on the role of the media in political evolutions in sub-Saharan Africa. Her recent works include *Elections and the media in post-conflict Africa* (London: Zed Books, 2011), *The media and conflicts in central Africa* (Boulder: Lyynne Rienner, 2007) and *Presse et democratie en Afrique francophone* (Paris: Karthala, 2000).

Nagwa Abdel Salam Fahmy is a Professor of Journalism in the Department of Mass Communication, Faculty of Arts, Ain Shams University, Egypt. She has also taught at the Communication College at Sharjah University (UAE). Her work on the Arab media has appeared in a number of journals, including the following: *Journal of Middle East Media, Egyptian Journal of Mass Communication Research, Egyptian Journal of Public Opinion Research* and *Egyptian Communication Research.*

Tendai Chari is a Lecturer in the Media Studies Department at the University of Venda, South Africa. Previously, he lectured at the University of Zimbabwe, where he coordinated the Media Programme, and at the Zimbabwe Open University, the National University of Science and Technology (Zimbabwe) and Fort Hare University (South Africa). His research interests are online media, political communication, media representation and media ethics. His other publications have appeared in the *Journal of African Media Studies, African Identities, Global Media Journal* and *Ecquid-Novi: Journal of African Media Studies.*

George Ogola (PhD) is a Senior Lecturer in the School of Journalism, Media and Communication at the University of Central Lancashire, Preston. He has published widely on the political economy of the media in Africa.

His research is also interested in understanding the impact of new media technologies on the broader media ecology in the developing world and how they address questions of power and democratisation.

Terje S. Skjerdal is Associate Professor at Gimlekollen School of Journalism and Communication, Kristiansand, Norway. He has spent several years researching journalism culture at the Horn of Africa and has also written generally about African media theory. His recent research has dealt particularly with professional identities in the Ethiopian state media.

Ahmed El Gody (PhD) is a Senior Lecturer in Media and Communication Studies and Director of Journalism Connected at Örebro University Sweden. He is the author of *Journalism in a Network: Role of ICTs in Egyptian Newsrooms*. He has also authored a number of book chapters and journal articles on issues around the Media in the Middle East, freedom of the press, censorship, new media and convergence.

Nathalie Hyde-Clarke (PhD) is an Associate Professor and Head of the School of Communication, University of Johannesburg, South Africa. She has conducted extensive research in new media studies and political communication. Her primary interest resides in war and peace media studies and how new media, such as mobile technology, may facilitate improved political engagement amongst the youth.

Ylva Rodny-Gumede (PhD) is a Lecturer in the Journalism programme in the School of Communication at the University of Johannesburg and a Senior Associate Researcher with the Stanhope Centre for International Communications Policy Research at the London School of Economics. She holds a PhD from the School of Oriental and African Studies, London University. Her primary research focus is on the role of the media in society with a special interest in the role of the news media in the monitoring of political figures and events.

Marenet Jordaan is a Lecturer in Journalism at the University of Pretoria, South Africa. She holds an undergraduate degree in Publishing, and a BPhil and Master's degree in Journalism from Stellenbosch University. Previously, she worked for around eight years as a newspaper journalist at *Die Burger* in Cape Town and *Rapport* in Pretoria. Her Master's thesis deals with the influence of social media on the cultures and news routines in two weekly South African newsrooms. She presented a paper on this topic at the 1st International Conference on Journalism Studies in Santiago, Chile (2012).

Johanna Mavhungu is a Researcher and Lecturer at the Sol Plaatje Institute for Media Leadership (SPI) at Rhodes University, South Africa. Her research looks at trends in media management and online and mobile media platforms in Africa. The SPI produces and uses data and knowledge to publish and to help develop the curriculum of Media Management courses. Johanna has worked with South African media organisations as a researcher and producer for broadcast television programmes on community development, which increased her involvement with research and development communication.

Index

For Product Safety Concerns and Information please contact our EU
representative GPSR@taylorandfrancis.com
Taylor & Francis Verlag GmbH, Kaufingerstraße 24, 80331 München, Germany